Foundation ASP.NET for Flash

Ryan Moore

friendsof

DESIGNER TO DESIGNER™

an Apress® company

Foundation ASP.NET for Flash

ISBN (pbk): 1-59059-517-3

Printed and bound in the United States of America 9 8 7 6 5 4 3 2 1

Distributed to the book trade worldwide by Springer-Verlag New York, Inc., 233 Spring Street, 6th Floor, New York, NY 10013. Phone 1-800-SPRINGER, fax 201-348-4505, e-mail orders-ny@springer-sbm.com, or visit www.springeronline.com.

For information on translations, please contact Apress directly at 2560 Ninth Street, Suite 219, Berkeley, CA 94710. Phone 510-549-5930, fax 510-549-5939, e-mail info@apress.com, or visit www.apress.com.

The source code for this book is freely available to readers at www.friendsofed.com in the Downloads section.

Credits

Lead Editors
Chris Mills and Matthew Moodie

Technical Reviewer
Joshua Bloom

Editorial Board
Steve Anglin, Dan Appleman,
Ewan Buckingham, Gary Cornell,
Tony Davis, Jason Gilmore,
Jonathan Hassell, Chris Mills,
Dominic Shakeshaft, Jim Sumser

Project Manager
Beth Christmas

Copy Edit Manager
Nicole LeClerc

Copy Editor
Liz Welch

Assistant Production Director
Kari Brooks-Copony

Production Editor
Ellie Fountain

Compositor and Artist
Katy Freer

Proofreader
April Eddy

Indexer
Broccoli Information Management

Cover Image Designer
Corné van Dooren

Interior and Cover Designer
Kurt Krames

Manufacturing Director
Tom Debolski

To my Mom, Dad, and Melissa, and Celeste.
To Lindsay.

CONTENTS

Chapter 10: Product Viewer Application 257

Chapter 11: Session State and Security 281

Chapter 12: Flash Remoting 309

ABOUT THE AUTHOR

After leading an artificial intelligence team at the University of Minnesota and graduating with a degree in electrical engineering and computer science, **Ryan Moore** started Green Lizard Computing in Minneapolis, Minnesota, in 1999, where he developed web applications using a combination of ASP, PHP, and Flash. In 2001, he cofounded Balance Studios in Green Bay, Wisconsin, where he is currently the technical director. At Balance Studios, Ryan architects and develops web-based applications using technologies ranging from Shockwave 3D to ASP.NET and Flash.

In 2003, Ryan also cofounded epicsoft, LLC, of Green Bay, Wisconsin, where he is the lead software engineer, designing and developing desktop and web-based applications for the creative and development communities using a combination of C# and Flash. Ryan is also a Certified Macromedia Flash Developer, teaches classes on Internet technologies at ITT Technical College, speaks at technology conferences, and authors articles for a variety of technology magazines. Ryan maintains an ASP.NET–Flash weblog, which can be found at http://blogs.ittoolbox.com/c/engineering/.

ABOUT THE TECHNICAL REVIEWER

Joshua Bloom has been working in various aspects of the software business for over eight years now. He has worked in areas as diverse as ERP systems, bar code labeling, and multimedia marketing. He developed his Flash and ASP.NET chops during his time with POPstick.

He is currently completing the final year of a baccalaureate program in industrial design. He hopes to combine his software engineering and critical thinking skills with his new degree in industrial design to create world-changing products and experiences.

If you have a problem . . . if no one else can help, and if you can find him, maybe you can hire . . . The A Team.

He occasionally blogs at www.bigbadcode.com and can also be found at www.jbloomdesign.com.

ABOUT THE COVER IMAGE DESIGNER

Corné van Dooren designed the front cover image for this book. Having been given a brief by friends of ED to create a new design for the Foundation series, he was inspired to create this new setup combining technology and organic forms.

With a colorful background as an avid cartoonist, Corné discovered the infinite world of multimedia at the age of 17—a journey of discovery that hasn't stopped since. His mantra has always been "The only limit to multimedia is the imagination," a mantra that is keeping him moving forward constantly.

After enjoying success after success over the past years—working for many international clients, as well as being featured in multimedia magazines, testing software, and working on many other friends of ED books—Corné decided it was time to take another step in his career by launching his own company, *Project 79*, in March 2005.

You can see more of his work and contact him through www.cornevandooren.com or www.project79.com.

If you like his work, be sure to check out his chapter in *New Masters of Photoshop: Volume 2*, also by friends of ED (ISBN: 1590593154).

ACKNOWLEDGMENTS

I would like to thank my family, who has always been supportive in my endeavors; Lindsay, who has been amazingly supportive and patient; and my coworkers and friends, who have provided a tremendous amount of guidance and knowledge. This book is truly a result of the extraordinary people who have surrounded me in all aspects of my life.

INTRODUCTION

Welcome to the world of Flash and ASP.NET.

In this stage in the evolution of the World Wide Web, the lay of the land has changed. Static HTML pages are becoming a thing of the past, and dynamic web applications that function much more like desktop applications are the platform of the future. This new breed of applications requires a new set of technologies that is not only capable of producing dynamic, interactive user interfaces, but also has access to a high-powered backend feature set, capable of performing complex functions such as databases access and web service integration.

As Flash developers are surely aware, Macromedia Flash provides developers with one of the most advanced environments for creating interactive user interfaces—with features that leave even the most advanced alternative web technologies in the dust. Where does the ASP.NET tie come in then? The Microsoft .NET platform is one of the newest and most advanced server-side programming languages available today, and can be used to provide Flash with an amazing, extended set of power and functionality. And one of the great things about the .NET platform is that it *focuses* on decreasing the time needed to develop complex functionality—allowing Flash developers to . . . develop Flash!

In this book, we'll take a look into the many ways that you can use Flash and ASP.NET together to develop some of the most powerful, interactive, and engaging applications available on the Web. I'm going to take for granted that you have a strong background in Flash and ActionScript programming, and are anywhere from a beginner to an advanced user of the .NET platform. In this book, I'll focus on ASP.NET development using the C# programming language (as compared to VB .NET), and do the C# development using Visual Studio .NET.

How this book is structured

- **Chapter 1** is an introduction to Flash and ASP.NET. In Chapter 1, we'll cover some of the basic concepts of the .NET Framework, and briefly touch on the concepts and methods used to communicate between Flash and ASP.NET. We'll also go through the setup of the .NET Framework, IIS, and SQL Server Express Edition.

- **Chapter 2** is a C# primer, explaining the basic elements of the C# programming language. This chapter is not a full explanation of the language (there are complete books for that!), but it will provide a good reference for C# development, and point out the similarities and differences between C# and ActionScript.

- In **Chapters 3** and **4**, you'll learn how to create your first ASP.NET website projects using Microsoft Visual Studio .NET. In these chapters, we'll also learn how to pass information from ASP.NET to Flash using two different methods: FlashVars and LoadVars. Along the way, we'll cover some ASP.NET concepts, including using server controls and sending mail messages from ASP.NET.

- In **Chapters 5–8**, we'll focus on Flash-ASP.NET interaction using XML documents and XML web services. By the end of these chapters, you'll know not only how to generate XML documents on the fly using ASP.NET, but also how to create ASP.NET web services, and even how to create your own interface to the Google search engine!

- **Chapters 9** and **10** cover one of the most important topics in Flash/ASP.NET development: accessing data using ASP.NET and retrieving that data using Flash. In these chapters, we'll learn how to connect to a Microsoft Access database and publish the data from a database as a web service, which we can connect to with Flash. Using this knowledge, we'll then create an example online store application, which will consist of a Flash interface, an ASP.NET web service, and data stored in an Access database.

- In **Chapter 11**, we'll discuss session management in ASP.NET and how it can be used to extend the online store application from Chapter 10. We'll also touch upon web service security and develop a method for providing more secure access to your web services, even without the use of Secure Socket Layers.

- **Chapters 12** and **13** are devoted to the understanding and application of Flash Remoting. In these chapters, we'll cover not only the ins and outs of Remoting, but also some exciting concepts, such as file uploading in Flash, and integrating databases into our applications. In the final example in Chapter 13, you'll create a "video weblog" application that will allow you to upload .flv video files to a web server and display them in a "blog" style, with full administrative capabilities!

What you'll need

To complete the examples in this book, you will need to be using Microsoft Windows 2000 or XP, and have the following software installed:

- Macromedia Flash MX 2004 or Flash 8 (Professional edition required for Chapters 7–13)
- Microsoft Visual Studio .NET 2003 or 2005
- IIS 5.0+
- SQL Server Express Edition (Chapter 13)
- Macromedia Flash Remoting MX (Chapters 12 and 13)

In Chapter 1, we'll walk through the installation of IIS and SQL Server. You'll find information on Flash Remoting installation in Chapter 12, where we'll walk through it step by step.

Sample files

The source code for this book is freely available to readers at www.friendsofed.com in the Downloads section.

Support

Questions about the examples in this book? Feel free to contact the author at flashnet@rymoore.com.

Chapter 1

PRIMING THE PUMP

What this chapter covers:

- The strengths and weaknesses of Flash
- Static web pages
- The strengths and weaknesses of dynamic web pages
- ASP.NET as a server-side technology
- SQL Server
- Accessing data using Flash
- The similarities between ASP.NET and ActionScript
- The .NET Framework
- Hosting ASP.NET on IIS
- Setting up your work environment

Welcome to the wonderful world of Flash and ASP.NET—a world created by two of the most powerful and intriguing World Wide Web technologies today. In this book we examine how these two technologies work together to create applications that are the next step in the evolution of the Web and how to create these applications in a fraction of the time required using similar technologies.

> *As an environment for developing ASP.NET 2.0 pages using C#, we will use Visual Studio .NET 2005, the most recent of Microsoft's Visual Studio development environment releases. Visual Studio .NET 2005 is the most powerful IDE available for development of ASP.NET pages and is built from the ground up with .NET development in mind. Although the examples in this book are displayed using Visual Studio .NET 2005, the code used is in no way Visual Studio–specific and can be used in any other C#/ASP.NET development environment.*

In this first chapter we cover a range of material to get you prepared for Flash/ASP.NET development. First, we offer a general overview of web technologies and explore how Flash and ASP.NET fit individually into the web model. After we see how ASP.NET and Flash function individually on the Web, we investigate the methods that can be used to integrate them into one, more powerful team. Finally, we take a look at the technologies and programs required to create ASP.NET applications and walk through the setup of these technologies so that you have an environment ready to tackle the world of Flash and ASP.NET!

Static web pages

In the early stages of the Web, web pages were mainly composed of static HTML documents. Static HTML pages are documents existing on a web server that are sent directly to the client when requested, without any interaction or modification by the web server. Static web pages typically come in the form of .htm or .html files, have almost no user interactivity, and rarely contain fresh content. Static web pages, by their nature, are a burden for web developers to maintain since the source HTML in the files must be modified and reposted to a web server for an update to be made.

An everyday example similar to a web server delivering static web pages is a candy bar vending machine. When you approach a vending machine, it advertises all of the merchandise it has to offer. This merchandise is not customized to your likes or dislikes and is the same for anyone who approaches the machine. When you have selected the candy bar that interests you the most, you enter your payment, select the product you want, and receive it from the machine—which possibly makes you a satisfied customer but not necessarily; after all, you may not be thrilled about the products you had to select from or the freshness of the goods you received. In order for you to receive fresh or different products, the candy bar vendor would have to physically open the machine and put new bars in . . . Vending machines don't know how to make candy bars (at least not in my neighborhood).

The same holds true for static web pages. When you request a static HTML web page in a web browser, the page responds and advertises the products it has available as text and links—you can request to see another product (in this case another HTML document), but there's no guarantee that the content you receive from the static page is current, and like a year-old candy bar, it is quite possibly a little stale. The page will also not have any interactivity and cannot be customized to fit your needs or respond to your interactions.

As a web developer (and candy bar vendor), the only way to keep static content fresh is to consistently update your inventory by replacing the old. In the early days of the Internet, the sites requiring frequent updates were manned by teams of webmasters who constantly made changes to page content and reposted files to the web server. This was an extremely arduous task and required many programmers skilled in HTML.

These static web pages also lacked the interactivity of modern-day desktop applications. Although we have become accustomed to it, the web browser interaction is generally not intuitive or responsive in the way that desktop applications are. When you click on a link in a static web page, the browser *refreshes* its display with the content of the newly requested web page. This refresh is similar to hitting a pothole while driving down a highway on a beautiful summer day—a thorn in the side of an enjoyable web experience.

Luckily, technologies evolved that have improved the web model for both the developer and the website end user. These technologies allow for the creation of web pages with both dynamically changing content and rich user interfaces . . . . which is where our friend Flash comes into play.

Flash

As I'm sure you're well aware, Flash is an exciting technology for creating applications ranging from JibJab animations to high-level business applications. Flash has come a long way from its low-level programming model in Flash 4 to the current version, Flash 8, which has many data-driven, high-level programming capabilities. ActionScript 2.0, released with MX 2004, is a powerful, object-oriented language, similar to other industry-standard development languages such as Java and C++.

As we discuss Flash and its integration into web applications, it's important to understand that Flash is a *client-side* technology. As such, Flash executes all of its ActionScript code on the system of the user who is viewing the Flash file, as shown in Figure 1-1.

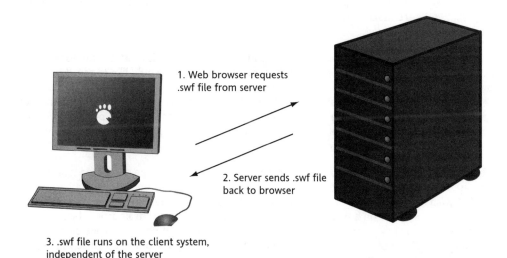

1. Web browser requests .swf file from server

2. Server sends .swf file back to browser

3. .swf file runs on the client system, independent of the server

Figure 1-1. Flash running on client machine, independent of web server

It is this client-side execution (among other things) that makes Flash such a powerful technology. Typical HTML-based web technologies are not able to perform processing on the client's computer and therefore are "dead" once sent to the client system. By executing on the client side, Flash can accomplish tasks such as creating reactive user interfaces, performing form validation, and loading images dynamically—features that are nearly impossible using standard technologies. Because it executes completely on the client side, Flash can also accomplish these features without the "road bump" of page refreshes I mentioned in the static web page technologies—a major accomplishment toward improving the web interaction model!

Being a client-side technology, though, Flash does have the limitation of not being capable of interfacing directly with information stored on web servers, such as databases and filesystems. Because of this limitation, Flash has been labeled in the past as a technology only useful for creating animations and banner ads. With Flash MX, though, many methods have been introduced that allow Flash to communicate with powerful server-side technologies, such as ASP.NET. With the help of server-side technologies, Flash is able to not only provide reactive, intuitive interfaces, but also to interface with server-side logic and data stores. This capability makes Flash an extremely powerful technology for building applications ranging from reservation systems to online storefronts.

Dynamically generated HTML

To overcome the limitations of static web pages, *dynamic* web page technologies have evolved. Dynamic web page technologies work differently than static web pages in that they allow developers to write code that generates HTML *when the page is requested* from the web server by a web browser. Again, I'll use an example to explain exactly how dynamic pages work as compared to static HTML pages.

Imagine an artist who paints pictures for a living. This particular artist paints the portraits in the comfort of her own home using her own ideas for the pictures, so when you see the works in a gallery, they are already completed. Again, like the candy bar machine example, this artist's work might be exactly what you were looking for, or it might be far from what you wanted, especially if you were in the market for a self-portrait.

Now imagine an artist who paints portraits on the street for a living. This artist can do his work in "real time," taking input from his customer about the type of portrait they would like to see. When you first meet the artist, all he has is a blank pad of paper, but by the time he is done, you might have a completed portrait of yourself. This artist's work is much more responsive to your desires than the work of the previous artist, who did not consider you at all before making the work. The point of purchase for this artist is significantly different also, in that the artist making the portraits did the work *when you requested it* rather than at an earlier time.

This "real-time portrait" is similar to the interaction of a dynamic web page compared to a static page. In the case of static web pages, the pages are prebuilt "pictures" that do not change based on your requests. Dynamic pages, on the other hand, are "portraits" built in real time, when you request them. These pages, as they exist on a web server, are similar to that of the portrait artist's blank slate—but when you request the page, and send along some indications of what you would like on the page, the web server "paints" the picture for you, generating the dynamic page based on what you requested, and possibly even "hot off the press" data from data sources.

Using dynamic technologies, developers can write pages that change their content based on other sources, such as user input or external data sources. Consider, for example the following page written in static HTML page:

```html
<html>
<head>
  <title>Foundation ASP.NET for Flash</title>
</head>
<body>
  <h1>Today's Date is 1/1/2005</h1>
</body>
</html>
```

Using this HTML, the same output will be displayed every time a user requests the page (Figure 1-2). Even if someone navigates to this page in 2024, the page will still say *Today's Date is 1/1/2005*. If you would like to make this page always show the correct date, it would be necessary to update it every day—a time-consuming task!

Figure 1-2. static.htm

Now, let's look at a similar page (Figure 1-3) written using a dynamic web page technology, *classic Active Server Pages (ASP)*:

```html
<html>
<head>
        <title>Foundation ASP.NET for Flash</title>
</head>
<body>
        <h1>Today's Date is <%Response.Write Date() %></h1>
</body>
</html>
```

Figure 1-3. simpledate.asp

You'll notice that the page, instead of containing a specific date, contains the code <%Response.Write Date() %>. What exactly is happening here? This doesn't look like standard HMTL . . . The <% symbol is telling the page "some ASP code will be executed starting here." Following this, Response.Write Date() is equivalent to saying "insert into the page the text value of the current date." This command is executed *on the web server, each time the page is requested.* And as a result, instead of containing a hard-coded date, the page now returns the current date each time the page is accessed—and you don't have to update the page every day!

This is just a simple example of the functions that dynamic web technologies can accomplish. They are also able to process many more complex functions such as database access, image, and file manipulation. The key to the dynamic technologies is that, as noted in the previous example, they are executing their functionality *on the web server, when the page is requested.* Because these technologies are executed strictly on the web server, they are known as *server-side* technologies. Again, this is the exact opposite of code executed by Flash, which occurs on the client's computer and is considered a *client-side* technology.

Since the inception of the Web, many server-side technologies have evolved for creating these dynamic web pages—the most recent of which is ASP.NET 2.0. Let's take a look at a few of these technologies to see where ASP.NET has come from and learn some competitive obstacles it has to overcome.

CGI

CGI (Common Gateway Interface) is the oldest and one of the most commonly used technologies for creating dynamic web pages. CGI is not a programming language or website architecture, but rather a mechanism for making a specific program run. CGI is typically written using the Perl programming language, although it can be written with languages such as C and C++. One of CGI's main advantages is that it is completely platform independent; it can run on nearly any type of web server.

ASP

In 1996, Microsoft released its first official web scripting language, ASP (Active Server Pages). ASP pages are written using either VBScript (as in the previous Date() example) or JavaScript. ASP pages are capable of accomplishing any of the tasks required from a modern web application, including database access and e-mail functionality. ASP went through three versions from 1996 to 2000, and is the predecessor of ASP.NET. ASP is now commonly referred to as *classic ASP*.

JSP

JSP (JavaServer Pages) is a web technology created by Sun Technologies that allows the Java programming language to be used to create dynamic HTML pages. JSP pages are typically hosted on Solaris or Linux platforms, but can be hosted on nearly any environment, including Windows.

ColdFusion

ColdFusion is a technology that was created by Allaire and was acquired by Macromedia in 2001. ColdFusion uses a tag-based scripting language called CFML (ColdFusion Markup Language). Since being added to the Macromedia family, ColdFusion has been made to integrate well with other Macromedia technologies, such as Flash.

PHP

PHP (PHP Hypertext Preprocessor) is an open-source dynamic web technology that is very similar to ASP in architecture and was built using a programming language similar to Perl. PHP receives much of its following from the open-source community and is commonly used on Linux platforms.

ASP.NET

Last, but certainly not least: ASP.NET! ASP.NET is the newest, best, and brightest of the web server technologies. ASP.NET is the successor to ASP and will be explained thoroughly in this book. In the next section, we'll take a detailed look at ASP.NET and compare it to the alternative technologies.

ASP.NET

ASP.NET is the latest in Microsoft's web development arsenal. Actually, to say ASP.NET is *Microsoft's* may be a bit misleading. ASP.NET—and more generally, the .NET Framework—was developed *by Microsoft*, but is an open standard, available for use by any software manufacturer on any platform. It just so happens that at the time of this book's writing, *Microsoft's version* of ASP.NET is the most popular and well-developed version available. (It's also the version we will be using in this book.)

With all of the other available technologies for creating dynamic web pages, why would a developer specifically choose ASP.NET?

- **Support for many popular languages:** One of the big accomplishments of the .NET Framework is that it allows developers to write ASP.NET code using one of many supported .NET programming languages. This is a huge benefit of .NET, since it does not lock a developer down into a single language or require a specific previous set of experience. .NET Framework applications can be coded using languages including (but not limited to) Visual Basic .NET, C#, J# (Java for .NET), Python, and Visual C++. When creating sites using ASP.NET, teams of developers can even be using different languages on the same project without interoperability issues. It also allows you, as a developer, to become focused on one particular language and not "pigeon-hole" yourself into the type of development you can do or the teams you can work with. In this book, we look specifically at C#, the newest of the .NET programming languages. As we'll see in this chapter, C# is a perfect match for a Flash developer since it is very similar to the ActionScript language, and is also very similar to any modern, object-oriented languages, including C++, Java, and Visual Basic.

- **Improved performance:** ASP.NET has implemented features that make it a much faster platform than previous-generation architectures. One of the reasons that it is faster than other architectures is because it makes possible the use of compiled code instead of inline scripting—an architecture of web programming used by languages like ASP and PHP. We will discuss this difference in detail throughout this book, but for now, just understand that when using inline scripting, the web server has to do more work to generate dynamic web pages than with compiled code.

- **Access to powerful functionality:** ASP.NET, being part of the .NET Framework, has access to a variety of powerful resources, allowing it to easily perform tasks ranging from database access to image manipulation. Having access to this "library" of functionality allows you, as a developer, to focus more on the functions you want your application to accomplish, instead of the underlying syntax of the back-end architecture.

- **Simplicity:** Let's be honest. As a Flash developer, you do not want to be required to spend copious amounts of time doing server-side programming instead of working in Flash. The server-side aspect of Flash-based applications should be an enhancement instead of a thorn. That's another one of the great things about C# and .NET—the .NET Framework handles many of the low-level programming processes for you, allowing developers to focus on the programming logic, instead of language-specific details. This feature, combined with the previous feature, brings up one of the goals of the developers of ASP.NET: to allow developers to accomplish complicated tasks more *efficiently*.

- **Scalability:** ASP.NET allows developers to make applications that are much more *scalable* than when developed using previous-generation technologies. A scalable web application is able to "scale up" in size without losing manageability. For a Flash developer, consider this similar to scaling up a bitmap image compared to a vector—the bitmap will lose clarity as it scales up, while the vector will maintain its structure no matter what size it is scaled to. The same is true with scalable web applications, when their scope is increased to serve "millions" of requests; they do not lose functionality, performance, or manageability.

- **Security:** With the importance of security on the Internet today, it's critical to choose a platform that will keep all sensitive information safe. ASP.NET, especially when combined with the Internet Information Services (IIS) platform, has the most extensive set of security features available in a server-side language.

- **Community:** ASP.NET has a tremendous developer community, with online communities, support groups, and tutorials readily available. Its features are well documented and training is readily available. ASP.NET has many community resources available at the website www.asp.net.

These are just a few of the benefits of using ASP.NET—we explore many more throughout this book. To put it in a nutshell, though, ASP.NET is a great choice for server-side development because, once you learn the technology, complicated tasks can be accomplished in a fraction of the time previously possible.

Flash/ASP.NET communication

As we've discussed, Flash by itself does not have access to the same functionalities as server-side technologies. One of the functionalities essential to modern-day web applications that Flash is incapable of on its own is database access. This is where the Flash-ASP.NET tag-team combination comes into play, making use of several methods for passing data back and forth between client-side Flash movies and server-side ASP.NET code.

A Flash movie on its own only has access to the data embedded within the .swf created by the developer. Let's say, for example, you want to make a web page with a Flash interface to display information about the products in a store's inventory. To accomplish this, you would have to individually enter that product's information as ActionScript into the Flash movie. This process would be very time consuming and unorganized, and cause the resulting Flash file to grow in size with each item entered.

This page would also be very "static," like the candy bar machine example earlier in this chapter. Once you have created the .swf and posted it to a web server, the inventory displayed on that site would be unchanging until you updated your ActionScript, republished the Flash movie, and reposted the .swf file to your web server. This process is time consuming, and probably not very realistic for a store with a large inventory, especially if the store's inventory needs to be updated often!

The way to get around this limitation is to use server-side technologies like the combination of ASP.NET and SQL Server to store and manage the store's inventory data and create methods for Flash to access this updated data as often as it wants. By housing the data storage and logic within the server-side technologies, your Flash file is now only responsible for the "presentation" logic—how to display the data. Now when you need to update the store's inventory, you don't even need to touch the Flash file; instead, the database can be updated and the Flash movie will load the updated information.

Methods of communicating between Flash and ASP.NET

Flash provides numerous methods for performing this communication with server-side technologies. In this book, we examine several of these methods and discuss the strengths and weaknesses of each. The methods we discuss are

- FlashVars
- LoadVars
- XML object
- Web services
- .NET Flash Remoting

FlashVars

FlashVars are a method of communicating between ASP.NET and Flash that uses tags embedded within HTML to exchange data. FlashVars only allow for one-way communication—from the server to the Flash movie. Because of this, FlashVars are not an alternative for applications that require data to be sent from a client-side application to a web server, such as an e-mail form. FlashVars, however, are a very fast and efficient form of communication and are often overlooked in circumstances where small amounts of data need to be sent to a Flash movie.

FlashVars are unique among the methods discussed in this book in that the data they contain is sent *along with* the .swf file when requested by the client browser, instead of in a separate load *after* a Flash movie is loaded. This concept will be covered in depth in Chapter 2.

LoadVars

The LoadVars object is much more versatile than FlashVars in terms of the direction and amount of data that can be exchanged. The LoadVars object is capable of either sending data to the server for processing, loading data from the server, or sending data to the server and waiting for a response from the server in one operation. The LoadVars object uses *name-value pairs* to exchange data between the client and server. The LoadVars object is best used in a scenario that requires two-way communication between the Flash movie and server-side logic, but doesn't require large amounts of data to be passed.

XML object

The Flash XML object is another option for communication between a web server and Flash client. The XML object is very similar to the LoadVars object in functionality; it can both send data to the web server and receive data from it. The difference between the XML object and the LoadVars object is the format in which the data is sent and received. Whereas the LoadVars object expects a name-value pair as a response, the XML object sends and receives a well-formatted, structured XML document. Structured XML data makes the XML object much more suitable than the LoadVars object for handling larger amounts of data.

9

Web services

Introduced with Flash MX 2004 Professional edition, web services are the newest method for communicating between Flash and ASP.NET. Web services use Simple Object Access Protocol (SOAP), an XML-based format, to transfer data between the client and server. Web services are an industry standard for exposing proprietary "services" for others to use in their applications. An example of a web service is the search method offered by Google. By using this method through web services, it is possible for you to create a Flash application that makes use of the Google search engine. Web services are also a strong point of ASP.NET and make it easy to publish web service functionality.

Flash Remoting

Flash Remoting is the most powerful and versatile of the options for communicating between a Flash movie and a .NET web server. Using Flash Remoting, it is possible to directly access data from an ASP.NET web application in a secure, quick, and efficient way. Using Flash Remoting does come with a price tag, however. Flash Remoting for ASP.NET is a standalone server-side component not included with Flash MX 2004, and it costs $999.

Three-tier architecture

Now that we understand the strengths and limitations of Flash, static web pages, dynamic web pages, ASP.NET, and Flash/ASP.NET communication, let's take a little more in-depth look at how the combination of these technologies fits together to create next-generation web applications. In order to describe how these technologies work together, I'd like to introduce a web application architecture known as a *three-tier application architecture*.

In a three-tier web application architecture, the processes occurring in the application are divided into sections, or *tiers*. These tiers are organized by the functionality they attempt to accomplish.

As an easy way of understanding application tiers, imagine a medieval army consisting of three units: front-line infantry, cavalry, and archers (see Figure 1-4). If the individual members of these units are not kept separate and are allowed to intermingle, the army's success will be limited. Archers, for example, will have a hard time shooting over the cavalry and the infantry, which risk being trodden by the cavalry. When the units are separated, though, the archers can do their work first, followed by the cavalry as an entire unit, and finally the infantry. By accomplishing a logical separation of the units, they are much more efficient and easy to manage.

Unorganized Army with
Mixed Division

Organized Army
Separated by Functionality

Figure 1-4. Three-tier army

The same is true for web applications, which is why these applications are divided into a three-tier architecture. With the three-tier architecture, the units of the application designed to accomplish similar tasks can be grouped into a single tier, making it easier to manage and maintain. In a three-tier web application, the tiers of the application are typically divided into the following:

- **Data tier:** The data tier is the "data store" for the application that houses the data that will be consumed by the application. In most application architecture today, the data tier is separated from the other tiers in an application. The data tier of a web application typically consists of database technologies such as MySQL, SQL Server, or Oracle. In this book, we use Microsoft Access and SQL Server 2005 Express edition as our data tier.

- **Logical tier:** This tier is also commonly referred to as the "business logic" or "middle" tier. The logical tier does most of the application's "grunt work," performing the majority of the computation and processing of the web application. The logical tier also provides the application with access to the data tier. In a web application, this tier exists on the web server and is typically one of the dynamic web languages I have previously mentioned. In the case of Flash/ASP.NET applications, ASP.NET will be our workhorse, performing the work in the logical tier.

- **Presentation tier:** The presentation tier is, as it sounds, the component of the application that takes care of the interface that is presented to the application's end user. The presentation tier typically contains processing functions related to the user interface, but not database access or "business logic" type functions. The presentation tier in web applications is typically accomplished using HTML. In this book, though, we will talk about one of the most powerful presentation-tier technologies available, Macromedia Flash.

In previous generation web technologies, these functional units, especially the presentation and logical tiers, were often combined into one, making it very difficult to manage and update any single element within the application. The combination of ASP.NET, SQL Server, and Flash, however, maintains a clear division between these tiers, and each unit provides us with the most powerful of its type available today. Figure 1-5 shows a visual representation of the three-tier architecture. When shown visually, it's easy to see why ASP.NET is an essential "translator" for database integration with Flash.

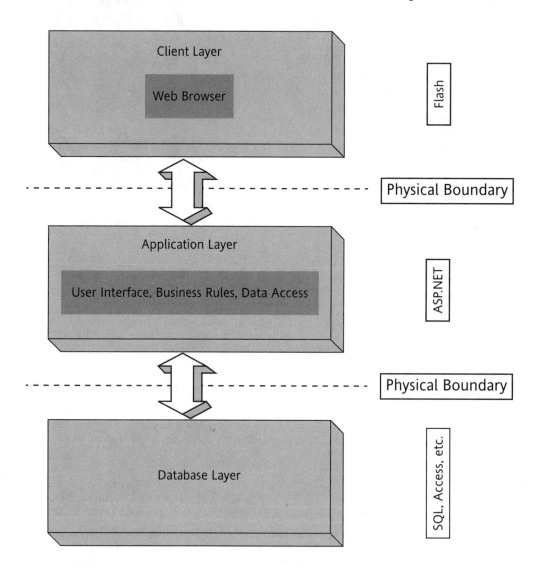

Figure 1-5. Three-tier application architecture using Flash, ASP.NET, and SQL Server

Let's use a simple example to take a look at the process that occurs when these tiers work together to accomplish a task in a web application. In this example, we'll build a theoretical plan for a digital photo gallery that has a user interface that displays images for its users, allows the user to cast a vote for a specific image in the gallery, and tallies these votes in a database. Even with a vague project definition like this, we can easily define which tiers will accomplish each portion of the task, and then pick the technologies that will compose those tiers:

- **Data tier:** The data tier will store information about the images in the gallery, such as width, height, name, author, location, and the number of votes that image has received.

- **Logical tier:** The logical tier will handle the access and modification of the data from the data tier, the formatting of that data, the storage of the images in the gallery, and any search-type functionality needed.

- **Presentation tier:** The presentation tier will handle the user interface. This tier will be required to communicate with the logical tier to retrieve a list of images in the gallery, lay out these photos, and add interactive elements in the interface. When a user selects an image to cast a vote for it, the presentation tier will need to send a notification to the logical tier indicating that the specified image has received a vote.

In this example application (and for the rest of the book), we will use Flash as our presentation tier, ASP.NET as the logical tier, and Microsoft Access or SQL Server as the data tier. Normally in a Flash/ASP.NET project, it is very important to weigh the benefits of each method of communication and choose a single method accordingly. We probably don't have enough information to knowledgably pick a method for this example, but to accomplish the task, it will have to be one of the methods that is capable of exchanging fairly large amounts of structured data—either LoadVars, the XML object, web services, or Flash Remoting.

Let's take a look at the steps that take place when the interaction occurs between the tiers in this application as a user requests the initial page of the gallery:

1. The user requests the web page that hosts the application. When this request occurs, the web server sends the Flash file in the form of an .swf to the client browser for display.

2. The browser receives the .swf file and executes it in its *Flash Player*. At this point, though, no images from the gallery are contained in the .swf file, so . . .

3. The .swf file communicates back to the web server (using one of the methods I've briefly described), requesting a list of the photos to display in the initial page of the gallery.

4. The web server receives this request and sends a *query* to the SQL database to retrieve the file names of the images in this page of the gallery.

5. ASP.NET formats this data (depending on the method of communication the application is using) and sends it back to the .swf file.

6. The .swf file receives this data from the ASP.NET logical tier and extracts the file names of the gallery images from it.

7. At this point, the .swf file knows what the names of the images it should be displaying are. The .swf file now loads those images (as thumbnails) and displays them on the user interface.

No problem, right? The Flash file in this example contains very limited "application logic" and instead contains the logic used in presenting the interface to the user. ASP.NET waits for a request from the presentation tier, and when it receives that request, it sends a message to the data tier to retrieve the necessary information and then sends the information back. That's it—the functionality is carried out in a very organized, effective, and structured manner, with the functional blocks clearly divided. Now, let's take a look at what happens when a user attempts to "vote" for an image in the gallery:

1. The user clicks the "vote" button in the Flash interface.

2. The .swf file receives this click, and responds by sending a message to the web server and ASP.NET. This message contains an indicator of the image the user voted for.

3. ASP.NET receives this message and again sends a query to the SQL database. This time, though, the query doesn't need to return values, but instead increments the value of the number of votes for a specified image in the gallery.

4. The SQL database increments the value and indicates to the ASP.NET that the value was incremented successfully.

5. ASP.NET forwards this indication on to the .swf file.

6. The .swf file receives the verification that the vote was registered successfully and passes the message on to the user of the application through the application's interface.

These steps, used to update the value of a database entry, are almost identical to the steps used to retrieve a list of the images in the gallery. It is almost exactly this same process that will be used many times throughout this book to allow Flash, ASP.NET, and SQL Server to work together to create powerful web applications.

C#

If we're going to be learning about using Flash with ASP.NET, where does C# come into the mix? Like many other dynamic web technologies, ASP.NET itself is not a programming language but a web application architecture. In this book, we will use the C# programming language to create ASP.NET applications.

> ASP.NET applications can be written using other .NET-compatible languages, including VB .NET and JScript. I have chosen C# for this book because of its similarities to the ActionScript 2.0 programming language and the third-party support for the C# language.

C# (pronounced *see-sharp*), is the newest language in the C family of languages. C# is a "best-of-breed" language, combining the most popular features of the C++, Java, and Visual Basic languages. If you are already familiar with C++ or Java, you will have no problem with C# due to its similar object-oriented structure.

C#, although designed by Microsoft, is a European Computer Manufacturers Association (ECMA) standard. This means that, like the .swf standard, C# is a public standard and companies other than Microsoft can release *compilers* for C#. This open standard adds to the popularity of the language, since entities other than Microsoft can provide a C# development implementation. This also adds the potential of exposing C# development to the open-source community (see the section "Developing and executing on other platforms" at the end of this chapter). Microsoft's specific implementation of the C# standard is known as Microsoft C# .NET.

Although we will use C# only for web-based development in this book, C# can be used for both web and Windows desktop development. This is a great reason to select C# as your language of choice since the knowledge you gain in learning the basics of C# can be applied to web page, web services, and Windows Forms applications. As the barrier between web and desktop applications gets broken down (which we'll be trying to do in this book), it will become increasingly important for a developer to understand both types of program architecture.

C# is also the most widely supported of the .NET languages for development on non-Microsoft operating systems (see "Developing and executing on other platforms" later in this chapter). This capability makes C# a much more "universal" language than languages such as Visual Basic, which are historically more specific to the Windows platform.

As we work through examples in this book, I will cover the syntax of C# as well as many of its features—but space prohibits us from covering them all. For more information on C#, check out Andrew Troelsen's *C# and the .NET Platform* (Apress, 2001), which provides a great analysis of many of the additional features of the C# language.

Similarities between C# and ActionScript 2.0

Although it might seem that Flash and C# have very little in common, they actually have very similar origins and architectures. Because of these similarities, it is fairly easy for programmers familiar with ActionScript 2.0 to make the jump to C# (or vice versa). As we go through the examples in this book, I will try to point out these similarities (and differences) so that the transition between languages is a smooth one.

ActionScript's origins follow very closely those of JavaScript, a technology that emerged in 1996. In its original release, JavaScript had very little *object-oriented* functionality, but rather used a *procedural* architecture. As ActionScript developed from its 1.0 to 2.0 versions, it followed the trends of the time and implemented more and more object-oriented functionality in its architecture. Today, with version 2.0, ActionScript is fully object-oriented and implements such features as an event-driven model, which puts it on par with the improvements of other modern languages.

Active Server Pages (ASP), the predecessor of ASP.NET pages, were "born" in the same year as JavaScript and follow the same architectural model. As a matter of fact, ASP pages can be built *using* JavaScript! (Talk about similar origins!) C#, a member of the C family of languages, also has a language structure similar to that of JavaScript, since JavaScript's origins closely resemble that of the C languages. C#, although following in the footsteps of procedural languages like C, was built from the ground up as a fully object-oriented language.

It is because of these similar origins and evolutions that C# and ActionScript 2.0 are so much alike in syntax and functionality. One major difference between ActionScript and C# is that in ActionScript you can "fudge" the rules of ActionScript 2.0 and use the more flexible rules of 1.0 without any penalty, whereas C# is much stricter in the enforcement of its object-oriented rules. Table 1-1 lists some of the other specific similarities and differences between these languages.

Table 1-1. ActionScript 2.0 vs. C#

Feature	ActionScript 2.0	C#
Arrays	Allows nonsequential indexes	States that arrays must have sequential elements
Variable typing	Recommended (but optional) strict typing	Strict typing
Syntax for type declaration	myString:String	string myString
Case-sensitive	Yes	Yes
Object-oriented	Yes	Yes
Event-driven	Yes	Yes
Dot-syntax	Yes	Yes
Complex collection objects	Limited	Yes
Backward language compatibility	Yes	No

Throughout the rest of this book, I will point out these and other similarities and differences between the C# and ActionScript programming languages.

The .NET Framework

So far, we've established that ASP.NET is a dynamic web development architecture and that C# is a language that can be used to develop ASP.NET applications. But what exactly is the .NET Framework? The .NET Framework (see Figure 1-6) is the entire development and execution environment used to create and deploy ASP.NET (and Windows Forms) applications. This framework is composed of a *Framework Class Library (FCL)* and a *common language runtime (CLR)* on which the ASP.NET architecture is based.

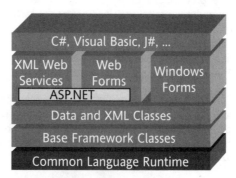

Figure 1-6. The .NET Framework

The common language runtime (CLR)

Okay, what the heck is a "common language runtime"? Not to worry, it's nowhere near as complicated as it sounds. In order to explain what the CLR is and how it relates to C#, let's take a look at something we're already familiar with: .fla files, .swf files, and the Flash Player.

As you probably already know, files you create using the Macromedia Flash development environment are saved in the .fla format. This .fla format cannot be "executed" by any other program other than the Flash IDE and is used mainly for the creation process. When you "publish" an .fla file, the combination of code and timeline-based objects you have created are *compiled* into a more compact format, .swf. The .swf format is no longer editable, but is now capable of being executed using the Macromedia Flash Player. When the .swf file is embedded into an HTML page and displayed in a web browser, the Flash Player on the client's system provides the *runtime environment* for the .swf file to execute in. This runtime environment acts as an interface between the .swf file and the low-level functionality of the client system, allowing it to accomplish functions such as displaying graphics and playing sounds.

The same general methods apply to C# and the common language runtime. When you create a C# file in Visual Studio .NET (or another program), it is purely in the form of source code, as an .fla file is. In order for this file to be in an "executable" format, it has to be *compiled* into a **.dll** file, similar to the way an .fla file is published to create an .swf file. Once this .dll is compiled, it can be executed on a web server (or any other system) that has the common language runtime installed. The CLR provides the interface between the .dll file and the system's underlying architecture, just as the Flash Player does for .swf files. Figure 1-7 demonstrates the similarities between ActionScript code compilation and the Flash Player, and C# code compilation to the common language runtime.

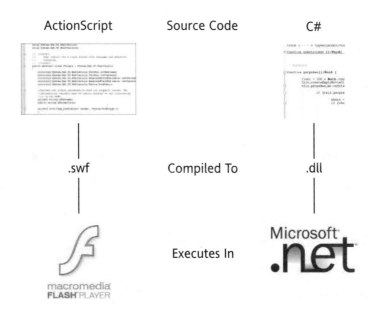

Figure 1-7. ActionScript and C# compilation compared

> *Since ASP.NET is a server-side technology, only the web server is required to have the .NET Framework installed. Unlike Flash, which requires the Flash Player to be installed, client machines that attempt to view ASP.NET pages are not required to have the .NET Framework installed.*

The Framework Class Library (FCL)

Again, here's a .NET term (along with another acronym!) that sounds complicated but that's not really all that difficult to understand. The FCL is a library of objects that can be reused throughout your projects. These objects provide standard functionality that allows you to accomplish tasks in C# without "reinventing the wheel." The FCL is very similar to the prebuilt classes and components provided in Flash such as MovieClip, Button, and the variable types such as String and Number. The libraries in the FCL include tremendously powerful collections, such as ADO.NET (the .NET Framework's data access libraries) and ASP.NET (the libraries that give .NET the ability to create and distribute web applications). As we go through the examples in this book, you'll start to get a feel for the scope of the FCL and its (hopefully) intuitive architecture.

Setup

Before we can start working with ASP.NET and Flash, it's important to have a development environment set up to perform all the necessary code compilation and testing. Listed here are the components needed to create the examples in this book:

- .NET Framework
- .NET SDK
- Internet Information Services
- SQL 2005 Express Edition
- Visual Studio .NET 2005 (or equivalent)
- Flash MX 2004 or higher

> *We assume that you already have the Flash development environment installed. If you do not have Flash installed, you can obtain a 30-day trial from the Macromedia website:* www.macromedia.com/cfusion/tdrc/index.cfm?product=flash_mx2004_pro.

Installing the .NET Framework

The .NET Framework is the essential element to compiling and running an ASP.NET application on your development machine. This framework will also need to be installed on any web server you intend to deploy an ASP.NET application to.

If you are planning on installing Visual Studio .NET 2005, this step may be skipped as it will be installed along with Visual Studio.

1. Download the .NET Framework 2.0 package as shown in Figure 1-8. The exact URL of this download will change as the release version of the .NET Framework is posted, so I recommend doing a Google search for ".NET Framework 2.0" to find the exact download URL.

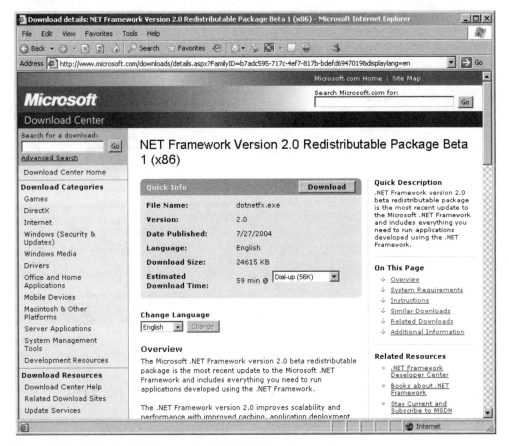

Figure 1-8. Installing the .NET Framework redistributable package

Once you have completed downloading the redistributable framework, run the dotnetfx.exe file and follow the prompts to install. There's really no configuration required, just download and let it go!

2. Download the .NET Framework 2.0 SDK. Again the exact location of this download is unsure at this point, but a quick Google search for ".NET Framework 2.0 SDK" should get you there easily.

3. Once the download has completed, run the setup.exe file and continue through the installation of the .NET Framework SDK. When the installation package prompts for the installation of the Software Development Kit and the SDK Examples, I recommend installing both. The SDK examples installs many sample files in C# useful for future ASP.NET reference.

And that's it! You now have the .NET Framework installed. If you are interested in testing the installation (or making sure the files are really there), you can check by navigating to the `Microsoft.NET/Framework/`directory in your system's base Windows directory (`C:\WINNT` on my system), as in Figure 1-9.

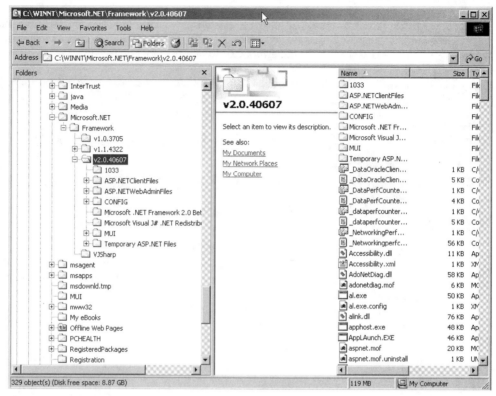

Figure 1-9. Checking your .NET Framework installation

Setting up Internet Information Services (IIS)

In order to host ASP.NET web applications, we need a web server supporting the ASP.NET framework. In general, ASP.NET pages can be hosted on any Microsoft Windows 2000+ server with the .NET Framework installed. Since the .NET Framework is cross-platform compatible, it is also possible to host ASP.NET on non-Microsoft operating systems, such as Linux or Sun, which we cover in the section, "Developing and executing on other platforms," later in this chapter.

For development purposes, ASP.NET can also be hosted on Internet Information Services (IIS) running on a desktop operating system, such as Windows 2000 or Windows XP. For the examples in this book, we will install IIS on a local computer to host our sample applications.

> *Visual Studio .NET 2005 also includes an integrated development web server. If you are using this web server, IIS is not required for creating and testing ASP.NET pages.*

Installing IIS

Installing IIS with support for ASP.NET on your Windows development system is relatively easy. If you don't already have IIS running, here's a quick and easy way to get it going:

1. First, make sure you have the most recent version of the .NET Framework installed (see the previous "Installing the .NET Framework" section).

2. Go to the Add/Remove Programs screen in the Windows Control Panel, as shown in Figure 1-10.

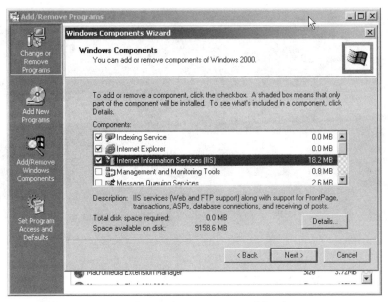

Figure 1-10. Selecting IIS in the Windows Components Wizard

3. Select Add/Remove Windows Components.

4. Select Internet Information Services (IIS) and click Next. This may require that you insert the operating system disk of the system you are working on.

And again, that's it—you now have Internet Information Services running on your system. Once you have IIS running on your system, you will need to run the aspnet_regiis.exe tool, which "starts up" ASP.NET on IIS. This tool can be run from the command prompt by going to the .NET Framework SDK command prompt, as shown in Figure 1-11, and running the command aspnet_regiis.exe –I, as shown in Figure 1-12.

Figure 1-11. .NET Framework SDK Command Prompt launched from the Start menu

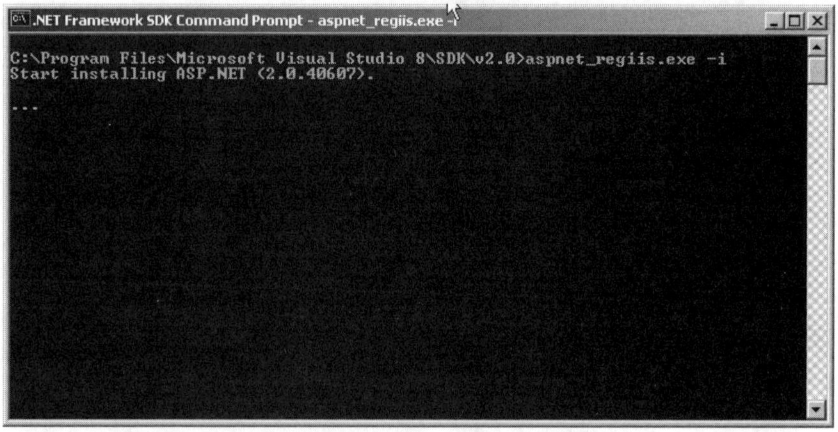

```
C:\Program Files\Microsoft Visual Studio 8\SDK\v2.0>aspnet_regiis.exe -i
Start installing ASP.NET (2.0.40607).

...
```

Figure 1-12. Starting the ASP.NET process

Testing your IIS/ASP.NET installation

Once you have IIS installed on your local system, you will be able to access your local IIS web server by navigating to http://localhost/ as shown in Figure 1-13.

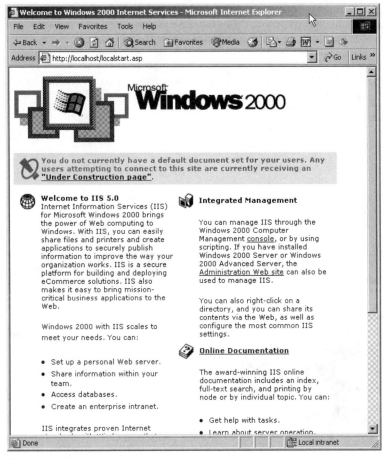

Figure 1-13. IIS successfully running

This test proves that we have IIS running, but not necessarily support for ASP.NET. We will be performing our first the ASP.NET installation test in the next chapter, when we develop our first ASP.NET web page.

Installing SQL 2005 Express Edition

Since many of today's web applications require database integration, it's also necessary to choose a database technology when deciding on a server-side web programming technology. ASP.NET is capable of integrating seamlessly with nearly every database technology on the market today, including Microsoft Access, MySQL, Oracle, and Microsoft SQL. In the later chapters of this book, I will focus on Microsoft's SQL Server, which is the most closely integrated with ASP.NET and the .NET Framework. Specifically, we will work with SQL Server 2005 Express Edition, which is a free version of SQL Server that can be installed right on your desktop system. Microsoft SQL 2005 Server's support of such advanced features as stored procedures, relationships, and indexes makes it a very powerful database technology.

Microsoft SQL 2005 Express Edition is a full-featured version of SQL Server, with some limitations in reporting features and analysis services. The Express Edition is designed for development purposes and is not meant to be used in a production environment.

> Because SQL Server 2005 is in Beta 2 at the writing of this book, the download/install process may change as the final version is released.

Here's how to install Microsoft SQL 2005 Express Edition:

1. Navigate to http://lab.msdn.microsoft.com/express/sql/ (see Figure 1-14).

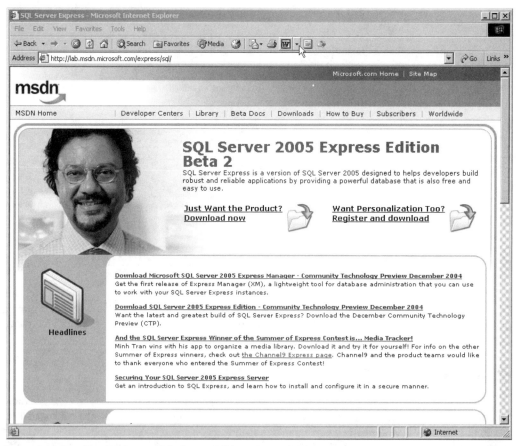

Figure 1-14. Installing SQL Server 2005 Express Edition

2. Click the Download Now link, then click the Download link on the following page.

3. When prompted to save the file, save it to a location on your system. After the download has finished, run the SQLEXPR.EXE file.

4. Continue through the installation process.

And that's all it takes—you now have a database environment installed on your desktop system! Databases created on SQL Server 2005 Express can be easily transferred to production web servers or even exported as Access databases for easy deployment.

Visual Studio .NET 2005

Microsoft Visual Studio .NET is the most powerful development environment for creating ASP.NET applications on the market today and the first to support ASP.NET 2.0 development. Visual Studio .NET is the complete package for writing, debugging, and deploying ASP.NET apps in the shortest amount of time possible. Using Visual Studio .NET, it is possible to easily develop not only ASP.NET web pages, but also ASP.NET web services and .NET Windows applications and services.

Specifically for ASP.NET developers, Visual Studio 2005 provides the following features:

- **IntelliSense everywhere:** IntelliSense (see Figure 1-15) is one of the coolest features of Visual Studio .NET. IntelliSense provides pop-up code hints in the Visual Studio environment while you are typing the code, making object-oriented programming much easier to learn and develop.

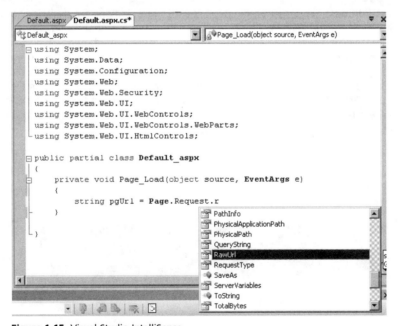

Figure 1-15. Visual Studio IntelliSense

- **Integrated debugger for Web applications:** Visual Studio .NET provides a unique web debugging model that makes it easy to debug the ASP.NET code you have written. Using Visual Studio and Internet Explorer, it's even possible to debug client-side scripts like JavaScript.

- **Integrated FTP support:** In previous versions of Visual Studio, any remote file access had to be done either using FrontPage extensions or through third-party software. Visual Studio .NET 2005, however, has a built-in FTP client, useful for connecting to remote ASP.NET websites and deploying local sites using FTP connections.

- **Built-in web server:** ASP.NET web applications can be built and tested on your local development machine without the need for IIS. This is an important feature for developers using operating systems like Windows XP Home Edition, which does not allow IIS installations.

- **WYSIWYG editor:** Visual Studio .NET 2005 provides extensive design support for creating ASP.NET files. This WYSIWYG is comparable to the tools provided by other products such as Dreamweaver.

- **Drag-and-drop data access:** Using Visual Studio .NET, you can create powerful database functionality through the use of drag-and-drop designers and code wizards. This feature takes many of the arduous tasks associated with data access out of the hands of the ASP.NET developer and allows you to focus on code functionality.

Visual Studio .NET 2005 editions

With the release of Visual Studio 2005, Microsoft has changed the structure of its release versions. In the Visual Studio .NET family, four versions are now available: the Express versions, the Standard version, the Professional version, and the Team version. Since choosing between these versions may seem like a tricky task in itself, I will highlight the strengths and weaknesses of each:

- **Express Editions:** The Visual Studio .NET 2005 Express Editions are designed to be high-level development environments for the "hobbyist, enthusiast, or student" and are perfect for easing into .NET development. These editions come with a more limited set of development tools than the Professional or Team Editions, but offer more than enough tools for you to learn and deploy .NET projects. Unlike the other editions of Visual Studio .NET, the Express Editions are broken down specifically by the type of development you will be doing (as shown in Figure 1-16). For the ASP.NET developer, the Visual Web Developer 2005 Express is the product of choice. At the time of the release of this book, the price for the Express products had not been set, but it is expected to range anywhere from "free" to $99.

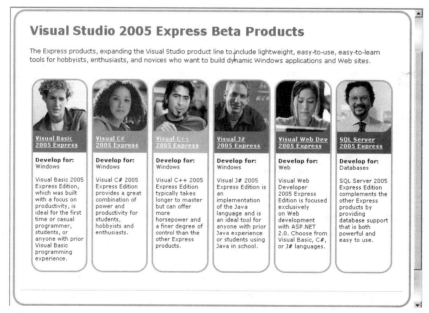

Figure 1-16. Visual Studio Express Editions

- **Standard Edition:** The Standard Edition of Visual Studio .NET is the first step into the "Professional" level of Visual Studio products. The Standard Edition, as compared to the Express Editions, has features such as mobile design support, improved deployment tools, and improved documentation. For the ASP.NET/Flash developer, the Standard Edition provides only slight improvements over the Visual Web Developer Express Edition. At the time of this book's writing, the price of the Standard Edition is unknown.

- **Professional Edition:** This version of Visual Studio is the real "step-up" for ASP.NET developers. The Professional Edition provides extended database connection functionality, enhanced SQL Server integration, and remote server debugging, and also ships with developer versions of both SQL Server 2005 and Windows Server 2003—perfect for creating an ASP.NET development environment.

- **Team Edition:** The Team Edition of Visual Studio is very similar to the Professional Edition with the addition of "team collaboration" and project management capabilities. The Team Edition is perfect for developing in group environments. This edition also provides additional features (not needed for ASP.NET/Flash development) such as Office development integration.

Installing Visual Studio .NET 2005

Installing Visual Studio .NET 2005 is a painless process. For this book, I will use the Visual Studio .NET 2005 Beta 1 release, codenamed "Whidbey." Installing Whidbey requires very little configuration, with the only configuration options shown in Figure 1-17.

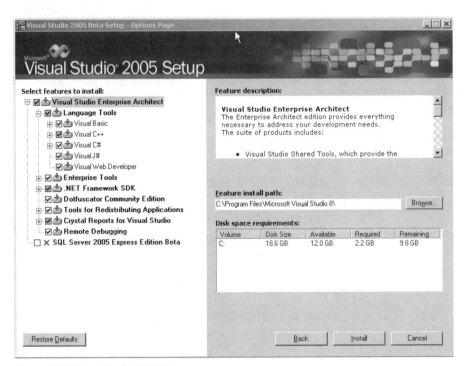

Figure 1-17. Visual Studio 2005 Setup

Notice that in this figure, I have installed Visual Studio with the default options. The only additional install we will need for the examples in this book is the SQL Server 2005 Express Edition.

Exploring the Visual Studio interface

Once you have Visual Studio .NET installed, let's take a look at the web designer interface. The default Visual Studio interface consists of *dockable* windows that allow you to customize your interface—a feature similar to the Flash MX 2004 IDE. In Chapter 2, we walk through the process of starting a new project using Visual Studio .NET, but for now, let's jump forward and take a quick look around the interface. In the default Visual Studio development interface, shown in Figure 1-18, you will notice (from top to bottom, left to right) the following windows:

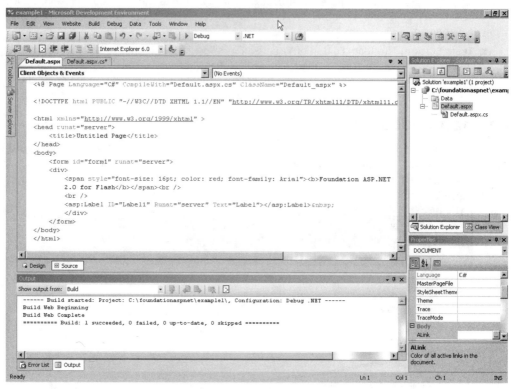

Figure 1-18. Visual Studio interface

- **Server Explorer (hidden on the left as a button):** The Server Explorer is a visual database design tool that allows .NET-compatible databases to be created and modified from right within the Visual Studio .NET environment. Database connections can typically be made in an application by simply dragging-and-dropping a database table from this explorer window to the design interface.

- **Toolbox (hidden on the left as a button):** The Toolbox is, just as it sounds, a storage bin for drag-and-drop WYSIWYG components that can be used in the Visual Studio design environment. The toolbox contains components ranging from text input fields to data access controls.

- **Design window (docked behind the Source window):** The Design window is a visual representation of the components in your ASP.NET web page. The Design window attempts to render the interface as closely as possible to what it would look like in a browser window. The Design window does not, however, execute any code when displaying this view.

- **Source view:** The Source view displays the HTML code that is being displayed by the Design view. Using the Source view, you can directly edit the HTML source of an ASP.NET web page.

- **Solution Explorer:** The Solution Explorer (Figure 1-19) is a list of all files within your current ASP.NET project. These files are grouped by two categories—Solutions and Projects, which we discuss more in the next chapter. Options relevant to projects, solutions, and files can be accessed in the Solution Explorer by simply right-clicking on the element.

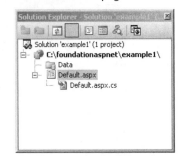

Figure 1-19. Visual Studio Solution Explorer

- **Class view (docked behind Solution Explorer):** The Class view allows developers to view a visual representation of .NET library and custom classes.

- **Error list (docked behind the Output window):** This window displays the errors encountered when building a .NET project.

- **Output:** Displays the textual output from a .NET compilation or operation.

- **Properties window:** Displays the properties of the current object selected in the Design window. This window provides easy access to component properties and events.

In the following chapters, we will touch upon some of the features of Visual Studio, but I'll try to focus more on the features of the C# language than features specific to the Visual Studio IDE. For more information about using Visual Studio .NET, check out its home page at http://msdn.microsoft.com/vstudio/.

#Develop: A free alternative to Visual Studio .NET

#Develop (pronounced sharp-develop) is a free development environment used to create C# and VB .NET projects. #Develop is created under the GPL open source license, and if you're interested, you can get involved in helping out with the product development. Although we will not be using #Develop for the development of ASP.NET pages in this book, it's great to know that, like other server-side web technologies, ASP.NET has open-source development alternatives (see Figure 1-20).

Some of the features of #Develop specific to web development include

- ASP.NET site creation
- Web services creation
- Code syntax highlighting
- HTML Editor
- Templated "wizards" for code creation

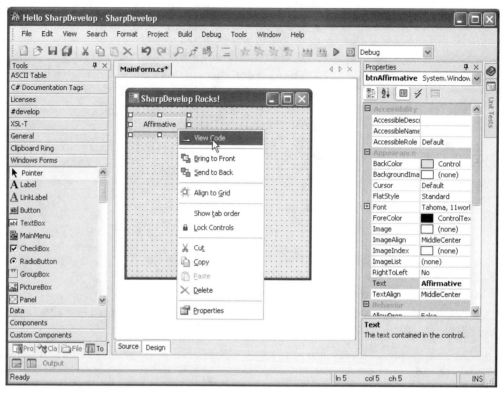

Figure 1-20. #Develop interface

Developing and executing on other platforms

It's important to note that although we will be discussing development and deployment of ASP.NET pages on Windows platforms, it is also possible for ASP.NET pages to be created and hosted on non-Microsoft platforms. This flexibility is available because the .NET Framework is completely platform independent—it can be installed on any OS that has a .NET Framework implementation.

One example of a non-Windows implementation of the framework is called the Mono Project. The Mono Project is an implementation of the .NET Framework for a variety of operating systems that allows those systems to execute the majority of the functionality provided by Microsoft's implementation of the .NET Framework. The Mono Project brings the .NET Framework to the following platforms:

- Mac OS X – 10.3
- Sun Solaris
- Red Hat 9.0, x86
- Slackware 10
- Fedora Core Linux 2, x86
- SUSE Linux 9.1, x86

The Mono Project is an open-source project sponsored by Novell that includes a compiler for the C# language, the CLR, and .NET class libraries.

> At this time, Mono ONLY includes support for the C# programming language. Mono plans to include support for Visual Basic and JScript in the future. At the time of this book's writing, Mono also implements only the .NET 1.1 Framework.

Mono also contains the class libraries for ADO.NET (which we will discuss in Chapter 8) and ASP.NET, making Mono a viable alternative for hosting ASP.NET web applications on non-Windows platforms such as Linux. Mono has an Apache module available, called mod_mono, which allows Apache to serve ASP.NET web pages.

The Mono Project also includes a development tool for creating ASP.NET (and other .NET) projects. This tool is called MonoDevelop, and is available at www.monodevelop.com. Using MonoDevelop, ASP.NET applications can be developed on *-nix based operating systems (including OS X). MonoDevelop does not, at this point, include a visual designer interface or many of the features of Visual Studio .NET, nor does it support the .NET 2.0 Framework.

Summary

In this chapter, we've covered a lot of ground. We established the need for the combination of Flash and ASP.NET, discussed some of the advantages of a three-tier application architecture, covered some of the specifics of C# and the .NET Framework, and got a good development environment set up. It is on these foundations that the next chapters move into the creation of ASP.NET/Flash applications. Hang on, it's going to be a fun ride!

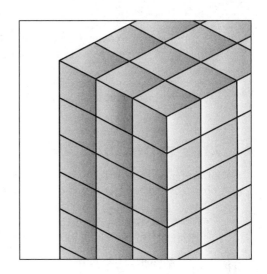

Chapter 2

C# PRIMER

What this chapter covers:

- Data types in C#
- Object-oriented programming concepts
- Strings
- Conditional logic
- Looping
- Enumerations
- Collections
- Dates

Before we get started working with ASP.NET, it's important to understand the fundamentals of the C# programming language. In this chapter, we'll cover some of the basics of C#, including data typing, memory allocation for variables, and some object-oriented programming concepts. From these concepts, you'll also get a better idea of the similarities between data types and object-oriented programming in C# and ActionScript 2.0.

Data types in C#

Data types, in general, are the foundation of any programming language. For those unfamiliar with the concept of data types (data typing is not necessary for ActionScript 1.0 programmers), a data type is a descriptor of a variable that defines that variable as being of a specific type, similar to declaring "this variable will be a number" or "this variable will be a date." An example of a variable declared as a *string* data type in both ActionScript and C# is shown here:

```
ActionScript 2.0:
myString:String;
C#:
string myString;
```

As you can see, this data type declaration is very similar in ActionScript 2.0 and C#, with ActionScript using the Java-based varName:varType syntax instead of the C-based declaration used by C#. Data types in all .NET languages are based on the same *primitive data types*. Primitive data types are types that are the basis of the language and can represent nearly anything a developer could need. Table 2-1 shows a list of the primitive data types in C#.

Table 2-1. C# primitive data types

C# Data Type	Description	ActionScript Equivalent
sbyte	8-bit signed integer	Number
byte	8-bit unsigned integer	Number
char	Represents a Unicode character	None
float	32-bit floating-point variable	Number
decimal	128-bit floating-point variable	Number
double	64-bit floating-point variable	Number
ushort	16-bit unsigned integer	Number
uint	32-bit unsigned integer	Number
int	32-bit signed integer	Number
ulong	64-bit unsigned integer	Number
long	64-bit signed integer	Number

C# Data Type	Description	ActionScript Equivalent
bool	Represents a true/false value	Boolean
string	Represents a series of Unicode characters	String
object	The base class that all classes in .NET inherit from	Object

Data typing becomes a very important concept in Flash and ASP.NET development since data must be reinterpreted each time it is exchanged from ASP.NET to Flash, or vice versa. For example, if you are writing an ASP.NET web service (see Chapter 7) that requires an integer as an input parameter, it is important to understand that, when using this service from Flash, you would need to pass a variable of number type since there is no direct ActionScript equivalent to integer.

Variables and memory

In .NET, and more specifically, C#, data types come in two different forms: *value types* and *reference types*. Of the primitive data types presented in the previous section, all are value types except for two: the string and object types. What's the difference between value and reference types? In order to completely understand the difference, it is first necessary to understand two concepts central to memory management in any programming language: the stack and the heap.

The stack

The stack is an area of a system's memory that is reserved by an application for its execution. All .NET variables that are of value type are stored on the stack. When these variables go *out of scope*, the variable is removed from the stack and is therefore deleted from the system's memory. (A variable is typically out of scope when the code's execution has left the codeblock in which that variable was defined.) To demonstrate what this means, let's take a look at our first C# method:

```
private void ValueTypeTest()
{
  int x=0;
  x++;
  int y=0;
  y++;
}
```

Doesn't look too bad, right? Structurally it is very similar to methods or functions in ActionScript. For the moment, let's ignore the syntax of the first line—this is a method declaration and we'll be talking more about these soon—and look at the first two lines that define and manipulate a variable:

```
int x=0;
x++;
```

In the first line, three things are really happening:

- A new variable, x, is created.
- x is declared as being of the integer data type.
- x is initialized with a value of 0.

In the second line of the previous codeblock, the increment operator, ++, is used to increment the value of the x variable. The increment operator in C# works in the same way as the ActionScript increment operator, adding one to an integer data type. Like ActionScript, C# also has a decrement operator, –. This operator works just the same as the increment, except it decreases the value of an integer variable by one. Since the variables x and y are declared in the ValueTypeTest method, it is within this method that they are considered to be *in scope* and, since they are value type variables, are *pushed* onto the stack. When this method completes its execution, these variables are considered *out of scope* and therefore no longer relevant to the program's execution. At this point, when the method has completed its execution, something interesting happens with the variables that have been created on the stack and are now out of scope—those variables are *popped* from the stack in the reverse order in which they were created. That's the way the stack works when storing variables, in a method called *last-in, first-out* (LIFO).

In this way, the stack is very similar to a deck of playing cards. When a card is added to the deck, it is always placed on the top of the deck. When a card is removed, it is also removed from the top—the same card that was last added to the deck.

When a method is called from within another method, a very common occurrence in object-oriented programming, the variables within the scope of the called method are placed on top of the original method's variables, or "on top of the deck." When this method completes, its variables are removed from the stack (or from the deck), and the stack is left with the original method's variables on top.

Because of their existence on the stack, value type variables have a feature that makes them fundamentally different than reference type variables. When a value type variable is created, it *must* have some value assigned to it, since it needs to exist on the stack. Therefore, value type variables are automatically given a default value by C# when they are created and not immediately assigned a value. For example, consider the following codeblock:

```
Bool bTest;  // bTest will be equal to false
Int iTest; // iTest will be equal to 0
```

In these two lines, we have initialized two value type variables without assigning them a value. Because they are of value type, C# will give the Boolean variable an initial value of false, and the integer a value of 0.

The heap

The heap is another section of memory, but this time, the memory is specifically designated for the creation of objects and reference type variables. As we've just discussed, when a variable of value type is created, a single instance of that variable is created in the stack, which is immediately discarded if the variable goes out of scope. When a variable is created that is of reference type, however, entries are actually created in *both* the stack and the heap. The entry that exists on the heap is an actual instance of that object and the entry on the stack is a *pointer* to that location in the heap. Although this may sound confusing, I'll try to explain it more clearly with examples throughout this book.

Because reference type variables have two separate entries in two separate memory locations, these variables must be declared in two steps, as in the following C# example:

```
myObjectType myObject; // create a reference on the stack
myObject = new myObjectType(); // create a new myObjectType on the heap
```

In the first line, a new variable named myObject is created. This variable creation actually creates the entry I've mentioned in the stack—a pointer that at this moment points to . . . nothing, otherwise known as a *null reference*. In the following line, this pointer is given a location on the heap to point to when a new entry on the heap is created, of the myObjectType type. Well, if value type variables get "recycled" when they go out of scope, what do you think happens to the more disjointed reference type variables? As with the value type variables, the pointer of the reference type variable that resides on the stack is destroyed when that variable goes out of scope. The heap entry, however, remains intact as a "floating" object—nearly useless without a pointer to track its location. This heap entry will, at some point, be cleaned up by the *.NET Garbage Collector*.

The .NET Garbage Collector is a process that runs in the background of the .NET Framework any time you have a .NET program running. This garbage collector periodically makes the rounds through the heap and other areas, finding unreferenced values and destroying them. The garbage collector is a godsend for developers familiar with C and C++, which rely on the developer to "clean up after themselves" by performing their own object recycling.

Object-oriented programming in C#

If you are an experienced ActionScript 2.0 developer, you probably already have a good idea of how object-oriented programming works, as ActionScript 2.0 is an object-oriented language. C# is also completely object oriented—as you'll realize after working with C# for a while, *everything in C# is an object*! What exactly does this mean? To understand better, let's examine exactly what an "object" is.

An object, in the context of object-oriented programming, is not too much different from an object in the "real world." An object in object-oriented programming is a collection of *properties*, *methods*, and *events* that represents an entity in your code. Although this might sound complicated, it's really not. Let's suppose that we wanted to represent an everyday item like a car as an object. In order to do this, it would be useful to first make a list of all the elements that describe the characteristics of the car, which would be known in object-oriented programming as the car's *properties*. For a car, some properties could be

- Color
- Doors
- Make
- Year
- Model

These properties help describe things about a car, such as what the car looks like and when it was made. Properties of objects do not necessarily have to be as simple as the car example I just mentioned. For example, a car could also have an Engine property that defines the type of engine in the car. That engine could itself be an object with its own properties, methods, and events. The car object would not necessarily have to know anything about the engine object, except how to interface with it. This ability for objects to interact with other objects without knowing the underlying dirty work going on inside that object is one of the keys of object-oriented programming (known as *abstraction* in object-oriented programming).

Methods, on the other hand, describe the actions that an object is able to perform. For our car example, some methods could be the following:

- Go forward
- Go backward
- Stop

Methods very typically require *parameters* that let the method know exactly how to perform an action. In the case of the "Go Forward" method, for example, a parameter might be "How Fast" or "How Far", depending on the job the method is intended to perform.

Events describe occurrences that can happen *to* an object. Events are different than methods in that they react to something instead of act upon it. Some events that could happen to our car object are

- Started
- Stopped
- Accelerating

An object's properties, methods, and events are collectively known as the *members* of the object. Now that we've defined these members, let's rewrite their names in a syntax that's a little bit more code-applicable and descriptive of the type of member they represent. Let's also define the type of data these properties would represent or the parameters that the methods would take as an input.

- Properties
  - Color—String data type
  - Doors—Integer data type
  - Make—String data type
  - Year—Integer data type
  - Model—String data type
- Methods
  - GoForward—Parameter: how fast
  - GoReverse—Parameter: how fast
  - DoStop—Parameter: no parameter
- Events
  - OnStart
  - OnStop
  - OnAccelerate

> *Method names, typically describing an action, are typically verbs or contain a prefix like Go or Do. An event, on the other hand, often begins with a prefix like On.*

Since each of these members is "generic" to all possible types of cars, this collection of properties, methods, and events gives us a *template*, or blueprint, for creating a car. Using this template, it's possible to create any number of different cars, such as a blue two-door 1956 Ford Mustang or a red four-door 2001 Honda Civic. Each instance of the car template will have similar "abilities"—GoForward, GoReverse, and DoStop, as well as the ability to react to events in its life cycle, like OnStart.

When a template is created using C#, it is known, as it is in ActionScript, as a *class*. A class is simply a way of defining a reproducible model of "something" that can have properties, methods, and events associated with it. Once a class is used in C# or ActionScript (like creating a '56 Mustang), it is known as an *object*—or an instance of a class.

To get an understanding of how C# implements objects, let's take a look at what this car object might look like as a class created in C#. (I have omitted the events from the class at this point; we will be covering them more thoroughly in Chapter 3):

```csharp
public class car
{
  private string _color;
  private int _doors;
  private string _make;
  private string _model;
  private int _year;

  public void GoForward(int speed)
  {
    // code to make the car move forward
  }
  public void GoReverse(int speed)
  {
    // code to make the car move backwards
  }
  public void DoStop()
  {
    // code to make the car stop
  }
  public string Color {
    get { return _color; }
    set { _color = value; }
  }
  public string Doors {
    get { return _doors; }
    set { _doors = value; }
  }
```

```
        public string Make {
          get { return _make; }
          set { _make = value; }
        }
        public string Model {
          get { return _model; }
          set { _model = value; }
        }
        public string Year {
           get { return _year; }
          set { _year = value; }
        }
    }
```

Again, if you know ActionScript 2.0, this C# class will look very familiar. In the first line of this example, the name of the class is defined, along with the class's *access level*, public. (Access levels will be further discussed in the "Code-behind files" section of Chapter 3.)

```
    public class car
```

Once the class is defined, the next block of code defines the private variables internal to the car class. These variables are used to internally store the values of the car's parameters and can't be used from outside the class (more on this in Chapter 3).

```
    private string _color;
    private int _doors;
    private string _make;
    private string _model;
    private int _year;
```

Since object-oriented programming discourages direct access to the internal properties of a class, C# (and also ActionScript 2.0) classes use *getter* and *setter* methods to provide controlled access to these parameters. Getter methods provide a way of retrieving the value of a property, and setter methods provide a way to set the value of a property. In C#, a property's getter and setter can be defined in a single codeblock, as for the color property:

```
    public string Color {
        // getter method
        get { return _color; }
        // setter method
        set { _color = value; }
    }
```

You'll notice that C# setter methods make use of the value keyword to obtain the value to set the property to. In ActionScript 2.0 classes, getter and setter methods of properties have a slightly different syntax, making use of the get and set keywords. Listed here is the ActionScript 2.0 equivalent to this Color property's getter and setter methods:

```
function get Color():String {
    return this._color;
}
function set Color(pColor:String):Void {
    this._color = pColor;
}
```

You'll also notice that the ActionScript setter method appears to take its input as a parameter, instead of using the value keyword—this notation is slightly deceptive, as an ActionScript property does not require a parameter as a method would, but can be assigned a value, just like a C# property, as shown in the following statement:

```
MyObject.Color = "Red";
```

You'll also notice a difference in the way that methods are created in C# compared to ActionScript. Whereas the ActionScript syntax includes the function keyword:

```
Function GoForward (speed:Number):Void { .. }
```

C# does not require a keyword at all, but rather specifies an access level and return type before the name of the method:

```
Public void GoForward(int speed) { .. }
```

To implement the entire car object we have created, let's take a look at how a new instance of the C# car class is created, and send a new instance forward at 65mph using the GoForward method.

```
car myCar = new Car(); // create new instance of the car class
myCar.Color = "Silver"; // set the car's color to Silver
myCar.Doors = 2; // set the car's number of doors to 2
myCar.Make = "Cadillac"; // set the car's make to Cadillac
myCar.Model = "Convertible"; // set the car's model to Convertible
myCar.Year = 1968; // set the year of the car's make to 1968

myCar.GoForward(65); // make the car go forward at 65mph
```

And just like that, we have a new '68 Cadillac created with C#! In this example, you'll see that, as in ActionScript, a new instance of a C# object is created using the new keyword. Also, like ActionScript 2.0, the new object's properties and methods are referred to using the dot-syntax.

When using the classes in the .NET base class library, you are constantly creating new instances of classes, just like in the car example shown earlier, and it is with these object instances that you are able to access the full depth of the .NET functionality. We will be covering some other features of object-oriented programming in C#, such as operator overloading and partial classes, as we move through the examples in this book. There are some more advanced topics in C# object-oriented programming that we won't be able to cover in this book. For more information on these topics, check out *A Programmer's Introduction to C# 2.0* (Apress, 2005), by Eric Gunnerson and Nick Wienholt.

Structs in C#

C#, unlike ActionScript 2.0, has another user-defined type available, called a struct. A struct is very similar to a C# class, the main difference being that structs are a value type instead of a reference type. Because they are a value type, structs are generally more quickly accessed than classes, but storing large amounts of data on the stack (where value types are stored) can slow application performance. Like classes, structs can contain properties and methods, and require a new keyword to instantiate a new instance, as in the following example:

```
struct House {
    Private string _color;
    Public string Color {
        Get { return _color; }
        Set { _color = value; }
    }

    Public void Build() {
        // build the house
    }
}

House myHouse = new House();
```

Looks just like a class, right? If structs look and perform almost exactly like classes, how do we know when to use each? For our use in this book, structs will be used only in the circumstance that we need to pass complex data values—a circumstance that they are well suited for because they are of value data type. For any other application object creation, classes are generally a better fit since they require less space on the stack. We'll actually be using structs extensively in the web services–based chapters of this book to pass complex data from ASP.NET to Flash.

Strings in C#

The .NET string data type is a very important, useful, and unique type. As with ActionScript programming, strings are often used to store a group of single characters. With the string data type, this group of characters can be referred to either as a single object or as an array of character data types (we'll be discussing arrays in Chapter 5). The string data type is a .NET primitive data type, although unlike most of the primitive data types, just like the ActionScript 2.0 string class, it is implemented as a reference type instead of a value type.

Because the string type is a reference type rather than a value type, when a string instance is created, entries are placed in the stack and heap portions of the system's memory. Therefore, in the circumstance that a string's value is changed, .NET actually creates a new instance of the string on the heap and the string's reference on the stack is reassigned. This function is performed by .NET "behind the scenes," and therefore isn't noticeable during development. But because of the memory consumption required by this operation, extensive string manipulations can cause a decrease in code performance at runtime. To overcome this problem, the StringBuilder class, which we will discuss shortly, can be used to perform extensive string manipulations.

Although the string data type is an object, the new keyword that is typically used to create instances of objects is not required to create a new instance of a string, as shown in the following example:

```
string myString = "Foundation ASP.NET for Flash";
```

Whereas a value type variable will have a default initial value, if a string is not initialized upon creation, its initial value is null, as it is with reference types:

```
// the value of myInt will be 0
int myInt;
// the value of myString will be null
string myString;
```

Comparing strings

In many instances, it is necessary to determine whether two strings are identical. In C#, there are several ways to make this comparison. The main difference between the options for comparing strings is whether or not you would like to consider case sensitivity when making the comparison. Let's first take a look at the most common method of string comparison, using the == comparison operator.

```
string myString1 = "Foundation ASP.NET 2.0 for Flash";
string myString2 = "Foundation ASP.NET 2.0 for FLASH";
if (myString1 == myString2)
{
  // do something
}
```

This comparison operator will perform a *case-sensitive* comparison between the two strings, in this case returning false since the strings are not the same based on the case of the word "Flash".

A method that can be used to perform a case-insensitive comparison is the string.Compare method. The string.Compare method takes as parameters two strings to be compared and a Boolean value that determines whether case sensitivity should be considered. This method returns a –1 if the first string comes alphabetically before the second, a 0 if the strings are identical, and a 1 if the first string comes alphabetically after the second. The string.Compare method considers the lowercase character to come before the uppercase, so an *a* character would be considered earlier in the alphabet than the *A* character. The string.Compare method is used without case consideration in the following example:

```
string myString1 = "Foundation ASP.NET 2.0 for Flash";
string myString2 = "Foundation ASP.NET 2.0 for FLASH";
// the string.Compare method is passed false as
// its third parameter, telling it to ignore the
// case of the strings, and in this example
// returns 0
if ((string.Compare(myString1, myString2, false)==0)
{
  // will execute if myString1 is equal to myString2
}
```

The final method for comparing strings, string.CompareOrdinal, is very similar to the string.Compare method, but differs in that it considers the uppercase letters to exist earlier in the alphabet than the lowercase. This method actually converts the characters of the string into their ASCII equivalent for comparison.

```
string myString1 = "FlAsh";
string myString2 = "Flash";
// the string.CompareOrdinal method considers
// the uppercase "A" to be before the lowercase
// "a", and will return a -1 in this comparison
int comp = string.CompareOrdinal(myString1, myString2);
switch (comp)
{
  case -1:
    // myString1 comes before myString2
  break;
  case 0:
    // myString1 and myString2 are equal
  break;
  case 1:
    // myString2 comes before myString1
  break;
}
```

Manipulating strings

String instances have a number of useful methods for manipulation and testing of the string. Several of these methods are listed in Table 2-2. As you'll notice, many of these methods are very similar to the methods available in the ActionScript 2.0 string class, with the addition of some very useful methods like Replace and Join.

Table 2-2. Methods of a string instance

Name	Description
String.Insert	Inserts a specified instance of String at a specified index position in this instance
String.Remove	Deletes a specified number of characters from this instance beginning at a specified position
String.Replace	Replaces all occurrences of a specified Unicode character or String in this instance, with another specified Unicode character or string
String.Split	Identifies the substrings in this instance that are delimited by one or more characters specified in an array, and then places the substrings into a String array
String.Substring	Retrieves a substring of the instance of the string

Name	Description
String.ToCharArray	Copies the characters of the String to a Unicode character array
String.ToLower	Returns a copy of the String in all lowercase characters
String.ToUpper	Returns a copy of the String in all uppercase characters
String.IndexOf	Reports the index of the first occurrence of a String, or one or more characters, within this instance

Here is an example that assigns a string a value using the String.Replace method of another instance:

```
string myString1 = "My father drives a car";
string myString2 = myString1.Replace("drives a car", "rides a bike");
// myString2 now equals "My father rides a bike"
```

The string class itself (as compared to a specific instance of a string) also has several methods for manipulation. Table 2-3 lists a few of these methods.

Table 2-3. Methods of the string class

Name	Description
string.Concat	Returns a string that is the concatenation of two instances of string (or the string representation of two objects)
string.Join	Returns a string that is the result of the concatenation of an array of strings with a specified separation string between each member of the array
string.Compare	Compares two string objects (as discussed in the previous section)

An example of a string created using the String.Concat method is

```
string myString1 = "My father";
string myString2 = " drives a car";
string myString3 = String.Concat(myString1, myString2);
// myString3 now equals "My father drives a car"
```

Again, it should be mentioned that string operations are very processor consuming and can cause code performance decreases. In the next section, we will talk about the much more "energy-efficient" StringBuilder class.

StringBuilder

As previously mentioned, strings are immutable—once they have been assigned a value, a developer cannot simply reassign that string a new value without a new string object being created in memory. This causes string-manipulation techniques to be very costly, especially when done on a large scale. For these types of operations, the StringBuilder class is much more efficient and should be used whenever possible.

> *The* StringBuilder *class, although more efficient when doing many string-manipula-tion operations, is not more efficient when doing only one or two operations. In this case, the* string *class should be used.*

A StringBuilder can be initiated by creating a new instance of the StringBuilder and passing the StringBuilder's original value through the constructor:

```
System.Text.StringBuilder myStringBuilder =
➥new System.Text.StringBuilder("I would like to count to 100");
```

Notice here that the StringBuilder class is a member of the System.Text namespace—so if you would like to use the StringBuilder class, you have to either include the System.Text namespace by including the statement

```
using System.Text;
```

at the beginning of your C# file, or by referring to the fully referenced System.Text.StringBuilder class. (Namespaces are described in more detail in Chapter 2.)

Table 2-4 shows a number of StringBuilder's methods.

Table 2-4. Methods of StringBuilder

Name	Description
Append	Appends a string to the end of the current StringBuilder
AppendFormat	Replaces a format specifier passed in a string with formatted text
Insert	Inserts a string or object into the specified index of the current StringBuilder
Remove	Removes a specified number of characters from the current StringBuilder
Replace	Replaces a specified character at a specified index

As you will notice, the StringBuilder does not have nearly the number of manipulation methods that the string class does. For this reason, it is not always possible to replace string operations with the StringBuilder.

An example of the StringBuilder's Append method is as follows:

```
System.Text.StringBuilder myStringBuilder = new
➥System.Text.StringBuilder("I would like to count to 100 . . .");
for (int x=0; x<100; x++)
{
  myStringBuilder.Append(x.ToString() + ", ");
}
```

In order to retrieve a specific character from a string builder, the StringBuilder has a zero-indexed character array property:

```
StringBuilder myStringBuilder =
➥new StringBuilder("I would like to count to 100");
// returns the 5th character in the StringBuilder,
// 'u'
char myChar = myStringBuilder[5];
```

Dates

In C#, dates and times are created and manipulated using the DateTime and TimeSpan structures. The DateTime object is a value type that represents a specific point in time from 12:00:00 midnight, January 1, 0001, AD to 11:59:59 P.M., December 31, 9999, AD. Thankfully, .NET has allowed us to plan for the future! The TimeSpan object, rather than representing a specific moment in time, represents a period of time. The difference between a DateTime and TimeSpan is similar to the difference between the concepts of "November 15, 2005, 8:00 A.M." and "1 hour." The former represents a specific point in time while the latter specifies a time duration. If, for example, you subtract one DateTime instance from another, the result is a TimeSpan as in the following example:

```
// create a new DateTime object which represents
// Jan 1, 2000
DateTime myDateTime1 = new DateTime(2000, 1,1);
// create a new DateTime object which represents
// the current Date
DateTime myDateTime2 = DateTime.Today;
// subtract the second object from the first
// to find the TimeSpan since Jan 1, 2000
TimeSpan myTimeSpan = myDateTime1 - myDateTime2;
```

In this example, we've used the DateTime.Today property, which is one of the most useful members of the DateTime object. The DateTime.Today property can be used to retrieve the current date from the system on which the .NET code is running. Another similar property is DateTime.Now, which retrieves the current date and the current time. Table 2-5 contains a number of the useful DateTime properties, followed by Table 2-6, which contains DateTime methods (this difference between properties and methods will be explained further in the next chapter).

Table 2-5. DateTime properties

Name	Description
Day	Gets the day of the month.
DayOfWeek	Gets the day of the week from 0=Sunday to 6=Saturday.
DayOfYear	Gets the number of days elapsed in the current year.
Hour	Gets the hour component of the date.
Millisecond	Gets the millisecond component of the date.
Minute	Gets the minute component of the date.
Month	Gets the month component of the date.
Now	Gets a DateTime that is the current date and time.
Second	Gets the second component of the date.
Ticks	Gets the number of ticks in the date. A tick is equal to 100 nanoseconds.
Time of Day	Gets the time of day in the date.
UtcNow	Gets the current date and time adjusted to UTC (Universal Time Coordinated) value.
Year	Gets the year component of the date.

Table 2-6. DateTime methods

Name	Description
Add	Adds a TimeSpan to the DateTime instance
AddDays	Adds a certain number of days
AddHours	Adds a certain number of hours
AddMilliseconds	Adds a certain number of milliseconds
AddSeconds	Adds a certain number of seconds
AddMinutes	Adds a certain number of minutes
AddTicks	Adds a certain number of ticks
AddYears	Adds a certain number of years

Name	Description
Compare	Compares two DateTime instances and returns their relative values
DaysInMonth	Returns the number of days in a specified month in a specified year
IsLeapYear	Returns a Boolean indication of whether the specified year is a leap year
Subtract	Subtracts a specified time or duration from the instance
ToLocalTime	Converts a time from UTC to local system time
ToString	Converts the instance into a string value

Conditional logic in C#

Two of the most basic and essential operations in any programming language are conditional operators and selection statements. These logical functions allow a developer to compare a variable with another variable of the same data type and make an appropriate response based on this comparison. In C#, comparison operators and selection statements are almost identical to ActionScript 2.0.

Comparison operators

As we have mentioned in the previous sections, *value* data types can be compared using comparison operators. The comparison operators in C# include the ==, !=, <, >, <=, and >=. Comparison operators compare two variables and return a Boolean value indicating the result of the comparison. Table 2-7 describes the comparison operators in C#. Although this table is for the C# comparison operators, it is also relevant for the ActionScript comparison operators.

Table 2-7. C# comparison operators

Operator	Description
x == y	Returns true if x and y are equal, false otherwise
x != y	Returns true if x and y are not equal, false otherwise
x < y	Returns true if x is less than y, false otherwise
x > y	Returns true if x is greater than y, false otherwise
x >= y	Returns true if x is greater than or equal to y, false otherwise
x <= y	Returns true if x is less than or equal to y, false otherwise

When multiple comparison statements are used together to create a more complex comparison, two additional operators can be used to join conditional statements: the && and || operators. The && operator performs a *conditional and* on two conditional statements. A conditional and will return true if both of the conditional statements in question evaluate as true, but will return false otherwise. An example of the && operator is shown here:

```
(x==y) && (y==z)
```

The || operator is similar to the && operator, except that it performs a *conditional or* function on its parameters. In a logical or function, the statement will return true if either of the relevant statements is evaluated to be true. An example of the || operator is shown here:

```
(x==y) || (y==z)
```

Selection statements

Selection statements in C# are used to execute specific blocks of code in an application based on a condition. These statements are similar to those used in most programming languages, including ActionScript.

if-else statement

The if statement selects a codeblock to execute based on the value of its conditional expression. The if statement is the most common of the selection statements and is used by nearly every developer at some point. An example if-else statement is as follows:

```
if (x==5)
{
   // do something
}
else
{
   // do something else
   // this "else" statement is optional
}
```

In this example, if x==5 is evaluated to be true, the first section of code is executed, but if x==5 is false, then the second section of code is executed.

As you'll notice in the previous example, the code to be executed by the if statement is enclosed in brackets ({}). It is not necessary to enclose the code in brackets if there is only one statement to be executed by the if statement, as in the following example:

```
if (x==5)
   // only one statement
```

The if-else statement can also accommodate multiple conditions by nesting if-else statements:

```
if (x==5)
{
   // do something
}
else if (x==10)
{
   // do something else
}
else if (x==15)
{
   // do another something else
}
```

In situations where more than two if statements are nested, code gets very confusing and hard to follow. In this case the switch statement is a better choice.

switch statement

In the circumstance where many (more than three) conditions need to be evaluated, it is best to use the switch statement. The switch statement can be used with any of the following data types: sbyte, byte, short, ushort, int, uint, long, ulong, char, string, or enum (we will be discussing enums in the next section). The switch statement provides a much more legible structure than the nested if statement by executing different codeblocks for each condition encountered.

```
switch (x)
{
   case 5:
      // do something for 5
      break;
   case 10:
      // do something for 10
      break;
   case 15:
      // do something for 15
      break;
   case 20:
   case 25:
      // this will execute for 20 and 25
      break;
   default:
      // this will execute if none of the above
      // are true
}
// the line after the switch statement
```

When the switch statement evaluates the value of x, it determines whether there is a corresponding case statement that corresponds to this value. If there is, the codeblock for that case is executed until the break statement is encountered. When the break statement is encountered, execution continues with the line after the switch statement. If the value of x is not handled by any of the case statements, the code execution jumps to the block within the default case. The default case is not required, however, and if it is not provided, the execution will jump directly to the statement after the switch statement if no case is applicable.

It is also possible to define a common handler for multiple cases as in the following lines:

```
case 20:
case 25:
   // this will execute for 20 and 25
   break;
```

In this code, the handler for both 20 and 25 is defined as the same codeblock, which can be very useful in eliminating redundant code. Again, with the switch statement, C# and ActionScript's syntax are identical.

Looping in C#

Looping is an essential part of any programming language. It allows a developer to accomplish logic like "As long as this condition exists, do this," or "do this 100 times," or "Go through all the items in a group and do this to them." Looping in C# is very much like looping in ActionScript—the main difference is the foreach loop, which we will cover here and which does not exist in ActionScript.

Looping in C#, as in any other language, can also be a dangerous task if not done correctly. If a loop is started and never meets a condition that will cause it to exit the loop, an "infinite loop" is encountered and will cause an application to "hang" and probably crash.

In C#, there are four main looping commands: while, do-while, for, and foreach. Each of these commands has a specific circumstance it is best suited for, and careful thought should be taken when choosing a looping command. The first looping command we'll examine is the while loop.

while statement

The while loop is considered a "pretest" loop in that it tests the value of a condition before entering the loop itself. Because of this pretest, the while loop might never actually execute, based on the value of the looping condition when entering the while loop. A "pseudo-code" example of a while loop is as follows:

```
while (I'm still too warm)
{
   turn down the temperature
}
```

In this example, when the while loop initially executes, it will evaluate the "I'm still too warm" statement and consider "Are you too warm?" If this evaluates to true (you are warm), the while loop will begin executing the code inside of its codeblock—"turn down the temperature". After executing this code once, the while loop reevaluates the "Are you too warm?" consideration and, if this is true, reexecutes the codeblock. However, if this is false (you're not too warm anymore), the while loop finishes execution and the program continues with the line after the while loop.

Here's a more "real" example of a while loop, which increments an integer value each time through its codeblock and continues execution if that integer is less than 20:

```
int myInt=0;
ArrayList myArrayList = new ArrayList();
while (myInt<20)
{
  myArrayList.Add(myInt);
  // after 20 times through the while loop, myInt
  // will be greater than 20 and will exit the
  // while loop
  myInt++;
}
```

do-while statement

Another looping command in C# (and ActionScript) is the do-while loop. The do-while loop is extremely similar to the while loop except that the loop condition is tested *after* executing the loop's code. Because of this, the do-while loop will always execute its code once, since the loop condition is not tested until after the first time through the code.

```
int myInt=19;
ArrayList myArrayList = new ArrayList();
do
{
  myArrayList.Add(myInt);
  // in this circumstance, the loop will only
  // execute once since myInt will equal 20
  // after the first execution
  myInt++;
} while (myInt<20)
```

for statement

The for loop is a looping command designed to execute a block of code a specific number of times. This is very useful for a scenario when you know (or can find out) the number of times you'd like to execute something. The syntax for the for loop is as follows:

```
for (variable = initial value; condition; next)
{
  // do something
}
```

53

For example, if you know that there are nine players on a baseball field, you might want to execute a for loop like

```
for (int x=0; x<9; x++)
{
    // give the xth player a glove
}
```

As you can see, the variable that is being tracked—x—can be initialized within the for loop, with the int x=0 code. The for loop could also be configured to count down by using the decrement operator (--) instead of the increment operator (++), or could be told to increment by a larger value by replacing x++ with x=x+4.

foreach statement

The foreach statement is extremely useful for looping through a collection or an array in C# (which we'll be covering next!). The foreach statement executes, as its name suggests, once for each element in the collection in its conditional statement. Building on the baseball player example we used in the for loop section, the foreach statement could be used if we have an array of baseball players as follows:

```
player[] team = new player[9];
foreach (player currentPlayer in team)
{
    currentPlayer = new player();
    currentPlayer.GiveGlove();
}
```

In this example, the foreach statement will execute once for each player in an array of players called team. Within the foreach codeblock, the value of the player we are currently looking at is referred to as a player called currentPlayer. In this way, the players could all be created and given gloves, even if we didn't know how many players were on the team (since the foreach loop would execute once for each entry in the array, no matter how many were there!).

Enumerations

Enumerations allow a developer to create a friendly name to define a group of related constants. In simpler terms, enumerations allow you to assign names to numbers so the numbers make more sense while coding. ActionScript, unlike C#, does not have built-in support for enumerations. An example of a useful enumeration is the days in a week:

```
enum DaysInWeek
{
    Sunday = 1,
    Monday = 2,
    Tuesday = 3,
    Wednesday = 4,
    Thursday = 5,
    Friday = 6,
    Saturday = 7,
}
```

As you can see, each day in the week can be assigned a specific integer, which is the default data type for enumeration members. However, the members can be assigned any of the integral data types in C#—byte, short, int, or long—or they can be assigned nothing at all, in which case they will automatically be assigned incremental integers, as in the following example:

```
enum DaysInWeek
{
   Sunday, // automatically assigned 0
   Monday, // automatically assigned 1
   Tuesday, // automatically assigned 2
   Wednesday, // automatically assigned 3
   Thursday, // automatically assigned 4
   Friday, // automatically assigned 5
   Saturday,// automatically assigned 6
}
```

Enumerations can be used within methods and as parameters for methods, as in the following example:

```
void MarkCalendar(DaysInWeek day)
{
   if (day==DaysInWeek.Monday)
   {
      // do something
   }
}
```

Arrays

C# allows developers to create groups of objects using arrays, though each object should be of the same type. Arrays in C# are zero-indexed (meaning that the first element in the array is actually the zero-th element). Unlike ActionScript, when you're creating an array in C# the array must be initiated, setting the number of elements that the array will contain. Also unlike ActionScript, an array in C# cannot be dynamically resized—once you declare the size of an array, it cannot be changed unless you specifically re-declare the array's size.

As shown next, an array can be created and initiated in the same statement. The following array is a single-dimensional array created with 15 elements:

```
int[] myArray = new int[15];
```

It is also possible to initialize an array in a separate step from the declaration of the array, as shown here:

```
int[] myArray;
   . . .
myArray = new int[15];
```

When arrays of value type objects are created, the constructor for that value type is called, typically setting that instance to a zero value. Arrays of reference types, however, are assigned a null reference to that type when initialized. In order to fill the array with members, it is necessary to either create a new object and assign it to the array's element or assign an existing object of that type. The following statement creates an array of myObjects (a user-defined object), creates 15 new instances of that object, and assigns them to the array:

```
myObject[] myArray = new myObject[15];
for (int x=0; x<myObject.Length; x++)
{
  myArray[x] = new myObject();
}
```

C# also supports the creation of multidimensional arrays. Multidimensional arrays can be thought of as a group of data cells arranged by the dimensions of the data—in simpler terms, multidimensional arrays are arrays of arrays. For example, a two-dimensional array would be similar to a table, consisting of rows and columns. A three-dimensional array would consist of three dimensions (when created visually), as shown in Figure 2.1. An array with any more than three dimensions cannot be visualized, but can be very useful for storing complex data in C#.

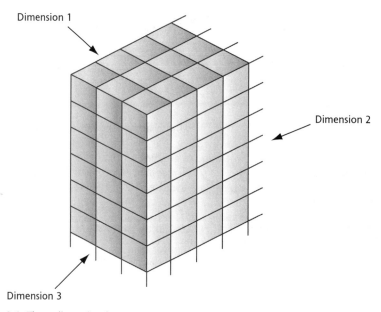

Figure 2-1. Three-dimensional array

C# supports multidimensional arrays in two different formats—rectangular and jagged. Rectangular arrays are arrays with more than one dimension in which each member of each dimension has the same length. In the case of a two-dimensional array, for example, each row will have the same number of columns (as compared to each row having a varying number of columns). An example of a three-dimensional array, created with each dimension containing five members, is shown here:

```
string[ , , ] = new string[5,5,5];
```

In a jagged array, each member of each dimension can have a different number of members. In the case of a two-dimensional jagged array, each row could have a different number of columns associated with it. In essence, a jagged array is an array of arrays. An example of a two-dimensional jagged array with three members in one dimension and a "variable" number in the second dimension is as follows:

```
string[][] myArray = new string[3][];
myArray[0] = new string[] {"string11", "string12",
➥ "string13", "string14"};
myArray[1] = new string[] {"string21", "string22"};
myArray[2] = new string[] {"string31", "string32
➥ ", "string33", "string34", "string35"};
```

As you can see, each new member can be assigned a new array of strings by using the curly brackets, { }. In this example, the first row will have four elements, the second will have two, and the third will have five. These jagged arrays can be used in an instance such as storing CD titles released by a band. If a band is represented by an array of strings, each subsequent row can have a different number of columns indicating the CD releases by that specific band.

Collections

The .NET Framework provides a number of objects called collections, which provide advanced functionality for managing groups of objects. One of the main features of these collections is to allow dynamic resizing of a group of objects, a feature that arrays do not achieve. If, for example, the necessary size of an array is unknown at design time, a collection may be a good alternative since it can be declared without a size specification and dynamically added to or subtracted from at runtime. Some of the collections provided by .NET are shown in Table 2-8. Each of these collections provides unique functionality for accomplishing common group-related tasks. (In this book, we'll only be examining the ArrayList collection.)

Table 2-8. Collections provided by .NET

Class	Description
ArrayList	Organizes a group of objects and allows dynamic adding and removal of those objects
SortedList	Represents a collection of key-and-value pairs that are sorted by the keys and are accessible by key and by index
BitArray	Manages a compact array of bit values, which are represented as Booleans (0=false, 1=true)
HashTable	Represents a collection of key-and-value pairs that are organized based on the hash code of the key
Queue	Represents a first-in, first-out collection of objects
Stack	Represents a simple last-in, first-out collection of objects

ArrayList

The `ArrayList` class provides a significant amount of general functionality for managing groups of objects. Unlike normal arrays, the `ArrayList` class can be dynamically resized and can contain objects of any type—including user-defined objects. Like arrays, `ArrayList` members can be accessed using an indexer. In the following example, an `ArrayList` is created and an object is added to it:

```
ArrayList myArrayList = new ArrayList();
myObject obj = new myObject();
myArrayList.Add(obj);
```

When an item is added to an `ArrayList`, it is placed at the end of the zero-indexed list of items. If you would like to add an item to a specific index in the `ArrayList`, it is also possible to use the `InsertAt` method, which inserts the object at a specific position, as in the following example:

```
ArrayList myArrayList = new ArrayList();
for (int x=0; x<5; x++)
{
  // Insert an integer with the value of x at the
  // first (zero-th) element in the ArrayList
  myArrayList.Insert(0, x);
}
```

Accessing a specific member item in an `ArrayList` is accomplished in the same way as with arrays:

```
int myInt = (int)myArrayList[0];
```

When an item in an `ArrayList` is accessed using an indexer, a generic object is always returned. This is a case where casting is useful in extracting the original data type from the `ArrayList`.

It is also possible to remove a specific item from an `ArrayList` using the `Remove` or `RemoveAt` method. The `Remove` method removes a specific object (if that object is contained in the collection) from the `ArrayList`. If the object is not contained in the `ArrayList`, the `Remove` command is ignored.

```
ArrayList myArrayList = new ArrayList();
myObject obj = new myObject();
myArrayList.Add(obj);
// this command will remove the myObject obj from
// the ArrayList
myArrayList.Remove(obj);
```

The `RemoveAt` method, on the other hand, removes an item from a specific location in the `ArrayList`. An example is as follows:

```
ArrayList myArrayList = new ArrayList();
for (int x=0; x<5; x++)
{
  myArrayList.Add(x);
}
// remove the second element from the ArrayList
myArrayList.RemoveAt(1);
```

When the second element is removed from the ArrayList, the list is automatically resized, leaving a list of four elements.

Another important feature of ArrayLists is the ability to create a typed array from the ArrayList using the ToArray method. Using ArrayLists and the ToArray method, it is possible to make use of the dynamic sizing features of ArrayLists when creating a list, then convert that ArrayList into a typed array, as in the following example:

```
int x=0;
while (x<10)
{
  myArrayList.Add(x);
  x++;
}
int[] myIntArray = (int[]) myArrayList.ToArray(typeof(int));
```

Here, an ArrayList has items added to it within a while statement, each dynamically changing the size of the list. After the list has been created (and the size of the collection is known), an array of integers is created using the ToArray method along with the typeof operator, which extracts the System.Type object for a specific type, in this case int. Notice also, that this list must be cast as an array of integers, since it, by default, returns an array of objects.

Summary

In this chapter, we have covered some of the basics of C#, from data types and object-oriented concepts to string manipulation and collections. As we move forward into Flash and ASP.NET interaction, we'll apply this basic knowledge and learn some more about other classes in the C# base class library. In the next chapter, we'll be using our C# knowledge to create our first ASP.NET application!

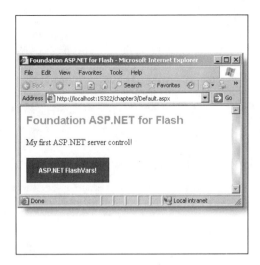

Chapter 3

BASICS OF AN ASP.NET PROJECT

What this chapter covers:

- Setting up an ASP.NET web project in Visual Studio .NET
- Using ASP.NET server controls
- Using server controls
- Understanding code-behind, code-beside, and inline code
- Embedding Flash in ASP.NET pages
- Passing data from ASP.NET to Flash using FlashVars

Now that you've got your development environment set up and ready to go, and you understand some of the basic concepts of C#, we're ready to move forward into ASP.NET and the creation of your first ASP.NET page. As we walk through the process, we'll investigate the ASP.NET code-behind model and how it can be used to manipulate ASP.NET *server controls*. Using this knowledge, we'll then walk through a basic example of embedding an ASP.NET Flash server control into an ASP.NET web page and passing data from ASP.NET to a Flash movie using the FlashVars method of communication.

Getting started in ASP.NET

Now that we have a good understanding of object-oriented programming concepts and have a C# development environment set up, let's get started with some ASP.NET basics. Visual Studio .NET 2005 has made the process of creating an ASP.NET project and jumping right in an easy one. Much of the setup work is done for you or can be configured through rich interfaces. First things first, let's use VS .NET to create a new ASP.NET website.

1. Open VS .NET 2005 and select File ➤ New ➤ Website.

2. In the New Web Site dialog box, select Visual C# as the project type, ASP.NET Web Site as the project template, and a directory of your choice for the location, as shown in Figure 3-1. In this book, I will use the c:\foundationaspnet\ directory for my example files.

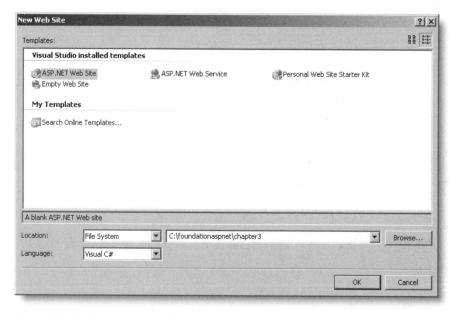

Figure 3-1. Creating an ASP.NET website using Visual Studio .NET 2005

3. Click OK, and just like that, you have created your first ASP.NET web project!

If your installation is like mine, your default screen will look similar to Figure 3-2. This screen is displaying the HTML Source view of your first ASP.NET web page. As you can see by looking at the Solution Explorer in the upper-right dockable window, the name of this first file is Default.aspx. Before moving further into the coding of an ASP.NET page, let's take a closer look at the windows in the Visual Studio interface that I mentioned in Chapter 1.

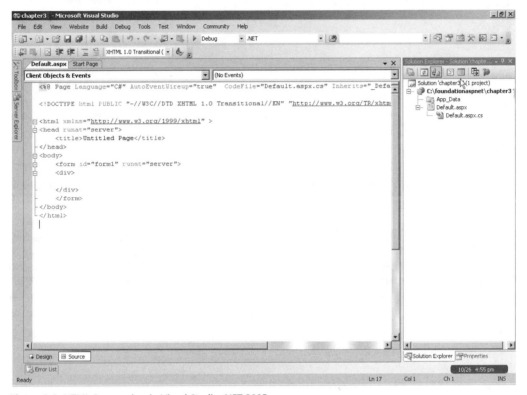

Figure 3-2. HTML Source view in Visual Studio .NET 2005

First, let's examine the Design view of the Document window. If you are currently in the Source view, you can easily access the Design view by clicking the Design button at the lower left of the Document window, as shown in Figure 3-3.

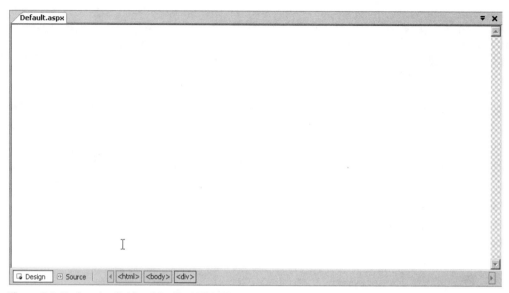

Figure 3-3. Design view in Visual Studio .NET 2005

The Design view in Visual Studio is similar to many other WYSIWYG (What You See Is What You Get) editors. The visual representation of an ASP.NET page in the Design view is as similar as possible to what your page will look like when published for the Web. As a first test, let's try typing some text directly on the design interface. Figure 3-4 shows the Design view, after the text "Foundation ASP.NET for Flash" has been typed directly onto the screen.

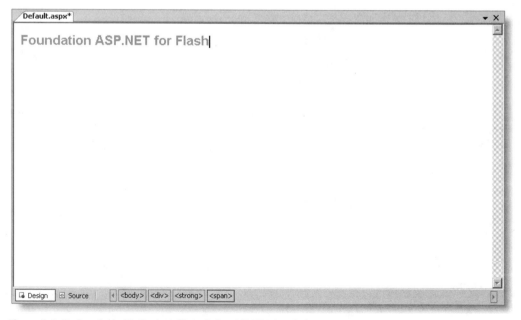

Figure 3-4. Design view with the text "Foundation ASP.NET for Flash"

As you can see, I have also formatted this text using the Formatting toolbar in the top tray of Visual Studio. This toolbar, shown in Figure 3-5, functions very similarly to one in the Flash IDE or Microsoft Word, providing options such as font formatting and linking.

Figure 3-5. The Formatting toolbar

Now that we have an ASP.NET page with some text created in the Design view, let's take a look at what Visual Studio has done behind the scenes for us by selecting the Source tab at the bottom of this window, as shown in Figure 3-6.

```
Default.aspx*                                                        ▾ ×
Client Objects & Events                    ▾  (No Events)                      ▾
    <%@ Page Language="C#" AutoEventWireup="true" CodeFile="Default.aspx.cs" Inherits="Default2"

    <!DOCTYPE html PUBLIC "-//W3C//DTD XHTML 1.1//EN" "http://www.w3.org/TR/xhtml11/DTD/xhtml11.c

  <html xmlns="http://www.w3.org/1999/xhtml" >
  <head runat="server">
        <title>Foundation ASP.NET for Flash</title>
  </head>
  <body>
      <form id="form1" runat="server">
      <div>
          <strong><span style="font-size: 16pt; color: #ff0000; font-family: Arial">Foundation
              ASP.NET for Flash<br />
              <br />
          </span></strong>      </div>
      </form>
  </body>
  </html>
```

Design   Source

Figure 3-6. The Source view

This Source view displays the HTML that has been generated by Visual Studio from your design. If you are familiar with other web WYSIWYG editors like Macromedia Dreamweaver, this concept should be pretty familiar to you. As you can see, Visual Studio has enclosed the formatted text I've written in span tags with a specific style defined. In this way, the Visual Studio Design and Source views can be used to easily create HTML-based ASP.NET pages—a concept we will not focus on much in this book since we will use Flash as our presentation layer *instead* of HTML-based elements. What we will instead focus on in the Visual Studio design interface are ASP.NET *server controls*.

Server controls

Server controls in ASP.NET are very similar to components in Flash—they are drag-and-drop tools that encapsulate a set of functionality. Server controls typically do much of the underlying grunt work of common tasks for you, allowing you to focus on the logic of the program (instead of HTML or JavaScript syntax, for example). Let's take a look at how server controls work by adding one of the most basic controls, Label, to our example.

To do this, we need to access the Toolbox in Visual Studio, which is cleverly hidden in a tab on the left side of the screen. By rolling over this tab, you can access the Toolbox and find the preinstalled server controls that can be used in the Design view, as shown in Figure 3-7.

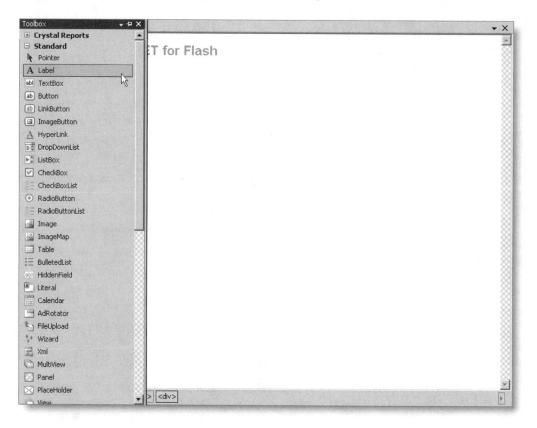

Figure 3-7. Accessing the Toolbox

To use the Label control, simply drag Label from the Toolbox (see Figure 3-7) onto the Design view. The Label is simply a control that renders text onto an ASP.NET web page. Once the Label is added to the design, you have access to all of its properties through the Properties window at the lower right of the Visual Studio interface. This Properties window is similar to the Component Inspector window in Flash. As you will notice in Figure 3-8, I have undocked the Properties window and repositioned it on the screen to make it easier to view. To make your life easier, you can reposition any of the toolbar and Explorer windows in the Visual Studio environment.

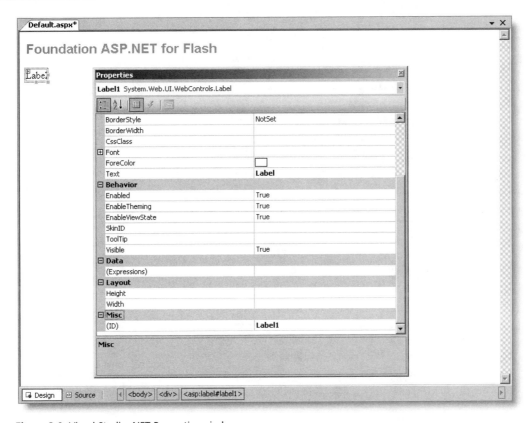

Figure 3-8. Visual Studio .NET Properties window

In the Properties window, find the property titled Text, listed under the Appearance category. As you can see, the default value for the Text property is the word Label, which also appears on the design interface. Let's try changing this value to a new value, My first ASP.NET page. If you hit *ENTER* after you type this value, you will see the text in the design interface change from Label to My first ASP.NET page (Figure 3-9). So, what's the advantage of using the Label control instead of just typing this text into the design interface like we did when displaying Foundation ASP.NET for Flash? Unlike with the HTML text generated when we type directly onto the design interface, when using the Label control we can access attributes like text color, width, height, and font style through our back-end code.

> *Before we take the dramatic jump into controlling this page using back-end code, it's important for me to emphasize that the page we have created so far is all part of the presentation layer we discussed in Chapter 1. As part of the presentation layer, nothing we have written yet is executing code on the web server.*

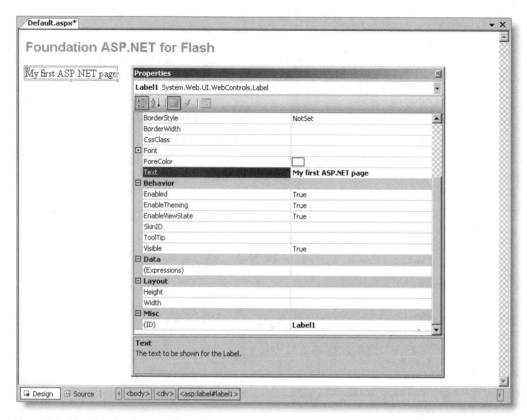

Figure 3-9. Changing the Text property value

Next, let's try viewing our newly created page in a web browser. If you are a Flash developer, you are probably used to the process of testing your Flash movie in a browser just by going to the Preview in Browser menu, which brings up the new HMTL page in a web browser. In Visual Studio, it's just as easy, although the back-end process is not quite as simple.

As we've discussed in Chapter 1, ASP.NET pages contain code that needs to be processed with a server before being sent to the browser for display—they can't just be run from your local filesystem. Server-side technologies, in general, need to be executed using a web hosting environment such as Internet Information Services (IIS) and cannot be run as just a file off your system. To demonstrate this point, let's try opening the .aspx page we've just created in a web browser without "hosting" it on a web server, as shown in Figure 3-10.

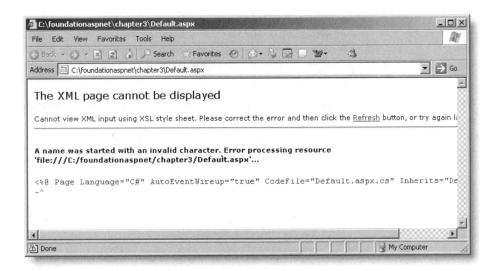

Figure 3-10. The browser cannot display the page.

Ouch! Not only did my browser not display the page correctly, but it also thought it was XML! Why is Internet Explorer having a hard time with this page? Let's take a quick look at the source code that the browser was trying to display to see why it didn't work. This can be done by selecting the Source option from the View menu in Internet Explorer. Figure 3-11 shows the result.

```
Default.aspx - Notepad
File  Edit  Format  Help
<%@ Page Language="C#" CompileWith="Default.aspx.cs" ClassName="Default_aspx" %>
<!DOCTYPE html PUBLIC "-//W3C//DTD XHTML 1.1//EN" "http://www.w3.org/TR/xhtml11/DTD/xhtml11.dtd">
<html xmlns="http://www.w3.org/1999/xhtml" >
<head runat="server">
    <title>Untitled Page</title>
</head>
<body>
    <form id="form1" runat="server">
    <div>
        <span style="font-size: 16pt; color: red; font-family: Arial"><b>Foundation ASP.NET
        2.0 for Flash</b></span><br />
        <br />
         
        <asp:Label ID="Label1" Runat="server" Text="My first ASP.NET page"></asp:Label>
        </div>
    </form>
</body>
</html>
```

Figure 3-11. Displaying the source code in Internet Explorer

Hmm . . . Looks eerily similar to the code we looked at in the Source view of Visual Studio—and it's pretty obvious to anyone familiar with HTML that <asp:Label is not a valid tag! Keep this thought in mind as we test this page in a browser using Visual Studio's built-in web server. You'll see that the web server actually takes these non-HTML tags and turns them into HTML-formatted tags that your browser has no problem reading.

Now, let's try viewing this page in a web browser after firing up Visual Studio's built-in web server. As I mentioned, doing this is pretty easy; just click the arrow labeled Debug, as shown in Figure 3-12.

Figure 3-12. Launching the site in Debug mode in Visual Studio .NET

When you click this Debug arrow, Visual Studio should prompt you with a message similar to the one shown in Figure 3-13.

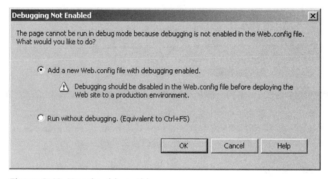

Figure 3-13. You should see this message.

This message is making reference to the web.config file, a file used to configure the settings of ASP.NET websites. We will cover the web.config file more thoroughly later in this chapter, but for now, feel safe selecting the Add a new Web.config file with debugging enabled option.

Once Visual Studio has created this new web.config file, two things happen to start the debugging process of your ASP.NET web page. First, the Visual Studio Visual Web Developer Web Server is started as a behind-the-scenes process, as Figure 3-14 shows.

Figure 3-14. The Visual Web Developer Web Server

The Visual Web Developer Web Server is a standalone web server used to host your ASP.NET projects on your local development machine. As you'll notice, the server is configured to host files at `http://localhost:18437`. You might be looking at the URL listed on the second line and thinking, "This doesn't look exactly like a normal URL, what does it mean?" The localhost section of the URL indicates that this site is coming off your local machine (`http://localhost/` on your coworker's machine would display a website running on their computer, not yours). The number after the word localhost indicates the port that your page will be served through. By default, a normal web server hosts pages using port 80—as you can see here, Visual Web Developer Web Server is using port 18437. Where did it come up with that? The Visual Web Developer Web Server is configured to find a "safe" port on your system that is not being used by another process. This is a great advantage for developers attempting to debug a site on their local system while at the same time using that system to test other sites.

Figure 3-15. Assigning a static port

By default, Visual Studio will assign your sites a "dynamic" port each time you open the project. This behavior can be difficult for interacting with Flash, since we need to hard-code some URLs into our ActionScript. Luckily, the Visual Web Developer Web Server can be forced to stick to a single port by changing the `Use Dynamic Ports` property of the web server to `false`, as shown in Figure 3-15.

Once Visual Studio has fired up the local web server, it turns its attention to the browser that it will be displaying your page in. Visual Studio fires up a browser window and directs the URL of that window to the "new" URL created by your Visual Web Developer Web Server, in this case `http://localhost:18437/chapter3/Default.aspx`, as shown in Figure 3-16.

> If your computer is not configured with Internet Explorer as the default browser, Visual Studio will not be able to perform many of its advanced debugging capabilities. To change the default browser in Visual Studio (but not change it on your system), select File ➤ Browse with, choose Internet Explorer, and click the Set as Default button.

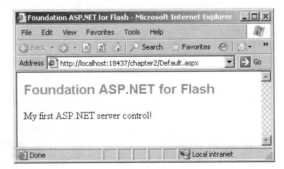

Figure 3-16. Your first ASP.NET page!

And as easy as that, you have your first ASP.NET web page! Let's take a look at the HTML source for this page to see how it differs from the page we viewed before, without using the local web server. As you can see in Figure 3-17, the HTML source of this `.aspx` page now contains a <span tag instead of an `<asp:Label` as it did previously. Now that we've executed this page using the web server, the server's ASP.NET handler has rendered the Label server control as HTML.

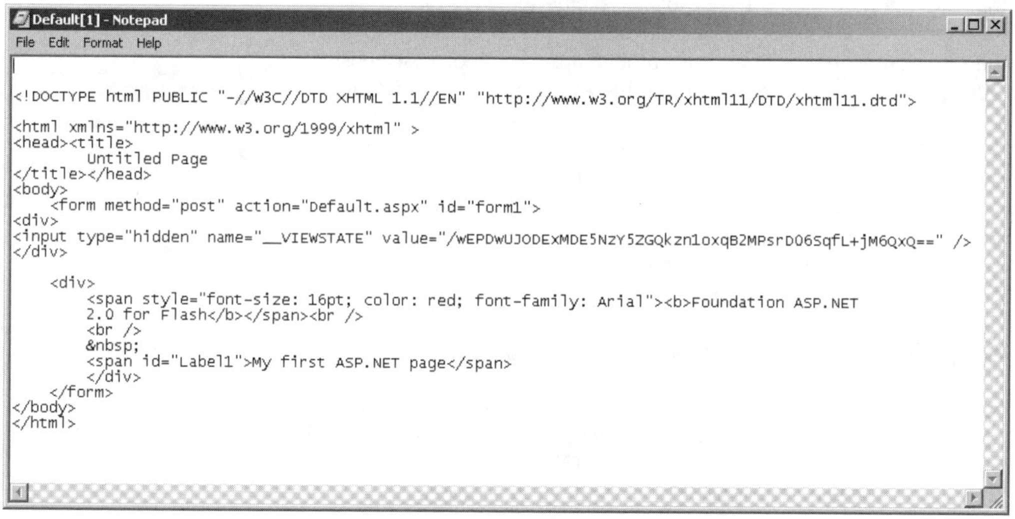

```
<!DOCTYPE html PUBLIC "-//W3C//DTD XHTML 1.1//EN" "http://www.w3.org/TR/xhtml11/DTD/xhtml11.dtd">

<html xmlns="http://www.w3.org/1999/xhtml" >
<head><title>
	Untitled Page
</title></head>
<body>
    <form method="post" action="Default.aspx" id="form1">
<div>
<input type="hidden" name="__VIEWSTATE" value="/wEPDwUJODExMDE5NzY5ZGQkzn1oxqB2MPsrD06SqfL+jM6QxQ==" />
</div>

    <div>
        <span style="font-size: 16pt; color: red; font-family: Arial"><b>Foundation ASP.NET
        2.0 for Flash</b></span><br />
        <br />
         
        <span id="Label1">My first ASP.NET page</span>
        </div>
    </form>
</body>
</html>
```

Figure 3-17. The HTML source of our `.aspx` page

Code-behind files

Okay, now that you've gotten a feel for creating an ASP.NET page in the Visual Studio design environment, it's time to take the big dive into the world of server-side programming using C#. In the examples we will look at in this chapter, the server-side programming will be used to manipulate server controls like the Label control we just discussed.

ASP.NET, unlike nearly any other server-side web technology, uses *code-behind files* to separate the presentation layer from the logical layer of a web application. Code-behind files are files written in C# (or another .NET-compatible language) that contain the programming logic for that page. Using code-behind files, it is possible to execute any of the functions in the .NET Framework, as well as manipulate the presentation-layer `.aspx` files that are "connected" to these code-behind files. This code-behind model is very similar to the ActionScript 2.0 class model; each of them can execute behind-the-scenes functions, as well as control user interface elements.

If you're familiar with another server-side programming language, like PHP or classic ASP, you are probably used to the concept of *inline scripting*, as mentioned in Chapter 1. Using inline scripting, server-side code is typically mixed in with user interface HTML elements. Using this methodology results in problems similar to those encountered when scripts are applied directly to button and MovieClip instances in Flash—the code becomes very hard to maintain since bits and pieces of it are scattered throughout your files.

With code-behind, though, this code is kept completely separate, allowing for more functional, easy-to-maintain applications. The code-behind model of ASP.NET is also an advantage over the inline-scripting model of other languages in that it compiles its code before a user accesses it, whereas inline-scripted code compiles *when it is requested*. Again, to relate this example to Flash, it would be like posting an .fla file on a web server that needed to be "published"—or compiled—into an .swf file each time a user requested that Flash movie. This would be a very ineffective process that could be made more efficient by just compiling the .swf *before* it is requested by a client browser—which is exactly what ASP.NET code-behind files do!

To access the code-behind file of an .aspx file in Visual Studio .NET, you can do one of two things:

1. Right-click on the page in the Design view and select the View Code option, as shown in Figure 3-18.

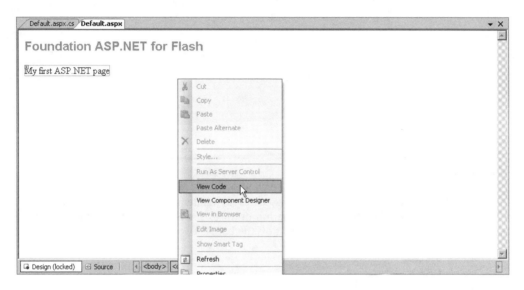

Figure 3-18. Selecting View Code

2. Double-click on the file in the Solution Explorer that sits "behind" the .aspx page you'd like to edit, as shown in Figure 3-19.

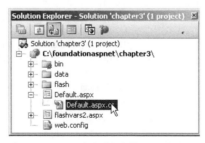

Figure 3-19. Code-behind file in Solution Explorer

When you have selected this page, you will be moved to a new type of Source view in Visual Studio .NET, and quite possibly, a new concept in web development altogether. This view, shown in Figure 3-20, is used to create and edit code-behind files and, more generally, class files.

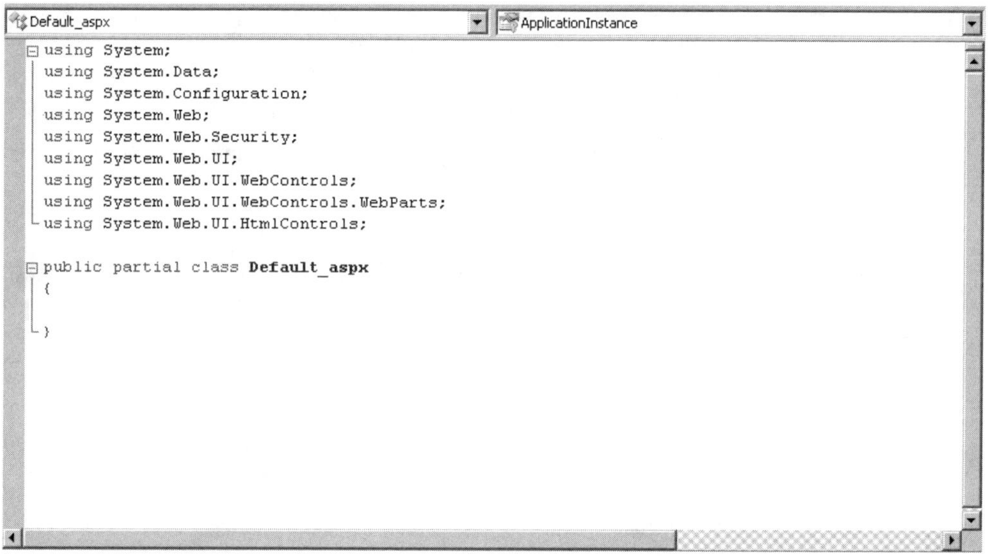

Figure 3-20. Code-behind file

This file, Default.aspx.cs, is a class that executes in tandem with the presentation-layer file, Default.aspx. Let's examine this file from the top down to see exactly what is happening. The first nine lines of this file might look confusing right off the bat:

```
using System;
using System.Data;
using System.Configuration;
using System.Web;
using System.Web.Security;
using System.Web.UI;
using System.Web.UI.WebControls;
using System.Web.UI.WebControls.WebParts;
using System.Web.UI.HtmlControls;
```

If you're familiar with the concept of OO programming or #include files in ActionScript 2.0, this might look familiar. These lines are telling the .NET Framework "I might be using some of the prebuilt classes you have stored in these libraries." As I mentioned in Chapter 1, one major part of the .NET Framework is the base class library. This is a HUGE library of classes that perform many of the arduous tasks of everyday programming. When you include these classes in your C# code-behind classes by using the using keyword, you are able to access those classes in an easy notation.

> It is not necessary to include these base classes in a .NET file in order to use them. Contrary to other programming languages (like ActionScript), which actually insert the code of included files into your code, the C# using statement actually only makes your development with those classes easier, as we'll see in the following examples. Whether or not you include a class from the base class library in a C# file with the using keyword, you will always have access to that class in your code.

These class libraries in .NET are grouped into larger collections, referred to as *namespaces*. For example, the line using System.Web.Security is including the System.Web.Security namespace in your page. As you can see, Visual Studio by default includes quite a few of these commonly used namespaces in your ASP.NET web page for you; some of them are much more specific to the ASP.NET/HTML presentation layer than ASP.NET/Flash development. As we use code-behind in the following chapters, I'll try to point out some of the namespaces that are most useful for ASP.NET/Flash development.

The next (and last!) section of code in the Default.aspx.cs page is as follows:

```
public partial class Default_aspx
{
}
```

Again, if you're familiar with classes in ActionScript 2.0, this *class declaration* should look pretty familiar. The first word in this line, public, is referring to the level of access that is allowed to this class. Access levels are not only assigned to classes, as in this example, but also to methods, properties, and events, as we will see throughout this book. As an ASP.NET code-behind page, a class must be declared as public in order to function correctly.

The next word in this class declaration is an important one. partial, a new concept in ASP.NET 2.0, tells the .NET Framework "This class is just one part of a class. When you execute the code for this page, use it *along with* the other parts of the class." Where, then, is the other mysterious half of this class and what does it do? The other, inaccessible half of an ASP.NET page's code-behind files contains much of the behind-the-scenes work in an ASP.NET page. This work includes defining *event handlers* and control properties. The use of partial classes in ASP.NET pages reduces the amount of code necessary in any code-behind page and lessens the risk of design-time "wiring" issues in ASP.NET development.

Finally, the code class Default_aspx defines the name of a class that will be functioning as the code-behind for the ASP.NET web page—which brings up a good question: How does the Default.aspx file "know" that Default.aspx.cs contains the code to use as its code-behind? The fact that it sits "behind" it in Visual Studio does not mean much to the .NET Framework, so there must be another "hint" provided by one of these files to indicate how they are connected. This hint resides back in the HTML Source view of the Default.aspx page, as shown in Figure 3-21.

```
<%@ Page Language="C#" CompileWith="Default.aspx.cs" ClassName="Default_aspx" %>
```

Figure 3-21. This doesn't look like valid HTML.

Once again, a line in the Default.aspx page that doesn't look like valid HTML—what is it? As you can see, this line starts with the <% delimiter. Again, if you are familiar with development in another server-side language, this might look familiar; it is a special sequence of characters that tells the web server "Anything that is listed within these delimiters should be 'read' by ASP.NET when this page is executed." The next few characters, @ Page, tell ASP.NET "The text in this tag will contain information about the file characteristics of this page," followed by Language="C#", which defines the programming language that will be used in this page. The next two attributes, CompileWith and ClassName, define the name of the file and the class that contains the code-behind file for this page. As you can see, this ClassName attribute is the same as the name of the class that was defined in Default.aspx.cs.

Page_Load

The first event we'll look at is the ASP.NET page's Page_Load event. Page_Load is an event that occurs, as you might guess, every time a page loads. Because of this convenient timing, the Page_Load event is a perfect place for the initial logic and ASP.NET page.

The easiest way to create the Page_Load event handler in Visual Studio .NET 2005 requires you to go back to the Design view of Default.aspx and double-click anywhere on the screen (except on the label that you created). Once you do this, Visual Studio creates the Page_Load event handler for you in the Default.aspx.cs file, as shown in Figure 3-22.

Figure 3-22. The Page_Load event handler

Going back to the OO concepts I discussed earlier in this chapter, Page_Load is now a new *member* of the Default_aspx class. Again, this event handler will fire every time the page is loaded, so let's use this handler to set some properties of the Label server control we've created.

Just as MovieClips that exist on the _root timeline are "members" of the _root timeline, the server controls that are created in an ASP.NET page are actually considered members of the code-behind page's class. Since they are members, it's easy to access them from within a code-behind class using the this.myControlName notation. In this case, to refer to the Label control that was named Label1, you can simply type this.Label1 to refer to this control. It is at this point that you'll start to see the power of Visual Studio's IntelliSense. As shown in Figure 3-23, IntelliSense picks up as you are typing and gives you code hints about the member of an object you might be looking for.

```
  using System.Web.Security;
  using System.Web.UI;
  using System.Web.UI.WebControls;
  using System.Web.UI.WebControls.WebParts;
  using System.Web.UI.HtmlControls;

public partial class Default_aspx
  {
      void Page_Load(object sender, EventArgs e)
      {
        this.l
      }                    Label1                          Label Default_aspx.Label1
                           Load
  }                        LoadComplete
                           LoadControl
                           LoadControlState
                           LoadPageStateFromPersistenceMedium
                           LoadTemplate
                           LoadViewState
                           MaintainScrollPositionOnPostback
                           MapPath
```

Figure 3-23. IntelliSense gives you code hints.

As you are typing, if you realize that Visual Studio has "guessed" the word you are looking for, you can hit either the *ENTER* or *TAB* key to auto-complete the spelling of those words. For example, as shown in Figure 3-23, I have typed this.l, which has prompted Visual Studio to bring up Label1, the name of the Label control we added to the ASP.NET page. Even after just typing the l, I can hit *ENTER* and have a successful reference to the server control I was looking for.

Now that we're on a roll, let's keep it going—after the word Label1, type another period to bring up the members of the Label class. As you can see, all of the properties (and more) that were accessible from the Property Explorer in the design interface are now available as members of the Label1 object through code! For this example, start typing Text, as shown in Figure 3-24.

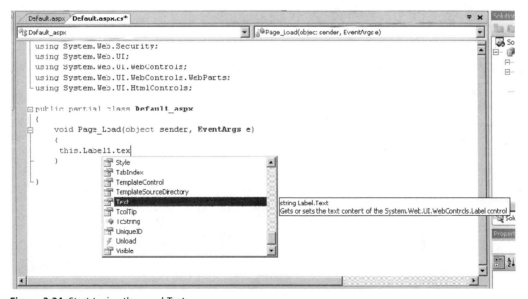

Figure 3-24. Start typing the word Text.

In the case of Text, it takes IntelliSense a little longer to figure out exactly what word you're looking for, since there are a number of T members in the Label class. Notice that, when you have found the Text property of the Label1 control, Visual Studio brings up the description of that property next to the property name. In this case, the Text property has the description

string Label.Text

Gets or sets the text content of the System.Web.UI.WebControls.Label control.

IntelliSense really is pretty amazing! As we are typing the Text property, IntelliSense is telling us that the Label.Text property is a string data type, and that it is used to either set or retrieve the value of the text in the Label control. Again, as you near completion of the word Text, hit either the TAB or ENTER key to complete the spelling of the word and to correct any case-related errors you had—remember, C# is case-sensitive!

Now that we have successfully created a reference to the Text property of the Label1 server control on the Default.aspx page, let's try setting the text value of that Label control to a new value, My first ASP.NET server control!. To accomplish this, all you need to do is assign the Text property to a string value, as shown here:

```
void Page_Load(object sender, EventArgs e)
{
this.Label1.Text = "My first ASP.NET server control!";
}
```

Notice here that, as is the case with ActionScript, C# requires a semicolon after each line of code. As you're typing in VS .NET 2005, you'll even notice that IntelliSense picks up on your typing the semicolon and corrects the indentation of your line of code since you have successfully completed a line of code.

It is great that we have set the Text value of the Label control to a value, but at this point it seems that we may have run into a problem: We have now set the value of the Text property of the Label control twice. First, we set it using the Property Explorer and now we have set it again using the Page_Load event of the code-behind file. Certainly, both values can't be accepted, so which will display as the Text property's value when the page is displayed? The answer is a simple one: Any server control property value set through the Page_Load event occurs *after* the value set using the Property Explorer in the ASP.NET page life cycle and therefore overrides that value. To prove this, let's try testing the page in a browser and see what it does.

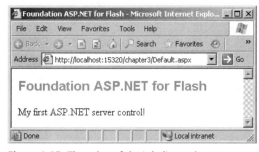

Figure 3-25. The value of the Label's text is as we entered it in the code-behind file.

Again, to view the page in a browser, click the Start button at the top of the Visual Studio interface. Figure 3-25 shows the resulting page displayed in a browser.

As you can see, the value of the Label's text is now as we entered it in the code-behind file. We have successfully "controlled the puppet" using an ASP.NET server control!

Taking things a step further, it would also be easy to control other properties of the Label server control, such as the background color, font style, or tooltip, but as mentioned earlier, an extensive examination of HTML-based elements in ASP.NET isn't required for ASP.NET/Flash use—we will hardly be using them! An ASP.NET server control that will be useful for ASP.NET/Flash development is one that will allow us to embed Flash movies directly into ASP.NET pages and access the properties of these movies dynamically.

Flash server control

We've taken a look at how to use server controls to create HTML-based user interface elements, so now let's apply this knowledge with a different type of server control that can be used to integrate Flash movies into ASP.NET web pages. A control of this type does not come "built in" to the .NET base class library or Visual Studio .NET, but several are available as third-party components. Specifically, the component we will use in this book is the epicFlashControl component by epicsoft.

The epicFlashControl is, as I mentioned, a server control that can be used to embed .swf files into an ASP.NET web page and dynamically change the properties of that .swf file. This type of functionality is extremely useful for situations where the web application you are developing is not *completely* a Flash interface. By using a Flash server control, you can combine Flash interface elements with other HTML-based ASP.NET controls and manipulate all of these controls using C#.

The epicFlashControl is free for development use (any testing done on the localhost domain), and costs only $10 for unlimited usage on all other web domains. The epicFlashControl is available as a download from www.epicsoft.net/products/flashnet/, as shown in Figure 3-26.

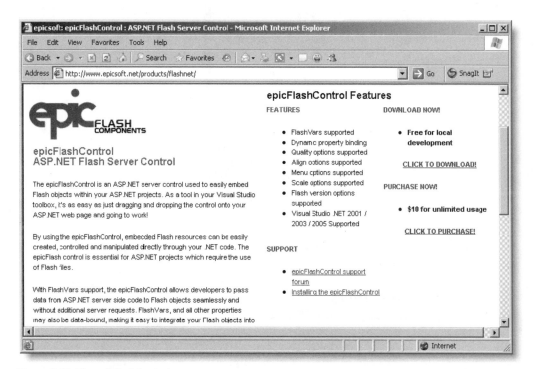

Figure 3-26. The epicFlashControl

Adding a control to the Toolbox

Here are the steps needed to get the epicFlashControl installed as a component in your Visual Studio toolbox:

1. Download the epicFlash component from www.epicsoft.net/products/flashnet/.

2. Unzip the epicFlash package to a folder on your system. I used the `c:\epicFlash\` directory to store these files on my system.

3. In Visual Studio .NET 2005 Design view, go to the ToolBox, right-click, and select Choose Items, as shown in Figure 3-27.

Figure 3-27. Selecting Choose Items

4. In the Choose Toolbox Items window, click Browse and browse for the `epicFlashControl.dll` file you saved on your system.

> *Note: There might be a significant delay after selecting the* Browse *button.*

5. Click OK, and the epicFlashControl will appear in your Toolbox! (See Figure 3-28.)

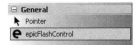

Figure 3-28. The epicFlashControl now appears in your Toolbox.

In this example, I have chosen to add the epicFlashControl to the General tab of my Toolbox. If you would like to create a new tab for this (and other) controls, it's as easy as right-clicking in the Toolbox, typing the name of the new tab, and dragging the control into this tab, as in Figure 3-29.

Figure 3-29. You can change the tab name.

Using the epicFlashControl

Now that you have the epicFlashControl added to your Toolbox, let's try creating a Flash file and using the epicFlashControl to add it to an ASP.NET web page. First, let's create a very basic Flash file to use in our example. I'm going to create this file in Flash MX 2004 Professional edition, although the features specific to the Professional edition are not necessary for this example.

In this Flash file, let's just create a small rectangle and some text, as in Figure 3-30.

Figure 3-30. First create a small rectangle and some text.

You'll notice that in this Flash file, I've changed the size of the canvas to 162×49 to remove any extra space from the Flash file. In order to use this Flash file with your first example ASP.NET web application, let's create a new folder within the same directory as your ASP.NET application and save this file in that directory. Since I chose to house my example application in the C:\foundationaspnet\ chapter3 folder, I'm going to create a folder in this directory called Flash that I'll use to house the Flash files in this application. Let's name this Flash file statictest and save it in that directory. Once you have the file saved, let's also publish the file to create an .swf that we can use in our example. It is not necessary to publish any accompanying files with the .swf, such as an .html file.

Now that we have a sample file to use, let's try adding the epicFlashControl to the Default.aspx page in the same way that we added the Label control: by dragging it onto the Design view in Visual Studio .NET. Once the epicFlashControl is added to the design interface, it's possible to change the properties of this control using the Property Explorer as we did with the Label control. Figure 3-31 shows the epicFlashControl on the Default.aspx web page with the Property Explorer opened to display some of the control's properties.

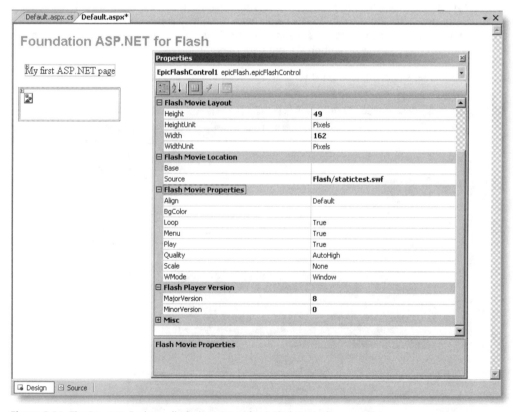

Figure 3-31. The Property Explorer displaying some of epicFlashControl's properties

As shown in Figure 3-31, many of the default options for embedding a Flash object into a page are exposed as properties using the epicFlashControl. Some of the most notable properties are listed here:

- **MajorVersion:** The "major" version number of the Flash Player that should be embedded into the page. For example, if you want to embed a Flash 7 file, the MajorVersion would be 7.

- **MinorVersion:** The "minor" version number of the Flash Player that is required for the embedded .swf file. For example, if you were publishing a Flash file that required 7,0,19,0 the MinorVersion would be 19.

- **Source:** The source of the Flash .swf file. This property can be a relative path or URL to a Flash file.

- **Height:** The height of the .swf file.

- **HeightUnit:** The unit base to use for the height. Either pixels or percent.

- **Width:** The width of the .swf file.

- **HeightUnit:** The unit base to use for the width. Either pixels or percent.

- **BgColor:** The background color of the .swf file.

- **Menu:** Whether or not to display the user-options menu when a user right-clicks on the .swf file in a web browser.

When you set these properties correctly, the epicFlashControl can be used to display any Flash file in an .aspx page. For this example, let's change the width, height, and source values of the epicFlashControl to the following:

- **Width:** 162
- **Height:** 49
- **Source:** Flash/statictest.swf

This should be all that is required to embed a Flash file in an .aspx page using Visual Studio. At this point, let's try testing the page again to see how the control works (see Figure 3-32).

Figure 3-32. Testing the control

And just like that, we have a Flash .swf file embedded into an ASP.NET web page as a server control.

Although it is great to be able to embed Flash within ASP.NET pages with Visual Studio, it really doesn't accomplish too much until we are able to communicate between the ASP.NET server-side code and the Flash file. Through the use of the epicFlashControl, it's possible to use one of the methods of communication mentioned in Chapter 1: FlashVars.

FlashVars

FlashVars can be a very effective method of communication between ASP.NET and .swf files. Passing data to the client using FlashVars is very similar to the methods used to pass data using standard dynamic web page technology in that FlashVars are embedded tags in the HTML page sent to the client. Because of this feature, FlashVars are useful mainly for onetime communication since FlashVars require a page refresh to change values. It is also because of this feature that FlashVars are particularly useful. In many circumstances, relatively small amounts of data are needed by the client application and this data, once sent, does not need to be reloaded. FlashVars are sent to the client browser using name-value pairs that are placed into attributes of the <EMBED> and <OBJECT> tags used to embed the .swf file in the page passed to the client browser. These variables are then available on the _root timeline of the Flash movie when loaded on the client machine. Consider the following HTML code used to embed a Flash movie into a web page:

```
<OBJECT classid="..." codebase="..."
WIDTH="300" HEIGHT="100" id="myMovie">
<PARAM NAME=movie VALUE="myMovie.swf">
<PARAM NAME=FlashVars
 VALUE="var1=Testing%20Variable1&var2=Testing%20Variable2">
<EMBED src="myMovie.swf" WIDTH="300" HEIGHT="100"
NAME="myMovie"
FLASHVARS=" var1=Testing%20Variable1&var2=Testing%20Variable2"
TYPE="..." PLUGINSPAGE="...">
</EMBED>
</OBJECT>
```

This HTML should look pretty familiar if you've ever embedded Flash movies in HTML. If you haven't worked with FlashVars before, you may not have seen the <PARAM NAME=FlashVars VALUE= "var1=test1&var2=test2"> and <EMBED ... FLASHVARS="var1=test1&var2=test2" ...> lines. These are the lines essential to communication using FlashVars. In these lines you see the name-value pairs that pass the variable data to the .swf. When the .swf is loaded, it will have available on its _root timeline the variables var1 and var2, which will be set to Testing Variable1 and Testing Variable2, respectively.

There are some important things to note when using FlashVars in a web page:

- Both the <EMBED> and <PARAM> tags must be included for the variables to work on all browsers.
- The length of the string embedded in the FlashVars tags must be less than 64KB in length.
- Variables must be separated by an & sign.
- Special characters must be encoded with a % sign followed by their two-digit hexadecimal value. A list of these hexadecimal values is available at www.macromedia.com/cfusion/knowledgebase/index.cfm?id=tn_14143.

Embedding FlashVars using the epicFlashControl

In order to make use of FlashVars in our example files, let's make a couple of modifications to our Flash file. First, let's change the static text field to a dynamic text field, with an instance name of Text1_txt, as in Figure 3-33.

Figure 3-33. Changing the static test field to a dynamic text field

Let's also create a new layer on the Flash timeline called Actions, and in the first frame of that layer, add a new piece of ActionScript:

```
Text1_txt.text = txtval;
```

This line will be used to take the value of a new variable, txtval, that we will be passing from ASP.NET to the Flash movie and displaying it using the Text1_txt field. Let's jump back to our ASP.NET page and take a look at how to pass this variable to the Flash file.

To pass values using FlashVars and the epicFlashControl, it's necessary to use the code-behind file, as when we set the value of the Text property of the Label component. Again, let's open the Default.aspx.cs file and add some code to the Page_Load event handler. Now that we have added a new control, EpicFlashControl1, to our page, this control will be accessible in the page's code-behind.

As we did with the Label control, let's start by typing this. to get IntelliSense on the right track toward showing us this page's members. In this page's members, you will now see the EpicFlashControl1 member, which you can select, as shown in Figure 3-34.

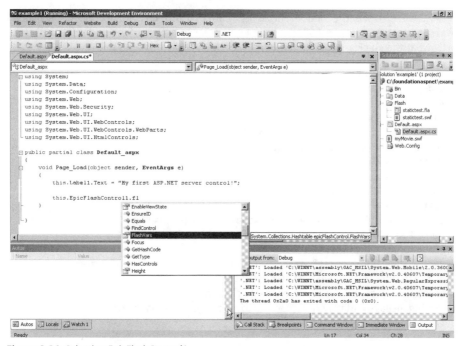

Figure 3-34. Selecting EpicFlashControl1

Once you have the reference to the EpicFlashControl1, FlashVars name-value pairs can be added through the FlashVars property's Add method:

```
this.EpicFlashControl1.FlashVars.Add("txtval", "ASP.NET FlashVars!");
```

This line of code will create a new FlashVars entry to pass to the .swf file from your C# code. The first parameter, passed in our code as txtval, is the name of the variable as it will appear on the root of the .swf's timeline, and the second parameter, ASP.NET FlashVars!, will be the value of that variable. Again, let's test this page in a browser to see if our FlashVars communication worked successfully (Figure 3-35).

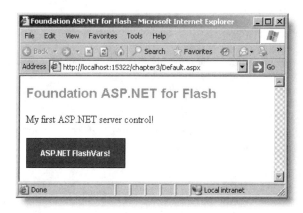

Figure 3-35. Testing our page

And finally, we can see the first example of ASP.NET/Flash communication—the value ASP.NET FlashVars was passed from an ASP.NET code-behind file to an .swf file for display! Let's take a look at exactly what the epicFlashControl rendered as HTML in the .aspx page:

```
<object classid="clsid:D27CDB6E-AE6D-11cf-96B8-444553540000"
codebase="http://download.macromedia.com/pub/shockwave/cabs/flash/
➥ swflash.cab#version=8,0,0,0" width="162" height="49"
id="EpicFlashControl1">
<param name="movie" value="Flash/flashvarstest.swf">
<param name="quality" value="autohigh">
<param name="menu" value="true">
<param name="play" value="true">
<param name="loop" value="true">
<param name="scale" value="noborder">
<param name="flashvars" value="txtval=ASP.NET+FlashVars!">
<embed src="Flash/flashvarstest.swf" quality="autohigh"
play="true" loop="true"
width="162" height="49" name="EpicFlashControl1" scale="NoBorder"
➥ flashvars="txtval=ASP.NET+FlashVars!"
menu="True" type="application/x-shockwave-flash"
➥ pluginspace="http://www.macromedia.com/go/getflashplayer">
</embed></object>
```

Here we can see the FlashVars embedded into the HTML of the resulting .aspx file by the epicFlashControl. The control took the parameters we passed and created name-value pairs, which were passed to the .swf file.

A practical example

To demonstrate a real-world example of how this combination of ASP.NET and FlashVars can be used in an application, we'll take a look at a site navigation bar created using these technologies. In this example, we'll create a Flash file that will take FlashVars from ASP.NET and use the values passed to create a button navigation system.

First, let's list, generally, what should happen in this example:

1. A Flash movie will be embedded into an .aspx web page.

2. The Flash movie should be about 650 pixels wide and 40 pixels high to make a good navigation bar.

3. The ASP.NET web page will embed FlashVars into the Flash movie using the epicFlashControl. These FlashVars will be used to pass a list of button titles and links.

4. The Flash movie will have a function to iterate through these titles and links and attach buttons with the specified title and link (using the getURL command). As an additional specification, let's say that the Flash movie can handle no more than six button values.

Sounds pretty simple, right? Let's get started by creating the Flash movie that will accept the FlashVars and create the buttons for the navigation. The first thing I've done, after starting a new Flash movie with a width of 650 and height of 40, is to create a new symbol in this movie, as shown in Figure 3-36. I have named this symbol GrayButton and have selected it to have a linkage identifier and class association of GrayButton as well.

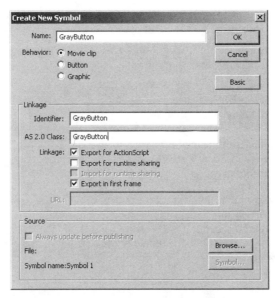

Figure 3-36. The Create New Symbol dialog box

Next, I have created two layers on the Flash timeline of the GrayButton symbol, one called Button, which will house a button, and another called Text, which will contain the text that will reside on that button. In the Button layer, I have created a small box on the stage using the rectangle tool. I've made this box 100×30 so that six of them can easily fit across our navigation bar, with a width of 650 pixels. I have then converted this box into a button with an instance name of Nav_btn. I've also added a slightly darker color of gray to the rollover state of the button for visual purposes.

In the Text layer, I have created a dynamic text field with an instance name of Text1_txt. As shown in Figure 3-37, I have set the fonts of this text field to be embedded Arial 12 point.

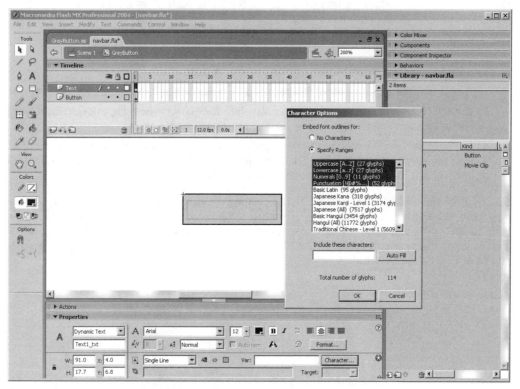

Figure 3-37. Setting the fonts for the text field

And that's about it for the Flash timeline! As you'll notice in this book, we will be doing as little work as necessary on the timeline in Flash, instead focusing our efforts on the more efficient use of the ActionScript 2.0 object-oriented syntax.

I have also created an external ActionScript 2.0 .as file, GrayButton.as. If you're not familiar with external .as files, they are very similar to writing ActionScript on the timeline in Flash, but allow for a more organized, object-oriented approach. To create a new .as file in Flash MX 2004 is as easy as going to the File ➤ New ➤ ActionScript File menu. For the examples in this book, we'll save all of the .as files in the same directory as the Flash files, although it is also possible to designate specific directories to store .as class files.

Here is the class I have created in the GrayButton.as file:

```
dynamic class GrayButton extends MovieClip {
  private var myLink:String;
  function GrayButton() {
  // create an onPress event for the button
    this["Nav_btn"].onPress = this.OpenURL;
  }
  function SetTitle(theTitle:String) {
    // set the text of the Text1_txt field to the new title
    this["Text1_txt"].text = theTitle;
  }
  function SetLink(theLink:String) {
    // set a private variable to the button's link
    this.myLink = theLink;
  }
  function OpenURL() {
    // when the button is pressed, open the link!
    _parent.getURL(_parent.myLink);
  }
}
```

As you'll notice, I've made the GrayButton class extend the built-in ActionScript class. When a class is made that extends another class, the "extended" class obtains the functionality of the original class and adds additional members to that class. For example, the GrayButton class now has all of the functionality of the MovieClip class, which it extends as well as the additional methods that I have added to it.

This is a great time to point out a couple of similarities and differences between class files in ActionScript 2.0 and C#:

- **Similarity:** Just like .NET has the base class library, ActionScript has "built-in" classes, like the MovieClip class that can be used and extended to make programming tasks easier.

- **Difference:** When extending a class in Flash, the extends keyword is used. In C#, a class would be extended using the following syntax:

```
public class GrayButton:MovieClip { .. }
```

Let's take a look at the methods of the GrayButton class:

```
function GrayButton() {
  // create an onPress event for the button
  this["Nav_btn"].onPress = this.OpenURL;
}
```

89

This function is the *constructor* for the GrayButton class. A constructor function, in either C# or ActionScript 2.0, is automatically executed when an instance of that class is created. Initialization functions are often placed within a class's constructor as well as declarations that prepare the class for execution. In this example, I have given the Nav_btn button an onPress event handler: the OpenURL function in the GrayButton class. This means simply that whenever someone clicks on the Nav_btn instance, the OpenURL function will fire.

```
function SetTitle(theTitle:String) {
  // set the text of the Text1_txt field to the new title
  this["Text1_txt"].text = theTitle;
}
```

I am using this method to set the text of the button once an instance of the GrayButton class is created. By calling the SetTitle method and passing a string value, the text field Text1_txt's text value is set to that value.

```
function SetLink(theLink:String) {
  // set a private variable to the button's link
  this.myLink = theLink;
}
```

This method performs a similar function to the SetTitle method, except that instead of setting the property of a TextField instance, the SetTitle method sets the value of a variable private to the GrayButton class. This variable will be of use in the OpenURL method here:

```
function OpenURL() {
// when the button is pressed, open the link!
  _parent.getURL(_parent.myLink);
}
```

This method, which handles the onPress event of the Nav_btn button instance, simply opens the URL as set by the SetLink function. Notice that this function refers to _parent for both the getURL method and the myLink property since this function's "home" becomes the Nav_btn instance, and therefore the _parent is the GrayButton instance.

You'll notice that, although I created a GrayButton symbol in the library, I have not created an instance of this object at all on the timeline. I have specifically done this to show the similarity between symbols in Flash and classes in C#. The symbol in the library is, at this point, a "blueprint" for future GrayButton instances that can be created at design time by dragging them onto the stage or at runtime by using the AttachMovie function. On the _root timeline, let's try testing the GrayButton out using the AttachMovie method:

```
attachMovie("GrayButton", "gb", 50);
this["gb"].SetTitle("Gray Button");
this["gb"].SetLink("http://www.friendsofed.com");
```

In the first line, attachMovie("GrayButton", "gb", 50), an instance of the GrayButton symbol, is attached to the _root timeline. By default, this instance will be placed at an x and y value of 0 on the stage when the movie is tested. I have also used the SetTitle method to set the text of the button and the SetLink method to set the page that will open when the button is "pressed." Let's take a look at what happens when this code is tested in the Flash IDE (see Figure 3-38).

Figure 3-38. Testing our button

All right! We've got an instance of the GrayButton on the stage with the text set correctly and (although I can't show it here) a link to the friends of ED website! We will be using this process:

1. Create a symbol in the Flash library with a Linkage identifier and assigned AS 2.0 class.

2. Create an AS 2.0 class to assign functionality to that symbol.

3. Create instances of this symbol dynamically at runtime.

4. Set properties and calling methods of the symbol at runtime.

If this process is unfamiliar to you, three of the easiest stumbling blocks in these steps are as follows:

1. Making sure to set a linkage identifier when creating the symbol in the library

2. Naming the ActionScript (.as) class file the same name as the AS 2.0 class you have defined in the symbol definition

3. Naming all UI elements so they can be referenced from your AS 2.0 class

Now that we've got a good start on the Flash side of our Flash/ASP.NET navigation example, let's move to the ASP.NET side and work with some FlashVars. Oops, don't want to forget to save! Let's save this Flash file as navbar.fla in the same Flash folder in the main directory of your first ASP.NET website directory. For my example, this directory is C:\foundationaspnet\chapter3\Flash. Also, let's "Publish" the Flash file at this point to create an .swf. Note: I'm going to leave our "test code" on the _root timeline for now for testing purposes in our ASP.NET development.

Moving the navbar to ASP.NET

As we move back to the Visual Studio interface, you'll notice that the Solution Explorer in Visual Studio has noticed the .fla and .swf files that we have created in the Flash folder in our first example's directory, as shown in Figure 3-39.

Figure 3-39. The Flash folder

To display our new navigation bar (which isn't quite functional yet), let's create a new `.aspx` page. Creating this page is simple in Visual Studio .NET, accomplished by right-clicking on the site's directory name and selecting Add New Item, as shown in Figure 3-40.

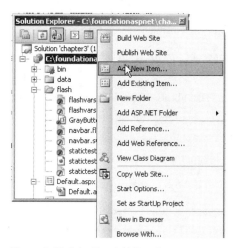

Figure 3-40. Selecting Add New Item

Once you have selected Add New Item, select Web Form in the following dialog box and name the new `.aspx` file FlashVarsNav.aspx. Make sure that you have C# selected as the language and Place code in a separate file enabled, as shown in Figure 3-41.

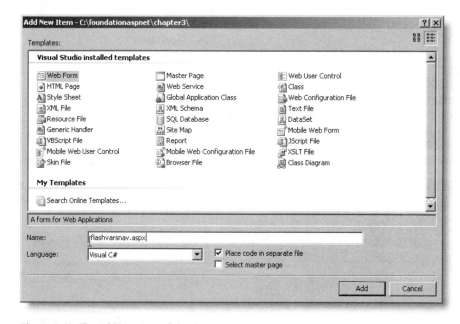

Figure 3-41. The Add New Item dialog box

Now that we have a new `.aspx` web page, we can embed the Flash file into it, again using the epicFlashControl. When I created the new web form, Visual Studio started me out in the Source view for that form. If this is the case for you, switch from the Source view to the Design view by clicking the button below the Document window. Next, go back to your Toolbox and find the epicFlashControl you added earlier in the chapter. When you find the epicFlashControl, drag it out onto the Design view. As you will notice, the epicFlashControl defaults to a size of 100×100 pixels, so we're going to want to set new values.

With the epicFlashControl selected, go to the Properties window and find the Width and Height properties. Set the width of the control to 650 and the height to 40, which are the dimensions we gave our Flash movie. Once the width and height are set, find the Source parameter in the same epicFlashControl and set this value to the relative path of your Flash movie: `Flash/navbar.swf`. At this point, your screen should look similar to Figure 3-42.

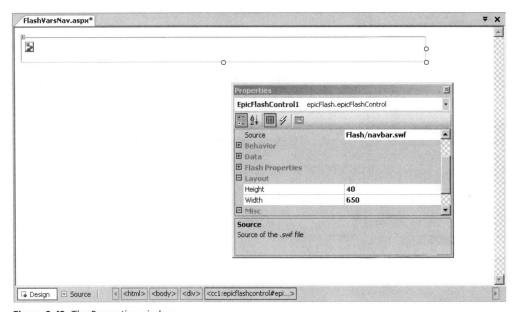

Figure 3-42. The Properties window

And, although it doesn't look like much at this point, you now have the "navbar" Flash movie embedded within this new page! Let's test the page again to prove that it is set up correctly. Again, select the Start button at the top of the screen to launch the page in a browser. Figure 3-43 shows the `navbar.swf` file embedded in the `.aspx` page.

Figure 3-43. navbar.swf embedded in the .aspx page

The first test of our first Flash–ASP.NET skills are successful! The navbar.swf Flash file is embedded within the FlashVarsNav.aspx page—now we can start with the FlashVars.

Back in the Visual Studio interface (with the debugging browser window closed, of course), let's go to the Page_Load event handler in the code-behind for this page. Again, this can be accessed by double-clicking anywhere on the design interface in Visual Studio.

At this point, if we are going to pass FlashVars to our Flash movie, we need to decide how we want to format the variable names and values before passing them to Flash. Since the buttons that the Flash file will be creating require both a title and a URL, these seem like obvious values to pass from ASP.NET to Flash. For formatting of these variables, let's use the following syntax:

```
title1=[First title];
url1=[First URL];
title2=[Second Title];
url2=[Second URL];
title3=[Third Title];
url3=[Third URL];
...
```

Using this syntax, it should be easy to pass the variable values from ASP.NET to Flash, as the epicFlashControl and ASP.NET take care of much of the work for us. Again, passing the FlashVars to the epicFlashControl involves using the Add method of the epicFlashControl's FlashVars property. Using this property, embedding a list of title and URL variables into the epicFlashControl instance (which by default was named EpicFlashControl1), is as easy as the following:

```
EpicFlashControl1.FlashVars.Add("title1", "Button1");
EpicFlashControl1.FlashVars.Add("url1", "http://www.friendsofed.com");
```

Creating the button names on our page then, along with navigation links, can be accomplished using this code:

```
void Page_Load(object sender, EventArgs e)
{
  // button 1
  EpicFlashControl1.FlashVars.Add("title1", "Microsoft");
  EpicFlashControl1.FlashVars.Add("nav1", "http://www.microsoft.com");
  // button 2
  EpicFlashControl1.FlashVars.Add("title2", "Macromedia");
  EpicFlashControl1.FlashVars.Add("nav2",
  ➥ "http://www.macromedia.com");
  // button 3
  EpicFlashControl1.FlashVars.Add("title3", "friends of ED");
  EpicFlashControl1.FlashVars.Add("nav3",
  ➥ "http://www.friendsofed.com");
  // button 4
  EpicFlashControl1.FlashVars.Add("title4", "ASP.NET");
  EpicFlashControl1.FlashVars.Add("nav4", "http://www.asp.net");
  // button 5
  EpicFlashControl1.FlashVars.Add("title5", "epicFlashControl");
```

```
      EpicFlashControl1.FlashVars.Add("nav5",
   ➥ "http://www.epicsoft.net/products/flashnet/");
      // button 6
      EpicFlashControl1.FlashVars.Add("title6", "Visual Studio .NET");
      EpicFlashControl1.FlashVars.Add("nav6", "flashvarsnav.aspx ");
   }
```

As you can see, I've added 12 FlashVars to the epicFlashControl, 6 of which define new button titles, and 6 that define the URL to open when that button is clicked.

Now that we've got some FlashVars being passed to the Flash movie, let's jump back to the Flash movie and get it ready to receive these variables and put our buttons out on the stage based on these variables. Back in the navbar.fla file, I have deleted the original test ActionScript we placed on the first frame of the _root timeline and replaced it with the following:

```
      function init() {
        var x:Number;
        for (x=1; x<=6; x++) {
          // get the name of the button
          var fvName:String;
          fvName = "title"+x.toString();
          // get the link for the button
          var fvLink:String;
          fvLink = "nav"+x.toString();
          // check to make sure there is a title available!
          if (this[fvName] != undefined) {
            // attach a new instance of GrayButton
            var butName:String = "but"+x.toString();
            attachMovie("GrayButton", butName, 100+x);
            // set the x value of the new button
            this[butName]._x = (x-1)*105;
            // set the title of the new button
            this[butName].SetTitle(this[fvName]);
            // set the URL of the new button
            this[butName].SetLink(this[fvLink]);
          }
        }
      }
      init();
```

Let's take a look at this init function line by line and see what's happening:

```
      var x:Number;
      for (x=1; x<=6; x++) {
```

The first line, var x:Number, declares a new variable, x, and declares this variable as a Number data type. This is ActionScript 2.0 demonstrating *strict typing*, as we mentioned earlier in Chapter 1. In the following line, that Number is used in a for loop, which is set to loop six times. We will cover looping more in the next chapter, but for now, if you're unfamiliar with for loops, just understand that everything inside the curly brackets, {, will be executed repeatedly six times, with six different values for the x variable, 1–6. We are doing this, of course, since we know that, due to physical size limitations, the maximum number of buttons our navbar can accept is six.

```
// get the name of the button
var fvName:String;
fvName = "title"+x.toString();
// get the link for the button
var fvLink:String;
fvLink = "url"+x.toString();
```

These lines are setting the stage for the rest of the init function. The fvName:String line is declaring a new variable, fvName, that will be used to retrieve the title of the buttons, and in the following line, is assigned to be the string "title" concatenated with the current value of the x variable. Since this code is looping six times, this variable will have the values of "title1", "title2", "title3", "title4", "title5", and "title6" as the for loop executes. As you'll notice, these values are the same as the names of the FlashVars we're passing into this Flash movie—that's not a coincidence! The next lines accomplish the same function, but with the fvLink variable and the nav FlashVar. So, each time through the for loop, we'll now have variables containing the names of the FlashVars being passed in.

```
if (this[fvName] != undefined) {
    // attach a new instance of GrayButton
    var butName:String = "but"+x.toString();
    attachMovie("GrayButton", butName, 100+x);
    // set the x value of the new button
    this[butName]._x = (x-1)*105;
```

In these lines we see the magic starting to happen! The first statement, using the if conditional statement (which we'll also be covering further in the next chapter), is checking to see if there is a variable on this timeline that has the name contained by the variable fvName. Seem like a mouthful? Really, it's not too bad at all—for example, the first time through the for loop, the value of x will be 1 and therefore, the value of fvName will be "title1". Checking if this[fvName] is undefined is essentially saying "check if there is a variable on this timeline that has the name *title1*". Of course, if we pass in a FlashVar from ASP.NET with a name of title1, this[fvName] will not be undefined and therefore the if statement will pass the test.

In the following line, I am declaring a new variable, butName, which will be the name for the new button instance that will be attached to the _root timeline. Since we will be attaching six buttons, we have to come up with six different button names—a perfect place to use the incrementing x variable. As the for loop executes, the values of butName will be "but1", "but2", "but3", "but4", "but5", and "but6".

The next line, like the example ActionScript in the earlier example, uses the attachMovie method to attach a new instance of the GrayButton symbol to the _root timeline. Instead of a hard-coded value, the attachMovie method will name the new symbol instance whatever the current value of the butName variable happens to be. Again, using the x variable from the for loop, the attachMovie method will put the newly attached movie at a depth of 100 plus the current value of x.

Finally, the line this[butName]._x = (x-1)*105 works to set the x-position of the newly attached buttons. Since our for loop starts with x=1, we want the to use one less than the current x value when setting the x-position. For example, when x=1, (x-1) will equal 0 and therefore 0*105=0, which will be the x-position of the first button. For the second and subsequent buttons, the x-position will be spaced by 105 pixels, slightly bigger than the width of the buttons.

```
// set the title of the new button
this[butName].SetTitle(this[fvName]);
// set the URL of the new button
this[butName].SetLink(this[fvLink]);
```

In this final block of text, we use the fvName and fvLink variables to set the text on the buttons and the URL that opens when the buttons are clicked. These methods, SetTitle and SetLink, come from the .as file that we included with the GrayButton instance in the symbol library.

This should be all we need in the Flash file for now. Let's take a jump back to Visual Studio .NET and try testing our new code in a browser to see if the combination of ASP.NET, FlashVars, and our Flash movie worked correctly—as you can see in Figure 3-44, the Flash movie creates the buttons with the correct text values and displays them. When these buttons are clicked, they also open to the links specified in the FlashVars we passed in from ASP.NET.

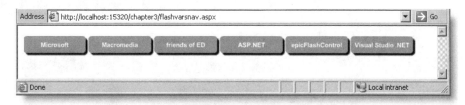

Figure 3-44. The Flash movie displays the buttons.

Summary

Although this may seem simple to a casual observer, the fact that we have created our first "connection" between ASP.NET server-side code and a client-side Flash movie is very exciting. As you have seen, the C# programming language closely resembles that of ActionScript 2.0 in a way that makes it easy to switch back and forth between the programming languages, as is required for a Flash/ASP.NET developer. Now that we have a basic understanding of C# syntax and Flash/ASP.NET communication, let's move forward into more powerful, two-way communication between Flash and ASP.NET.

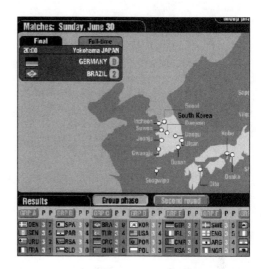

Chapter 4

TWO-WAY ASP.NET/FLASH COMMUNICATION

What this chapter covers:

- The request-response model
- The C# Request object
- The C# Response object
- try-catch-finally statements
- Sending mail using C# and ASP.NET
- Using loadVars with ASP.NET
- Asynchronous communication with Flash
- Processing an e-mail form with Flash loadVars and ASP.NET

With a basic knowledge of C# and ASP.NET under our belts, we're now ready to move forward into some more powerful, two-way communication between Flash and ASP.NET. Two-way communication between Flash and ASP.NET is superior to "traditional" HTML client-server communication because it allows server-side code to be triggered and executed by the Flash interface without requiring the user to experience a page refresh. This feature makes for a much more user-friendly interface, with all of the power of the ASP.NET back-end.

In this chapter, we'll take a look at Flash/ASP.NET communication using the Flash loadVars object. We'll also take a look at some new C# objects—Request, Response, and Mail—and how they can be used in conjunction with loadVars to create applications that are able to send data between a Flash client and server-side ASP.NET code. As a final example in this chapter, we'll tie all of these new concepts together to produce a very practical example: a Flash-based e-mail contact form.

The request-response model

As discussed in Chapter 1, ASP.NET, and web technologies in general, use a *request-response* model for serving web pages to client browsers. This model, which you are probably familiar with (even if you don't realize it), consists primarily of the following steps in order to fulfill a request for a web page made by a web browser:

1. The client browser submits a URL request to a domain name server (DNS).
2. The domain name server sends the Internet Protocol (IP) address of the server hosting the requested URL back to the client browser.
3. The browser connects to port 80 on that IP address.
4. The browser sends a **request** to the web server for a page (or other data).
5. The server processes the request and sends a **response** back to the browser.

In this section, we'll take a look at the nature of the page request and response, as well as ASP.NET's ability to read and modify the data sent in these transmissions. We'll then see how this ability can be used to communicate with Flash in the form of the Flash LoadVars class.

HTTP request

In the request-response model, a client browser requests a web page from a web server by sending a packet of information to the web server. This packet, known as a *request header,* specifies two things: information about the client machine requesting data from the server, and additional data about the nature of the page requested. An example of a request header sent from a client browser to the friends of ED web server is shown here:

```
GET / HTTP/1.1
Host: www.friendsofed.com
Connection: close
Accept: image/gif, image/x-xbitmap, image/jpeg, image/pjpeg,
application/vnd.ms-powerpoint, application/vnd.ms-excel,
application/msword, application/x-shockwave-flash, */*
Accept-Language: en-us
User-Agent: Mozilla/5.0 (Windows; U; Windows NT 5.0; en-US; rv:1.7.5)
  Gecko/20041107 Firefox/1.0
```

As you can see, this request header sends quite a bit of information about the nature of the request. In the first line, GET /HTTP/1.1, the browser specifies the type of operation it would like to perform, in this case a GET operation, as well as the version of HTTP it will use in this transaction. In the second line, Host: www.friendsofed.com, the request header specifies the name of the domain from which it is requesting web data. The following lines describe details about the client browser to help the web server determine the type of content it can or cannot send to the browser. You'll notice specifically that the Accept parameter contains an entry called application/x-shockwave-flash. This parameter tells the web server that the browser making the request has the Flash Player installed.

GET and POST variables

Along with this information about the nature of the request, a page request also transmits *GET* or *POST* variables associated with the request. GET and POST variables are the traditional method for passing information from an HTML web form to a web server for some form of server-side processing. This information could be data from an HTML-based credit card application, or search strings sent to a web search engine.

In case you're not familiar with the terms GET and POST variables, let's take a minute to get acquainted with them. GET and POST variables, as defined in HTML standards, are methods for passing data from an HTML web form to a web server. These variables are sent either through the *query string* (GET variables), or through the *HTTP message body* (POST variables). Even though you might not know it, you're already used to seeing GET variables in action. Any time you see a web page URL with *name-value pairs* that look similar to the following:

http://www.someserver.com/mypage.aspx?**name1=value1&name2=value2**

you're seeing values passed as GET variables. The name1=value1&name2=value2 part of this URL is known as the *query string* and can be used to pass information from the client browser to the web server.

POST variables, which are passed through the HTTP message body, are more "invisible" in their travels. POST variables are sent in essentially the same way as name-value pairs, but are not included as part of the query string, like GET variables. One of the main advantages that POST variables have over GET variables is the amount of data that can be passed from client to server using this type of variable. Whereas POST variables do not have a limitation to the amount of data that can be sent, GET variables are limited to about 2,000 characters, making them a poor option for sending large amounts of data.

GET variables are also generally dangerous to use because of the security risks they can potentially pose. When a page uses GET variables, it is not hard for a page's end user to manipulate those variables, simply by changing the address line in their browser. Doing this could possibly have drastic repercussions for your application, including destroying a database or access to unauthorized information. For this reason, GET variables should only be used in low-security-risk environments.

It is for this same reason, though, that GET variables can be very useful. GET variables, unlike POST variables, can be used to help maintain application state in your web page. If a user wants to make a bookmark to a page that contains query string variables, your server-side code will still be able to access those variables when the user comes back to the page. POST variables, however, are not saved with a bookmark or when a URL is copied; therefore, the current state of your application is lost. Using GET variables along with FlashVars (see Chapter 3), data that is contained in the query string can also be passed directly to a Flash movie embedded in a page.

GET and POST variables are also very relevant to Flash/ASP.NET communication because two of Flash's communication methods use GET and POST variables to "talk" to server-side applications. Later in this chapter, we'll take a look at one of those methods, loadVars, which can use GET or POST variables to send information from a Flash movie to server-side code, like ASP.NET.

HTTP response

For every request, there must be a response . . . right? The HTTP response header works on the opposite end of the web page request—when a page is requested by a client browser, an HTTP response is sent back to the browser from the web server to describe the content it will be delivering. An example of an HTTP response header is shown here:

```
HTTP/1.1 200 OK
Server: Microsoft IIS/6.0
Content-Type: text/html
Content-Length: 1408
```

In this response header, the first line, HTTP/1.1, is confirming the version of HTTP it will be using to transmit data to the browser. The 200 OK is a code sent to the browser to confirm that all went well with the HTTP request. It is through this code that you receive the painful "404 Page not found" status code, as well as others. The line Content-Type: text/html specifies the type of the data transmitted to the client browser. As in this example, this data could be HTML, or it could be other formats (which we will discuss in later chapters), such as text/xml.

This response header appears in the page response *before* the page's HTML (or other format) data, typically just separated by a line space as in the following example:

```
HTTP/1.1 200 OK
Server: Microsoft IIS/6.0
Content-Type: text/html
Content-Length: 59

<html><body>Foundation  ASP.NET for Flash</body></html>
```

Typically, you won't see the response header of a page by just looking at that page's source code. To view a response header, special tools are available, such as the liveHTTPheaders Firefox extension, available at http://livehttpheaders.mozdev.org/.

ASP.NET Request object

ASP.NET provides an object, Request, that allows you to access the data sent in these request headers, for use within your application. Using the Request object, it is possible, for example, to find out information about the type and capabilities of the browser being used to view your ASP.NET page. Some of the properties of the Request object that describe the type of request generated appear in Table 4-1.

Table 4-1. Header properties of the Request object

Property	Description
AcceptTypes	Gets an array of strings denoting the list of MIME types supported by the web client.
Browser	Gets an HttpBrowserCapabilities object that contains information about the client's browser.
HttpMethod	Gets a string denoting the HTTP method used in the request. This string could be "GET", "POST", or "HEAD".
UserAgent	Gets a string that identifies the browser. This string uses the User-Agent field of the request header mentioned earlier.

The ASP.NET Request object also provides properties for accessing variables, files, and cookies sent in the page's request header. These properties are very important for ASP.NET/Flash communication, as many of the methods for ASP.NET/Flash communication make use of either GET or POST variables. Table 4-2 lists a few of these properties.

Table 4-2. Variable, file, and cookie properties of the Request object

Property	Description
ClientCertificate	Gets an HttpClientCertificate object that contains information about the client's security information settings
Cookies	Gets an HttpCookieCollection object representing the cookies sent by the client
Files	Gets an HttpFileCollection object representing the files uploaded by the client
QueryString	Gets a NameValueCollection object containing all of the query string variables sent by the client
UserHostAddress	Gets the IP address of the client's machine

Aside from these methods used to retrieve information from the page's request headers, the ASP.NET Request object also has an easy notation used to retrieve the value of any GET or POST variable submitted to the page. This notation requires just that you know the name of the GET or POST variable that was submitted, and using that name, the value of that variable can be accessed. As you'll see in the examples later in this chapter, this method will be one of the most useful of the ASP.NET Request object's methods for Flash/ASP.NET loadVars communication.

```
string ReqValue = Request[name];
```

This Request[name] notation will *always* return a string value, regardless of how the variable was passed to the page. Back to the example URL we used earlier:

```
http://www.someserver.com/mypage.aspx?name1=value1&name2=value2
```

If we wanted to access the value of the name1 variable, we could do this in the mypage.aspx's code-behind by using the code:

```
string theVal = Request["name1"]; // theVal will be "value1"
```

As we'll see in the examples later in this chapter, this shorthand notation makes the passing of variables from Flash to ASP.NET using GET and POST variables an almost seamless operation!

ASP.NET Response object

The Response.Write method is used, as the name implies, to write characters to an ASP.NET page's *output stream*. This means that, when the Response.Write method is called, ASP.NET will write the string passed to it as a parameter to the HTML page it is generating. Although this method is not all that useful when using HTML-based elements as an ASP.NET presentation layer, it is extremely effective when passing values to the Flash loadVars object, which we will be exploring in this chapter. A simple example of the Response.Write method is as follows:

```
// will write 'var1=Flash' to the page's output stream
Response.Write("var1=Flash");
```

The Response.Redirect method is a method that can be used to redirect a user's browser to another URL. This method is similar to the ActionScript getURL method, with the exception being that the redirection occurring using the Response.Redirect method is being initiated server-side instead of by the client, in the case of the getURL method. An example of the Response.Redirect method is as follows:

```
If (Request["redir"]!=null)
{
 // will redirect page to the value of the 'redir' Request variable
  Response.Redirect(Request["redir"]);
}
```

Using the Request and Response objects

Let's take a look at an example that makes use of the Request and Response objects in ASP.NET. In this example, we will use the Label server control, introduced in Chapter 3, as well as two new server controls, the Button and TextBox. The functionality of the example will be simple: A value can be typed into an ASP.NET TextBox control, and when a Submit button is clicked, the value from the TextBox is displayed in a Label control.

This example can be created in the same web project that we used for the previous examples. On my system, this is in the C:\foundationaspnet\chapter4 folder. In the web project, create a new web form, called requestresponse.aspx, by right-clicking on the name of the project in the Solution Explorer, as in Figures 4-1 and 4-2.

Figure 4-1. Adding a new item using Solution Explorer

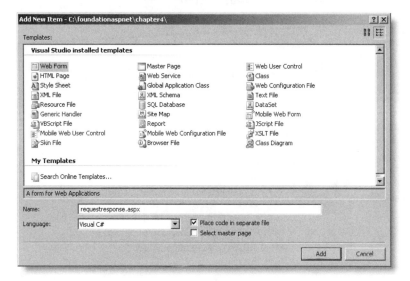

Figure 4-2. The Add New Items dialog box

In this newly created .aspx page, we'll add three ASP.NET server controls from the Visual Studio Toolbox. The first server control will be the TextBox control, as shown in Figure 4-3.

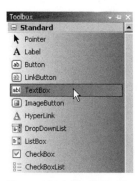

Figure 4-3. Adding a TextBox control

Using the Property Inspector, I have changed the name of this TextBox control to tbText. Next, add a Button control, and finally a Label control to the design interface. When you drag these controls onto the design window, they will not be arranged nicely as they might be if you dragged controls into the Design view of the Flash IDE. To accomplish this, it is necessary to go into the HTML Source view by selecting the Source tab at the bottom of the design interface and creating HTML that will result in a more structured layout. Here is the HTML source of the page I have created in the Source view:

```
<%@ Page Language="C#" CompileWith="requestresponse.aspx.cs"
ClassName="requestresponse_aspx" %>
<!DOCTYPE html PUBLIC "-//W3C//DTD XHTML 1.1//EN"
"http://www.w3.org/TR/xhtml11/DTD/xhtml11.dtd">
<html xmlns="http://www.w3.org/1999/xhtml">
<head runat="server">
    <title>Request-Response Example</title>
</head>
<body>
    <form id="form1" runat="server">
        <div align="center">
            <asp:Label ID="Label1" Runat="server" Font-Size="Large"
              ForeColor="Red"></asp:Label>
            <br />
            <br />
            <table cellpadding="1" border="0">
                <tr>
                    <td bgcolor="#000000">
                        <table cellpadding="3"
                          cellspacing="0" border="0">
                            <tr>
                                <td bgcolor="#CCCCCC">
                                    <strong>Enter a value
                                    </strong></td>
                            </tr>
                            <tr>
                                <td bgcolor="#FFFFFF">
                                    <asp:TextBox ID="tbText"
                                    Runat="server"></asp:TextBox></td>
                            </tr>
                            <tr>
                                <td bgcolor="#FFFFFF" align="center">
                                    <asp:Button ID="Button1"
                                    Runat="server" Text="Submit"
                                    OnClick="Button1_Click" /></td>
                            </tr>
                        </table>
                    </td>
                </tr>
            </table>
        </div>
    </form>
</body>
</html>
```

As you can see, I have created an HTML table to position the Button and TextBox elements, and placed the Label control above this table. I have also changed the Label's Font-Size and Color properties for visual purposes. The Design view of this HTML source is shown in Figure 4-4.

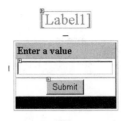

Now that we have created the interface, let's move to the page's code-behind and the use of the Request and Response objects. First, we'll need to create an event handler to react to our new page's Page_Load event. As we learned in Chapter 3, the easiest way to do this in Visual Studio .NET is to double-click anywhere on the Design view. The result should be the creation of the Page_Load event in the page-behind file for this ASP.NET page, as shown here:

Figure 4-4. The Design view

```
public partial class requestresponse_aspx
{
  void Page_Load(object sender, EventArgs e)
  {
  }
}
```

Inside of this Page_Load event handler, let's create some code that will determine if there has been a variable sent in the page's Request header through the use of GET or POST variables, and if there is such a variable, we need to set the value of the Label's Text property to that variable. This can be executed through the following code:

```
public partial class requestresponse_aspx
{
  void Page_Load(object sender, EventArgs e)
  {
    if (Request["txt"] != null)
    {
      Label1.Text = Request["txt"];
    }
  }
}
```

In the first line of this code, the shorthand notation of the Request object is used to determine whether there is a GET or POST variable with the name "txt" present. This is accomplished by using the != comparison operator and the null keyword—if the Request["txt"] statement does not evaluate to be null, or is nonexistent, then the following lines will execute. In the next line, we simply set the Text property of the Label1 Label instance to the value returned by the Request object's Request["txt"] operation.

We now have code written that tests for the existence of a POST or GET variable in the page's Request header and sets the value of a Label's Text property to this variable each time the page loads. Now, let's write code that will generate a GET query string value based on the text entered into the page's TextBox control. To do this, we will set up a new event handler that will respond to the Button's Click event, and redirect the page using the Response object.

In order to generate the Button's Click event and event handler, go back to the Design view of the `requestresponse.aspx` page and double-click on the Button control. This will, by default, generate the following code in the code-behind page:

```
void Button1_Click(object sender, EventArgs e)
        {
        }
```

This Button_Click event in the page-behind file will automatically execute when a user clicks the button. This is similar to the functionality of the on(Release) event of a Flash button. In this event handler, we'll place code that will access the text entered into the TextBox control, and redirect the page with this value passed as a query string variable, as shown in the following code:

```
void Button1_Click(object sender, EventArgs e)
{
   Response.Redirect("requestresponse.aspx?txt=" + tbText.Text);
}
```

As you can see, this call to Response.Redirect will redirect the page back to the same page, `requestresponse.aspx`, with a new name-value pair appended to the URL. Because we have already set this page up to respond to a variable passed through the query string, our page is now complete. The result of this code is shown in Figure 4-5.

Figure 4-5. Our page is now complete!

Success! The page now takes as input, a value in the TextBox control. When the Submit button is clicked, this value is then displayed in the page's Label control. Let's take a look at the life cycle of this page in relation to the request-response model:

1. The browser sends a request to the web server for `requestresponse.aspx`.

2. The server sends the response with HTML-rendered output.

3. After text is entered into the TextBox and the Submit button is clicked, the browser sends a request to the web server, this time with the data in the TextBox submitted to the server as a POST variable.

4. The C# code on the web server detects that the button has been clicked and uses the Response.Redirect method to redirect the page to the same URL, but with a new query string variable appended to the page name.

5. When this newly requested page (with a query string variable) loads, the C# code in the Page_Load sets the value of the Label's Text property using the Request object.

6. The page's rendered HTML output is sent back to the browser through an HTTP response.

In the Flash e-mail form example at the end of this chapter, we'll take a further look at the use of the Response and Request objects, and their relationship to Flash communication.

The try-catch-finally statement

As any developer knows, writing code that executes flawlessly 100 percent of the time is a near impossibility—especially in systems that depend on external resources for execution, such as databases or mail servers. Because of this reality, one of the essential features in modern-day programming languages is the ability to gracefully respond to errors within code execution. Those familiar with previous generations of Microsoft Windows know what it's like to have code that *doesn't* respond gracefully to errors—the infamous Blue Screen of Death or application crash. In an application that has graceful error response, rather than crashing the program (or system), the application will inform users of the error and try to direct them to a proper fix for the problem.

For web applications, graceful error handling can mean anything from a friendly error message to a description of why the error occurred or redirection to a customer service representative. The key is to *not* leave the application in a state that is unusable—at worst, the familiar "Page cannot be displayed" or "Application error."

C# provides a feature for responding gracefully to errors called the try-catch statement. Using the try-catch statement, a block of code can be executed, and if an error is encountered, the code execution can jump to a second block that "handles" the encountered error. By using the try-catch statement, it is possible to "protect" portions of your code that you know might encounter errors because they depend on external factors, such as user input or database connections.

The syntax of the try-catch statement is as follows:

```
try
{
 // code to try here
}
catch
{
 // code that will execute if code within try fails
}
```

In this scenario, the code in the *try block* will execute until one of the lines in its execution encounters an error. If this happens, the code in the try block discontinues execution and transfers execution to the *catch block*. Code is placed in this catch block that will handle the try block's error gracefully and either attempt to fix the error or relay the error to the user (without "breaking" the application).

It is also possible to obtain information about the nature of the error encountered in the try block by using the System.Exception object in the following syntax:

```
catch (System.Exception e)
{
    // retrieve information about the error through the Exception object
}
```

Using this System.Exception class, you can obtain information such as the type and description of the error generated. This is useful not only for program stability, but also for debugging purposes.

Another, optional section of the try-catch statement is called the finally codeblock. The finally block appears after a try-catch statement and will *always* execute after a try-catch statement, whether or not the try block encountered an error.

```
try
{
    // try to execute some code
}
catch
{
    // do something else if the try section didn't work
}
finally
{
    // do this after both code blocks have completed
}
```

Let's take a look at two simple ASP.NET pages, one that makes use of a try-catch statement, and another that does not. In these examples, I will purposely write code that will generate an error upon execution: In one page, you'll see a "nasty" error message, and in the page making use of the try-catch statement, a much friendlier reaction to the error.

For this example, I have created a new ASP.NET page, called trycatch.aspx, that will take a text input from a user and, using the String object's Substring method, return the fifth through tenth characters of this string. The danger of performing such an operation is the fact that you can't say for sure how long the string will be that the user will enter—if it's under 10 characters, the Substring method will generate an error.

To create this page, I have added four server controls to the Design view in Visual Studio, as shown in Figure 4-6—a TextBox control called tbInput, a Button control named Button1, and two Label controls, named lbResult and lbError.

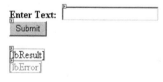

Figure 4-6. Our four server controls

I will skip the details of this page's creation (since they are very similar to the previous Response-Request example), but the HTML source for the page is shown here:

```
<%@ Page Language="C#" CompileWith="trycatch.aspx.cs"
ClassName="trycatch_aspx" %>

<!DOCTYPE html PUBLIC "-//W3C//DTD XHTML 1.1//EN"
 "http://www.w3.org/TR/xhtml11/DTD/xhtml11.dtd">

<html xmlns="http://www.w3.org/1999/xhtml" >
<head runat="server">
    <title>Try-Catch Example</title>
</head>
<body>
    <form id="form1" runat="server">
    <div>
        <strong>Enter Text:</strong>  
        <asp:TextBox ID="tbInput" Runat="server"></asp:TextBox>
        <br />
        <asp:Button ID="Button1" Runat="server" Text="Submit"
        OnClick="Button1_Click" />
        <br />
        <br />
        <asp:Label ID="lbResult" Runat="server"></asp:Label><br />
        <asp:Label ID="lbError" Runat="server"
         ForeColor="Red"></asp:Label>
        <br />

    </div>
    </form>
</body>
</html>
```

I have also created a Button Click event in the page's code-behind file to perform the Substring function:

```
void Button1_Click(object sender, EventArgs e)
{
  this.lbResult.Text = "Characters 5-10 are: "
  + this.tbInput.Text.Substring(5, 10);
}
```

In Figure 4-7, you see this page about to be executed with an input string with fewer than 10 characters. Figure 4-8 shows the result of this execution.

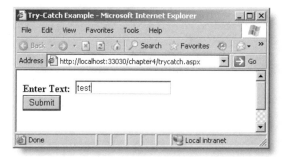

Figure 4-7. The results of testing with an input string with fewer than 10 characters

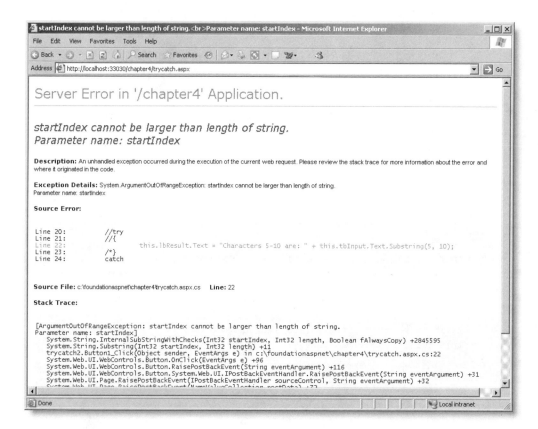

Figure 4-8. trycatch.aspx without try-catch statements

Ouch, not a friendly result to a user input error! An error page like this doesn't leave a user with many options or descriptions of what they did wrong. Let's try adding a try-catch statement to the page's code-behind that will provide a better reaction to an application error:

```
try
{
  this.lbResult.Text = "Characters 5-10 are: "
   + this.tbInput.Text.Substring(5, 10);
}
catch
{
  this.lbError.Text = "! You must enter at least 10 characters!";
}
```

As you can see in Figure 4-9, this is a much more acceptable response to invalid user input than in the previous example. When using the try-catch statement, it's possible to gracefully respond to potential errors in the ASP.NET side of our application. In the e-mail form example at the end of this chapter, we will take another look at the try-catch statement, and use it with the ASP.NET SmtpMail object, which we will be examining next.

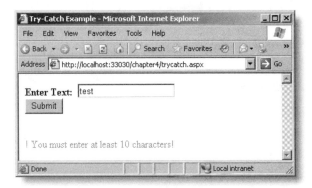

Figure 4-9. trycatch.aspx with try-catch statements

Sending mail using ASP.NET

One of the most common needs in any web application is the ability to send e-mail. E-mails from web applications have many uses, ranging from contact submission forms to online store receipts. ASP.NET has a built-in object for sending e-mails and also has many third-party components that provide extended functionality. In this chapter, we will be looking at the SmtpMail object of the .NET base class library's System.Web.Mail namespace for sending e-mails using ASP.NET.

As with e-mail client programs, like Outlook Express or Thunderbird, sending mail using ASP.NET is a pretty easy process, fundamentally consisting of two steps:

1. Create an instance of an e-mail message, consisting of a subject, body, recipient, and optionally, attachments, cc fields, and bcc fields.

2. Send the e-mail using an SMTP e-mail server.

In ASP.NET, an e-mail message can be created using the System.Web.Mail.MailMessage object. This object contains all of the necessary properties we listed earlier for creating e-mail messages. Table 4-3 lists some of the properties of the MailMessage object.

Table 4-3. Properties of the MailMessage object

Property Name	Description
Attachments	Specifies the collection of attachments that are transmitted with the message.
Bcc	Gets or sets a semicolon-delimited list of e-mail addresses that will be sent blind carbon copies of the e-mail.
Body	Gets or sets the body of the e-mail message.
BodyFormat	Gets or sets the content type of the e-mail message. The content type of an e-mail can be either HTML or text formatted.
Cc	Gets or sets a semicolon-delimited list of e-mail addresses that will be sent carbon copies of the e-mail.
From	Gets or sets the e-mail address of the e-mail's sender.
Subject	Gets or sets the subject of the e-mail message.
To	Gets or sets a semicolon-delimited list of e-mail addresses that the e-mail will be sent to.

Creating a new e-mail message is as simple as creating a new instance of this object using the following syntax:

```
System.Web.Mail.MailMessage MailMsg =
  new System.Web.Mail.MailMessage();
```

and then adding the properties of the e-mail as in the following example:

```
MailMsg.Subject = "Foundation ASP.NET for Flash";
MailMsg.Body = "Testing ASP.NET e-mail";
MailMsg.To = "test@test.com;test2@test.net";
MailMsg.From = "anothertest@anothertest.com";
```

As shown in this example, an e-mail can be specified to have multiple recipients by separating the recipient e-mail addresses with a semicolon. Sending this new e-mail message is accomplished then using the Send method of the System.Web.Mail.SmtpMail object, as in the following line:

```
System.Web.Mail.SmtpMail.Send(MailMsg);
```

By default, .NET uses the SMTP server built into the Windows operating system, but an external SMTP server can be specified for sending the e-mail through using the SmtpServer property of the SmtpMail object, as in this example:

```
System.Web.Mail.SmtpMail.SmtpServer = "smtp.myserver.com";
System.Web.Mail.SmtpMail.Send(MailMsg);
```

In order to send an e-mail through an external mail server, the server originating the e-mail typically has to be "authorized" to relay mail through that server.

Configuring IIS to relay mail

If you are on a system that has IIS installed (if not, please see the "Installing IIS" section of Chapter 1), you should be able to configure your local IIS installation to relay mail from your ASP.NET applications. This can be accomplished on Windows 2000 or Windows XP Professional by executing the following steps:

1. Go to the Internet Information Services Management Console, as shown in Figure 4-10. You'll find this in the Administrative Tools folder of Control Panel.

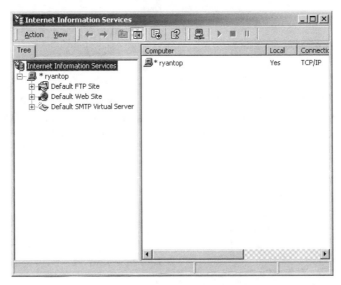

Figure 4-10. The Internet Information Services Management Console

2. Select the Default SMTP Virtual Server node, right-click, and select Properties.

3. Select the Access tab of the Default SMTP Server Properties window, and click the Relay button, as shown in Figure 4-11.

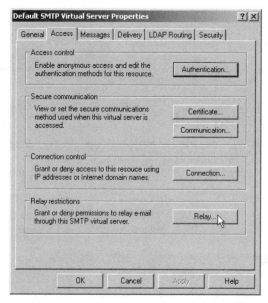

Figure 4-11. Click the Relay button.

4. In the next window, titled Relay Restrictions, click the Add button.

5. In the next window, select the Single Computer radio button and type 127.0.0.1 into the IP Address text box, as shown in Figure 4-12. This will configure the IIS server to allow messages to be relayed as long as they are coming from the local machine (which is, by default, IP address 127.0.0.1).

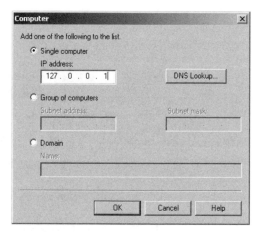

Figure 4-12. Type the IP address.

After hitting OK, your local system will be properly configured to send e-mail using ASP.NET. In the example at the end of this chapter, we'll test out this configuration by sending an e-mail from ASP.NET that has been requested by a Flash form. But first, we have to tackle another form of Flash/ASP.NET communication: loadVars.

Using loadVars to call an ASP.NET page

As our first example of communicating between Flash and an ASP.NET web server, let's take a look at the Flash loadVars object. The loadVars object provides a method for sending data from a Flash movie to an ASP.NET page and receiving data back from that page through name-value pairs. When communicating using the loadVars object, each direction of communication is optional—you could either just send data to the server, or just load data from the server; it's not necessary to do both. The data that is exchanged between the client and server, however, must be initiated by the Flash client; it cannot be "pushed" to the Flash movie by the ASP.NET code.

> *A method is available for pushing data from server-side ASP.NET code to client-side Flash movies: the XML Socket Server. Several commercial .NET socket servers are available for use with Flash communication.*

The loadVars object was introduced into Flash in version 6 as an alternative to the loadVariables action. The loadVars object provides a more object-oriented approach to client-server communication than the loadVariables method and provides events that signal the occurrence of certain actions, such as the receiving of data. The key feature of the loadVars object is that it both sends and receives variables in a name-value pair, much like that of the query string variables I have mentioned in earlier chapters. The name-value method of data exchange has both advantages and disadvantages. The main advantage is that it is very easy to create, and the major disadvantage is that it is hard to organize large amounts of data and, when exchanging large amounts of data, is very processor intensive.

The loadVars object, like the rest of the communication methods that will be discussed in this book (but *unlike* FlashVars, presented in Chapter 3), uses *asynchronous* communication to communicate with server-side code. Asynchronous communication, mentioned in Chapter 1, is a feature that gives Flash a huge advantage over HTML as a presentation-layer technology, allowing Flash to communicate with the logical layer without removing control of the user interface from the user. As an example of asynchronous communicating using Flash, take a look at the 2002 FIFA World Cup Game Tracker Flash application in Figure 4-13.

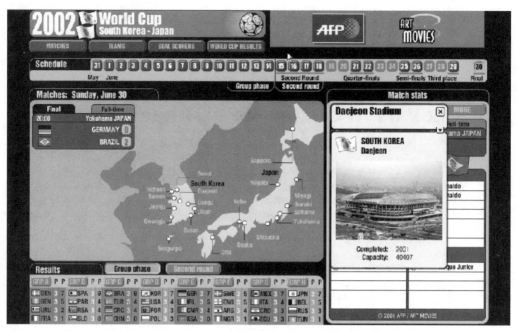

Figure 4-13. FIFA Game Tracker (www.cbc.ca/sports/afp/wc-flash/2/gametracker.html)

This web application, used to provide real-time data about the World Cup games in 2002, makes use of loadVars to perform two-way communication between its interface and server-side data. Because of the nature of two-way communication between Flash and ASP.NET using loadVars, the user of the application can look up game scores and data without requiring a page refresh between each lookup. If a similar application were to be designed using only HTML as the presentation layer, the page would be required to refresh each time the user made a selection on the screen—not a fun experience!

To understand how loadVars work with ASP.NET, let's take a look at the steps that occur when a browser makes a request for a page that contains a Flash movie that uses loadVars:

1. The page is requested by the client browser from the server.

2. The ASP.NET page is processed by the server and the HTML is sent to the client browser.

3. The browser requests the .swf files that are embedded in the HTML file.

4. The server sends the .swf files to the client.

5. The page is displayed to the user while the .swf file is loading.

6. After the .swf has loaded, actions such as button clicks occur in the .swf, triggering a loadVars call.

7. The loadVars object calls the ASP.NET web page to request data.

8. The ASP.NET page processes data (if required) and (if required) generates name-value pairs to return to the loadVars object.

9. The Flash movie processes the loadVars object and displays the results in the interface.

In this process, the key point is that additional data is loaded from ASP.NET *after* the initial .swf file is loaded onto the client system, which is impossible using purely HTML-based interface elements.

Let's take a look at the methods, event, and property of the Flash loadVars object to see how data can be transferred to and from ASP.NET (see Tables 4-4, 4-5, and 4-6).

Table 4-4. Methods of the Flash loadVars object

Method	Description
load	Loads name-value pair variables from a specific URL
getBytesLoaded	Returns the number of bytes loaded from a load or sendAndLoad command
getBytesTotal	Returns the total number of bytes that will be downloaded in a load or sendAndLoad command
send	Sends loadVars variables to a URL
sendAndLoad	Performs a send command followed by a load command to retrieve the server's response to the send
toString	Returns a URL encoded string of the variables in the loadVars object

Table 4-5. Event of the Flash loadVars object

Event	Description
onLoad	Fires when data is loaded from a load or sendAndLoad operation

Table 4-6. Property of the Flash loadVars object

Property	Description
loaded	Boolean value indicating whether a load or sendAndLoad has completed

As you can see, the loadVars object provides several methods for exchanging data with ASP.NET. The load method does not send any data to the ASP.NET page; instead it just loads the name-value pairs from that page. The send method, on the other hand, only sends data, as name-value pairs to the ASP.NET page for processing, expecting no response from the page. sendAndLoad combines these two functions by sending data to an ASP.NET server page (probably for processing of some sort), and then waiting for a response from that page. This is the method that we will be focusing on in this book for communicating using loadVars.

The getBytesLoaded and getBytesTotal methods are available for monitoring the progress of a load or sendAndLoad request. For example, if you have made a load request that retrieves a large amount of data from an ASP.NET page and would like to have a progress bar that indicates the percentage of this data that has been transferred, you could use these methods to retrieve this value.

The onLoad event is extremely useful, as it fires when the Flash file has completed loading the data from a load or sendAndLoad call. Once this event has fired, you can move forward with the processing of the data—but in the meantime, you can leave your application's presentation layer in the control of the user or display an indication, such as a progress bar, that the application is currently performing an operation.

Let's take a look at an example of a loadVars object that uses the sendAndLoad method to send and retrieve variables from an ASP.NET server:

```
var myUrl_str:String = "mypage.aspx";
var send_lv:LoadVars = new LoadVars();
var load_lv:LoadVars = new LoadVars();
load_lv.onLoad = function(success:Boolean) {
  if (success) {
    // sendAndLoad processed successfully!
  } else {
    // sendAndLoad had an error
  }
};
send_lv.param1 = "test variable";
send_lv.param2 = "test 2";
send_lv.sendAndLoad(myUrl, load_lv, "POST");
```

The first three lines of this code are simply creating new variables, myUrl_str, send_lv, and load_lv. myUrl_str is a string which is initially assigned a value, "mypage.aspx", that is the name of the ASP.NET page that the loadVars object will be communicating with. send_lv and load_lv are new loadVars objects that will be used to communicate with the ASP.NET page. As you'll notice, we're actually using two loadVars objects to execute a sendAndLoad operation. Using two loadVars objects is not necessary for a sendAndLoad but can help make your code more manageable.

In the next section of code, the load_lv.onLoad event is defined as a function that takes a Boolean value as a parameter. Using this Boolean value, we can determine whether the load method executed successfully and respond accordingly.

Finally, in the last three lines of this code, the send_lv object is assigned two variables, param1 and param2, and the sendAndLoad method of this object is executed. You can see here that the sendAndLoad method takes three parameters:

1. The URL of the page to communicate with.

2. The loadVars object that will handle the response of the ASP.NET page.

3. The method for sending the variables to the ASP.NET web page. This method can be either GET or POST. In most cases, it is best to use the POST method, which is capable of passing a larger amount of data than the GET method.

Before moving on to the ASP.NET side of loadVars, let's take a look at one last method of the loadVars object, the toString method. The toString method returns the URL encoded name-value pair string that will be passed to the ASP.NET page. URL encoded, in this case means that Flash will replace special characters, such as spaces and commas, with their HTML-equivalent value. In the previous example, if we replace the line

```
send_lv.sendAndLoad(myUrl, load_lv, "POST");
```

with the line

```
trace(send_lv.toString());
```

we'll see that the name-value pairs that will be sent to the ASP.NET page are

```
param2=test%202&param1=test%20variable
```

Here we can see that the loadVars object has converted the spaces in the variables to %20, their HTML equivalent, and combined the variables into a single string separated by & signs.

Example: Using loadVars in the navbar

Now that we understand how loadVars work, let's try modifying the navbar example from the previous chapter using loadVars instead of FlashVars. (In this example, I am going to remove the buttons' links for simplicity in testing). In last chapter's example, variables were passed from ASP.NET to the Flash movie *along with* the page's HTML. In this example, the exchange of data will change, as the Flash movie will have to specifically request it before the ASP.NET page will send it.

For this example, create a new WebSite project in a folder called Chapter 4. Within this folder, create a new folder called Flash and copy the navbar.fla and GrayButton.as file into this folder. For this example, however, we will not need to embed the Flash movie in an .aspx file, so change the publishing settings of the navbar.fla file to publish an .html file called navbar.html when published.

In the navbar.fla file, we will have to make some changes to allow the loadVars to work properly. Listed here is the code necessary to change this Flash movie to load its button names using loadVars instead of FlashVars. I have placed this code on the first frame of the _root timeline, replacing the code that was on the _root timeline of the navbar.fla file from Chapter 3.

```
function gotVars(suc) {
if (suc) {
  var x:Number;
  for (x=1; x<=6; x++) {
  // get the name of the button
  var fvName:String;
  fvName = "title"+x.toString();
  // check to make sure there is a title available!
  if (this[fvName] != undefined) {
    // attach a new instance of GrayButton
    var butName:String = "but"+x.toString();
    _root.attachMovie("GrayButton", butName, 100+x);
```

```
      // set the x value of the new button
      _root[butName]._x = (x-1)*105;
      // set the title of the new button
      _root[butName].SetTitle(this[fvName]);
      }
    }
  } else {
    trace("Call failed!");
  }
}
var myUrl:String = "http://localhost:33030/chapter4/navbar.aspx";
var load_lv:LoadVars = new LoadVars();
load_lv.onLoad = gotVars;
load_lv.load(myUrl);
```

Let's take a look at this code line by line and see what's happening. Actually, let's examine this code from the "bottom-up" as it will make more sense.

```
var myUrl_str:String = "http://localhost:33030/chapter4/navbar.aspx";
var load_lv:LoadVars = new LoadVars();
```

These lines are very similar to the Flash loadVars example earlier in this chapter. Two variables are declared here, myUrl_str and load_lv, with myUrl_str defining the new URL we will be using to test our application. In this URL, I have specified navbar.aspx as the name of the page that we will be calling to load the name-value pairs into the loadVars. Don't worry if you haven't created this page yet; we will be doing that next. The load_lv variable is simply creating a new loadVars object that we will use to load in the names of the buttons to be displayed in our navigation bar.

```
load_lv.onLoad = gotVars;
```

In this line, I'm defining the onLoad event of the newly created load_lv loadVars object to a new function, gotVars. If you're not familiar with this syntax, this line is essentially saying "when the loadVars object has loaded its data (or failed to load its data), run the gotVars function." As you'll notice, I have defined the gotVars function *before* this definition and call to the loadVars' load method. This is a good practice because Flash has the possibility of running into problems if a function is referenced before it occurs at runtime.

```
load_lv.load(myUrl_str);
```

Finally (well, not quite finally) we tell the load_lv loadVars object to load the name-value pair contents of the myUrl_str URL. Again, once the data from this call has been loaded, the gotVars function will be fired.

```
function gotVars(success:Boolean) {
if (success) {
    . . .
  if (this[fvName] != undefined) {
```

The gotVars function, by default, takes a Boolean value as a parameter that lets us know if the load method executed successfully. In the second line, if (success) {, I am testing this parameter to determine whether the data loaded is valid. If it is valid, we can move forward with placing the buttons on the interface.

I have omitted the next few lines of code, since they are identical to the example in Chapter 3, but the following line, although the same as the example from Chapter 3, actually functions differently. Since the function gotVars is a function that handles the result of an object's event (in this case, the load_lv's onLoad event), a reference to this within this function will actually refer to the load_lv instance instead of the _root timeline on which the function resides. This is very important to keep in mind as it can save hours of debugging.

In the line if (this[fvName] != undefined), the reference to this[fvName] is actually referring to the parameter in the load_lv loadVars object with the name contained in the variable fvName.

Next, let's create a new ASP.NET page that will respond to the Flash loadVars request with name-value pairs that will provide a listing of the button names for the navigation bar. I have created this page in the same manner as the previous examples—an ASP.NET web form with a C# code-behind file. I have named this file navbar.aspx, and within the Page_Load event for this page, I have created the following codeblock:

```
void Page_Load(object sender, EventArgs e)
{
  string outputString;
  outputString = MakeLoadVar("title1", "Home");
  outputString += MakeLoadVar("title2", "Photos");
  outputString += MakeLoadVar("title3", "Videos");
  outputString += MakeLoadVar("title4", "Links");
  outputString += MakeLoadVar("title5", "About");
  outputString += MakeLoadVar("title6", "Contact");

  Response.Write(outputString);
}

private string MakeLoadVar(string name, string value)
{
  return "&" + Server.HtmlEncode(name) + "="
    + Server.HtmlEncode(value);
}
```

This code should look pretty straightforward. I have created a new method called MakeLoadVar, which assembles a name-value pair string from values that are passed as parameters. This method first adds an & to the beginning of each name-value pair, and then encodes the name and value in their HTML-safe equivalent using the Server object's HtmlEncode method. When, for example, the second line of the Page_Load's codeblock executes, the outputstring variable will be equal to &title1=Home. After each call to the MakeLoadVar method, another name-value pair is appended to the outputstring variable, with the final value of outputstring being

```
&title1=Home&title2=Photos&title3=Videos&
title4=Links&title5=About&title6=cContact
```

Finally, once we have a full name-value pair string created, we can write that string to the page's output stream using the Response.Write method so it can be read by the Flash loadVars call. When the Flash application is now executed, we get the same values for the button names as we did in Chapter 3, but this time, we got them through loadVars instead of FlashVars (see Figure 4-14).

Figure 4-14. navbar.fla created using loadVars

Example: Flash e-mail form

In this chapter, we've covered quite a variety of topics, ranging from the C# Request, Response, and Mail objects to the concept of loadVars in Flash. Let's now take a look at an example that combines all of these technologies for a practical application: a Flash contact form. In this contact form, we'll acquire specific information from a user—their name, e-mail, phone number, and where they heard about our site. Using loadVars, we'll transmit this information to an ASP.NET page, which will generate an e-mail to inform us of the user's information. In the ASP.NET page, we'll also generate a response e-mail to the page's end user, thanking them for their submission.

Before getting started, let's list the steps required to make this application:

1. Create a Flash "Form" that uses Flash TextInput and ComboBox components to acquire information from the page's user.

2. Create a Submit button on this form using a Flash Button component that triggers an event when clicked.

3. When this Submit button's event is fired, a new loadVars object should be created, containing the user's information as properties.

4. This loadVars object should then perform a sendAndLoad operation, sending the user's information to an ASP.NET web page.

5. Upon receiving the variables from the Flash movie, the ASP.NET web page should generate two e-mails, one containing the values passed from the Flash movie to be sent to us, and a second "thank you" e-mail that will be sent to the e-mail address provided by the form.

6. The ASP.NET page should then output a name-value pair indicating whether the e-mail was sent successfully.

7. Back in the Flash movie, this name-value pair will then be loaded by the load portion of the loadVars' sendAndLoad operation.

8. If the value returned to Flash is true, indicating the e-mail was generated successfully, the Flash movie will present a "Thank You" dialog box to the form's user; otherwise, it will present an Error dialog box.

Let's start this example by creating the Flash form. As mentioned, let's make this form using the Flash TextInput, ComboBox, and Button components, along with some basic interface elements. In Figure 4-14, you can see the interface I've created.

Figure 4-15. Our Flash form

I've also given each of these interface elements an instance name as follows:

- `InputFirstName`
- `InputLastName`
- `InputEmail`
- `InputPhone`
- `ComboHow`
- `ButtonSubmit`

In order to perform the form's initialization functions, I have created a new function, `init()`, in the first frame of a new layer called Actions I have created in the Flash movie. In this function, we can fill the combo box with initial values, using the ComboBox's `addItem` method as follows:

```
function init() {
  ComboHow.addItem("--");
  ComboHow.addItem("Google");
  ComboHow.addItem("Yahoo");
  ComboHow.addItem("Friend");
  ComboHow.addItem("Other");
}
```

The next step we need to take is to "hook up" the Submit button to respond to a click. Doing this requires adding an event listener to the item, so a specific event can be handled. In the case of the Submit button, the Click event can be handled using the following code, again on the first frame of the Actions layer:

```
var ObjectForm:Object = new Object();
ObjectForm.click = function(ev:Object) {  . . . }
ButtonSubmit.addEventListener("click", ObjectForm);
```

In these statements, the addEventListener method is "hooking up" the Click event of the Submit button to be handled by the newly created ObjectForm object. Then, by creating a Click event handler for the ObjectForm's Click event, using the ObjectForm.click = function(ev:Object) statement, we can respond to this event accordingly.

Once we have the button's Click event handled, the next step is to create the loadVars object that will send these input parameters to an ASP.NET page and assign the parameters to that loadVars object:

```
ObjectForm.click = function(ev:Object) {
   var Form_lv:LoadVars = new LoadVars();
   Form_lv.firstName = InputFirstName.text;
   Form_lv.lastName = InputLastName.text;
   Form_lv.phoneNumber = InputPhone.text;
   Form_lv.emailAddress = InputEmail.text;
   Form_lv.how = ComboHow.selectedItem.label;
}
```

As you can see, I have assigned parameters to the loadVars object just like in the examples earlier in this chapter. Next, let's create a new loadVars object that will receive the response from the ASP.NET page, when we perform a sendAndLoad call:

```
var Response_lv:LoadVars = new LoadVars();
   Response_lv.onLoad = function(success:Boolean) {
   if (success) {
      //
   }
}
```

Next, let's make the call to the loadVars' sendAndLoad method to send these parameters to the ASP.NET page we will be creating:

```
var Url_str:String = "http://localhost:33030/chapter4/emailform.aspx";
Form_lv.sendAndLoad(Url_str, Response_lv, "POST");
```

Let's put all of these lines together in the FormObject's Click event handler and rearrange a bit:

```
ObjectForm.click = function(ev:Object) {
   // the URL 'localhost:33030' will be replaced by
      // the URL of your development server
   var Url_str:String =
    "http://localhost:33030/chapter4/emailform.aspx";
   var Response_lv:LoadVars = new LoadVars();
   Response_lv.onLoad = function(success:Boolean) {
      if (success) {
         //
      }
   };
   var Form_lv:LoadVars = new LoadVars();
   Form_lv.firstName = TextFirstName.text;
   Form_lv.lastName = TextLastName.text;
   Form_lv.phoneNumber = TextPhone.text;
```

```
      Form_lv.emailAddress = TextEmail.text;
      Form_lv.how = ComboHow.selectedItem.label;
      Form_lv.sendAndLoad(Url_str, Response_lv, "POST");
   }
```

And for now, let's leave the Flash emailform.fla file.

ASP.NET loadVars handler page

With the form created to accept the user's input, now we can create an ASP.NET page that will handle this input as sent by the Flash loadVars object. Again, to do this, we will be using the C# Request and Response objects, as well as the Mail namespace that was presented earlier in this chapter.

Listed next is the HTML code for the .aspx page I have created. You will notice again that I have removed the "guts" of this page, as we will be replacing the HTML response with a name-value response to the Flash movie.

```
<%@ Page Language="C#" AutoEventWireup="true"
    CodeFile="emailform.aspx.cs" Inherits="emailform" %>
<html></html>
```

I have saved this page as emailform.aspx, with the code-behind page named emailform.aspx.cs, as shown in the CodeFile directive above. In the code-behind file, I have created the following code to handle the request from the Flash file, send off the necessary e-mails, and respond to the Flash movie with an indication of whether or not the e-mail was sent successfully.

```
using System.Web.Mail;

public partial class emailform2 : System.Web.UI.Page
{
  void Page_Load(object sender, EventArgs e)
  {
    string msgText =
    "You have received a new contact submission:<br><br>";

    msgText += "<b>First Name:</b> " + Request["firstName"];
    msgText += "<b>Last Name:</b> " + Request["lastName"];
    msgText += "<b>Phone #:</b> " + Request["phoneNumber"];
    msgText += "<b>E-mail Address:</b> " + Request["emailAddress"];
    msgText += "<b>Found Us Through:</b> " + Request["found"];

    MailMessage msg = new MailMessage();
    msg.BodyFormat = MailFormat.Html;
    msg.Subject = "Flash E-mail Form Submission";
    msg.Body = msgText;
    msg.From = "";  // your e-mail address #1
    msg.To = "";   // your e-mail address #2

    try
    {
```

```
        SmtpMail.SmtpServer = "my SMTP server here";
        SmtpMail.Send(msg);
        Response.Write("success=true");
    }
    catch
    {
        Response.Write("success=false");
    }
```

In this page, I have included the System.Web.Mail namespace, which provides easy access to the ASP.NET mail classes we will be using in the example. In the first few lines of the code within the Page_Load delegate, the text for a new e-mail message is created by using the Request object to obtain the values passed by the Flash movie through POST variables. The titles of the Request objects in this case correspond directly to the names of the variables we created as a part of the loadVars object. For example, when we made the following statement in the Flash movie:

```
    Form_lv.firstName =  . . .
```

we can access this parameter by referencing the same name, firstName, of the ASP.NET Request object.

Notice that, in order to concatenate the lines of the e-mail together, I'm using the shorthand notation of +=. The += operator, when applied to a string, simply adds a value to the end of that already existing string. Also, it may seem strange that I have included HTML tags in this e-mail. When creating HTML formatted e-mails (as we are doing here), you can add HTML tags, which will display just as they would in a browser, as long as the client receiving the e-mail has an HTML-compatible e-mail client.

In the lines

```
        MailMessage msg = new MailMessage();
        msg.BodyFormat = MailFormat.Html;
        msg.Subject = "Flash E-mail Form Submission";
        msg.Body = msgText;
        msg.From = "";  // your e-mail address #1
        msg.To = "";    // your e-mail address #2
```

the mail message itself is created with the line MailMessage msg = new MailMessage(). This object can be created without using the full System.Web.Mail.MailMessage syntax since I have included the using System.Web.Mail statement in this class, as in the following code:

```
    using System.Web;
      . . .
    using System.Web.Mail;
```

In the next line, msg.BodyFormat = MailFormat.Html, I have declared the format of the body of the mail message to be HTML formatted. MessageFormat is an enumeration—like we talked about earlier in the chapter. This enumeration has two possible values: Html or Text.

The following lines, which define the To and From properties of the MailMessage object, should be set to the e-mail addresses you would like this e-mail to be sent from and the address you would like it sent to.

The next section of code in this method performs the action of sending the e-mail to the recipient, followed by the response to the Flash movie with a name-value pair, using the Response object.

```
try
{
  SmtpMail.SmtpServer = "my SMTP server here";
  SmtpMail.Send(msg);
  Response.Write("success=true");
}
catch
{
  Response.Write("success=false");
}
```

In the line SmtpMail.SmtpServer= "my SMTP server here", I am defining the SMTP server that we will use to send the e-mail through. This could be a local machine (the machine you're developing this code on), or an external web server. The following line, SmtpMail.Send(msg), is performing the action of sending the e-mail message through the defined SMTP server. It is this line that will determine whether the ASP.NET page will return the success=true or success=false lines. If the SmtpMail.Send method encounters an error, such as an invalid SMTP server, the code execution will immediately exit the try block and continue execution in the catch block, responding to the Flash movie with success=false.

That's going to be it for the ASP.NET page in this e-mail form example. To recap, the ASP.NET page does the following:

1. Obtains the e-mail form values using the Request object and creates a string e-mail message with them.

2. Creates a new MailMessage object and defines the MessageType, Body, Subject, To, and From parameters of this object.

3. Tries sending the MailMessage using the SmtpMail.Send method through the defined SmtpServer, and writes a name-value pair of success=true to the output stream if the method executes successfully, and a value of success=false if the method fails.

Back to the Flash form

We now have the ASP.NET page that will respond to the Flash e-mail form created, so let's finish up the code of the Flash e-mail form by creating the code in the loadVars onLoad event handler. In our previous code, the onLoad event handler looked like this:

```
Response_lv.onLoad = function(success:Boolean) {
  if (success) {
    //
  }
};
```

What we'll need to do now is handle the result of the ASP.NET page, based on the three possible results:

1. The ASP.NET page returns a value of success=true.

2. The ASP.NET page returns a value of success=false.

3. The ASP.NET page cannot be called for some reason.

We can handle the first two of these possibilities by adding the following lines within the if (success) statement we have created:

```
if (success) {
  if (Response_lv.success == "true") {
    // success!
  } else {
    // mail couldn't be sent!
  }
}
```

Since the Boolean variable suc indicates whether or not the loadVars object executed the sendAndLoad successfully, the third scenario can be handled with an else statement corresponding to the same if (suc) statement, as shown here:

```
if (success) {
  ..
}
else
{
  // sendAndLoad didn't work!
}
```

Now that we have all of the potential responses handled in our code, it's time to create a message dialog that will relay this result to the e-mail form's user as a "pop-up" form.

> *Another great thing about using Flash as a presentation tier: You don't have to worry about pop-up windows in Flash being blocked by pop-up blockers!*

In order to make a pop-up window, I have created a new MovieClip using the Insert ➤ New symbol command in Flash. As you can see in Figure 4-16, I have assigned a linkage value to this new MovieClip, as well as an AS 2.0 class for the methods and properties we will be assigning to this pop-up.

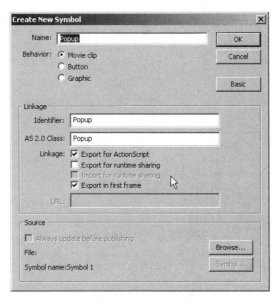

Figure 4-16. The Create New Symbol dialog box

On the timeline for this MovieClip, I have created four layers: one titled "Text" for text fields, one titled "Button" for an OK button, one titled "Background" for the visual background elements, and another titled "Shadow," which holds the shadow placed underneath the background. The completed pop-up MovieClip is shown in Figure 4-17.

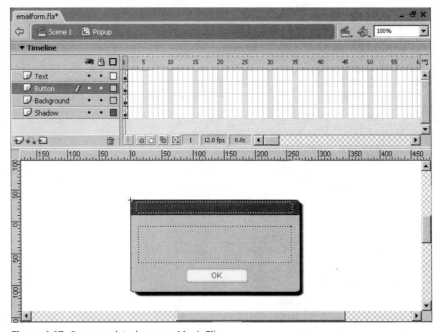

Figure 4-17. Our completed pop-up MovieClip

In this MovieClip, I have created two dynamic text fields, Title_txt and Msg_txt. The Title_txt field is the field in the blue header of the pop-up form and will contain a short message describing the nature of the pop-up window—whether it is an error or success message. The Msg_txt field will contain the textual description of the error or success that the e-mail form has encountered.

The Button I have created is a Flash Button UI component with an instance name of ButtonOk. We won't define any handler or events for this button instance, though, as we will do it all in the .as class file for this pop-up MovieClip.

To create the functionality of this pop-up MovieClip, let's create another .as file, popup.as, and save it in the same directory as the emailform.fla file. In this .as file, we'll need to define methods that allow the pop-up form to

1. Set a message that notates "success"

2. Set a message that notates "error"

3. Responds to the click of the OK button and closes the pop-up form

The first two requirements of this form can be accomplished by defining a single method within the pop-up class, as follows:

```
dynamic class Popup extends MovieClip {
  function SetMessage(msg_str:String, error:Boolean) {
    if (error) {
      this["Title_txt"].text = "ERROR";
      this["Title_txt"].textColor = 0xFF0000;
    } else {
      this["Title_txt"].text = "Thank you!";
    }
    this["Msg_txt"].text = msg_str;
  }
}
```

This function, SetMessage, takes two parameters as input, msg_str and error. The msg_str parameter will be displayed directly in the Msg_txt text field to display a short message to the user. The Boolean error parameter will determine the "type" of pop-up that we would like to create. As shown in the lines

```
if (error) {
    this["Title_txt"].text = "ERROR";
    this["Title_txt"].textColor = 0xFF0000;
} else {
    this["Title_txt"].textColor = 0xFFFFFF;
    this["Title_txt"].text = "Thank you!";
}
```

the Title_txt field's text value and color will change based on the value of the error variable. So, for example, if we called this function with the parameters "Error accessing SMTP server!" and true as in the following line:

```
SetMessage("Error accessing SMTP server!", true);
```

132

the Msg_txt field would display the "Error accessing SMTP server" message, while the Title_txt field would display, in red (0xFF0000), "ERROR", since the Boolean error parameter was set to true.

The only thing we have left to do in this pop-up form is define the functionality of the OK button. All this button needs to accomplish is to close the pop-up form. Since we will be attaching this form dynamically using the attachMovie method, this can be accomplished using the Flash MovieClip's removeMovieClip method. First, though, we need to create a handler to catch the Click event of the Button. This will be done in a new event handler defined in the .as class, onLoad.

```
dynamic class Popup extends MovieClip {
  var ObjectForm:Object;
  public function onLoad():Void {
  this.ObjectForm = new Object();
  this.ObjectForm.click = this.CloseMe;
  this["ButtonOk"].addEventListener("click", this.ObjectForm);
}
function CloseMe(ev:Object) {
  removeMovieClip(this);
}
```

The onLoad event handler is one of the events built into the MovieClip class, and therefore available when we use the extends MovieClip syntax when defining the popup.as class file. It is important that we perform initialization type functions on Flash components within the onLoad event handler rather than in the class's constructor function as shown here:

```
dynamic class Popup extends MovieClip {
  public function onLoad():void {
    // component initialization functions can be performed here
  }
  public function Popup () {
    // Popup constructor function
    // component initialization functions can't be placed here
    // because the component hasn't been created yet!
  }
}
```

If you do try to perform functions on a component within a class's constructor function, you will find yourself doing endless hours of troubleshooting because the component hasn't been created yet—therefore you cannot access any of its members.

Back to the onLoad function, within this function I have defined a new object, ObjectForm, that will handle the Click event of the ButtonOK instance. I have actually defined this object outside of the onLoad method, so it will be available to the entire Popup class, and initialized the object within the onLoad event. Once the ObjectForm object is created, I have defined the Click method of that object to be a new function that we will create, CloseMe. This function will perform the actual action of closing the pop-up form. Finally, within the onLoad method, I have added an event listener to the ButtonOK instance using

```
this["ButtonOk"].addEventListener("click", this.ObjectForm);
```

This line "hooks up" the ButtonOk instance to the ObjectForm object and sets that object to handle the Click event of the button.

Once we have created this connection between the ButtonOk instance, the ObjectForm object, and the CloseMe function, we can create the CloseMe function to remove the Popup instance from the Flash movie:

```
function CloseMe(ev:Object) {
  removeMovieClip(this);
}
```

More information on the removeMovieClip method can be found in the Flash documentation, but essentially, it removes any MovieClip that was added to a Flash movie using the attachMovieClip or duplicateMovieClip method. As you will see soon, we will be using the attachMovieClip method to create this instance of the Popup MovieClip, so the removeMovieClip method will work perfectly to "close" this pop-up form.

Tying it all together

With the Popup MovieClip created, we can now go back to loadVars onLoad code in the _root time-line and attach an instance of the Popup MovieClip as needed when a response is received from the ASP.NET web page. With this pop-up form added, the new onLoad event looks a little bit different:

```
Response_lv.onLoad = function(success:Boolean) {
attachMovie("Popup", "popup", 10);
this["popup"]._x = 100;
this["popup"]._y = 100;
if (success) {
  if (Response_lv.success == "true") {
    this["popup"].SetMessage("Your information
    was submitted successfully.", false);
  } else {
    this["popup"].SetMessage("There was
     an error sending your information.", true);
  }
} else {
  this["popup"].SetMessage("There was
  an error sending your information.", true);
  }
};
```

In the first line of this function, we now are attaching a new instance of the Popup MovieClip using the attachMovie method. In the following lines, this new instance's position is set to [100, 100], to center it on the e-mail submission form. (If we do not set these values, the pop-up form will default to [0, 0] when attached.) Once this pop-up form is attached to the Flash movie's _root timeline, the SetMessage method of this instance can be called with the necessary parameters, depending on whether the information was sent successfully or not.

And that's it. We have successfully created an e-mail form using Flash and ASP.NET. The result of our form, when tested using the Flash IDE's Test Movie function, is shown in Figure 4-18.

Figure 4-18. Testing our form

Summary

In this chapter, we've covered a lot of information, ranging from the ASP.NET Request and Response objects to the Flash loadVars object and sending e-mail using ASP.NET. These communication methods are great for certain, non-data-intensive Flash/ASP.NET applications. In the next chapters, we cover more advanced ASP.NET features, as well as some of the more advanced methods of Flash/ASP.NET communication.

```
<table>
  <tr><td colspan="2"><b>War and
Peace</b></td></tr>
  <tr><td>Author:</td><td>Leo
Tolstoy</td></tr>
  <tr><td>Pages:</td><td>1424</td></tr>
  <tr><td>Publisher:</td><td>Modern
Library</td></tr>

<tr><td>ISBN:</td><td>0375760644</td></
tr>
</table>
```

Chapter 5

XML

What this chapter covers:

- The history of XML
- The XML standard

One of the biggest challenges in creating applications with ASP.NET and Flash, and with web technologies in general, is the formatting of data for exchange between two systems. Without a standardized language for formatting data, communication between applications becomes nearly impossible. XML provides a standardized universal language for describing data that allows applications from anywhere in the world to communicate.

For ASP.NET and Flash, XML provides a more structured and robust format for exchanging data between server-side and client-side applications than unstructured methods like LoadVars. In this chapter, we'll take a look at a brief history of XML as well as the basics of creating an XML document. In the next two chapters, we'll take a look at methods of communicating between Flash and ASP.NET that use XML as the "language" for interaction.

The history of XML

XML, or e**X**tensible **M**arkup **L**anguage, is a markup language, similar to our friend, HTML. XML and HTML are actually both *subsets* of the same, larger language, SGML. SGML—the **S**tandardized **G**eneral **M**arkup **L**anguage—was "invented" in 1969 by Dr. Charles Goldfarb, to help format documents for publishing purposes. This language was intended by Goldfarb to be a *universal* language that would assist in both the exchange and formatting of data.

It is this universality that makes SGML and its descendants so powerful. SGML could be used to provide formatting description to nearly any document and still be reliably interpreted by another system. In the world of document formatting and publishing, SGML is similar to establishing a universal and all-encompassing language that can be spoken throughout the world. This language breaks down interpretation barriers and provides a reliable form of communication.

SGML, being so powerful, is also very complex. Imagine a spoken language that encompasses the words in all languages around the world—it would become so vast that the creation of a dictionary would be almost an impossibility. This is the case with SGML—a document formatted with SGML can become so complex that the software reading it cannot reliably display it. A very simple SGML document is shown here; as you can see, a lot of work is required to just exchange two bits!

```
<!doctype simp [
<!element simp o o (bit*)>
<!element bit - - (#PCDATA)>
<!attlist bit name id #required>
]>
<bit name=one>1</bit>
<bit name=two>2</bit>
```

In the 1991, Tim Berners-Lee invented a method for document exchange, now known as the World Wide Web. For his invention, he needed a standard for document formatting that could be used to format a wide variety of documents, but also one that was simple enough to be easily interpreted by any client running his World Wide Web browser. For this task, he chose a subset of the complex SGML language, HTML—HyperText Markup Language.

HTML was initially chosen for document exchange on the World Wide Web because of its simplicity and lightweight nature. Unlike SGML, HTML was not overly complex, and consisted of a tightly grouped set of tags for document formatting, allowing for reliable document exchange and interpretation. This simplicity made it fairly easy to exchange documents like academic papers and scientific journals—the purpose for which it was originally intended. It was also lightweight enough that it could be reliably displayed in browsers without taking a significant amount of processing time. HTML was originally intended, however, for formatting and displaying textual elements, and not the "multimedia" elements that we expect today—images, animations, and video, for example (the reason that we use Flash as a presentation tier!)

This need for visual display improvements caused HTML to stray from its SGML roots as a data-descriptive language into a display-friendly language that does not do a good job of describing the data that it formats. Consider the following HTML table that contains information on the book *War and Peace*:

```
<table>
  <tr><td colspan="2"><b>War and Peace</b></td></tr>
  <tr><td>Author:</td><td>Leo Tolstoy</td></tr>
  <tr><td>Pages:</td><td>1424</td></tr>
  <tr><td>Publisher:</td><td>Modern Library</td></tr>
  <tr><td>ISBN:</td><td>0375760644</td></tr>
</table>
```

Although this table does a reasonable job of displaying this data, it does not contain any *description* of the data. Imagine, for example, that you are in charge of designing a "web-bot" that will be able to scan web pages and extract information about books. Even though this page contains all of the data your bot might need, it would have a hard time finding and extracting the data in a reliable way, since the data is not described in any way—the <td> tags containing the book's title, author, and publisher are not noted as containing this data, making their contents indistinguishable from any other <td> tags that your web-bot might find on the Internet.

This is where XML comes into play—and where it differs from HTML. Although not used to *display* data, XML can be used to masterfully *describe and exchange* data. Whereas a book's information could become lost within display-intended tags in HTML, with XML this information can be properly tagged and described, as in the following example:

```
<book>
  <title>War and Peace</title>
  <author>Leo Tolstoy</author>
  <pages>1424</pages>
  <publisher>Modern Library</publisher>
  <isbn>ISBN</isbn>
</book>
```

In this example, the tags, rather than performing visual formatting, are used to describe the textual data in the document. Because of this description, your web-bot would have no problem finding the book's title, author, and publisher in this document, as long as it knows what it is looking for.

One of the great powers of the XML language is that the language itself is extensible. For our book example, I have created my own implementation of the XML language—I was not constrained by having to use certain tags to describe my data, but could instead invent tag names, like <isbn>. Because of this extensibility, it is possible to describe nearly any set of data for communication between different parties all over the world, as long as each party understands what the data inside each tagged element means.

Elements of an XML document

Like HTML documents, XML documents are composed of tags that mark up or describe data. Although XML is completely extendible (unlike HTML), certain rules must be followed when creating XML documents to make them *valid*. Let's take a look at some of these rules, as well as the elements that compose a valid XML document.

Text elements

As mentioned, an XML document is created with a combination of *character data* and *markup*. Markup is data residing within the familiar HTML-like tags, such as <book>, whereas character data resides outside, or more properly, *between* these tags, such as the word "Hello" in <message>Hello</message>.

Again, like HTML, an XML document is made up of a hierarchy of *elements*. Elements can be nested inside other elements, creating a further level of description for each element. Each element must consist of a *start tag* and an *end tag*, and may optionally contain *attributes*, which will be described later in this chapter. An example of an XML element is as follows:

```
<book>Foundation ASP.NET for Flash</book>
```

As a rule, every XML document must have a single *root element*—the first and highest-level element in the XML document. Here is an example of an XML document with a properly formatted root element:

```
<inventory>
  <book>Foundation ASP.NET for Flash</book>
  <book>The Odyssey</book>
</inventory>
```

An example of an improperly formed XML document (because it violates the one-root rule) is as follows:

```
<book>Foundation ASP.NET for Flash</book>
<book>The Odyssey</book>
```

Since each XML document has a single root element, every XML document can be considered to be just a single element, consisting of any number of child elements. You can think of this in terms of the bookstore inventory represented in the previous example—even though there may be thousands of books in a store's inventory, the inventory can still be referred to as a single unit "inventory."

Start tag

Each element in an XML document must begin with a start tag. A start tag is a way of telling the software (or other agent) reading the XML document "I'm starting to describe an element here." A valid start tag must have the following characteristics:

- Begin with the < character
- End with the > character
- Contain a tag name between the two previous characters

Following these rules, a valid start tag is as simple as

    <book>

The start tag's name is not a unique identifier but rather an identifier describing the type of element that it will be describing. Like Flash MovieClips, XML element names must adhere to certain restrictions:

- It cannot begin with the letters XML or xml.
- It cannot begin with a number.
- It cannot begin with a dot (.) or dash (-).

Table 5-1 contains examples of legal XML tag names, and Table 5-2 shows examples of illegal names.

Table 5-1. Legal XML start tag names

Name	Description
INVENTORY	Capital letters are legal.
book	No problem here!
sub_title	Underscores are legal and are commonly used to replace spaces.
sub_title2	Numbers are legal in a name as long as they're not the first character.
book_xml	*xml* is legal in a name, as long as it does not begin the name.

Table 5-2. Illegal XML start tag names

Name	Description
123name	Cannot begin with numbers
.text	Cannot begin with a .
-person	Cannot begin with a -
xmlTag	Cannot begin with xml
my inventory	Cannot have a space in the name

End tag

An XML end tag is very much like an end tag in HTML—it denotes the end of a specific element. Unlike HTML, though, *every* element must have an end tag. For example, the HTML shorthand break or paragraph notations are not valid in XML since they do not have an end tag:

```
<br>
<p>
```

To make an element like a <br> valid in terms of XML, the tag can be closed within the start tag using the following notation:

```
<br />
```

> The newest generation of HTML—XHTML—applies XML rules to HTML documents. HTML development using Visual Studio .NET defaults to this XHTML format.

End tags, by definition, contain no information about the element of which it is a member. You cannot, for example, put an attribute (which we'll be covering next) within an end tag:

```
<book> ... </book title="War and Peace">
```

An end tag must follow these rules:

- Begin with a </
- End with a >
- Contain the name of the element it is closing

End tags in XML, also unlike end tags in HTML, are case-sensitive and must have exactly the same characters as the start tag. The following line, for example, would be invalid:

```
<book> .. </Book>
```

Nested end tags must also be closed in the same order as their start tags were created, as in the following example:

```
<inventory>
  <book> ... </book>
</inventory>
```

Table 5-3 shows examples of both properly and improperly formatted XML tags.

Table 5-3. Properly and improperly formatted XML tags

Properly Formatted	Improperly Formatted	Description
`<book></book>`	`<Book></book>`	Character casing must be exact.
`<book />`	`<book>`	If no end tag is provided, the element must contain /> in the start tag.
`<book />`	`<book />..</book>`	If the start tag is "closed," an end tag is illegal.
`<inventory><book>..</book></inventory>`	`<inventory><book></inventory></book>`	Improper end tag nesting.

Attributes

Attributes are used within elements in XML to provide additional description of an element. Attributes are passed using the familiar name-value pairs, as shown here:

```
<book title="Foundation ASP.NET for Flash" />
```

An element can contain an unlimited number of attributes, as long as there is only one instance of each attribute (a book cannot have two titles). Attributes must adhere to the following rules:

- Must be enclosed with quotation marks
- Must use = between name and value
- Cannot contain a < character
- Cannot contain a " character *within* the attribute

Table 5-4 shows examples of both properly and improperly formatted attributes.

Table 5-4. Properly and improperly formatted attributes

Properly Formatted	Improperly Formatted	Description
`title="Foundation..."`	`title=Foundation...`	Quotation marks are required.
`image="&lt;img src=&quo; http://friendsofed.com/ images/..&quo;&gt; "`	`image="<img src=" http://friendsofed.com/ images/..">"`	Contains illegal < and " characters.

Character data

Character data is generally the data *not contained* within the start and end tags. The character data of an element is meant to contain the majority of the data in the element, whereas the markup (the information in the tags) is meant to add structure to the document. Character data is used in the following format:

```
<message>Hello</message>
```

Character data content can contain any characters except the < and & characters, which are specific to XML tags. These characters must be delimited with their ASCII or HTML equivalent.

Table 5-5 shows examples of both properly and improperly formatted character data.

Table 5-5. Properly and improperly formatted character data

Properly Formatted	Improperly Formatted	Description
<message>4<8 = true</message>	<message>4<8 = true</message>	Illegal < character

Comments

Comments can be used in XML in a way similar to the way they are used in ActionScript or C#. Comments are made purely for human use—to make your XML document make more sense to you or someone else who is reading it. They do not have any use when being read by software, such as Flash, and are typically ignored. XML comments are created between <!– and –> using the following syntax:

```
<!-- Comment text goes here -->
```

Comments must appear in an XML document outside of any markup that you have created (again, markup being anything within tags). The following XML comment, for example, is not valid:

```
<book <!-- still need price --> name="War and Peace">
```

Another rule for XML comments limits the use of double dashes, --, within the comment. The following XML comment, is also invalid:

```
<book><!-- Remember -- find the name of this book! --> </book>
```

Summary

In the next several chapters, we will be investigating methods for using XML documents to transfer properly formatted data between server-side ASP.NET code and client-side Flash movies. As we will see in these chapters, XML is a good option not only because it allows data to be described and exchanged, but also because it is a standard format that can be used to exchange data between applications around the world.

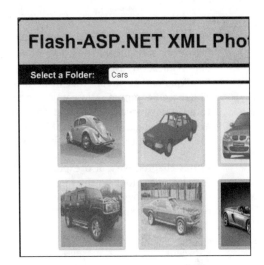

Flash-ASP.NET XML Pho[t]

Select a Folder: Cars

Chapter 6

COMMUNICATING USING XML

What this chapter covers:

- Flash animation using the Zigo engine
- The C# System.IO namespace
- The C# Server.MapPath method
- The Flash XML object
- The C# System.Xml namespace
- Flash/ASP.NET communication using XML

Now that we've gotten a good understanding of Flash/ASP.NET cooperation using LoadVars and FlashVars, and understand some of the basics of XML, in this chapter we'll examine Flash/ASP.NET communication using XML documents. This type of communication has many advantages over LoadVars and FlashVars that make it a more attractive communication method. The advantages of XML-based communication are rooted in the fact that XML documents provide a more logically structured, human-readable format for exchanging data. Since XML is also an industry standard for exchanging data, support for XML document creation is built into the .NET base class library, making the formatting of XML data a simple task with ASP.NET.

In this chapter, we'll also explore the .NET System.IO namespace, which contains methods for performing operations on the filesystem of the web server, such as reading, writing, and listing files and directories. Knowledge of the System.IO namespace will be necessary for many of the examples in the rest of this book, and one of the most useful features of Flash and .NET interaction.

At the end of this chapter, we'll make use of the XML communication and System.IO namespace knowledge to create a "self-powered" image viewer application. The foundation concepts we'll be using in this chapter will be the basis for the following, more advanced forms of Flash/ASP.NET interactions using XML web services and Flash Remoting.

Flash animation using the Zigo tweening engine

With all of the data-driven functionality that we'll cover in this chapter (and the rest of this book), I feel like we're missing out on half of the fun of writing Flash applications—creating interactive, animated interfaces. For the animations used in the examples for the remainder of this book, I'm going to make use of one of the handiest third-party ActionScript libraries available: the Zigo tweening engine (formerly known as the Flash MovieClip Tweening Prototype). The Zigo engine, originally written by Ladislav Zigo (www.laco.wz.cz) and currently maintained and updated by Moses Gunesch (www.mosessupposes.com), is an ActionScript 2.0 component that allow developers to easily create MovieClip animation, traditionally done on the timeline, with code. A newer extension called Fuse makes it simple to lace multiple tweens together sequentially, and for advanced developers, it acts as a production syntax for any complex set of tweens and timed method calls. The Zigo engine and Fuse kit, fully compatible with Flash 8, can be downloaded at www.mosessupposes.com/Fuse.

Installation of the Zigo engine is easy. If you have the Macromedia Extension Manager installed, you can simply download the .mxp file from this site and open the file, and the libraries will be installed automatically. Once they're installed, you should see a new section in your Flash Help menu (available by pressing F1 in Flash), called ZigoEngine + Fuse. In this section, you'll see descriptions and examples of the methods included in the classes. You will also have three new components (in your Components panel in a folder called FUSE – mosesSupposes). To make use of the Zigo engine, simply drag the component to the stage (be sure it's in a frame on or after your classes export frame) and you are ready to go.

Using the Zigo engine, nearly any property of a TextField, Button, or MovieClip can be animated over time using a very simple and intuitive syntax. Listed in Table 6-1 are some of the most useful methods of the Zigo engine.

Table 6-1. Useful methods of the Zigo engine

Method	Description
tween	Animates any of the applicable properties of the MovieClip, TextField, or Button instance. This is the most general of the prototype methods and can be used in place of any of the other methods in this table.
alphaTo	Animates the alpha transparency of the specified instance over time.
sizeTo	Animates the size of the specified instance over time.
slideTo	Animates the position of the specified instance over time.
scaleTo	Animates the scaling of the specified instance over time.
rotateTo	Animates the rotation of the specified instance over time.
colorTo	Animates the color of the specified instance over time.

Each of these tweening methods generally makes use of the same parameters. Here is the usage syntax for the tween method:

```
my_mc.tween([property1name, property2name, ...],
[property1end, property2end, ...],
seconds, animationtype, delaytostart, callbackfunction)
```

Although this statement might look a little daunting, it's really pretty easy to use. For example, let's say that we have a MovieClip that we want to move from its initial position at [0,0] to a final position at [300,300]. Along the way, let's say we also want the MovieClip to animate its original alpha transparency from 50 up to a final transparency of 100, and that we want this animation to happen over a course of 1 second. This could be accomplished with the following use of the tween method:

```
my_mc.tween(["_x", "_y","_alpha"], [300,300,100], 1);
```

Pretty easy! I have just placed each property name that I would like to animate within quotes, enclosed in brackets [], and done the same for the final destinations of those properties. This animation, when executed, will have the my_mc MovieClip moving from [0,0] to [300,300], in a linear fashion, immediately when the script is executed. Now, let's say we want to have a little more control over the animation. I'd like the animation not to move in just a linear fashion, but instead ease out as it nears its final destination. I'd also like the animation to wait for a little over a second before it starts. This more advanced function can be accomplished by adding two more parameters to the tween method:

```
my_mc.tween(["_x", "_y","_alpha"], [300,300,100], 1, "easeOut", 1.2);
```

In this example, I've made use of one of the "animation type" parameters to control the easing of the animation. In this example, I've used the easeOut animation type, which gives the desired "slowing" effect I was looking for. There are many more animation types that can be used with the Zigo engine, all based on Robert Penner's easing equations (which can be found at www.robertpenner.com/easing/). The following is a list of these easing types:

```
"easeInQuad", "easeOutQuad", "easeInOutQuad", "easeOutInQuad",
"easeInCubic", "easeOutCubic", "easeInOutCubic", "easeOutInCubic"
"easeInQuart", "easeOutQuart", "easeInOutQuart", "easeOutInQuart",
"easeInQuint", "easeOutQuint", "easeInOutQuint", "easeOutInQuint",
"easeInSine", "easeOutSine", "easeInOutSine", "easeOutInSine",
"easeInExpo", "easeOutExpo", "easeInOutExpo", "easeOutInExpo"
"easeInCirc", "easeOutCirc", "easeInOutCirc", "easeOutInCirc",
"easeInBack", "easeOutBack", "easeInOutBack", "easeOutInBack",
"easeInBounce", "easeOutBounce", "easeInOutBounce", "easeOutInBounce",
"easeInElastic", "easeOutElastic",
"easeInOutElastic", "easeOutInElastic", "linear"
```

Now that you grasp the core tween method, you can easily use any of the other extensions:

```
// move the MovieClip to 100,20
my_mc.slideTo(100, 20, 1, "easeOutElastic");
// fade the MovieClip to an _alpha of 0
my_mc.alphaTo(0, 3, "easeInQuint");
// bring the brightness of the MovieClip to -100 (black)
my_mc.brightnessTo(-100, 2);
```

Finally, suppose we want to be able to react to the *completion* of an ActionScript-based animation—something that's pretty difficult to do with timeline-based animation without creating some very disjointed ActionScript code. This can be accomplished using the Zigo engine's callback parameter, as shown in the following example:

```
function myCallback(param1, param2) {
  // handle the animation callback
}
var p1:Number = 12;
var p2:Number = 15;
my_mc.tween(["_x", "_y","_alpha"], [300,300,100], 1, "easeOut",
            1.2, "myCallback(p1,p2)");
```

In this example, the myCallback function will be executed as soon as the tween function has completed (and after the 1.2 second initial delay). As you can see, I have also passed parameters to the callback function, using a very intuitive syntax.

Although it's not possible to use these ActionScript-based MovieClip tweening classes for *every* animation, they do come in very handy when creating responsive user interfaces, as we'll be doing in this book. Since they are created in ActionScript 2.0, they also follow a syntax that will be very familiar to C# development—something that timeline-based animation certainly is not!

C# System.IO namespace

One of the many advantages to having ASP.NET as a server-side counterpart for Flash is the ability for server-side code to interface with the filesystem on a web server. With this ability, applications can perform more low-level functions, like creating, listing, and deleting directories or files. In C#, the System.IO namespace provides a wealth of methods for executing such tasks.

In this section, we're going to take a look at a couple of specific members of the System.IO namespace: the System.IO.Directory and System.IO.File classes. Using these members, we will be able to perform tasks such as listing directory contents, creating new directories, checking for the existence of files, and deleting files or directories.

System.IO.Directory

The System.IO.Directory class provides methods for creating, listing, and removing directories on a web server's filesystem (it also provides other methods that we won't get into here). Some of these methods are listed in Table 6-2.

Table 6-2. Selected System.IO.Directory methods

Method	Description
GetDirectories	Lists all of the subdirectories in a directory
GetFiles	Lists all of the files in a directory
CreateDirectory	Creates a directory
Delete	Deletes a directory and everything in it
Exists	Determines whether a directory exists

The methods that we will make the most use of in this chapter are the GetDirectories and GetFiles methods. Each of these methods takes a directory as a parameter and returns a string array listing all of the files or directories that exist within a specified directory. An example of the GetFiles method is shown here:

```
// GetFiles will return a string array of files in a directory
string[] files = Directory.GetFiles("C:\\foundationaspnet\\");
```

You'll notice that in this example, a single forward slash (\) is replaced with a double forward slash (\\) in this directory string. This is required in C# because the forward slash is a reserved string character, used to notate special characters inside of a string quotation. Because it's so easy to forget this notation when dealing with directories or file strings, C# allows the use of the @ sign before a string to remove the need for double slashes, as shown in the following example:

```
// GetDirectories will return a string array of the directories
// found within the c:\foundationaspnet\ folder
string[] directories =
  Directory.GetDirectories(@"C:\foundationaspnet\");
```

Server.MapPath

As shown in the GetFiles and GetDirectories examples in the previous section, when specifying directories in ASP.NET, it is often necessary to provide a complete path, rather than a path relative to the ASP.NET website root. Many times, when you're placing code onto a web server, you aren't necessarily aware of the full file structure or the folder that your application resides in, making it difficult to hard-code a directory path into your application logic. Additional issues can also occur if you hard-code path names into your code that refer to a directory on your development machine—when transferred to a new machine, your code will no longer be accurate. For these reasons, the ASP.NET Server object's MapPath method, used to retrieve a full path to a file or directory when passed a relative directory from a website root, is essential for use with filesystem operations. The MapPath method, when passed a directory relative to the root of an ASP.NET site, returns the physical file path that corresponds to the specified virtual path on the web server.

For example, let's say that you wanted to list all of the files that resided in an uploads directory that resided in the root folder of your website. If you were to hard-code the path to this directory, you might use code similar to the following:

```
string[] files =
➥ Directory.GetFiles(@"c:\inetpub\wwwroot\mysite\uploads\");
```

which would work perfectly fine, provided you didn't move your application to another machine. Using the Server.MapPath method, however, you could modify this code to properly find the uploads directory in any site you place the code:

```
String path = Server.MapPath("~/uploads/");
String[] files = Directory.GetFiles(path);
```

In the first line of this codeblock, you'll notice that I used a tilde (~) before the uploads path. In ASP.NET, the tilde refers to the root of the current ASP.NET website, regardless of its physical location on the web server. This character can be very useful when performing operations like file uploads (which we'll be covering in Chapter 13).

System.IO.File

The System.IO.File class provides similar functionality to the System.IO.Directory class, except, as its name suggests, it works with files rather than directories. Some of the methods of the System.IO.File class that are relevant to the examples in this book are listed Table 6-3.

Table 6-3. Selected System.IO.File methods

Method	Description
Exists	Determines whether a file exists
Delete	Deletes a file
Copy	Copies an existing file to a new location

In the image gallery example at the end of this chapter, we'll be making use of the File.Exists method to determine whether a file we are attempting to create already exists—in which case we don't need to create it!

XML communication with the Flash XML object

In Flash 5, Macromedia introduced the XML object, a built-in set of classes for creating, reading, sending, and loading XML documents. The XML object is capable of sending and receiving data in a very similar fashion to the LoadVars object, but has extended functionality for creating and parsing XML documents.

The simplest way of creating an XML document using the Flash XML object is by creating a string of XML-formatted data, and initializing an XML document with this string, as follows:

```
var xml_str:String = "<team><player name=\"Shoeless Joe\" />
➥ <player name=\"Babe Ruth\"></team>";
var team_xml:XML = new XML(xml_str);
```

In this book, we will be using this syntax when we need to create XML documents in Flash. (XML documents can also be created using functions like createTextNode and createElement, which will not be covered in this book.) Once created, an XML document can be sent to a server-side program (ASP.NET!) using the XML.send or XML.sendAndLoad function, as shown here:

```
team_xml.send("mypage.aspx", "_blank");
```

Like LoadVars, an XML document can also be loaded from a source by using the XML.load or XML.sendAndLoad methods, as shown here:

```
team_xml.load("mypage.aspx");
```

Once a Flash XML object contains an XML document, its contents can be parsed using several properties and methods of the XML object—we will be examining these methods further in the ASP.NET/Flash XML examples in this chapter.

C# System.Xml namespace

For working with XML documents, C# provides a prebuilt library in the System.Xml namespace. This namespace contains a tremendous amount of tools for creating, reading, and manipulating XML documents—much more extensive than we need to cover for the use of Flash and ASP.NET communication. In this chapter we will cover two very useful classes within this namespace: the XmlTextReader and the XmlTextWriter.

XmlTextReader

As we'll discover later in this chapter, when a Flash movie communicates with server-side ASP.NET code using XML, the communicated XML data is sent through the POST variables of a page request. This XML document, upon arrival at the server-side ASP.NET code, will be in the format of a URL-encoded text string. C#'s XmlTextReader class provides a straightforward method for reading such an XML document so its data can be used in server-side processing.

When talking about XML processing, there is a very wide range of functionality that could be required by a developer. The C# XmlDocument class provides a wide range of functionality for creating, manipulating, and exporting XML documents, but comes with an overhead of being very complicated and memory inefficient. The XmlTextReader class, however, provides a more simplified and efficient, *non-cached*, *forward-only* method of accessing an XML document. Saying that the XmlTextReader is non-cached and forward-only means that as you are using the XmlTextReader to read, line by line, through an XML document, you are unable to go *back* through the data you've already read. Essentially, once you have moved past one line in a document, the XmlTextReader will flush that line from its memory, reducing the overall overhead of XML processing.

Another reason that the XmlTextReader is a very efficient method for processing XML data is because, like the XML object in Flash, the XmlTextReader does not provide *validation* of the XML data it is processing. Validation is the process of comparing an XML document to a Document Type Definition (DTD) file to ensure that the XML data is formatted in accordance with a predefined set of rules. The XmlTextReader does, however, enforce the rules of a well-formed XML document, decreasing the possibility for error in the data processing of the document.

The XmlTextReader has many methods available for reading XML documents, the most relevant of which are shown in Table 6-4. Table 6-5 contains the properties of the current element as selected with an XmlTextReader instance.

Table 6-4. Selected XmlTextReader methods

Method	Description
GetAttribute	Gets the value of an attribute
IsStartElement	Tests if the current node is a start tag
MoveToAttribute	Moves to a specified attribute
MoveToContent	Moves to the next piece of content in the XML document, skipping over whitespace, comments, and other noncontent tags
MoveToElement	Moves to the element that contains the current attribute node
MoveToFirstAttribute	Moves to the element's first attribute
MoveToNextAttribute	Moves to the element's next attribute
Read	Reads the next node in the document

Method	Description
ReadStartElement	Checks that the node is a start element and advances the node to the next element
Skip	Skips the children of the current node

Table 6-5. Properties of the current node in an XmlTextReader

Property	Description
AttributeCount	The number of attributes on the node
BaseUri	The base URI of the node
Depth	The depth of the node in the tree
HasAttributes	Whether the node has attributes
HasValue	Whether the node can have a text value
IsDefault	Whether an attribute node was generated from the default value defined in the DTD or schema
IsEmptyElement	Whether an element node is empty
LocalName	The local name of the node
Name	The qualified name of the node, equal to prefix:LocalName
NamespaceUri	The URI defining the namespace associated with the node
NodeType	The XmlNodeType of the node
Prefix	A shorthand reference to the namespace associated with the node
QuoteChar	The quotation mark character used to enclose the value of an attribute
Value	The text value of the node
XmlLang	The xml:lang scope within which the node resides

Example of using the XmlTextReader

Let's take a look at a simple example of Flash/ASP.NET communication using the Flash XML object and the C# XmlTextReader. In this example, we'll create a user login interface in Flash, which will send an XML document to an ASP.NET page using the Flash XML object's send method.

First, let's create a new ASP.NET project in Visual Studio .NET in a folder called `chapter6`, as shown in Figure 6-1.

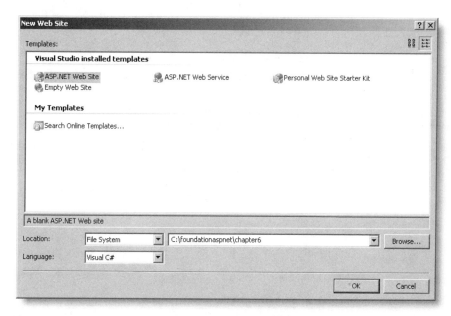

Figure 6-1. Creating a new ASP.NET project in the chapter6 folder

Next, we'll create a new ASP.NET page within this directory, called `loginxml.aspx`, as shown in Figure 6-2.

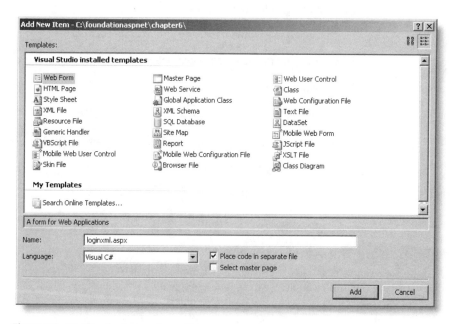

Figure 6-2. Creating the loginxml.aspx file

Now, with the ASP.NET site set up, let's jump into Flash to create a Flash login interface. To do this, I am creating a new Flash file, with a width of 210 pixels and a height of 165 pixels.

Within this new Flash file, I have created the interface shown in Figure 6-3 using the rectangle tool, text input boxes, and the Flash Button component.

In this interface, I have named the first text input box user_txt and the second pass_txt; the latter is a Flash password field. The Submit button I have given an instance name of submitButton.

Figure 6-3. The Flash login interface

The purpose of this interface is, fairly obviously, to receive text input from a user in the form of a username and password. When the Submit button is clicked, we want this textual input to be passed, through the use of an XML document, to a page that we will create in ASP.NET.

First, let's create the code which will handle the Submit button's click event. (Note that, since this is a simple, "nonreplicable" example, I will be placing the ActionScript code in a layer called Actions, rather than in an .as class file.) To handle the click event, it's first necessary to create a listener object that will wait for the Submit button's click event:

```
var SubmitListener:Object = new Object();
SubmitListener.click = function(ev) {
  //  place code to create XML
};
submitButton.addEventListener("click", SubmitListener);
```

Within the function that handles the click event, we want to place code that creates a new XML object that will be sent to our server-side ASP.NET page. In this example, we will first create the XML document as a string, and then load this string into a Flash XML object:

```
SubmitListener.click = function(ev) {
  var login_str:String = new String();
  login_str = "<login>";
  login_str += "<username>"+user_txt.text+"</username>";
  login_str += "<password>"+pass_txt.text+"</password>";
  login_str += "</login>";
  var login_xml:XML = new XML(login_str);
}
```

As you can see, by adding a trace(login_xml); statement, this code will create a simple XML document with the following format:

```
<login>
  <username>name entered in user_txt</username>
  <password>password entered in pass_txt</password>
</login>
```

With this XML object created, the next step is simply to send this object's data using the XML object's send method:

```
login_xml.send("loginxml.aspx", "_blank");
```

In this line, I have instructed the Flash XML object to open the loginxml.aspx page in a new window, through the use of the _blank parameter. In a real-world example, we probably would not want this to happen—which is why we will modify this example later on in the section on XmlTextWriter using the XML object's sendAndLoad method.

With all of this code put together, the first frame of the Actions layer on your timeline should contain the following ActionScript:

```
var SubmitListener:Object = new Object();
SubmitListener.click = function(ev) {
  var login_str:String = new String();
  login_str = "<login>";
  login_str += "<username>"+user_txt.text+"</username>";
  login_str += "<password>"+pass_txt.text+"</password>";
  login_str += "</login>";
  var login_xml:XML = new XML(login_str);
  login_xml.send("http://localhost:21509/chapter6/loginxml.aspx",
➥ "_blank");
};
submitButton.addEventListener("click",SubmitListener);
```

Now that we have the Flash interface created and code generated to handle the Submit button's click event and XML document creation, let's again jump to our server-side code in the loginxml.aspx page—but first, let's save this new Flash movie as login.fla in a folder called Flash within our new website's folder.

In the Design view of the loginxml.aspx page, let's create a very simple interface, used purely for debugging purposes, to see if our Flash/ASP.NET communication is working properly. Using the Visual Studio Toolbox, I have added to the Design view two Label controls to create the interface shown in Figure 6-4.

Figure 6-4. Adding the two label controls

As you'll notice in Figure 6-4, I have named these Label instances lblUsername and lblPassword. Once these Labels have been created, let's create a Page_Load event in the page's code-behind file that will execute when the page is requested. Again, this is most easily done in Visual Studio .NET by double-clicking on the page layout in the Design view, creating the following code:

```
public partial class loginxml_aspx
{   void Page_Load(object sender, EventArgs e)
  {

  }
}
```

Since the Flash XML object sends data through the use of POST variables, we are going to want to create a method for retrieving this data and use this data to create a new XmlTextReader object, which will read through it. In order to accomplish this, it will be necessary to make use of the Form parameter of the familiar Page.Request class, and the UrlDecode method of a class we have yet to experience, Page.Server.

The C# Server object consists of a number of low-level server-side functions, such as Transfer, which performs a function similar to the Response.Redirect method, and MapPath, which determines the physical path name of a file in an ASP.NET directory. (We will be using the Server.MapPath method in the photo gallery example later in this chapter.) Since, as we mentioned, the Flash XML object sends its data as URL-encoded POST variables (*URL-encoded* means that characters that could possibly cause errors on transmission are replaced with their ASCII hexadecimal equivalents), we will need to decode this data into its original state, using the Server object's UrlDecode method.

Using the UrlDecode method is simple, as it requires only one parameter, a string value to decode, and returns as a value the decoded string. For our example, the UrlDecode method can be used with the Request.Form parameter to retrieve any XML data sent through POST variables by using the following syntax:

```
string xString = Server.UrlDecode(Request.Form[0]);
```

When placed into the Page_Load event of the page, this line will create a new string with the URL-decoded value of any POST variables sent to the page (assuming there are POST variables sent to the page; if not this line will generate an error).

With this string created, we are just about ready to create a new instance of the XmlTextReader class—but the XmlTextReader cannot load its XML document directly from a string. Instead we must create an instance of another new class, the System.IO.StringReader class, to pass to the XmlTextReader. On a basic level, the StringReader class simply provides an interface for the XmlTextReader to read a string—and for the use of ASP.NET and Flash, that's about all that's necessary to understand about it!

Using the StringReader class to load a string and then create a new instance of the XmlTextReader is then as simple as this:

```
System.IO.StringReader sr = new System.IO.StringReader(xString);
XmlTextReader xmlReader = new XmlTextReader(sr);
```

And with this XmlTextReader created using XML data passed to the page using POST variable, we are now ready to read some XML! When attempting to read an XML file using the XmlTextReader, one of the most common methods for cycling through the elements within the document is by using the Read method in a while loop, as in the following example:

```
while (xmlReader.Read())
{
  // do something
}
```

This method will allow you to step through the elements of the document, one by one, and test each to determine if it contains the data that you are looking for. Using this method, along with the XmlTextReader's IsStartElement method and Name property, we can effectively read the XML document we have created in Flash, retrieving the values of the username and password as entered in the Flash interface.

```
string username="";
string password="";
while (xmlReader.Read())
{
  if (xmlReader.IsStartElement())
  {
    switch (xmlReader.Name) {
      case "username":
        username = xmlReader.ReadString();
        break;
      case "password":
        password = xmlReader.ReadString();
        break;
    }
  }
}
lblUsername.Text = username;
lblPassword.Text = password;
```

Let's take a look at this code, line by line, to see exactly what is being accomplished:

```
string username="";
string password="";
```

In the first two lines, I have created and initialized two string variables that will be used to hold the value of the username and password as they are extracted from the XML document.

In these lines:

```
while (xmlReader.Read())
{
  if (xmlReader.IsStartElement())
```

we begin reading the XML document, using the while loop. Again, this loop will execute once for each XML element in the document—including end elements. It is for this reason that the line if (xmlReader.IsStartElement()) is used—to make sure that the current element is a start tag rather than an end tag.

In these lines:

```
switch (xmlReader.Name) {
  case "username":
    username = xmlReader.ReadString();
    break;
  case "password":
    password = xmlReader.ReadString();
    break;
```

I am using a switch statement to set the value of the username or password strings based on the name of the current element. If the element has a name of username, then we know that the value of that element will be the username that was passed from the Flash interface, and similarly for the password. To retrieve the value from the XML element, I am using the XmlTextReader's ReadString, method, which reads the value of the element, with the assumption that it is a string value (which it is!).

Finally, for the purpose of this example, I am setting the Text properties of the Label controls we created earlier to display the results of our XmlTextReader's findings:

```
lblUsername.Text = username;
lblPassword.Text = password;
```

If, for some reason, the XmlTextReader cannot find the username or password in the XML document (possibly because it is not in the format we are expecting), the value of the Label's Text property will be blank.

This is all of the code required on the ASP.NET side of the XmlTextReader example code. With this completed, it is necessary to compile the website using the Build Solution command from the Build menu of Visual Studio, as shown in Figure 6-5.

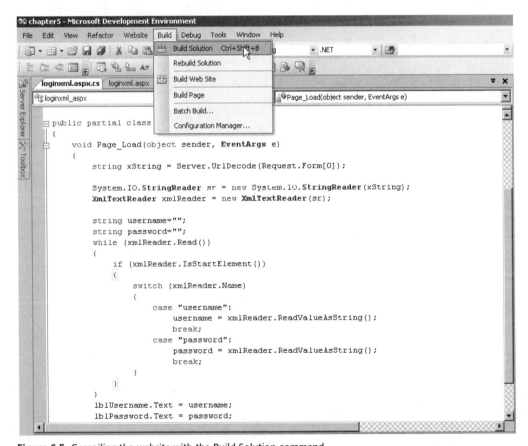

Figure 6-5. Compiling the website with the Build Solution command

And with this, the example is complete, with the exception of one minor tweak. When we created the Flash file, we passed the string "loginxml.aspx" as a parameter to the `login_xml`'s send method. Let's change this to the actual URL that our ASP.NET page will be executing from—the easiest way to determine this if you are using the built-in Visual Developer Web Server in Visual Studio .NET is to simply start your project for the first time and check the URL of the page that is launched. On my development system, this URL will be `http://localhost:21509/chapter6/loginxml.aspx`—so I will change the line in the Flash ActionScript to

```
login_xml.send("http://localhost:21509/chapter6/loginxml.aspx",
               "_blank");
```

Now, with our code complete, let's try testing our example, straight from the Flash IDE, using the Publish Preview command to launch the movie in an HTML page. Figure 6-6 shows this Flash movie launched in a browser, ready to submit.

> Be sure to test the Flash interface in an HTML page, since testing the movie in the Flash debugger will only allow the XML object to send values using GET variables, which will cause an error in our ASP.NET page.

Figure 6-6. A user is ready to submit their details.

When the Submit button is clicked and the data is sent to the ASP.NET page, a new browser is spawned with the result shown in Figure 6-7.

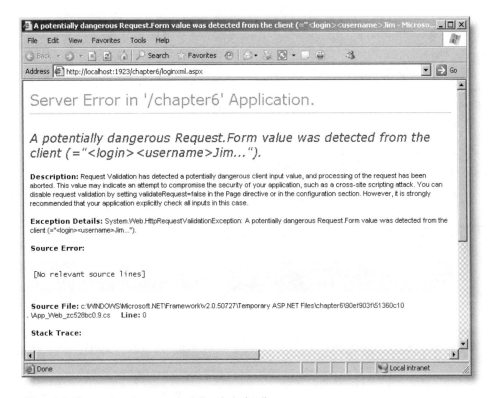

Figure 6-7. The results of a user submitting their details

Ouch—our example did not execute quite as well as planned! This is a result of a security feature built into the ASP.NET framework, and enabled by default. This security feature prevents "script-injection" attacks, in which a malicious user submits data to a website containing tags such as `<script>alert("Hello")</script>`, which could be used to manipulate data within a database. For the use of ASP.NET and Flash, however, we will disable this feature—this type of an attack is not nearly as likely on a page that is not readily exposed to a user's navigation. In order to disable this security feature, we just need to add an entry to the Page tag in the `loginxml.aspx` page, as shown here:

```
<%@ Page Language="C#" ValidateRequest="false"
        CompileWith="loginxml.aspx.cs" ClassName="loginxml_aspx" %>
```

With this line changed and the file resaved, the result of our example file looks a little bit better, as Figure 6-8 shows.

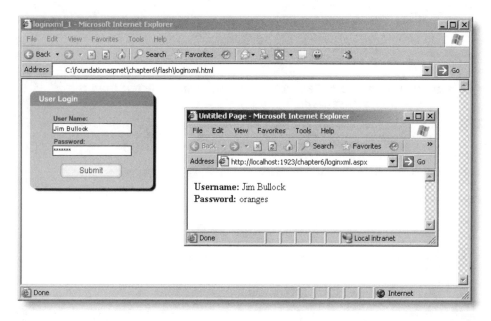

Figure 6-8. The website works as expected.

As you can see, we have successfully created an application that communicates between a Flash front-end and an ASP.NET back-end using XML as its method of communication and the XmlTextReader as the method for reading the XML document sent from Flash to our server-side code. Next, we will investigate a method for sending data back from our ASP.NET code to the Flash movie using the C# XmlTextWriter class.

XmlTextWriter

XmlTextWriter is a C# class that allows for the easy creation of XML documents—and directly pertaining to ASP.NET and Flash, write this document to the *output stream* or page output, which can be read using a Flash XML object's load or sendAndLoad method. XmlTextWriter, like the XmlTextReader class, operates in a forward-only, noncached manner, reducing the overhead of this class on the server-side memory. In many ways, XmlTextWriter makes it easier to create XML documents in C# than in ActionScript. With specific methods for starting documents, creating elements, and adding attributes, XmlTextWriter also reduces the possibility of error when creating XML documents in C#.

Table 6-6 lists a number of XmlTextWriter's methods used to create XML documents.

Table 6-6. Selected XmlTextWriter methods

Method	Description
WriteStartDocument	Used to start creating an XML document. This method will create the first line in an XML document that specifies the document as being an XML document and the type of encoding the document will be using.
WriteStartElement	Creates a new element within an XML document.
WriteElementString	Creates an XML element with specified text content.
WriteAttributeString	Writes an attribute within the current element.
WriteEndElement	Used to close an element created with the WriteStartElement method.
WriteEndDocument	Completes an XML document created using the WriteStartDocument method.
Close	Closes the XML document, writing the contents of the document to a specified location.

Let's take a look at the XmlTextWriter by extending the XmlTextReader login example we walked through earlier. In this example, we'll not only read in the XML document in ASP.NET, but also do a very simple username/password verification, and respond to the Flash movie with an XML-formatted document that can be read by a Flash XML object.

Starting this time from the ASP.NET side, the code we have created in the Page_Load event of the code-behind file can stay unchanged, with the exception of the "debugging" lines we used to output the results of our XmlTextReader to an HTML interface. With these lines removed, the Page_Load event will read as follows:

```
string username="";
string password="";
while (xmlReader.Read())
{
  if (xmlReader.IsStartElement())
  {
    switch (xmlReader.Name) {
      case "username":
        username = xmlReader.ReadString();
        break;
      case "password":
        password = xmlReader.ReadString();
        break;
    }
  }
}
```

After this code, we will add the logic necessary to "validate" the username/password combination and create an XML response indicating whether the user is "authorized." First, let's create an if statement to do the user authorization (in this example, there will only be one valid username/password combination).

```
bool isAuthorized = false;
if ((String.Compare(username, "Jim Bullock")==0) &&
    (String.Compare(password, "oranges")==0))
{
  isAuthorized = true;
}
```

In this code, I have created a new Boolean variable and have given it an initial value of false. If, after our XmlTextReader reads through the XML file, the value of the username variable is found to be Jim Bullock and the password variable is found to be oranges, then the isAuthorized variable will be set to true, indicating that the user is authorized. If any other combination is entered (remember that the String.Compare comparison *is* case sensitive!), the isAuthorized variable will remain false.

Next, let's start creating an XML document that will tell Flash whether or not the user has been authorized. The first step in creating such a document is to create a new instance of the XmlTextWriter class, as in the following code:

```
XmlTextWriter xmlWriter =
    new XmlTextWriter(Response.OutputStream, System.Text.Encoding.UTF8);
```

As you can see, I have passed to the XmlTextWriter's constructor the Response.OuputStream object, allowing the XmlTextWriter to output its contents directly to the page's output. The following parameter, System.Text.Encoding.UTF8, is required to create a new XmlTextWriter, and simply specifies the type of encoding that will be used to create the document.

With the XmlTextWriter successfully created, we can move forward and begin the creation of the document itself with the WriteStartDocument method:

```
xmlWriter.WriteStartDocument();
```

As mentioned earlier in this chapter, this method writes the first line of the XML document, which specifies that the document will be composed of XML content. The lines

```
xmlWriter.WriteStartElement("login");
xmlWriter.WriteAttributeString("authorized", isAuthorized.ToString());
xmlWriter.WriteEndElement();
```

perform the composition of the bulk of our (rather short) XML document. First, the WriteStartElement method is called, writing the start tag for an element with a name of login, which would look similar to <login. Next, I am adding an attribute to that login tag, with a name of authorized and a value of the string representation of the Boolean isAuthorized variable. In the scenario that isAuthorized is true (because the user entered Jim Bullock and oranges), the xmlWriter would now contain <login authorized="true". Finally, since this is all of the data that is necessary to pass back to the Flash movie, the WriteEndElement method closes the login tag, making it ready for delivery as a single-element XML document. The document at this point (with the initial line from the WriteStartDocument call included) looks similar to:

```
<?xml version="1.0" encoding="utf-8"?><login authorized="True" />
```

To complete this document, we just need to add a little cleanup work:

```
xmlWriter.WriteEndDocument();
xmlWriter.Close();
```

Those lines will close out the XML document and send its contents to the page's output stream. But we're not quite done with the ASP.NET end of this example yet. In order for the loginxml.aspx page to return XML data to a Flash movie, the page itself must be configured to have a *content type* of XML rather than HTML. In order to do this, we must go back to the loginxml.aspx page, and in the Source view, remove *all* of the page content except for the first line:

```
<%@ Page ContentType="text/xml" Language="C#"
        ValidateRequest="false" ... %>
```

As you can see, I have added an additional attribute to the Page tag, ContentType. This ContentType tag specifies the page as having a content type of XML data rather than HTML or otherwise.

With that done, we can move to the Flash side of the login form to complete our example! In our Flash movie, we need to set up the XML object we created in the XmlTextReader example now to not only send an XML message with the login information from the user interface, but also to wait for a response from the ASP.NET code and read that response. In order to do this, we will need to replace the login_xml.load call in the first example with a sendAndLoad call and a second, "receiving" an XML object, as shown here:

```
var result_xml:XML = new XML();
login_xml.sendAndLoad("http://localhost:21509/chapter6/loginxml.aspx",
                      result_xml);
```

Much like the LoadVars example in Chapter 3, when we execute the sendAndLoad method from the login_xml object, the XML data that was contained in the login_xml object will be sent to the ASP.NET page and the result_xml object will eagerly await the result. When the result XML is sent from the ASP.NET page, the onLoad event of the result_xml object will fire—which is where we will place our code to determine whether or not the login was successful, as shown here:

```
var result_xml:XML = new XML();
result_xml.onLoad = function(suc) {
  if (suc)
  {
     if (result_xml.childNodes[0].attributes.authorized == "True") {
         // authorized user
         // redirect to another URL!
       } else {
         // unauthorized user!
          }
  }
   else {
      // error in the XML call
   }
};
```

And with that, we have a combination of an XmlTextReader, XmlTextWriter, and Flash XML object being used to communicate between a Flash presentation tier and an ASP.NET logical tier! This login example is a very simple implementation of these technologies—you can easily extend this example to create a user login for a website back-end, protected area, or private image gallery (as you'll see in the next section).

Image gallery using XML

We've seen in this chapter how Flash and ASP.NET can communicate with each other through the use of the Flash XML object and the C# XmlTextReader and XmlTextWriter—now let's take a look at a full example, using these technologies to create a web-based image gallery. In this image gallery application, I'd like to be able to create folders in a directory on my web server, and within these folders, place a number of images (photos, etc.) for my friends and family to view. Then, I'd like to have a Flash interface where someone viewing the application can select a folder and, when the folder is selected, view thumbnail images of the images residing within that folder. Finally, I'd like to be able to click on a thumbnail to open the original high-resolution image in another browser.

Sounds pretty simple, eh? Using Flash and ASP.NET with XML as the communication format, it's not very hard at all! Let's take a look at the basic steps necessary for this application to execute:

1. The Flash movie calls an ASP.NET page using the XML load method.
2. The ASP.NET server-side code searches through an images directory within our site's root for folders that may contain images.
3. In each of those folders, the ASP.NET code will search for image files.
4. For each of the image files, ASP.NET will create a 100X100 "thumbnail" image (if it's not already created), giving this image the same name, but with an addition of _tmb before the extension (myimage.jpg would become myimage_tmb.jpg).
5. The ASP.NET page will generate an XML document describing the location and names of these folders and images and send it back to the Flash interface.
6. The Flash movie, upon loading the XML document, will cycle through the elements, recording the folders and images that reside within these folders.
7. After recording the folder names, the Flash movie will populate a ComboBox with these names for a user to select.
8. When a user selects a folder name from the ComboBox, Flash will place movie clips on the stage that will load the thumbnail images from the selected folder.
9. If a user selects a thumbnail image, the Flash movie will open the full-sized version of that image in a new browser.

Logical tier: ASP.NET server-side code

Since we already have a pretty good idea of what the Flash interface is going to require (an XML file that lists the folders and images on our web server), let's start the process of creating this application from the ASP.NET side. As in the examples earlier in this chapter, let's start out this application by creating a page that generates an XML document by using an XmlTextWriter. As in the previous examples, create a new ASP.NET web form called imagegallery.aspx and add it to your project. I have created this web form in the same chapter6 folder as the other examples in this chapter, but you could also create a new website folder for this example if you'd like.

With this page created, let's take care of some dirty work so we don't forget. Since this page will be returning XML data, as in the XmlTextWriter example earlier in this chapter, we need to remove the HTML code from the .aspx page and add the XML content type to the Page tag, as shown here:

```
<%@ Page ContentType="text/xml" Language="C#"
         CompileWith="imagegallery.aspx.cs"
         ClassName="imagegallery_aspx" %>
```

Again, we will create the Page_Load event for this page by double-clicking on the design interface in Visual Studio. As in the XmlTextWriter example earlier in this chapter, we'll begin this application by creating a new instance of the XmlTextWriter class:

```
using System.Xml;
using System.IO;
...

public partial class imagegallery_aspx
{
  void Page_Load(object sender, EventArgs e)
  {
    XmlTextWriter xmlWriter =
      new XmlTextWriter(Response.OutputStream,
➥ System.Text.Encoding.UTF8);
  }
```

Before we move too far forward with the creation of this XML document, let's stop and define the structure of this document. As we've discussed, we simply need to define folders and images within those folders, so the following XML format should work nicely:

```
<gallery>
  <folder name="name of folder">
    <image>name of image</image>
    <image>name of image 2</image>
  </folder>
  <folder name="name of folder 2">
    <image>name of image</image>
    <image>name of image 2</image>
  </folder>
</gallery>
```

In this example, the document's root element will be the <gallery> element. As you can see, only one of these elements is defined, as is the rule for root elements. Following the <gallery> element will be an unlimited number of <folder> elements, based on the number of folders in the images directory of our web application (more on this momentarily). The <folder> element will also contain a name attribute, which will pass the name of the folder to the Flash application. Within each <folder> element will be an undetermined (although this time limited, as you'll see when we get to the Flash interface) number of <image> elements. The text value of these elements will be the name of the image itself—myimage.jpg for example. And that is it for the XML document definition—again, not complicated, but extremely powerful in its capability to define large amounts of data in a structured manner.

With this definition complete, we can begin the creation of our XML document in C#.

```
xmlWriter.WriteStartDocument();
xmlWriter.WriteStartElement("gallery");
```

Again, the first line, xmlWriter.WriteStartDocument(), simply generates a line which declares that the document will consist of XML data. The following call to the WriteStartElement method writes the start tag for our document's root element, gallery.

At this point, the basic XML document setup is complete and it's time to begin the slightly trickier process of generating the folder and image elements based on the contents of the website's images directory. The first step in this process will be to get a list of the directories within the images directory of our website's root, using the System.IO.Directory namespace's GetDirectories method along with the Server.MapPath method, as shown next. Place this line directly within the Page_Load event handler of your code-behind file:

```
string[] dirs = Directory.GetDirectories(Server.MapPath("~/images"));
```

In this line, the GetDirectories method returns an array of string values, listing the directories that exist within a certain directory—this directory must be specified with its full path, such as C:\foundationaspnet\chapter6, which is why we must make use of the Server.MapPath method. The Server.MapPath method takes, as a parameter, a reference to a directory relative to the current website's root directory. As covered in the Server.MapPath section earlier, the ~ sign in ASP.NET is used to refer to the site root directory, so the reference to Server.MapPath("~/images") is the same as saying "Give me the full directory path of the images directory that resides in my website's root directory."

In order for this call to Directory.GetDirectories to return anything relevant, there must be directories that exist within the images directory in our site root (and the images directory must exist!). Let's create these directories now, as shown in Figure 6-9. The directories I have created are just examples—you can give your directories any names you'd like.

Figure 6-9. The directory structure of the image gallery application

At this point, we will have a new string array, dirs, that will contain the *full* directory paths to each of the directories in our images directory. For my specific example, dirs will contain the following elements (this is just an example, don't put it in your code!):

```
dirs[0] = "C:\foundationaspnet\chapter6\images\Apes\";
dirs[1] = "C:\foundationaspnet\chapter6\images\Cars\";
dirs[2] = "C:\foundationaspnet\chapter6\images\Houses\";
```

With this array created, we'll need to cycle through the elements, creating a new XML element in our XML document for each folder. Then, for each folder, we'll need to make a list of the images that reside within the folder and add those entries to the XML document as well. To cycle through the newly created string array, we'll use the foreach loop, presented earlier in this chapter:

```
foreach (string dirname in dirs)
{
```

The foreach loop, in this example, will execute the contents of its codeblock once for each string entry in the dirs array. When the code in the foreach codeblock is being executed, the value of the current string will always be referred to by dirname:

```
xmlWriter.WriteStartElement("folder");
xmlWriter.WriteAttributeString("name",
  dirname.Substring(dirname.LastIndexOf("\\") + 1));
```

Inside of the foreach codeblock, the first thing we'll do is create the start tag for a new folder XML element, followed by writing the name of the folder as an attribute of the <folder> element. In order to retrieve just the name of the folder that resides in the images directory, it is necessary to perform a little bit of slicing on the current directory path, dirname (that's because dirname currently contains a full path, not just the short name of the directory). The directory's name can be extracted from the full path by simply taking a substring of the full path, starting from one character past the last occurrence of a \ character—essentially removing everything from the path except the highest-level directory.

At this point, if we could take a sneak peek at our XML document, it would look like this:

```
<?xml version="1.0" encoding="utf-8" ?>
<gallery>
  <folder name="Apes">
```

Looks good so far! The next step in our application will be to get a list of all of the files within the current directory (the Apes directory in this case). If you haven't already, you'll want to save some .jpg image files into this directory. (As of Flash 8, Flash now supports dynamic loading of .png, .jpg, and .gif files, any of which can be used in this example.) In my Apes directory, I have saved five images, as shown in Figure 6-10.

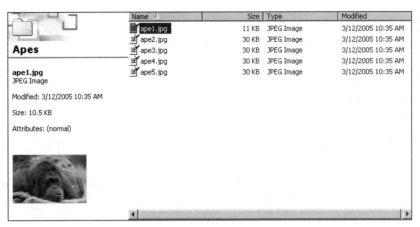

Figure 6-10. The five saved images in the Apes directory

Similar to retrieving a list of the directories within a directory, in order to get list of the images that reside within in a directory, we can use the `Directory.GetFiles` method, which returns an array of strings, as shown here:

```
string[] files = Directory.GetFiles(dirname, "*.jpg");
```

This method will return, again, the *full path* of each of the files within this directory, and with the `.jpg` extension specified, will only return the files that have a `.jpg` extension (just in case there are some imposter files in our directories!). Again, like the directory array, we can loop through this array of file names using the `foreach` loop:

```
foreach (string filename in files) {
```

It is at this point in our application that we must do some extra legwork. In our image gallery Flash presentation tier, we do not want to have to load all of the full-sized images in order to display a folder's contents to the user—it makes more sense to just load a thumbnail of the full-sized image and load the full-sized image when a thumbnail is selected. In order to do this, we're going to do some server-side image manipulation using the `System.Drawing.Image` namespace.

Let's take a look at the steps that we'll need to execute in order to do server-side thumbnail generation of the files in our directories:

1. Get an array of the files in a directory.
2. For each file, check to see if it is already a thumbnail—we'll know it's a thumbnail if the file name contains the `_tmb` characters, which we're going to insert into the file names of our thumbnail images.
3. If it's not a thumbnail (it's a full-sized image), check to see if a thumbnail of this image already exists (we've already created it).
4. If it doesn't exist, we want to create a new 100×100 thumbnail of this image, saved with `_tmb` *before* the `.jpg` file extension (again, `myimage.jpg` would become `myimage_tmb.jpg`).

In our code, we've already accomplished the first step of getting the array of files within each directory, so we can move ahead to the second step of checking to see if the current file *is a thumbnail* (in which case we don't need to put it in the XML document):

```
if (filename.IndexOf("_tmb") == -1) {
```

Again, using the IndexOf method, we can test to see if the file name contains the characters _tmb—if it does not, IndexOf("_tmb") will return -1, and we'll know that the current file is not a thumbnail image.

Once we know that the current file we are dealing with is not a thumbnail image, we'll need to perform step 3—checking to see if the thumbnail image for this file has already been created (we surely do not want to create a thumbnail image for each file every time this page is called!). Since we know what the name of the thumbnail file would be, we can test for its existence using the File.Exists method, as shown here:

```
string thumb = filename.Replace(".", "_tmb.");
if (!System.IO.File.Exists(thumb)) {
```

By using the string's Replace method, we have created a new string variable, thumb, which will contain the name of the thumbnail file for the current full-sized image, and by testing for the existence of this file, we know whether or not we need to create a thumbnail image for this file:

```
if (!System.IO.File.Exists(thumb)) {
    // create a new image instance by loading the full sized image
    System.Drawing.Image img = System.Drawing.Image.FromFile(filename);
    // create a 100X100 thumbnail of that image
    img = img.GetThumbnailImage(100, 100,
                                this.ThumbnailCallback, IntPtr.Zero);
    // save this thumbnail to the filename with the "_tmb" inserted
    img.Save(thumb, System.Drawing.Imaging.ImageFormat.Jpeg);
}
```

As you can see, image manipulation using C# is pretty easy because of the powerful classes included with the .NET class library. Let's take a look at these thumbnail creation steps, line by line. In this line

```
System.Drawing.Image img = System.Drawing.Image.FromFile(filename);
```

we are creating a new instance of the System.Drawing.Image object, which can be used to create, load, manipulate, and get information about images. In this application, we are loading an image from an already existing image, by passing the image's file name to the Image.FromFile method.

With the new Image object created, we can create a thumbnail of that image by using the Image object's GetThumbnailImage method:

```
img = img.GetThumbnailImage(100, 100,
                            this.ThumbnailCallback, IntPtr.Zero);
```

which returns a new Image object with the dimensions we specify. In this example, we'll make the thumbnail images for each image 100X100—this will NOT create a thumbnail scaled properly to the proportions of every image. For example, if the source image is 800X600 and a thumbnail is created at 100X100, the image will appear slightly "squished" because the width and height have both been scaled to 100 pixels (it will work perfectly with images with an equal width and height). If you'd like to try creating properly scaled thumbnail images, there are several third-party ASP.NET components for doing this, and it can also be accomplished by using more advanced features of the Image object.

There are a couple of tricky parameters that we have to pass to the GetThumbnailImage method: this.ThumbnailCallback and IntPtr.Zero. These parameters, although not actually used by the .NET code, *are essential*! It is also necessary to create a ThumbnailCallback method in this page, outside the Page_Load event handler, shown here:

```
private bool ThumbnailCallback()
{
  return false;
}
```

It is not necessary to know anything about the this.ThumbnailCallback or the IntPtr.Zero parameters, other than that they are necessary for the GetThumbnailImage method to execute.

Finally, the new thumbnail image can be saved as a file by using the image's Save method, specifying the name of the file to save to, as well as the ImageFormat we would like to save as, in this case, .jpg:

```
img.Save(thumb, System.Drawing.Imaging.ImageFormat.Jpeg);
```

And that's all the code that's necessary to create a thumbnail image for each file in each directory within our site's images directory! Again, because of the logic we have implemented, the thumbnail for each image will only be created the first time the page is requested, cutting down on the server-side resources needed. With the thumbnail created, the next step in our C# code is to add the name of the image to our XML document:

```
// add the file to the XML document
string shortFilename =
   filename.Substring(filename.LastIndexOf("\\") + 1);
xmlWriter.WriteElementString("image", shortFilename);
```

Again, to retrieve just the name of the image file (and not the entire file path), we can use the Substring method of the string object, retrieving the string starting from the last instance of the \ character. In this case, for the image XML element, we can make use of the WriteElementString method, which will create a new XML element containing a text value of the image's name, as shown in the example here:

```
<image>ape1.jpg</image>
```

Essentially, at this point, we are done with the creation of our XML document—all we need to do is some cleanup work, closing the created XML start tags we have created. The completed Page_Load codeblock is shown here:

```
void Page_Load(object sender, EventArgs e)
{
  XmlTextWriter xmlWriter =
    new XmlTextWriter(Response.OutputStream,
➥ System.Text.Encoding.UTF8);
  xmlWriter.WriteStartDocument();
  xmlWriter.WriteStartElement("gallery");

  string[] dirs = Directory.GetDirectories(Server.MapPath("~/images"));
  foreach (string dirname in dirs)
  {
    xmlWriter.WriteStartElement("folder");
    xmlWriter.WriteAttributeString("name",
      dirname.Substring(dirname.LastIndexOf("\\") + 1));

    string[] files = Directory.GetFiles(dirname, "*.jpg");
    foreach (string filename in files)
    {
      if (filename.IndexOf("_tmb") == -1)
      {
        string thumb = filename.Replace(".", "_tmb.");
        if (!System.IO.File.Exists(thumb))
        {
          System.Drawing.Image img =
            System.Drawing.Image.FromFile(filename);
          img =
            img.GetThumbnailImage(100, 100,
                                  this.ThumbnailCallback, IntPtr.Zero);
          img.Save(thumb, System.Drawing.Imaging.ImageFormat.Jpeg);
        }
        // add the file to the XML document
        string shortFilename =
          filename.Substring(filename.LastIndexOf("\\") + 1);
        xmlWriter.WriteElementString("image", shortFilename);
      }
    }
    xmlWriter.WriteEndElement();
  }
  xmlWriter.WriteEndElement();
  xmlWriter.WriteEndDocument();
  xmlWriter.Close();
}
```

And with that, we have an ASP.NET page that makes a "map" of the directories and images in the images directory of our website! By executing this page in a browser using Visual Studio .NET, the page shown in Figure 6-11 is displayed in Internet Explorer.

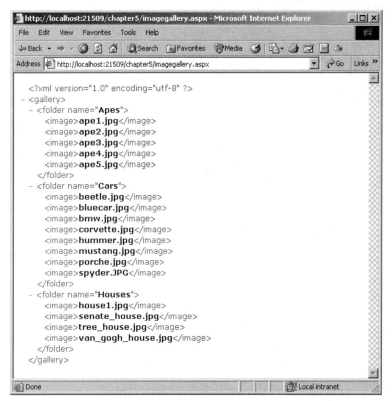

Figure 6-11. An XML map of the gallery directory structure

And with this page executed, if we look again at the files in the Apes directory, we will see that there is now a corresponding thumbnail file for each full-sized image in the directory (see Figure 6-12). You'll also notice that these files are much smaller in size than the original, making it a more pleasant user experience to download for preview.

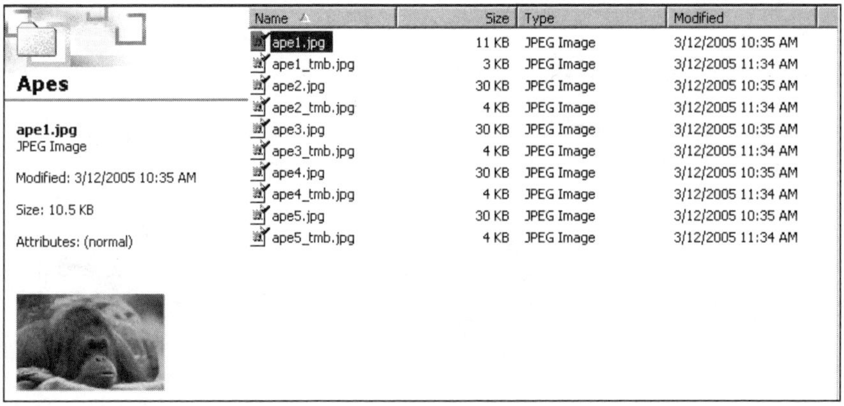

Figure 6-12. Each photograph has a corresponding thumbnail.

Presentation tier: Flash interface

With the majority of the grunt work done by our ASP.NET code, the rest of the tasks left in our image gallery application will involve the retrieval of the XML document created by ASP.NET and the creation of the user interface that will display the thumbnail images for the application's end user. Of course, to accomplish these tasks, we're going to use Flash and its XML object, as shown in examples earlier in this chapter.

First, let's create a new Flash movie with dimensions of 650×600 pixels, named `ImageGallery.fla`, saved within the `flash` directory of our ASP.NET site's root directory. In this Flash movie, let's start by creating a background for displaying the thumbnail contents of the folders that will be displayed in our application. Figure 6-13 shows the background I have created—feel free to be as creative as you'd like with this—it's your gallery!

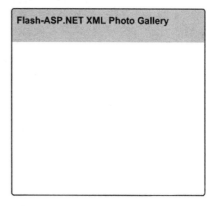

Figure 6-13. The background to the gallery

Next, we'll create a new MovieClip within this Flash file, called `Folder_List`. Make sure to create this MovieClip with Linkage Identifier and AS 2.0 Class settings, as shown in Figure 6-14.

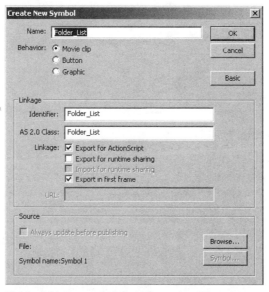

Figure 6-14. Ensure that the Linkage Identifier and AS 2.0 Class settings are correct.

177

It will be within this MovieClip's AS 2.0 class file that the majority of the magic in this application will happen—but before looking at this code, let's create a basic interface that will allow a user to select from a list of folders in our application. Again, you may choose to create the interface differently, but I have created the interface for the Folder_List MovieClip as shown in Figure 6-15.

Figure 6-15. The user can use this interface to select a folder.

In this MovieClip I have dragged an instance of the Flash ComboBox component from the toolbox, which I have named folder_cbo. This ComboBox will be used in our interface to display the list of folders that exist on the server. When a user selects a folder name from the list, the application should display the thumbnail images that exist within that folder.

As I'm sure you noticed, when we created the Folder_List MovieClip, we specified that this MovieClip would have an attached AS 2.0 class. Let's create this .as file now, in the same folder as the ImageGallery.fla file. Since this class is extending the Folder_List MovieClip, we'll begin this .as file as follows:

```
dynamic class Folder_List extends MovieClip {
}
```

Within this class, let's first define the ComboBox instance we have created with the following line of code:

```
var folder_cbo:mx.controls.ComboBox;
```

Next, let's create a few more variables within this class—folder_listener, myUrl, _folders, and _photos—as well as a constructor and onLoad function for this class. (You'll see how these variables will come into play momentarily.)

```
var folder_cbo:mx.controls.ComboBox;
var folder_listener:Object;
var myUrl:String;
var _folders:Array;
var _photos:Array;

private function Folder_List() {
   // Folder_List constructor function
}
private function onLoad():Void {
   // Folder_List onLoad function
}
```

Within the constructor function, let's do some variable initialization as follows:

```
private function Folder_List() {
  _photos = new Array();
  _folders = new Array();
  _global.folderLine = this;
  myUrl = "http://localhost:21509/chapter6/";
  image_xml = new XML();
  image_xml.onLoad = GotXML;
}
```

I have also added a new, global variable here, which will serve as a reference to a Folder_List MovieClip instance—we'll see in a moment how this will come in handy. I have also defined the myUrl variable to be the URL http://localhost:21509/chapter6/, which is the URL of the Chapter 6 example in my Visual Studio Visual Web Developer Web Server. You may need to modify this string in order to suit your application. I have also defined the onLoad event of the image_xml XML object to be a new function called GotXML—again, we'll catch up to this one momentarily. In the meantime, though, let's define some actions in this class's onLoad event which will initiate the loading of the XML generated by our ASP.NET code:

```
private function onLoad():Void {
  // add a "loading" item to the ComboBox
  _global.folderLine.folder_cbo.addItem("-Loading-");

  // start the loading of the XML!
  image_xml.load(myUrl + "imagegallery.aspx");

  // set up the ComboBox change event listener
  folder_listener = new Object();
  folder_listener.change = loadPhotos;
  folder_cbo.addEventListener("change", folder_listener);
}
```

In this function, I have first added an item to the ComboBox instance to indicate to the user of the application that the application is currently loading data. This is especially important because the first time that we run the application after adding new photos to the folders on the web server, the ASP.NET code will take slightly longer to return XML data, as it will have to generate thumbnail images for each of the images in the folders.

In the next line, image_xml.load(myUrl + "imagegallery.aspx"), we are beginning the loading process of the image_xml XML object. Since we have also declared the onLoad event handler of the image_xml object in the class's constructor, this XML object is all set to receive data.

Finally, in the onLoad function, I am setting up the folder_listener object to "listen" for the folder_cbo ComboBox change event. This event will be fired once we have filled the ComboBox with the folder values loaded from the ASP.NET code and a user selects a value from the ComboBox.

Next, let's create the function GotXML, which will be called when XML data has been loaded from the image_xml object. This function will be doing the majority of the processing in this application and will be in charge of making sense of the XML data sent from ASP.NET. We'll start the function with a very basic test to see if the XML page was loaded successfully. This can be determined by a default Boolean parameter that is passed to the onLoad event of the XML object:

```
private function GotXML(success:Boolean) {
  if (success) {
    // process the XML here!
  }
}
```

Since we now know that the XML document has been successfully passed from ASP.NET to Flash, we can begin "picking apart" the XML document, extracting the relevant data from the document's elements. The first thing that I'd like to do is create a new variable that will represent the first child node in the XML document. This is done since we know that the first node is the <gallery> node, and by creating a new reference to that node directly, we can remove redundant code.

```
var mNode:XMLNode = image_xml.childNodes[0];
```

Next, I'd like to put some initial data into the _folders and _photos arrays that we created in the constructor of our Folder_List class file. At this point, it would probably be a good idea to define exactly what the _folders and _photos arrays will be doing:

- _folders: Array that will hold a list of the folder names. This array will be used as the data source for the folder_cbo ComboBox instance.

- _photos: Two-dimensional array that will hold the photo names for each folder. For example, _photos[2][2] will hold the name of the third photo in the third folder.

With that said, I'm going to push initial values into these arrays to create a nonfunctional Select element in the ComboBox. This element will not perform any purpose, other than helping the user navigate the application. Since we don't want this ComboBox entry to load any images, we are going to push a blank space into the _photos array for this entry:

```
_global.folderLine._folders.push("–Select–");
_global.folderLine._photos.push("");
```

With this simple initialization complete, we can move forward to the control loop that will grab the data from the node elements of the XML document:

```
for (var x = 0; x<mNode.childNodes.length; x++) {
  var fNode:XMLNode = mNode.childNodes[x];
  _global.folderLine._folders[x+1] = fNode.attributes.name;
  _global.folderLine._photos[x+1] = [];
```

In this code, we are creating a for loop that will execute once for each of the child nodes in the mNode XMLNode—this is the equivalent of saying that it will go through each of the folders in the gallery, since we know that each folder is simply a child node of the <gallery> node (which is mNode), as shown here:

```
<gallery> <!-- this is mNode -->
  <folder><!-- this is mNode's first child element --></folder>
  <folder><!-- this is mNode's second child element --></folder>
</gallery>
```

Each time the for loop executes, we are creating a new variable, fNode, that will take on the value of mNode's xth child node. Again, this is done mainly to simplify the code legibility and to reduce redundant code. Since we know that fNode is now a folder element, we can extract the name attribute we created from this element and place it in our _folders array. You'll notice that we're placing this value at the [x+1] index, since we have already pushed a value into the _folders array, –Select–.

In the last line of the previous code, I am initializing the xth element of the _photos array to be a new array itself, ready to hold the photos for each folder.

Once we have the folder name extracted from the XML document, we can proceed to traverse the child nodes of this folder element, extracting the names of the images within the folder:

```
for (var x = 0; x<mNode.childNodes.length; x++) {
  var fNode:XMLNode = mNode.childNodes[x];
  _global.folderLine._folders[x+1] = fNode.attributes.name;
  _global.folderLine._photos[x+1] = [];
  for (var y = 0; y<fNode.childNodes.length; y++) {
    var fPhoto:String = fNode.childNodes[y].childNodes[0].nodeValue;
    var fFull:String =
      _global.folderLine.myUrl+"images/"
➥ +fNode.attributes.name+"/"+fPhoto;
    _global.folderLine._photos[x+1][y] = fFull;
  }
}
```

Again, this is easily accomplished using a for loop, executing once for each child node of the <folder> element. In the case of the image, we have passed the image name using the text value of the node, rather than an attribute, so the value of the image name is recovered using the nodeValue attribute of the node's first child node, as in the following line:

```
var fPhoto:String = fNode.childNodes[y].childNodes[0].nodeValue;
```

With this photo name extracted, we can easily build an exact URL to the image by using the myURL variable we initialized in this class's constructor function, along with the current folder name, as in the following line:

```
var fFull:String =
  _global.folderLine.myUrl+"images/"+fNode.attributes.name+"/"+fPhoto;
```

And with this value successfully extracted, we can create a new entry in the _photos array for each photo within a folder:

```
_global.folderLine._photos[x+1][y] = fFull;
```

With this line, our XML processing is complete—not overly complicated, but very orderly and reliable. With the _folder array full at this point, we have one more step to bind this data to the ComboBox control:

```
_global.folderLine.folder_cbo.dataProvider =
  _global.folderLine._folders;
```

The complete code for the GotXML function is shown here:

```
private function GotXML(success:Boolean) {
  if (success) {
    var mNode:XMLNode = image_xml.childNodes[0];
    _global.folderLine._folders.push("–Select–");
    _global.folderLine._photos.push("");
    for (var x = 0; x<mNode.childNodes.length; x++) {
      var fNode:XMLNode = mNode.childNodes[x];
      _global.folderLine._folders[x+1] = fNode.attributes.name;
      _global.folderLine._photos[x+1] = [];
      for (var y = 0; y<fNode.childNodes.length; y++) {
        var fPhoto:String =
          fNode.childNodes[y].childNodes[0].nodeValue;
        var fFull:String =
          _global.folderLine.myUrl
            + "images/"+fNode.attributes.name+"/"+fPhoto;
        _global.folderLine._photos[x+1][y] = fFull;
      }
    }
    _global.folderLine.folder_cbo.dataProvider =
      _global.folderLine._folders;
  }
  else
  {
    trace("Error loading XML");
  }
}
```

With this code created, let's try testing our Flash movie, loading the XML data from the imagegallery.aspx page for the first time—if you are using the built-in Visual Web Developer Web Server, make sure that it is running at this point! As you can see in Figures 6-16 and 6-17, once the Flash movie has loaded the XML file from our server-side ASP.NET file, the ComboBox is populated with the names of the folders that we created in the website's images directory.

Flash-ASP.NET XML Photo Gallery

Select a Folder: --Loading--   ▼

Figure 6-16. Loading the directories

Flash-ASP.NET XML Photo Gallery

Select a Folder: --Select--   ▼
                    --Select--
                    Apes
                    Cars
                    Houses

Figure 6-17. Choosing a directory

The next step in our application is to create the event handler for the change event of the folder_cbo ComboBox. This event handler will be in charge of determining which folder was selected, placing a new MovieClip onto the stage for each image that exists within that folder, and telling those new MovieClips to load the thumbnail image for a specific image. Before we move to the folder_cbo's change handler, though, let's create the MovieClip that will be used to display the thumbnail images. I will create this MovieClip with an Identifier and AS 2.0 Class of PhotoThumb, as shown in Figure 6-18.

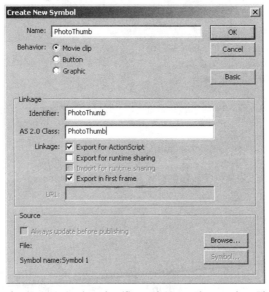

Figure 6-18. Setting Identifier and AS 2.0 Class to PhotoThumb

183

Again, the interface for this ThumbNail MovieClip is very simple—consisting only of a gray 110✕110 rounded rectangle background and a second MovieClip with an instance name of progBar, which will function as a load progress bar. The ThumbNail interface is shown in Figure 6-19.

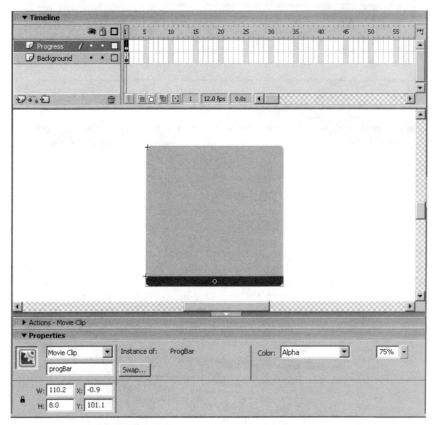

Figure 6-19. The thumbnail interface

And, like the folder_cbo MovieClip, we'll be doing the majority of the work on this MovieClip in a new AS 2.0 class, PhotoThumb.as, which we will save in the same directory as the ImageGallery.fla file:

```
dynamic class PhotoThumb extends MovieClip { .. }
```

Within this class, let's create a few new variables, as well as a constructor function, as shown here:

```
private var _loader:MovieClipLoader;
private var _photo:String;
private var _listener:Object;
private function PhotoThumb() { .. }
```

As you can see, we have created a new MovieClipLoader instance, _loader, which will be used to monitor the progress of the loading of the thumbnail images. The _photo string will contain the actual URL for the photo to load into this specific instance, and the _listener object will be created to handle the loading events of the _loader.

In the PhotoThumb constructor function, we'll also create a new, empty MovieClip, which will be used to load the image into:

```
private function PhotoThumb() {
    // create a new, empty MovieClip that the image will load into
    this.createEmptyMovieClip("loader", 10);
    this["loader"]._x=4;
    this["loader"]._y=4;
```

Next, we'll initialize the variables we created in this class and set up the _loader and _listener variables, as well as creating new events for the onRollOver, onRollOut, and onRelease events of this class:

```
    // intialize a few variables
    _photo = new String();
    _listener = new Object();
    _loader = new MovieClipLoader();
    // set up the MovieClipLoader and listener
    _loader.addListener(_listener);
    _listener.onLoadProgress = GotProgress;
    _listener.onLoadComplete = LoadComplete;
    // start the progress bar with a width of 0
    this["progBar"]._width = 0;
    // set up functions to handle the RollOver,
    // RollOut and Release events
    this.onRollOver = GotRollOver;
    this.onRollOut = GotRollOut;
    this.onRelease = GotClick;
}
```

Listed next are the GotRollOver, GotRollOut, and GotClick functions, which simply use the Zigo engine's alphaTo method to animate the _alpha value of the ThumbImage (in the case of the RollOver and RollOut) or open the full-sized image in a browser, in the case of the Click:

```
private function GotRollOver() {
    this.alphaTo(100, .3);
}
private function GotRollOut() {
    this.alphaTo(60, .2);
}
private function GotClick() {
    getURL(_photo, "_blank");
}
```

> Remember that since we're using the Zigo engine classes, an instance of the engine must be dragged onto the stage in the Flash movie!

And, for the _listener object, we'll set up the functions that handle the LoadProgress and LoadComplete:

```
private function GotProgress(target_mc:MovieClip, bytesLoaded:Number,
                            bytesTotal:Number) {
  target_mc._parent["progBar"]._width = 110*(bytesLoaded/bytesTotal);
}
private function LoadComplete(target_mc:MovieClip) {
  target_mc._parent["progBar"].alphaTo(0, .4);
}
```

The only thing left to define in the ThumbImage class is now the function that will allow the Folder_List class to tell the ThumbImage instance the URL of the image for it to load:

```
public function SetPhoto(photo:String) {
  _photo = photo;
  var loc:Number = _photo.lastIndexOf(".");
  // insert a "_tmb" in before the .jpg extension!
  var thumb:String = _photo.slice(0, loc)+"_tmb"+_photo.substr(loc);
  // tell the MovieClipLoader to start loading the image
  this._loader.loadClip(thumb, this["loader"]);
}
```

The most important line of this function is the line in which we create the local variable, thumb, by inserting a "_tmb" string into the _photo variable, before the .jpg extension. Without this line, we would actually be loading the full image into the thumbnail viewer—would not work out too well!

OK—now that we have the PhotoThumb MovieClip and class created, we can move back to the click handler of the Folder_List's folder_cbo ComboBox. If you remember back in the onLoad function we created for this class, we have already set up the folder_cbo ComboBox change event to call a function called loadPhotos, which we created with these lines:

```
folder_listener = new Object();
folder_listener.change = loadPhotos;
folder_cbo.addEventListener("change", folder_listener);
```

Let's create the loadPhotos event handler now to process the change in the folder selection and place the correct thumbnails on our interface:

```
private function loadPhotos() {
  // record the selected folder index
  var selInd:Number = _global.folderLine.folder_cbo.selectedIndex;
  // create a new Array to temporarily hold the current photos
  var photos:Array = _global.folderLine._photos[selInd];
```

In these lines, we first determine which folder was selected by obtaining the selectedIndex property from the folder_cbo instance. Since the items were placed into the _folders array (which is the folder_cbo's data source) in the same order as they were in the _photos array, we know that the selected index of the folder_cbo instance will reference the index in the multidimensional _photos array that should be displayed. In the following line, we have created a new array, called photos, which will be a one-dimensional array holding the values of the images to load.

Next, we'll perform the task of adding new instances of the ThumbImage MovieClip to the _root time-line, positioning their X and Y coordinates so that there are no more than four images in a row. We have also called the SetPhoto function created in the ThumbImage class to both set the image in the ThumbImage instances, and also to begin the load of the thumbnail image:

```
// xCount is the current count of images in the current row
var xCount:Number = 0;
// yCount is the current count of the number of rows
var yCount:Number = 0;

for (var x = 0; x<photos.length; x++) {
    // create a new name for a MovieClip to attach
    var nn:String = "photo"+x.toString();
    // attach a new instance of PhotoThumb
    // to the _root timeline with this new name
    _root.attachMovie("PhotoThumb", nn, 100+x);
    _root[nn]._x = 0;
    _root[nn]._alpha = 0;
    // start the new MovieClip moving to its destination
    _root[nn].tween(["_x", "_alpha"], [75+(xCount*130), 60],
                    .9, "easeOutBack", x*.2);
    _root[nn]._y = 130+(yCount*130);
    // set the photo in the new PhotoThumb instance
    _root[nn].SetPhoto(photos[x]);
    // increment the counter
    xCount++;
    if (xCount>3) {
        // if there are 3 items in this row, move to the next row
        xCount = 0;
        yCount++;
    }
}
_global.folderLine._photoCount = photos.length;
}
```

As you'll notice, in the last line of this function, we have created a new variable, _photoCount, on the _folderLine timeline. This variable is used to store the number of current images being displayed on the interface so, when a folder is selected, the existing ThumbImage MovieClips can be removed before adding the batch from the next folder. To perform this "clearing" of the photos currently displayed on the interface, let's create one last function within the Folder_List class, ClearOldPhotos, and add a call to this function within the loadPhotos function:

```
private function ClearOldPhotos():Void {
    if (_global.folderLine._photoCount>0) {
        for (var y = 0; y<_global.folderLine._photoCount; y++) {
            var nn:String = "photo"+y.toString();
            _root[nn].removeMovieClip();
        }
    }
}
```

```
private function loadPhotos() {
  ClearOldPhotos();
  ...
}
```

And with that, we have completed our photo gallery! Let's save all files one last time and test the `ImageGallery.fla` file—right within the Flash IDE is fine (see Figures 6-20 and 6-21).

Figure 6-20. The car gallery in the process of loading

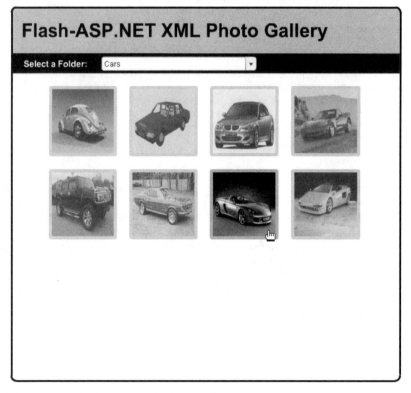

Figure 6-21. Selecting an image in the car gallery

As you can see, our image gallery application now performs all of the functions we defined earlier in the chapter:

1. Retrieving a list of directories and image files from the server's `images` directory
2. Generating a thumbnail image for each of these image (if there isn't already one created)
3. Creating an XML document that lists all of the directories and images
4. Loading this XML document into Flash
5. Parsing this XML document and creating a list of the folders that exist on the server
6. Displaying the thumbnail images of the files located in a folder when that folder is selected
7. Opening the full-sized image when a thumbnail is selected

Now, all you have to do is add images!

Summary

In this chapter, we've covered a lot of material—ranging from C# arrays to thumbnail generators. We've also covered the method of ASP.NET/Flash communication using XML documents, and we've seen the power of this communication in the image gallery example. In the next chapter, we'll take a look at how XML can be used in a slightly different way, web services, to communicate between ASP.NET and Flash, and also how XML web services can be used to communicate with applications from around the world.

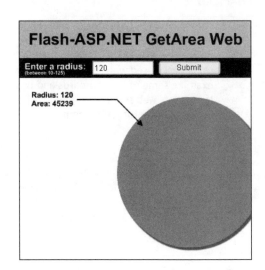

Chapter 7

WEB SERVICES

What this chapter covers:

- The concept of web services
- Web service standards
- Creating a web service using ASP.NET
- Calling a web service method from Flash

Now that we've learned some of the tricks of Flash and ASP.NET communication using the Flash XML object and ASP.NET XML classes, let's advance a step further and look at Flash and ASP.NET interaction using XML-based web services. In this chapter we'll learn about the concept of web services and briefly examine some of the standards and protocols related to web service technologies. We'll then see how to create a web service using ASP.NET and how to invoke methods of this service using the Flash Web Service Connector component.

> *The Flash Web Service Connector component is only available in Flash Professional editions. If you only have access to the Flash Standard edition (or a previous version of Flash), the Flash Professional 30-day trial can be downloaded from* www.macromedia.com/downloads/.

Introducing web services

Throughout the history of computing, programmers have experimented with technologies and exchange formats that would allow applications created using different programming languages, existing in different physical locations, to "talk" with each other, allowing one application to make use of resources created by another. While there have been many formats and methods designed to accomplish such tasks, web services have recently emerged as a standard format for this exchange, making use of a universal, XML-based protocol for communication and the far-reaching power of the HTTP protocol. Web services not only allow developers to create new applications that can be accessed by clients from around the world, but also extend existing applications, thus giving developers access to legacy functionality never before possible.

To get a better idea of what this means, let's take a look at how Amazon.com has used web services to extend the ability of third-party developers, like you or me, to access the Amazon databases. In the past, before Amazon.com implemented web services, many people making use of Amazon.com to sell their products did not have an easy means of monitoring their product on the Amazon site. A publisher, for example, who wanted to monitor the sales and reviews of their books would have to do so by creating a custom application that performed "screen scraping" to extract data from HTML pages. This is a very poor method for obtaining data, and the Amazon experience for the publishers was, in many cases, not up to par.

Amazon also obtains a large portion of sales from its associate sales vendors. These people make a percentage on Amazon product sales by referring visitors to the Amazon.com site. Before web services, these vendors had no easy way to get lists of Amazon.com products or perform searches on the gigantic Amazon.com product databases—features that would increase their sales, and the sales of Amazon.com overall. Figure 7-1 shows the relationship of Amazon.com to its affiliates and publishers.

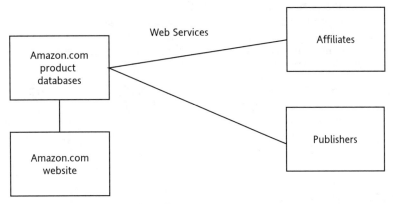

Figure 7-1. Amazon.com web services

With the inception of web services, Amazon.com was able to solve these two problems for publishers and affiliates and effectively increase their potential number of sales by giving people a tremendous amount of access to their products. Amazon.com web services are free and require only an account sign-up. Using web services, developers can now create applications that grab up-to-the-minute information from the Amazon.com product databases, perform product searches, and find product vendors. An example of such an application is the SellerEngine software shown in Figure 7-2.

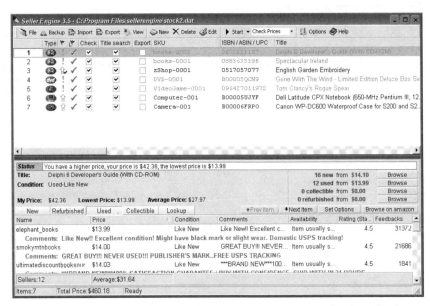

Figure 7-2. Amazon web services allow developers to access Amazon data in applications.

The desktop application shown in Figure 7-2 allows Amazon.com merchants to pull information quickly and easily for products, create new Amazon.com listings, and create item alerts—a far cry from the "screen scraping" applications available before Amazon web services. More information on the SellerEngine is available at www.sellerengine.com.

The most important concept to keep in mind is that developers were creating custom, inferior applications to help them sell Amazon.com products even though Amazon.com had, in its databases, all of the information those developers needed—they just didn't have a way to let the developers safely access it. By implementing web services, Amazon.com was able to extend their existing data to the developers, eliminating the need for the developers to "reinvent the wheel."

To clear the road before we move forward, I should point out that in the Flash/ASP.NET world, web services are *created* or *published* using ASP.NET and *consumed* by either Flash or ASP.NET (Flash does not create web services). In this chapter, we'll take a look at some examples of ASP.NET as a web service publisher with Flash as a consumer, and in the next chapter, we'll see how ASP.NET can become both a consumer and a publisher in the same application.

Web service standards

Like Ajax or ASP.NET, web services are not a specific technology in themselves, but rather a collection of standards that, when combined, create a technology. It is because of the fact that web services consist of universally accepted standards that their use is so widely accepted. These standards are the core of the common "language" that allows applications of many types to communicate using web services.

SOAP

When talking about web services, one of the most common terms you'll hear is SOAP. SOAP, or **S**imple **O**bject **A**ccess **P**rotocol, is a lightweight protocol often used to exchange information in web service operations (and, as a matter of fact, *is* used by Flash and ASP.NET). SOAP is an industry standard that uses XML to encode Remote Procedure Calls (RPCs). RPC refers to the action of an application (in this case, created in Flash) requesting methods from a remote application (in this case created in ASP.NET, residing on a web server), and receiving data back from that application without the need to understand the details of the network residing between the two applications.

SOAP, in the case of ASP.NET web services, is exchanged over HTTP, the same way that HTML web pages are. (The reason I say "in the case of ASP.NET web services" is because SOAP is not *required* to function over HTTP—SOAP doesn't specify the mode of transportation, just the way the message is constructed—as a simple XML file.) Because SOAP is exchanged over HTTP, it is an extremely powerful format, allowing it to function through "network roadblocks" like firewalls. Many other technologies that attempt to accomplish RPCs use methods that become blocked by firewalls and other network security measures, thus limiting their compatibility. (All of the methods for Flash and ASP.NET communication that we're investigating in this book use HTTP for communication. Another method for Flash/ASP.NET communication, the XML Socket Server, uses other standards that can encounter these firewall-related problems.)

Sound a bit complicated? Stated much more simply, SOAP can be thought of as an envelope in which you can place a message written in XML, allowing that XML message to be correctly interpreted by its recipient. And, to make life easier, when using Flash and ASP.NET web services, you won't ever have to "write" anything using SOAP, or even the XML message that the SOAP envelope encloses—Flash and ASP.NET take care of this work for you! That's one of the most obvious differences you'll see between the use of web services and the XML object, as in Chapter 6—with web services, it is not necessary for a developer to serialize and deserialize data that needs to be communicated. These functions are built into the web services framework of both ASP.NET and Flash, allowing you to focus more on the application logic and less on the extraction of data.

WSDL

WSDL is another acronym in the world of web services; it stands for **W**eb **S**ervices **D**escription **L**anguage. WSDL files are used to describe the types of messages that the methods of a web service will send and receive. WSDL files are again created in XML to provide a format that can be universally understood by any web service client. An example of a WSDL file (in pseudocode, rather than XML) would say something like this:

Hello, I'm a web service named "Flash Service." I have several methods that are available for your use:

- **ComputeDistance:** This method takes two parameters, zipcode1 and zipcode2, as integers and returns an integer that specifies the number of miles between zipcode1 and zipcode2.

- . . .

In short, that's exactly what a WSDL file does; it describes the features of the web service to any potential web service clients. Trying to create or read a WSDL file directly is not as easy as this example, though. The actual XML description of the web service can become very complicated, since it is describing a large amount of data. Lucky for us, ASP.NET and Flash again take care of both the creation and the reading of WSDL files, leaving us with an easy-to-read service description. In the next "HelloWorld" example, we'll see how WSDL files come into play and how easy it is to create them in ASP.NET.

Creating an ASP.NET web service

Creating an XML web service in Visual Studio .NET is a simple task—as a matter of fact, "ASP.NET Web Service" is one of the default website templates in Visual Studio .NET! In this example, we'll take a look at how to create a very basic web service in Visual Studio with a method that performs the traditional "HelloWorld" example, and a slightly more complicated "GetArea" method that will compute the area of a circle, given the circle's radius. Once we have created this service, we'll explain how to call it from Flash using the Web Service Connector component supplied by Flash Professional.

The steps needed to create an ASP.NET web service are very similar to those used to create the ASP.NET website projects in the previous chapters. Our first step is to start a new website project in Visual Studio .NET. This time, instead of selecting ASP.NET Web Site as the project type, select ASP.NET Web Service, as shown in Figure 7-3. I have created this project in a new folder called chapter7 in the foundationaspnet folder of my C: drive. *Again, be sure to select Visual C# as the project type or you'll end up getting a web services project set up for VB .NET!*

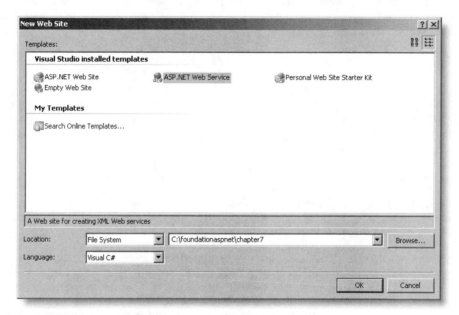

Figure 7-3. Creating a new web service project in Visual Studio .NET

Once I click OK, Visual Studio will begin a new web project in the chapter7 directory, creating the default App_Code and App_data directories, and a file with an extension that you may not have seen before, Service.asmx. This file is the "default" web service file that Visual Studio has created for you; the .asmx extension is the standard ASP.NET web service file extension. You'll also notice that, instead of displaying this page's .cs source file "behind" the page in Visual Studio's Solution Explorer, this web service's code-behind files are, by default, stored in the App_Code directory of your site's root, as shown in Figure 7-4.

Figure 7-4. The web service's code-behind files are stored in the App_Code directory.

This `.cs` file stored in the `App_code` directory instead of the root works exactly the same way as the code-behind model for `.aspx` pages—the only difference you'll notice is that the CodeBehind attribute for the page is simply set to reference the `.cs` file in this directory. Take a look at the HTML view of the `Service.asmx` file—if you don't already have `Service.asmx` open in Visual Studio .NET, you can access it by simply double-clicking on the file within the Solution Explorer.

```
<%@ WebService Language="C#" CodeBehind="~/App_Code/Service.cs"
               Class="Service" %>
```

In this line, you'll also notice that, instead of the `<%@ Page` tag used to initiate `.aspx` pages, ASP.NET web services start with the `<@ WebService` tag. This tag indicates to the ASP.NET processor that the page will need to output XML data instead of HTML.

Next, let's open up the `Service.cs` file by opening the `App_Code` folder, then double-clicking the file in Solution Explorer. In this file, you'll see that Visual Studio .NET has already created some C# code for us, to help get us started creating web services:

```
using System;
using System.Web;
using System.Web.Services;
using System.Web.Services.Protocols;

[WebService(Namespace = "http://tempuri.org/")]
[WebServiceBinding(ConformsTo = WsiProfiles.BasicProfile1_1)]
public class Service : System.Web.Services.WebService
{
    public Service () {

        //Uncomment the following line if using designed components
        //InitializeComponent();
    }

    [WebMethod]
    public string HelloWorld() {
        return "Hello World";
    }

}
```

Let's take a look at this code to see the difference between a web services project and a website project:

```
using System.Web;
using System.Web.Services;
using System.Web.Services.Protocols;
```

In these lines, three namespaces are included into this file: System.Web, System.Web.Services, and System.Web.Services.Protocols. (Namespaces are explained in Chapter 3.) As in ASP.NET website projects, the System.Web namespace contains the lowest-level support for creating web-based projects. This namespace is typically included in nearly every web-based project, including web pages and web services. You'll notice that the next namespace, System.Web.Services, is a sub-namespace to the System.Web namespace. The System.Web.Services namespace generally contains the classes necessary to create web services in ASP.NET. This namespace will be present in any ASP.NET web service application. The System.Web.Services.Protocols namespace consists of the classes that define the protocols used to transmit data across the Internet during the communication between web service clients and web services created using ASP.NET.

Next, the line

```
[WebServiceBinding(ConformanceClaims=WsiClaims.BP10,
                   EmitConformanceClaims = true)]
```

which might look rather confusing, is, in essence, telling a consumer of the web service that this service will be conforming to a standard for web service methods. This standard is created to make web services more interoperable—to make them all speak the same language. For use in our applications, this value can remain unchanged. More information on this topic can be found at http://msdn.microsoft.com/library/default.asp?url=/library/en-us/dnsvcinter/html/wsi-bp_msdn_landingpage.asp.

The line

```
public class Service : System.Web.Services.WebService {
```

is used to create a new class named Service. If you remember the HTML view of the Service.asmx file, the first line of that file specified that the class containing the code-behind for the web service be named Service:

```
<%@ WebService Language="C#" CodeBehind="~/App_Code/Service.cs"
               Class="Service" %>
```

This Service class, used to create the methods enclosed within a web service, *inherits* from the System.Web.Services.WebService class, meaning that it will contain all of the functionality of this class—making it a functional web service!

In this codeblock:

```
[WebMethod]
public string HelloWorld() {
    return "Hello World";
}
```

our first web service method is created for us. This method does not look any different from the methods we've looked at in the typical ASP.NET pages, with the exception of the first line, [WebMethod]. This line is a very important one—it is used to tell the service that we are creating a method that should be published as an accessible web method. We'll get a better idea in a moment exactly what this means.

The lines following this [WebMethod] declaration simply create a new method named HelloWorld, which takes no parameters and returns the string value "Hello World". Again, this method is preceded by a [WebMethod] tag; therefore, it will create an accessible web service method with this functionality.

And that's it! Without doing a bit of work, we have created our first ASP.NET web service with a single method, HelloWorld. Let's take a look at this service in a browser to get an idea of what has actually been created. Starting a web services project using the Visual Web Developer Web Server is done in the same way that a website project is started—by clicking the Start arrow in the Visual Studio .NET interface, pressing the F5 key, or selecting Start from the Debug menu in Visual Studio .NET. Starting this project will, by default, launch the Service.asmx page in a web browser, as shown in Figure 7-5.

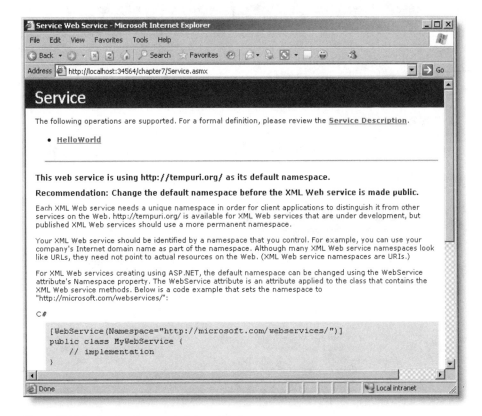

Figure 7-5. Viewing Service.asmx in Internet Explorer

Sure doesn't look like anything we've created, does it? Actually, this page is just a templated visual representation of a web service page, used to display human-friendly information about the web service and its methods. This page is never actually used by a web service client (such as Flash) that would connect to this service—it's just for human use.

The first, and one of the most important, lines that is displayed on this page is the first in the upper white section of the page. In this line, you'll see the Service Description link. This is a link to the WSDL file for this web service; you must know this location when you want to use the service from a client created in Flash or any other technology. As you can see in Figure 7-6, the location of the WSDL file for this specific web service is `http://localhost:34564/chapter7/Service.asmx?WSDL`.

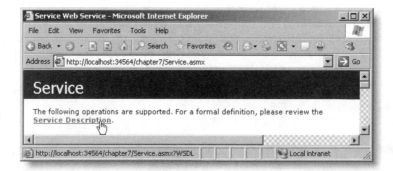

Figure 7-6. Selecting the Service Description link

Selecting this link will display the XML WSDL file for this web service, as shown in Figure 7-7. (I've minimized most of the sections of this WSDL file since even a simple web service like this one has a very long WSDL file, the details of which are not important at this point.)

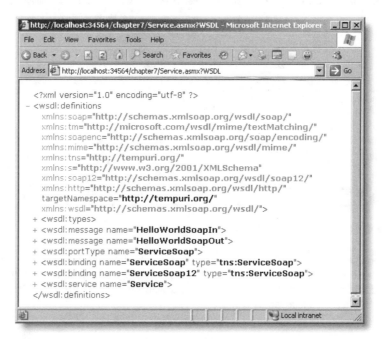

Figure 7-7. Viewing the Service.asmx WSDL file

This WSDL file, as mentioned earlier in this chapter, is not too much help for a human reader as it is very complicated and contains many prototype-specific instructions. Its details are, however, very important for a client preparing to execute one of the methods of the service.

Returning to the Service.amx file (you can get to this file again by simply hitting your browser's back button), the next important detail on this page is the "advertisement" of the methods that are presented by this web service. In this case, the HelloWorld method is the only method available and appears on the screen as an underlined link. Selecting this link will bring up the description of the HelloWorld method of this web service, as shown in Figure 7-8.

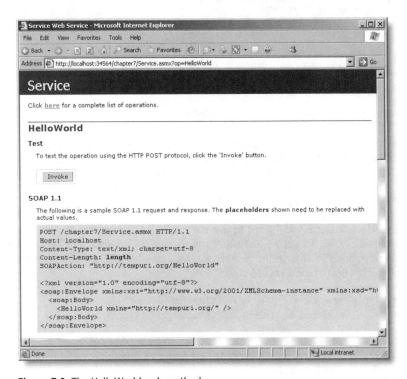

Figure 7-8. The HelloWorld web method

On this page are two interesting pieces of information—a button labeled Invoke, used to execute (test) the method, and a list of methods that can be used to call the method from a software client. The first entry on this list is SOAP, as you can see in Figure 7-6. This is the method that we will be using to call our ASP.NET web services when we set up our Flash client. Underneath the SOAP heading, ASP.NET has listed the SOAP Request and Response headers that are used in this web service method. These Request and Response headers are an example of a SOAP message, as mentioned earlier in the chapter. Again, this information is not necessary for us to create our ASP.NET/Flash application, but it is essential for the behind-the-scenes duties that the Flash Web Services connector will be performing when communicating with this web service.

Next, let's try clicking the Invoke button to execute this method of the web service. (Note that this Invoke button is only available when accessing the web service from your local computer—if someone is accessing the same page from a remote location, the Test section of the service, including the Invoke button is, by default, removed.) Figure 7-9 shows the output of the HelloWorld method.

Figure 7-9. Results of testing the HelloWorld web method

And with that, we have successfully executed our first web service method! As you can see, the service has returned the string "Hello World", enclosed in an XML document with some extra descriptive information. This tag currently contains the return data type of the method, string, as well as the default namespace for the web service, http://tempuri.org. Let's go back to the code for our web service and change this namespace so it better describes the location of the service we are creating.

When creating this namespace, you'll want to use the actual location of the domain you will be publishing your web service on. (If you're just using the service on localhost for testing purposes, any namespace will work fine.) To change the namespace, we'll need to add a new line to the Service.cs file, before the declaration of the Service class:

```
[WebService(Namespace = "http:/www.friendsofed.com/")]
public class Service : System.Web.Services.WebService {
```

This Namespace attribute is one of several attributes that can be used to describe the web service when published. Let's also add a Description attribute, used to give a human-readable description of the service:

```
[WebService(Namespace = "http:/www.friendsofed.com/",
Description = "An ASP.NET web service created in Chapter 7
➥ of Foundation ASP.NET for Flash!")]
```

And, let's also add a Description attribute to the [WebMethod] tag created to specify the HelloWorld method as an accessible web method:

```
[WebMethod (Description="Returns the string 'Hello World'")]
    public string HelloWorld() {
```

And with these changes complete, let's test the service again by pressing *F5* in Visual Studio .NET; Figure 7-10 shows the result.

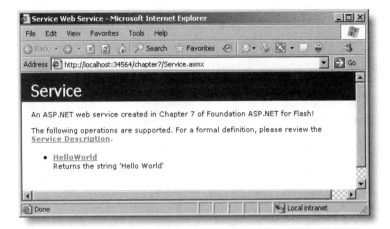

Figure 7-10. Adding a description to the HelloWorld web method

A much more legible and descriptive interface to our web service! Although these changes are not essential for creating a web service, they do make the service easier for you or another developer to understand—similar to code commenting. Now, if we select the HelloWorld link and hit the Invoke button, you'll notice that the result no longer contains the http://tempuri.org domain, but instead the domain you have placed in your web service Namespace attribute, as shown in Figure 7-11.

Figure 7-11. Results of changing the web service namespace

Creating the GetArea web method

Now, let's take what we've learned in dissecting the HelloWorld method and create our own method to be published as a web service. We'll make this service fairly simple, like the HelloWorld example, but in this method, we'll take in a parameter and, after manipulating that parameter, return a result. To be more specific, we'll create a method that returns the area of a circle when passed a value of that circle's radius.

Let's start this method by creating a new [WebMethod] tag similar to that in the HelloWorld method, but with a different description (I'm creating the code for this method right underneath the HelloWorld code):

```
[WebMethod (Description = "Takes a circle's radius as a parameter
➥ and returns the area of that circle")]
```

Next, let's create a method called GetArea, which takes a double value as a parameter and also returns a double value. In this method, we'll make use of the System.Math.PI constant and the Math.Pow method to compute the area of a circle (the Math.Pow method is used to raise a number to a given power):

```
public double GetArea(double radius)
{
    return Math.Pow(radius, 2) * System.Math.PI;
}
```

And with that, we've created our first web service method on our own. This service, unlike the last, will take an input parameter and return a value based on that parameter—providing a more useful function than the simple HelloWorld method. Figure 7-12 shows this method as published in a browser by ASP.NET.

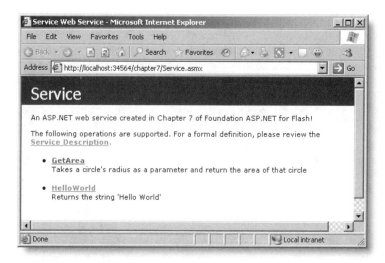

Figure 7-12. Web methods in Service.asmx

As shown in Figure 7-12, the Service.asmx file has now added an entry for the GetArea method we just created, with that method's description listed below it. When we select the GetArea link, the GetArea method's descriptive page appears, but this time with a new text input box, used to input a parameter used to test the method, as shown in Figure 7-13.

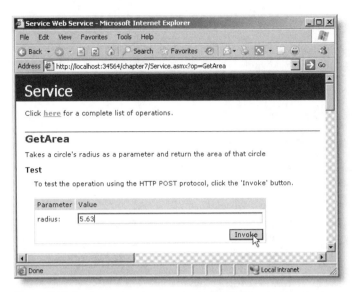

Figure 7-13. Passing an input parameter to the GetArea web method

This input box is used to input the radius parameter to the GetArea method. If the method we wrote involved multiple parameters, this page would contain multiple text input boxes for testing the method. Again, these input boxes, along with the Invoke button, only appear when we are viewing the web service from the localhost domain and are not visible when the page is viewed from a remote location.

As you can see in Figure 7-13, I have entered a value of 5.63 (a valid double value) into this radius input box and, by clicking the Invoke button, you'll see that our GetArea web method returns the area of a circle with radius 5.63 (see Figure 7-14).

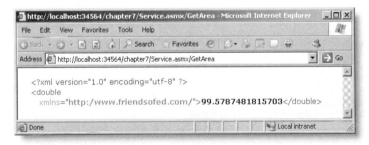

Figure 7-14. Results of the GetArea method

> Notice here that the text in Figure 7-13 says, "To test the operation using the HTTP POST protocol . . ." This is interesting because, instead of executing the method using SOAP, this use of the Invoke button is executing the method by passing the request through POST variables. As mentioned in the SOAP section in the beginning of this chapter, the POST method will not be used when connecting to the service using Flash. Both the POST and SOAP methods accomplish the same task and return the same result—just a different method of data transport.

Using the Flash XML Web Service Connector

Now that we've established the basics of creating an ASP.NET web service, let's move to the presentation tier and learn how to invoke and display the results of this service using Flash Professional. First, we'll inspect the methods available from the web service by connecting to the service's WSDL file, and then we'll create two examples: a simple interface for the HelloWorld method, and a more complex consumer of the GetArea method.

Defining a web service in Flash

The first step is to connect to the existing web service using the Flash IDE's Web Services panel. This way, we can inspect the methods of the service and use these methods with the Web Service Connector component.

Let's get started by opening the Web Services panel in the Flash IDE. It isn't necessary to start a new Flash movie yet—when you set up a web service in the Web Services panel, that service will be accessible in all of your Flash projects. This panel can be accessed by selecting Window ➤ Development Panels ➤ Web Services. Once you have this panel open, click the globe icon, titled Define Web Services, as shown in Figure 7-15.

Figure 7-15. Clicking Define Web Services in the Flash Web Services panel

When the Define Web Services screen shown in Figure 7-16 opens, we'll need to jump back to the Service.asmx page we created in the previous section to grab some information. If you don't have the Service.asmx page currently open in a browser, open it now by pressing *F5* from Visual Studio. On the Service.asmx page, we need to copy the location of the Service Description (or WSDL) link, as shown in Figure 7-16.

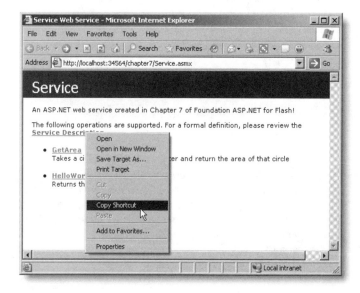

Figure 7-16. Copying the web service WSDL link

And, taking this copied shortcut back to the Flash Web Services panel, click the plus sign titled Add Web Service, and paste the URL currently in your clipboard into the input box, as shown in Figure 7-17.

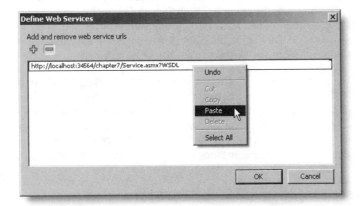

Figure 7-17. Adding a WSDL link in the Define Web Services panel

By letting Flash know where the WSDL file is for this web service, we enable Flash to understand all of the methods contained by this service, making it possible to inspect these methods at design time. Next, click OK; after a moment of processing, Flash will have loaded the data from the WSDL file, and your Web Services panel will look like Figure 7-18.

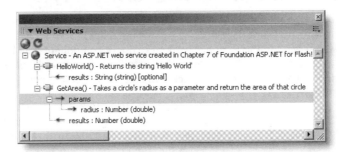

Figure 7-18. Inspecting the methods of the Service.asmx web service

As you can see, by loading and parsing the WSDL file for our service, Flash was able to load and display the methods of the service, as well as the description of the service itself, and the descriptions of the methods. It was even able to determine the data types of the method's input parameters and output results! You can now probably see a reason why web services might be an easier method for Flash and ASP.NET communication than the previous methods we've discussed—there is support in the Flash IDE for viewing the available methods, which takes care of much of the guesswork necessary when you are unable to directly inspect server-side methods.

Flash Web Service Connector component

The Flash Web Service Connector is a component available in Flash Professional that provides a "bridge" to web service methods. By using the Web Service Connector, you can interface with a web service method as if it existed in your Flash file, making web services extremely accessible for Flash developers. The Web Service Connector also allows you to easily pass parameters to web service methods and fires an event when the method result has been received.

The Web Service Connector makes calls to web service methods using SOAP. As discussed earlier in this chapter, this SOAP call is completely behind the scenes—taking much of the dirty work out of the hands of the developer. It's important to note that each instance of the Web Service Connector that you use in a Flash file can only be used for *one* web service method. This means that if you are making a Flash file that will be calling several web service methods, even if all of these methods are from the same service, you should have one instance of the Web Service Connector on the stage for each method you plan to call.

As with the rest of the components available in the Flash arsenal, there are a number of ways to make use of the Web Service Connector component, ranging from purely ActionScript based (no design time support) to purely component based, which requires very little ActionScript. In the following examples, we'll first use the Web Service Connector without involving any ActionScript at all in the HelloWorld example, and then we'll get a bit more in depth and use a more ActionScript-based approach in the GetArea example.

Connecting to the HelloWorld web service method

As a first example of using the Flash Web Service Connector component to connect to our ASP.NET web service, we'll make a simple interface that will call the HelloWorld web service method created in our Service.asmx web service. In this example, we'll make use of component data binding and behaviors, concepts that may be new if you have not worked with Flash components extensively before. By using these methods, making the call to the HelloWorld method will be extremely painless.

To set up the HelloWorld example, first create a new Flash file with a width of 200 pixels and a height of 120 pixels, and save it as helloworld.fla in a new directory called flash within the chapter7 directory you created earlier in this chapter. With this file created, drag new instances of the Button, TextArea, and, most important, the Web Service Connector components onto the stage, naming them callBtn, msgTxt, and helloService, respectively. Change the label of the Button instance to say Call Hello World! as shown in Figure 7-19.

Figure 7-19. helloworld.fla interface

As you can see in Figure 7-19, the Web Service Connector component displays visually as a globe with a plug on the stage—this is purely a visual placeholder. When the Flash file is published, all traces of the component will have disappeared.

Next, open the Component Inspector panel in Flash if it is not already open (you can open this panel by choosing Window ➤ Development Panels ➤ Component Inspector). Select the helloService component on the stage, and several items should display within the Parameters tab in the Component Inspector panel—WSDLURL, operation, multipleSimultaneousAllowed, and suppressInvalidCalls. At this point, we'll focus on the first two of these methods (more information on multipleSimultaneousAllowed and suppressInvalidCalls can be found in the Flash Help documentation).

Click within the WSDLURL's Value box, and a drop-down will appear with the WSDL URLs of the web service we created (and any others you've already added). Select the WSDL file we created, and then select the Value box of the operation property. This property should display a drop-down listing of each of the methods we created in our web service, HelloWorld and GetArea. Select the HelloWorld option from this drop-down, as shown in Figure 7-20.

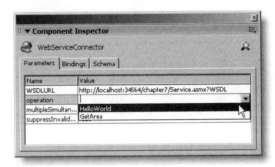

Figure 7-20. Selecting the HelloWorld operation

By selecting the HelloWorld option as the operation for our Web Service Connector instance, we have set this instance to become an interface with that specific method of the web service—able to make calls and receive results from this method.

Next, select the Bindings tab in the Component Inspector to view the current data bindings that have been created for this component (since we haven't created any yet, this tab should be blank!). Select the plus sign, titled Add Binding, to add a new binding to this Web Service Connector instance.

The Add Binding screen will show two parameters of the helloService instance that can be bound to: params and results, as shown in Figure 7-21.

Figure 7-21. Adding a binding to a component

Since our web service method requires no parameters, the params parameter of the service will be of little use in this case. The result returned from the service, however, is of interest—let's bind the result that is returned by the method to the msgTxt TextArea instance by clicking result, then clicking OK. Next, back in the Component Inspector, click the Bound To parameter, and in the following screen, click the msgTxt instance, as shown in Figure 7-22.

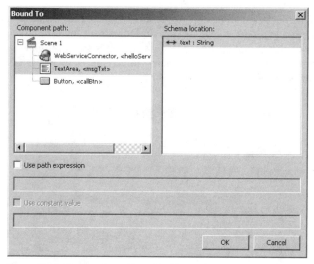

Figure 7-22. Binding the web method's results to a TextArea

In the right panel of this window, titled Schema location, you will see listed a single property of the TextArea component, text. By selecting this property (in this case we don't have any other choice!), we are deciding to display the results of the helloService's execution as the text of the TextArea instance. If, for example, we were using a different type of component to display the method's results, we might select a different schema location, such as Data Provider for a ComboBox component.

Again, click OK to return to the Component Inspector window for the helloService instance. The last thing we need to note to complete the binding of the results of the Web Service Connector is that the direction parameter of the binding is set to Out. This means, as you might guess, that this binding will be spitting a value out to our TextArea instance. If, however, we were using another component, such as a TextInput, to pass a parameter to a Web Service Connector instance, we would set this value to In, configuring it to pass a value into the params of the instance.

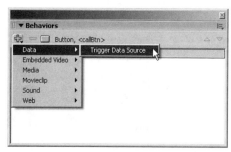

Figure 7-23. Adding a Trigger Data Source behavior to the Button

That's all of the configuration needed to set up the helloService instance output—all we have left to do in this example is configure the callBtn instance to trigger the Web Service Connector. To do this, we'll make use of the Flash Behaviors panel. This panel is available by choosing Window ➤ Development Panels ➤ Behaviors, and is used to create component-driven event triggering without the need for ActionScript. First, select the callBtn instance, then within this panel, select the plus sign. Then choose Data ➤ Trigger Data Source, as shown in Figure 7-23.

210

In the resulting Trigger Data Source window, select the helloService instance, and leave the Relative option selected, as shown in Figure 7-24.

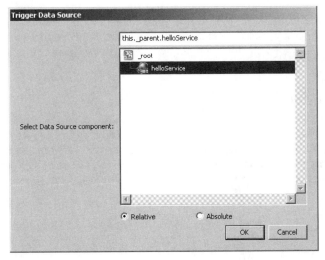

Figure 7-24. Triggering the helloService web service with the Trigger behavior

And, after clicking OK, we have successfully configured the Button to trigger the helloService when it is clicked—our example is complete!

Let's recap the steps that will occur in this example when the user of the application clicks the Call Hello World! button:

1. The user clicks the Button.

2. The helloService instance, configured to call the HelloWorld method of the Service.asmx web service, is triggered. This instance sends a request to the Service.asmx web service using SOAP to specify that it would like to execute the HelloWorld method.

3. The Service.asmx web service processes the web method request and returns the string "Hello World" to the Flash movie through SOAP.

4. The helloService Web Service Connector receives the result from the web service and, since we have bound the result to the msgTxt instance, outputs this value to the interface.

Next, let's test the HelloWorld.fla movie, as shown in Figure 7-25. When testing a web service project like this one, you can do so in the Flash IDE or in a browser.

And, in dramatic fashion, our file performs as expected, calling the HelloWorld web service and displaying the result in the TextArea!

Figure 7-25.
Viewing the result of helloworld.fla

GetArea web service example

Although the `HelloWorld` example is a good test for ASP.NET and Flash web service communication, it's not exactly a method that we'd use in an everyday application. In this example, we'll make a much more real-world use of web services by using the `GetArea` method to compute the area of a circle, and we'll create a Flash interface to display that circle to the user. In this example, we'll also learn how to use the Flash Web Service Connector using purely ActionScript instead of the Component Inspector and data binding.

Creating the interface

First, let's start a new Flash file and save it as `circle.fla` in the same `flash` directory as the one you created for the HelloWorld example. I'm going to leave the size and frame rate of the Flash file to its default values of 550×400 pixels and 12 fps. Within this new file, let's drag an instance of the Flash Web Service Connector component onto the stage and give the component an instance name of areaService (or another name you prefer), and label the layer the service is currently on as WebService, as shown in Figure 7-26.

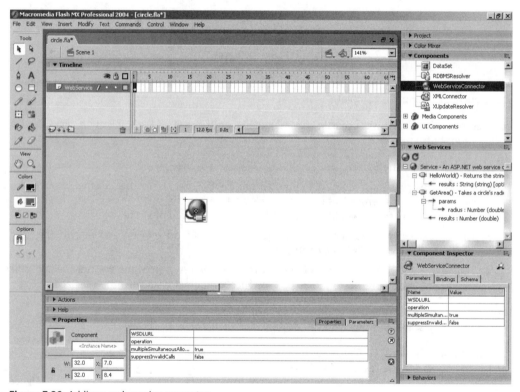

Figure 7-26. Adding a web service connector

Next, we need to create a text input in which the user can enter a circle's radius, as well as a Submit button for the user to click when they have finished entering the radius. To accomplish this, we'll use two more Flash components, the TextInput and Button. I have placed these two components in an interface background similar to the one created in the Chapter 6 image gallery example and given them instance names of inputTxt and submitBtn, respectively. Figure 7-27 shows the interface.

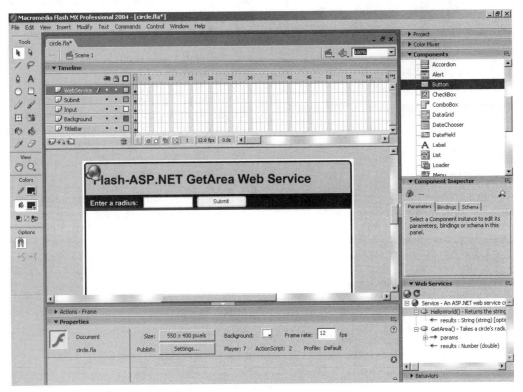

Figure 7-27. circle.fla interface

Next, let's create a new shape on our interface with a width and height of 250 pixels. Then, let's create a new MovieClip out of that shape, called Circle, with a registration point at the center of the MovieClip (for scaling purposes that we'll see soon), as shown in Figure 7-28.

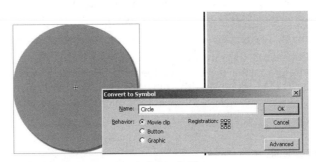

Figure 7-28. Creating the Circle MovieClip

213

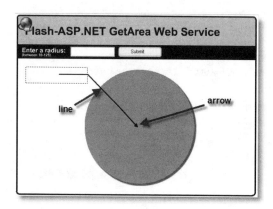

Figure 7-29. The line and arrow MovieClips

We're also going to create a new MovieClip called BlackArrow that will be used to point to the circle when displaying the circle's area. On the stage, we will give this MovieClip an instance name of blackArrow. Within this MovieClip, we'll break up the straight line and the arrow into two separate MovieClips—with instance names line and arrow, as shown in Figure 7-29. Lastly, we are going to add a dynamic text instance called msg_txt, which will display the results of our GetArea function.

In the linkage identifier for the Arrow MovieClip, let's specify an AS 2.0 class, Arrow.as, which will contain a basic function to change the length of the arrow as the radius of the circle varies.

Initializing

Now that we have the interface completed, let's create some new ActionScript on a new layer, called Actions, in the _root timeline. This function, init, will be used to initialize some of the basic elements of the interface, create event listeners for the Submit button, and most important, initialize the areaService component.

```
function init() {
    // restrict the input to numbers
    inputTxt.restrict = "0-9";
    // hide the circle and arrow until "submit" is clicked
    circle._alpha = 0;
    blackArrow._alpha = 0;
    // add an event listener to the submit button's click
    submitBtn.addEventListener("click", this);
    // add an event listener to the input text's focus
    inputTxt.addEventListener("focusIn", this);
    // set up the areaService
    areaService.WSDLURL =
        "http://localhost:34564/chapter7/Service.asmx?WSDL";
    areaService.operation = "GetArea";
    // add an event listener to the web service result
    areaService.addEventListener("result", res);
}
```

Let's take a look at the lines that are doing the configuration of the Web Service Connector, areaService. These lines are taking the place of the configuration that we did in the Component Inspector in the HelloWorld example—it's important to note that making these settings in ActionScript will override any settings you chose in the Component Inspector.

In the line

```
areaService.WSDLURL =
    "http://localhost:34564/chapter7/Service.asmx?WSDL";
```

we are setting the WSDLURL property of the Web Service Connector, specifying the WSDL file from our web service. Although it isn't quite as easy to specify the WSDL file using ActionScript (it doesn't appear in a drop-down menu), using ActionScript does make it easier to update the WSDL settings if the location of your WSDL file changes—for example, if you are publishing your website to a new domain. This is also a much more effective method when using more than one Web Service Connector in a single Flash file, as we will see in the Google web service example in Chapter 8.

Next, we specify the operation, or method, that the Web Service Connector will be using:

```
areaService.operation = "GetArea";
```

Again, this method is a bit more painstaking than setting the operation through the Component Inspector, since the method name *is* case-sensitive and must be spelled correctly.

And finally, we add a listener to the component that fires an event when the Web Service Connector returns a result from a method call:

```
areaService.addEventListener("result", res);
```

In the HelloWorld example, this event was handled "behind the scenes" by using data binding—in this example, we'll be able to see exactly how a web method's result is handled, using the res function.

Receiving the result

I've created the following res function in the same layer of the _root timeline as the previous code-blocks, defining the initialization functions:

```
var res:Function = function (evt:Object) {
    // get the radius from the input box
    var rad:Number = Number(inputTxt.text);
    // get the area from the web service results
    var result:Number = evt.target.results;
    var area:Number = Math.round(result);
    // set the text to display the radius and area
    msg.text = "Radius: "+rad.toString();
    msg.text += "\nArea: "+area.toString();
    // show the circle and arrow
    circle._alpha = 100;
    blackArrow._alpha = 100;
    // change the circle's size to the proper radius
    circle.tween (["_width", "_height"],
                  [rad*2, rad*2], .6, "easeOutBack");
    // change the arrow's size to suit the circle
    blackArrow.SetLength(170-rad);
};
```

This function, fired when the areaService instance has returned a result, does a variety of operations, the most important of which involve the evt parameter that is passed to the function. This parameter is an object that contains a property called target, which is a reference to the Web Service Connector instance for which the function is receiving a result, areaService. By accessing the areaService's results parameter, as in the line:

```
var result:Number = evt.target.results;
```

215

we are able to extract the value returned from the service, regardless of the value's type (in this case, we know it's a double). You might wonder at this point how it would be possible to return multiple values from a web service method to Flash—as we'll see in the Chapter 8 example, this can be done by using an array of objects.

In the remaining lines in this codeblock, the interface is updated to display the returned area in the msg dynamic text instance, as well as to change the size of the circle instance to reflect the radius entered. Again, I've used the Zigo engine classes (see Chapter 6) to accomplish the circle's size change. (Since we're using the Zigo engine, be sure to remember to drag an instance of the Zigo engine from the Component Library onto the stage of your Flash movie.) In the last line, we are calling a function of the blackArrow instance, which we'll define in a new Arrow.as file, used as the Arrow MovieClip's AS 2.0 file.

```
dynamic class Arrow extends MovieClip {
  function SetLength(nl:Number) {
    this["line"].tween(["_width"], [nl], .6);
    this["arrow"].tween(["_x"], [nl], .6);
  }
}
```

This function, when passed a number, will change the length of the diagonal portion of the arrow to the number specified. Notice that this is accomplished by changing the _width property of the line MovieClip in the Arrow, as well as the _x property of the arrow itself.

Completing the code

The last thing we need to do to complete this example is to write the event handler functions for the focusIn event of the inputTxt instance and the click event of the Submit button. In the focusIn event handler, all we want to do is clear the text in the text input for the user as in the following codeblock, which should be added to the _root timeline's Actions layer:

```
var focusIn:Function = function (evt:Object) {
  // clear the text
  evt.target.text = "";
};
```

And, for the click event of the submitBtn instance, we want to do a couple of things—validate the user's input to make sure it's within a specified range of values (an input greater than 125 will make a circle too big for our interface!), and trigger the areaService instance, passing the input radius as a value:

```
var click:Function = function (evt:Object) {
  var rad:Number = Number(inputTxt.text);
  if ((rad<10) || (rad>125)) {
    inputTxt.text = "– Out of Range –";
  } else {
    areaService.params = [Number(inputTxt.text)];
    areaService.trigger();
  }
};
```

In this codeblock, we see another important property of the Web Service Connector, params. This property is used to pass values as parameters to the web service method that is being called. These parameters are passed using the following syntax:

```
Webservice.params = [ param1, param2, param3, ... ];
```

In this case, the GetArea method requires only one parameter, radius, which is grabbed from the TextInput component. It's important to notice that this inputTxt.text property has been changed to a numeric value—even though Flash will convert the string to a number behind the scenes for you, it's a very good practice to do this before executing the method, as it reduces the potential for error when the method executes.

Finally, we fire the GetArea method by calling the areaService's trigger method. Calling this method tells the Web Service Connector component to call the method using SOAP, and since we have already set up an event listener, we are prepared to receive the result when it comes back from ASP.NET!

The final result of this example is shown in Figure 7-30.

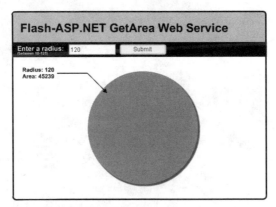

Figure 7-30. Results of circle.fla

This web service application is only a simple example of the power exposed by ASP.NET that can be accessed by Flash using web services. By using ASP.NET web services, Flash interfaces can gain access to the most complex functionality of the .NET Framework, including processor-intensive operations like cryptography or image generation. In Chapter 10, we'll learn how to use ASP.NET web services to access some more complex functionality—database access.

Summary

In this chapter, we've established the basics of web service creation and consumption using Flash and ASP.NET. Through these examples, you should be able to get an idea of how powerful the web service concept is, and how (relatively) easy it is to create web service communication in Flash and ASP.NET. In Chapter 8, we'll extend this basic use of web services by connecting to the Google web service, and then in Chapter 10, we'll create a database-driven online-store service.

Chapter 8

THE GOOGLE WEB SERVICE API

What this chapter covers:

- Creating web service proxies in ASP.NET
- Creating an Application class in Flash
- Using ASP.NET to consume the Google web API

One of the most exciting abilities that web services provide to developers is the capability to access functions that have been written by other developers—meaning that you don't have to reinvent the wheel to perform complex tasks! In this chapter, we'll explore the methods needed to access third-party web services from Flash, and introduce the concept of creating a web service proxy method in ASP.NET. By using ASP.NET web service proxies, we'll create a new, Flash-based interface to the Google web service API—talk about making good use of existing code instead of reinventing the wheel!

Consuming third-party web services

Building web services as we did in the previous chapter is an excellent example of Flash/ASP.NET communication, but it only begins to touch on the abilities made available by web services. In Chapter 7's examples, we learned how to consume web services that we create—now, we're going to look at consuming web services that *other people* create. By being able to access external web services made available by other people or companies, the capabilities of our applications improve dramatically. Thousands of web services are currently available, with features ranging from credit card validation to Morse code translation. A huge list of these web services is available at www.xmethods.net.

Although it is possible to consume a third-party web service directly using the Flash Web Service Connector, there are several security restrictions in the Flash sandbox that make this type of communication very difficult. As we saw in the previous chapter, it is very easy to consume a service that comes from *within the same domain* as the Flash file. In order to get around this Flash sandbox security issue, and call a web service from outside the local domain, it is possible to make a *web service proxy* using ASP.NET. A web service proxy created with ASP.NET actually calls the third-party web service for you and returns the result from that service, as shown in Figure 8-1.

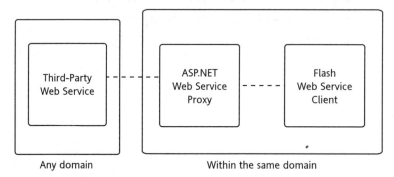

Figure 8-1. ASP.NET web service proxy

This web service proxy, provided by ASP.NET, is both a web service creator and a service consumer, consuming a web service from the third party, and republishing that service for use in your Flash movie, which requests it from within the same domain.

Creating a web service proxy in ASP.NET involves only three steps:

1. Adding a reference to the web service in ASP.NET. To do this, you must know the web service's WSDL URL, so ASP.NET knows how to communicate with the service.

2. Creating a web service method in ASP.NET that takes (optionally) the same parameters as the third-party web service—in essence, "mirroring" the service.

3. When the local ASP.NET service method is called, it must call the third-party web service method, passing the necessary parameters. When the result is received from the third-party service, the ASP.NET service should pass it on as its return value.

In this chapter, we're going to create a web service proxy for the Google web service, making the tremendous power of that service available to our Flash applications. Information about the Google web service is available at www.google.com/apis/. This is a free service provided by Google, allowing developers to create applications that make use of the Google search engine, as well as other functionality such as spelling correction and cached page information. The free version of the Google web service allows you to make up to 1,000 requests to the service per day—more than enough for our example!

Signing up for the Google web service API

In order to use the Google web service, it's necessary to first sign up for a Google account at www.google.com/apis/. Once you validate your e-mail address, Google will send you an e-mail with a "Web APIs License Key." Don't delete it! This license key will allow you to make use of the Google web service.

On this page (see Figure 8-2), you'll also see a link titled Reference that provides a detailed description of the methods available from the Google web service—this is a very useful reference, as the Google search method takes ten input parameters!

Figure 8-2. Google Web API signup page

221

Creating a web service proxy using ASP.NET

With your Google account created, let's move to Visual Studio .NET and learn how to create a web service proxy for this web service. Creation of a web service proxy in ASP.NET is actually not too much different than creating a web service. First, create a new web service project in a new folder called chapter8, as shown in Figure 8-3.

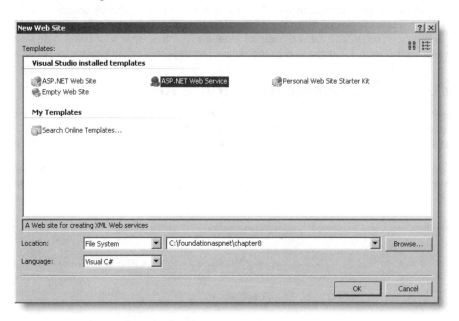

Figure 8-3. Creating a web service for Chapter 8

Again, Visual Studio .NET will create a default web service page, Service.asmx. With a bit of modification, this page will work just fine for our web service proxy example. Next, we'll need to add a web reference to our project, using Visual Studio .NET. Creating a web reference in Visual Studio allows you to use a third-party web service just like it is a local object within our project, disguising the fact that the code you are executing exists on a server across the Internet. To add a web reference in Visual Studio, go to the Solution Explorer window and right-click on the location of the web service project, then select Add Web Reference, as shown in Figure 8-4.

Figure 8-4. Right-click on the project name to add a web reference.

In the following screen, titled Add Web Reference, we'll need to specify the WSDL URL of the Google web service. According to the Google Reference documentation, this URL is http://api.google.com/GoogleSearch.wsdl. Place this value in the URL input of this form and click the Go button. Just like in the Flash Web Services panel, Visual Studio will load the information published by the Google WSDL file and display a list of the methods made available by that service, as shown in Figure 8-5.

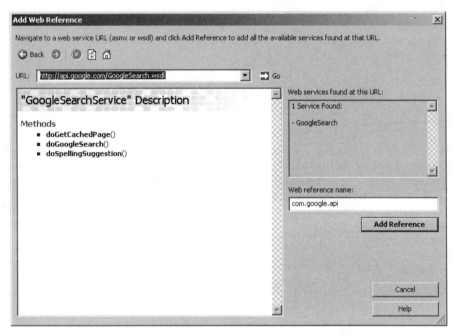

Figure 8-5. Adding the GoogleSearchService

Here we see that the methods available from the Google web service are doGetCachedPage(), doGoogleSearch(), and doSpellingSuggestion(). Hit the Add Reference button, and, with a little work, these methods will become available in our web service project!

Once you have added the Google web service to the project, you will see a new folder of files in the Solution Explorer, titled App_WebReferences. Within this folder are two files, GoogleSearch.discomap and GoogleSearch.wsdl (see Figure 8-6). These files contain information about the web service that we have connected to and do not need to be manipulated in order to use the web service.

Figure 8-6. The App_WebReferences folder

Next, let's create a new web method within the `service.asmx.cs` web service—actually, let's delete the `HelloWorld` web method created by Visual Studio, and save the [WebMethod] tag for our own use. Let's call this method `GoogleSearch` for now and make it without a return type or any parameters.

```
[WebMethod]
public void GoogleSearch() {
}
```

The next step we need to take involves creating an instance of the remote Google web service—made possible by the web reference we added to our project. Creating this instance is just like creating an instance of any other class in C#:

```
public void GoogleSearch() {
  com.google.api.GoogleSearchService serv =
    new com.google.api.GoogleSearchService();
}
```

You'll notice here that the namespace of this class, `com.google.api`, is the same name as we specified in Figure 8-5, and reflects the name of the folder listed in Figure 8-6. As we learned in Figure 8-5 (and we could find out from the Google Reference page), the Google web service has three accessible methods. In this ASP.NET web method, we're going to be making a "mirror image" of the `doGoogleSearch` method. Once we type the following in Visual Studio, IntelliSense will start and allow us to take a look at the return type and input parameters of the `doGoogleSearch` method of the `GoogleSearchService` class:

```
com.google.api.GoogleSearchResult searchRes = serv.doGoogleSearch(
```

IntelliSense will display the information shown in Figure 8-7 about the `doGoogleSearch` method.

GoogleSearchResult GoogleSearchService.doGoogleSearch(string key, string q, int start, int maxResults, bool filter, string restrict, bool safeSearch, string lr, string ie, string oe)

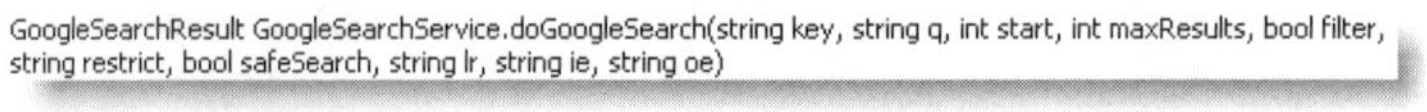

Figure 8-7. Visual Studio IntelliSense entry for the doGoogleSearch method

As we can see in Figure 8-7, the `doGoogleSearch` function returns a value of type `com.google.api.GoogleSearchResult`. This is a class specific to the Google web service, which we can use as a return type for our web method. We also get a glimpse here of the input parameters that the `doGoogleSearch` method takes—quite a load! For now, we'll just "mirror" these parameters in our method, and we'll take a closer look at them when we need to pass values to them from our Flash client. Continuing with our `GoogleSearch` method, we now know that the `doGoogleSearch` method has a return type of `com.google.api.GoogleSearchResult`:

```
public com.google.api.GoogleSearchResult
➥ GoogleSearch(string key, string query, int start, int results,
➥ bool filter, string restrict, bool safe, string languageRestrict,
➥ string ie, string oe)
{
```

```
    com.google.api.GoogleSearchService serv =
➥    new com_google_api.GoogleSearchService();
    com.google.api.GoogleSearchResult searchRes =
➥    serv.doGoogleSearch(key, query, start, results, filter,
➥    restrict, safe, languageRestrict, ie, oe);
    return searchRes;
}
```

In the first line of this codeblock, I have added both input parameters (again, mirroring the input parameters of the doGoogleSearch method), as well as a return type, com.google.api. GoogleSearchResult. These parameters will be passed directly to our new GoogleSearchService instance's doGoogleSearch method in the third line of this codeblock.

In the third line, we create a new instance of the com.google.api.GoogleSearchResult class, and set it equal to the result of the doGoogleSearch method. As you can see, we've also passed each of the input parameters of our method into the doGoogleSearch method. In the following line, we simply return the GoogleSearchResult instance just returned to us. And that's all that is involved in creating a web service proxy in ASP.NET! Let's review the steps we just went through in creating this proxy service:

1. Create a new web service.

2. Add a web reference of the third-party service to the web service project.

3. Create a method that "mirrors" a method of the web service, which takes the necessary input parameters and returns the service's results.

4. Repeat for as many methods of the service you'd like to use.

Four pretty simple steps to create a web service proxy—at this point, we've only completed three, though. Let's complete the fourth step by "mirroring" the functionality of the Google web service's doSpellingSuggestion method so we can also provide spelling suggestions from our Flash presentation tier.

Beginning in the same manner, let's create a new method with no input parameters or return type, until we can "feel out" the doSpellingSuggestion method for its parameters and return types:

```
[WebMethod]
public void GoogleSpell { }
```

And, in a similar fashion to the GoogleSearch method, we'll create a new instance of the com.google.api.GoogleSearchService with the following line:

```
    com.google.api.GoogleSearchService serv =
➥    new com.google.api.GoogleSearchService();
```

Following this line, all we have left to do is determine the input parameters and return types of the doSpellingSuggestion method, found easily enough to be the ones shown in Figure 8-8.

string GoogleSearchService.doSpellingSuggestion (string key, string phrase)

Figure 8-8. IntelliSense entry for doSpellingSuggestion

This method is much simpler than the doGoogleSearch method, requiring only two parameters and returning a string as a value. Using this information, we can complete our GoogleSpell method as follows:

```
[WebMethod]
public string GoogleSpell(string key, string phrase)
{
  com.google.api.GoogleSearchService serv =
➥ new com.google.api.GoogleSearchService();
  string spellRes = serv.doSpellingSuggestion(key, phrase);
  return spellRes;
}
```

And with that, we have completed our Google web service proxy. It should be pretty clear at this point what the proxy accomplishes—it calls the methods of a third-party web service and returns its results, unscathed.

Using an Application class in ActionScript

In the examples we've worked on up to this point in the book, we've created ActionScript 2.0 code in a couple of different locations—either in the first frame of a layer in the _root timeline or in an external .as file. I have presented the ActionScript code in this way as a transition for those who are not as familiar with writing ActionScript in purely external .as files. As we move forward in this and subsequent chapters, I'm going to present a more "C#" approach to ActionScript 2.0 object-oriented code architecture. Using this architecture, there will be almost no code on the timeline of our Flash movies, but rather just a line creating an instance of an Application class that will reside in an external .as file and will act as the "master" for our application. A typical Application class (named Application.as) will start with the following code:

```
dynamic class Application extends MovieClip {
  function Application(owner)
  {
    owner.__proto__ = this.__proto__;
    owner.__constructor__ = Application;
    this = owner;
    setup();
  }
  public static function main(createdBy:MovieClip) {
    var app = new Application(createdBy);
  }
  private function setup()
  {
    // perform setup functions
  }
}
```

which can be initiated on the _root timeline with this line:

```
Application.main(this);
```

When this Application class is initiated with this call to the Application.main function, the rather complex-looking lines

```
owner.__proto__ = this.__proto__;
owner.__constructor__ = Application;
this = owner;
```

will allow this Application class to function *as if it is the _root timeline*, making it easier to reference the members of the _root timeline through this class. Then, within the setup function, any initialization code can be placed for the class, just as you would in a constructor function in a .NET class, or in the Page_Load event handler of an ASP.NET page.

> *If you've ever attempted to create a .NET Windows Forms application using .NET 1.1 (before partial classes in 2.0), you'll notice that this setup (minus the __proto__ stuff) is very similar to the* static main *method in these applications.*

More information on this architecture, including video tutorials, can be found at the following locations on the FlashExtensions website (which is a great resource for all sorts of ActionScript tutorials!):

- **Building the Application class:** www.flashextensions.com/categories/fesup/index.php
- **Assigning Application as _root:** www.flashextensions.com/categories/as2i/APX_A/index.php

Creating a Flash presentation tier for the Google web service

Almost everyone who has used the World Wide Web has at one point used the Google search engine home page to do a web page search. The standard Google user interface, to its benefit, is very simple, displaying very little interactivity and a minimal amount of functionality. Although this helps to keep the Google search easy to use, we're going to make a Flash-based interface that has the same great search power of the Google search service (through the use of the Google web service) but a more interactive interface that we hope will result in an improved user experience for our search engine.

The code I have used to create the Flash interface to the GoogleSearch and GoogleSpell web methods is quite extensive, and it would be overkill to explain each section in great detail. Instead, since we have already covered the basics of calling web service methods and retrieving their results in the previous chapter (and we'll be examining them again in the next chapter), I will simply provide a brief description of the interface and ActionScript classes involved in each piece of my application.

> *The complete code for this file is available from the friends of ED website,* www.friendsofed.com, *in the Downloads section.*

The Flash interface that I am creating will consist of the following functional blocks:

- A TextInput field that will allow a user to input a search.

- A ComboBox that will store current searches by the user—allowing them to re-queue a previous search.

- Next and Previous buttons that will allow the user to navigate pages of results after a search is executed. Each page will consist of 10 result elements.

- A Did you mean field, which will appear if alternate text was found for the current search. If the user clicks on this field, the alternate search phrase is executed.

This interface, when coupled with the ASP.NET web service proxy that we just created, will be able to access the entire breadth of the GoogleSearch and GoogleSpell functionality. The final result of the interface is shown in Figure 8-9.

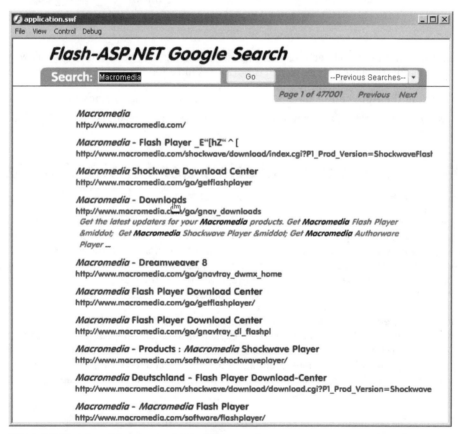

Figure 8-9. Flash-based Google search interface

To create this application, I have created several Flash MovieClips, each published with a linkage identifier. A list of these MovieClips is shown here:

- SearchBar: Contains the TextInput field, the Go button, and the Previous Searches ComboBox. This MovieClip uses the SearchBar.as file as its AS 2.0 class.
- SearchResult: This MovieClip encapsulates a single search result. It uses the SearchResult.as file for its AS 2.0 class.
- DYM (Did You Mean): This MovieClip is used to present the alternate spelling text. Uses the DidYouMean.as file for its AS 2.0 class.
- Loader: This MovieClip is used to provide the loading animation for the search interface.
- PageBar: This MovieClip is used to display the Next and Previous page buttons.

Listed next are the logical steps that occur in this application, along with some of the important web service–related codeblocks used.

Do some setup work.

Before a user can make a call to a web service, we should first create the Web Service Connector objects that will perform our web service operations. This is done in a very similar manner to that in Chapter 7, as shown in the following codeblock:

```
var gSearchService:WebServiceConnector;
var gSpellService:WebServiceConnector;
...

function init() {
  // global definitions
  _global._gUrl = "http://localhost:2052/chapter8/Service.asmx?WSDL";

  // google search service
  gSearchService.addEventListener("result",searchResult);
  gSearchService.WSDLURL = _global._gUrl;
  gSearchService.operation = "GoogleSearch";
  // google spell service
  gSpellService.addEventListener("result",dymResult);
  gSpellService.WSDLURL = _global._gUrl;
  gSpellService.operation = "GoogleSpell";
}

function searchResult(ev) {
  // code to handle the result of the GoogleSearch service
}
function dymResult(ev)
{
  // code to handle the result of the GoogleSpell service
}
```

In this codeblock, I have also specified the WSDL URL of the ASP.NET web service we have created, assigned the operation name of each of the web service connectors, and created the functions that will handle the results of the GoogleSearch and GoogleSpell calls.

229

Display the search bar.

Once we have done our setup work, we can just display the search bar to the user—then just hang back and wait for some interaction.

When the Submit button is clicked, call the GoogleSearch web method from the service.asmx web service.

Once we have received a search phrase from the user, we need to send that phrase to our ASP.NET web service (which will, in turn, forward it on to Google), and wait for a result. Just like in Chapter 7, this is accomplished by setting the proper parameters to send to our web service, and calling the trigger method of the gSearchService connector.

```
gSearchService.params = [{ my key number }, { the search phrase },
➡ { the starting record }, { the number of records we want (10) },
false, "", true, "lang_en", "", ""]; // a few more parameters
gSearchService.trigger();
```

After we have called the GoogleSearch method, call the GoogleSpell method to check for another search suggestion.

Just because we've sent off a request to the Google search service doesn't mean we're done with this search phrase. We should also send the phrase off to the GoogleSpell method to see if there's a possibility that the user misspelled a word. This method can be executed at the same time as the GoogleSearch method, since we have created two web service connector instances, each of which has its own "result" event handler. The call to the GoogleSpell service is a little bit easier to accomplish, as shown here:

```
gSpellService.params = [{ my key number}, {the search phrase}];
gSpellService.trigger();
```

Display a loading function while the search is occurring.

In my interface, I have created an animation that will execute while the user is waiting for the results of the GoogleSearch query. Figure 8-10 shows this animation in action, while a search is being performed.

Figure 8-10. Loading animation while search is being performed

When the result is returned by the GoogleSearch web method, format and display these results in the interface.

The most important step, right? After sending off the user's search phrase to our ASP.NET web service method, we receive a result back from the web method. This result will, as we specified in the web method definition, be an array of GoogleSearchResult objects. We can easily retrieve each of the results by using a for loop to cycle through each of the results.

```
function res (ev:Object)
{
  var tr:Array = ev.target.results;
  for (var x = 0; x<tr.resultElements.length; x++) {
    var elem:Object = tr.resultElements[x];
    var nn = "sr"+x.toString();
    // attach a "SearchResult" MovieClip for each result
    _root.attachMovie("SearchResult",nn,50+x);
  ...
}
```

And, within this function, the data from each result element can be obtained by accessing the properties exposed by the GoogleSearchResult:

```
var url:String = elem.URL;
var title:String = elem.title;
var summary:String = elem.summary;
var snippet:String = elem.snippet;
```

This information can then be displayed in the SearchResult MovieClips that are attached to the interface. I have created code to show a more detailed result when a user places the cursor over one of the result elements; this will display the summary, as well as the title and snippet (see Figure 8-11). If the user clicks on the result, a new browser window is opened to the result's URL.

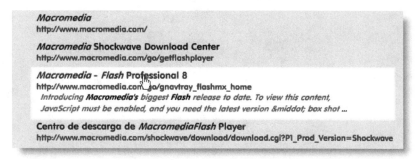

Figure 8-11. Full item description on rollover

If there are more than 10 results, display the PageBar MovieClip.

We want to allow the user to be able to navigate past the first 10 results, so, in order to do this, we'll add the PageBar MovieClip, which will allow them to navigate through the records. If the user selects the Next button, we'll make another call to our Google web service proxy, but this time request the next 10 records by changing the starting record parameter when we make the method call.

```
gSearchService.params = [{ my key number }, { the search phrase },
➡ { the starting record }, { the number of records we want (10) },
false, "", true, "lang_en", "", ""]; // a few more parameters
```

When a result is returned from the GoogleSpell request, show the Did You Mean? dialog box if the result is not a null string.

If our request to the GoogleSpell service proxy returned a value other than a null string (it will return a null string if there it has no suggestion), we should display this result in the Did You Mean dialog box. When a search phrase is clicked within the Did You Mean dialog box, a new search is initiated with the suggested phrase. This dialog box is shown in Figure 8-12.

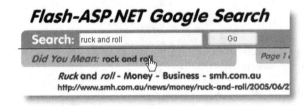

Figure 8-12. The Did You Mean dialog box

After a search is performed, record it in the Previous Searches ComboBox.

If a user is performing a number of searches, it is often useful to be able to jump back to the results of a previous search. By storing the user's previous search phrases in an array, and using that array to populate the values of a ComboBox, we can give the user this ability (see Figure 8-13). When the user selects a value from the ComboBox, the search function is called again, with the selected value.

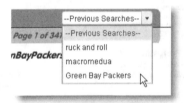

Figure 8-13. ComboBox displaying previous searches

Publish and embed the Flash file in an ASP.NET page.

After the Flash functionality has been completed, we're ready to go live with the revamped Google interface. By using the epicFlashControl (see Chapter 3), we can easily embed the .swf into a new ASP.NET web form, which I've named default.aspx—and the application is ready to go!

And, with these simple steps, we are able to create a presentation tier in Flash that consumes the Google web service proxy we created earlier in the chapter. Again, the complete source code for this example is available from the Downloads section of the friends of ED website, www.friendsofed.com. Using similar methods, you can integrate the Google services into your existing applications, or create new applications that consume any of the thousands of public web services available on the Web.

Summary

In this chapter, we've learned how to consume third-party web services using Flash and ASP.NET. By using web services from sources all around the world, it's possible to expand the capabilities of your applications to accomplish tasks that would otherwise be impossible. And, one of the amazing things about the combination of Flash and ASP.NET is how easy it is to connect to and consume these services. This chapter should spur some ideas for integrating web services into your future Flash/ASP.NET applications!

Chapter 9

DATABASE CONNECTIVITY

What this chapter covers:

- SQL statements
- ADO.NET
- Data access using DataReaders
- Data access using DataAdapter-DataSet

In the past several chapters, we've covered methods used to send information from an ASP.NET web server to a Flash client. One of the best uses of this communication is to transfer data from a database to a Flash client so it can be displayed in a rich interface. In this chapter, we'll take a look at .NET database access, ranging from SQL statements to ADO.NET—the data access core of the .NET Framework. Using ADO.NET's DataReader and DataSet objects, we'll then learn how to execute commands on a database and transfer data from a database to a Flash client using web services.

SQL

If you have experience using a relational database such as Microsoft Access, Microsoft SQL Server, MySQL, or Oracle, then you most likely have encountered SQL statements at some point. SQL, or Structured Query Language, is the international standard language for databases and allows you to perform such functions as selecting, updating, and inserting data in database tables.

In this section, we'll briefly cover some of the basic SQL statements: SELECT, UPDATE, INSERT, and DELETE. These statements are fundamental for creating database-driven applications using ASP.NET and Flash.

Using SELECT statements

SELECT statements are used to retrieve data from a database. Using a SELECT statement, you can specify which columns you would like to see and the conditions and sorting instructions for the data you'd like to retrieve. The use of SELECT statements can range from simple to extremely complex—in this book, we'll use the SELECT syntax, as shown here:

```
SELECT [ALL | DISTINCT] column_list FROM table
[ WHERE condition ] [ ORDER BY expression [ ASC | DESC ] ]
```

Using this syntax, the column_list parameter is a comma-separated list used to specify the columns that should be selected from the database. A wildcard character, *, can also be used in a SELECT statement to retrieve data from all columns. The ALL and DISTINCT keywords are used to specify whether the query should return all rows (ALL) or only rows that have nonduplicate values (DISTINCT). These keywords are optional, and if none is specified, the query will default to ALL.

```
SELECT DISTINCT Column1, Column2...
```

The FROM keyword is used to specify the table within the database that the data rows should be retrieved from. The FROM keyword is mandatory; after all, the database needs to know what table you are talking about!

```
SELECT DISTINCT Column1, Column2 FROM myTable
```

The WHERE condition is an optional section of a SELECT statement that allows you to specify a set of conditions that must evaluate to true for rows to be returned. When using the WHERE statement, the comparison operators shown in Table 9-1 are used to filter data from the database.

Table 9-1. Comparison operators in the WHERE statement

Operator	Description	Example
=	Equality	WHERE PostDate='1/1/2005'
<	Less than	WHERE HitCount<20
>	Greater than	WHERE Clicks>5
<=	Less than or equal	WHERE Age<=50
>=	Greater than or equal	WHERE Population>=100000
!=	Not	WHERE Color!='Red'
AND	And	WHERE (Color!='Red') AND (Size!='Large')
OR	Or	WHERE (Color='Green') OR (Color='Orange')

The AND and OR comparison operators can be used within a WHERE statement to combine comparisons, allowing you to be more specific with your SELECT statements.

The optional ORDER BY section of the SELECT statement can be used to order the data before it is returned to your .NET code. Allowing the database to sort data can often be a much more efficient process than obtaining unsorted data and performing sorting operations through code. In the ORDER BY statement, column(s) are specified; the first columns specified are the first sorted, and the ASC and DESC keywords are used to specify whether the columns should be sorted in an ascending or a descending manner. Consider the following example:

```
SELECT * FROM People ORDER BY LastName ASC, FirstName ASC
```

Here, the data rows returned will be sorted by the LastName column first, then any returned rows *that have the same* LastName value will be sorted by the FirstName column. Since ASC was specified as the sort order, the LastName and FirstName rows with the lowest values will be returned first.

Another useful keyword that can be used in SELECT statements is LIKE. If we use the LIKE keyword along with the % character, we can perform searches that meet not only specific conditions but also a range of conditions, such as "all last names that start with the letters *Sm*." An example of a SELECT statement that uses LIKE is shown here:

```
SELECT * From People WHERE LastName LIKE 'Sm%'
```

This SELECT statement will return all the rows from the People table that have a LastName column entry that begins with *Sm*.

Using UPDATE statements

The UPDATE statement is used, as its name implies, to update data that exists in a database table. Using this statement, it is possible to update one or multiple rows, specified by the WHERE condition, as in the SELECT statement. The syntax for the UPDATE statement is shown here:

```
UPDATE table SET column = value [ WHERE condition ]
```

When using the UPDATE statement, it's very important to specify the optional WHERE condition, because otherwise you will update every entry in the table you have specified (which can have disastrous results!). Here is an example of the UPDATE statement:

```
UPDATE Products SET Price=20 WHERE ProductId=12
```

This statement will update a table named Products, setting the Price to 20 of all columns that have a ProductId equal to 12.

Using INSERT statements

The INSERT (or INSERT INTO) SQL keyword is used to insert a single row into a database table. The INSERT statement uses the following syntax:

```
INSERT INTO table [(column1 [, column2] [, column3] [, ...])]
VALUES (value1 [, value2] [, value3] [, ...])
```

In the INSERT INTO statement, the values specified to the right side of the VALUES keyword will be inserted into the columns of a new database row. The values will be entered into the columns specified on the left side of the VALUES keyword and must be listed in the same order as the column names.

An example of using an INSERT statement to create a new row of data in a table called Products is shown here:

```
INSERT INTO Products (ProductId, ProductName, ProductPrice)
VALUES ('PRO121', 'Red Socks', 12)
```

In this example, a new row of data is created, with a ProductId of PRO12, a ProductName of Red Socks, and a ProductPrice of 12 (assuming that these columns exist in the Products table).

Using DELETE statements

Using the DELETE statement, rows can be deleted from a database table. Here is the syntax for the DELETE statement:

```
DELETE FROM table [ WHERE condition ]
```

Like the UPDATE statement, DELETE can be very dangerous when used without the optional WHERE condition, as it will delete *all* entries in a table! An example of a SQL DELETE statement is shown here:

```
DELETE FROM Products WHERE ProductId='PRO121'
```

Now that we've touched on the basics of SQL statements, let's move on to the .NET Framework's classes that deal with database access—generally referred to as ADO.NET.

Introducing ADO.NET

ADO.NET, or **A**ctive **D**ata **O**bjects for .NET, is a set of classes and objects in the .NET Framework that provides access to data sources. Since data access is so essential to .NET, these classes are part of the core of the .NET Framework, capable of providing data to all other elements of the framework. ADO.NET is the latest in the evolution of Microsoft's database-access technologies. This evolution started with the Open DataBase Connectivity (ODBC) API, which was designed to eliminate the differences between application-level SQL statements and internal database server query engines. With the inception of COM, this idea was merged into a technology called OLE DB, which, although very powerful and flexible, never gained widespread acceptance.

From OLE DB came a COM automated technology called Active Data Objects (ADO). ADO was implemented to make OLE DB access available to Microsoft-based technologies such as Visual Basic and ASP. If you've programmed using previous generations of Microsoft technologies, you have probably heard of ADO (without the .NET).

With the inception of the .NET Framework, ADO.NET was developed from the ground up—not based on previous ADO technologies—to perform the type of functions that ADO was created to do. Since ADO.NET is created with a new, more efficient architecture, it is much faster and more powerful than the "patched" ADO. ADO.NET is not an enhanced version of ADO, however; it is completely revamped. Whereas the concepts used in ADO hold true, most code written for ADO is not applicable for use with ADO.NET. The main reason that ADO.NET still has the ADO name is so that developers feel comfortable with ADO.NET as the means for database access using .NET.

Like many of the other .NET technologies, ADO.NET is built from the ground up and is based on XML. Although much of the XML structure of ADO.NET is behind the scenes, it's good to know that the fundamental structure of ADO.NET is based on XML, and therefore primed for use with XML-related functionality like web services, and generally for communicating with client-side technologies using XML as a common language.

DataSet vs. DataReader

When designing an application that will utilize ADO.NET to perform database operations, there are two common approaches—using a DataReader object or the combination of a DataAdapter and DataSet. Each of these methods has advantages and disadvantages that make them properly suited for specific situations. Generally speaking, the DataReader object is best used in situations where a single, fairly simple SQL instruction will to be executed. DataSets are better suited for situations that require you to perform multiple, potentially complex, operations on sets of data. Table 9-2 compares the DataSet and DataReader methods.

Table 9-2. Comparing the DataSet and DataReader methods

DataReader	DataSet
Read-only access of data	Read-write access
Forward-only access to data	Forward-backward access to data
Faster data access	Slower data access
Operations must be performed while connected to database	Operations performed while disconnected
Based on a SQL statement from a single database	Can include tables from multiple databases

Read-write access

If your project requires you to grab data from a database and store it locally so the data can be manipulated, then a DataSet is the way to go. The data contained in a DataReader cannot be written to, only read from.

Data direction

DataReaders, along with being read only, are only able to scan data in a forward manner as the data is retrieved from the database. DataSets, however, can move both forward and backward through retrieved data.

Database access

If you are performing an operation that requires retrieving data from tables residing in multiple databases, it is necessary to use the DataSet instead of the DataReader. The DataReader only allows operations to be run on a single database (at any one time).

Speed of access

Starting to sound like the DataReader is pretty limiting? Well, the limitations come with their advantages. The DataReader is able to access data much more quickly than the DataSet, mainly due to the fact that the DataSet temporarily stores its data as an object on the web server. The DataReader, on the other hand, doesn't store data as an object in your application; instead, it allows you to access data quickly and store only the data you need. If your application doesn't require the advantages of the DataSet we've listed, the DataReader will be a better option, since it is a more efficient method of access.

Connected vs. disconnected

When using a DataReader object, your application is required to be connected to the database the entire time you will be reading the data returned from a query. The DataReader uses a "firehose" connection—when it's on, you have fast access to data, but when it's disconnected, you don't have access to the data, unless you stored it manually. The DataSet object, on the other hand, only connects to a database when it is necessary to retrieve or update data, and makes a store locally. Therefore, it does not need to be connected in order to scan the data within the DataSet.

It's important to note that, although DataSets are very useful for performing complex database operations, it is not possible for Flash to read a DataSet return type from a .NET web service (as we'll see in Chapter 12, it *is* possible using Flash Remoting), nor is it discussed in the "Using DataSets" section of this chapter. There is a method for "reformatting" a DataSet in a way that can be exported by a .NET web service and read by a Flash client.

In this book, we won't cover DataSet examples that make use of multiple databases or that make use of the DataSet's InsertCommand or UpdateCommand properties—essentially, we will make use of the DataSet as an alternative to the DataReader for retrieving data from a database.

Working with ADO.NET data providers

The ADO.NET classes within the .NET Framework contain four *data provider* classes that function as a "bridge" between your code and the underlying database you would like to communicate with. These data provider classes are intended to be very lightweight components—providing a minimal amount of interference between your C# code and the data source. The four basic .NET data provider classes are listed here:

- **SQL Server Data Provider:** Used to connect to Microsoft SQL Server 7.0 and later.
- **Oracle:** Used to connect to Oracle—supports all of its data types.
- **OLE DB Data Provider:** Used to connect to OLE DB data sources such as SQL Server 6.5 or earlier, Microsoft Access, Oracle, or any other database that has an OLE DB provider.
- **ODBC Data Provider:** Used to connect to ODBC data sources such as Oracle, Microsoft Access, or any other database where an ODBC driver is available and is the only alternative.

Of these four data providers, only the first two, SQL Server and Oracle, are attached to a specific database type. The second two, OLE DB and ODBC, are able to access a variety of different database types using existing OLE DB and ODBC providers.

> *SQL Server and Oracle are not the only database types that we can connect to using the native ADO.NET providers. Other databases, such as MySQL, can be easily accessed using providers available from* www.mysql.com *or third-party components, such as the MySqlDirect.NET provider from* www.crlab.com *or the ByteFx provider from* http://sourceforge.net/projects/mysqlnet/.

Data provider elements

For each of these types of data providers, there are four core elements: Connection, Command, DataAdapter, and DataReader. These four core elements provide the essential components needed to perform database operations using ADO.NET. Each of these elements has a different name within the scope of each data provider. For example:

- SqlConnection
- OleDbConnection
- OdbcConnection
- SqlCommand
- OleDbCommand

The four core elements provide functionality as listed here:

- Connection: Establishes a connection to a data source
- Command: Executes a command on a data source
- DataReader: Reads a forward-only, read-only stream of data from a data source
- DataAdapter: Connects to a data source to fill a DataSet and makes updates to the data source

Using these four classes, along with the System.Data.DataSet class, we'll be able to accomplish nearly any interaction between Flash and ASP.NET requiring database operations.

Connections

The ADO.NET Connection classes (SqlConnection, OleDbConnection, and OdbcConnection) provide the most fundamental and important element of database access—the connection between your .NET code and the database. Each of the other ADO.NET classes makes use of the Connection class to provide access to the database that they are reading or manipulating.

The most important property of the Connection class is the ConnectionString property. This property provides information to the Connection class about the specifics of the connection to a specific database, including the name and location of the database and security credentials. The ConnectionString property is a string value that can be set either through the constructor for a Connection class or after an instance of that class has been created. Two examples of the ConnectionString property are shown here, one set through the constructor of a SqlConnection and another using the ConnectionString property of a SqlConnection instance:

```
// Connection with ConnectionString set through constructor
OleDbConnection conn =
  new OleDbConnection("Provider=Microsoft.Jet.OLEDB.4.0;
➥ Data Source= chapter9.mdb;Persist Security Info=False");

// Connection with ConnectionString set using ConnectionString property
OleDbConnection conn  = new OleDbConnection();
conn.ConnectionString =
  "Provider=Microsoft.Jet.OLEDB.4.0;Data Source= chapter9.mdb;
➥ Persist Security Info=False";
```

As you can see in these examples, ConnectionStrings have a number of parameters separated by semicolons. These parameters are listed in Table 9-3.

Table 9-3. ConnectionString parameters

Parameter	Description
Provider	Used to specify which OLE DB provider to use. This parameter is only used in conjunction with the .NET OLE DB data provider.
Data Source	The name or location of the database server to connect to.
Persist Security Info	Specifies whether to resend security information if a connection is reopened.
Connection Timeout	The number of seconds to wait for a server reply. The default value for this parameter is 15 seconds.
Initial Catalog	The name of the database to connect to. (Note that this is different from the Data Source in that the Initial Catalog specifies the name of the database on the Data Source.)
User ID	The username to connect with when using SQL authentication.
Password	The password to connect with when using SQL authentication.
Trusted Connection	Specifies whether the connection is going to be encrypted.

Connecting to an Access database

As a first step in learning how to perform database access using ASP.NET, let's take a look at a simple connection to a Microsoft Access database using the C# OleDbConnection class. In this example, we'll create a web service method that will open a connection to an Access database and return a Boolean value indicating whether the connection was completed successfully. In this example, we're using web services only because they provide an easy interface for us to test a method—this method could be written in any other C# class file.

For this example, I have created a new Web Services website project in Visual Studio .NET, in a folder called chapter9. Within the App_Data folder, which is automatically created by Visual Studio, I have created a new Access database called chapter9.mdb. This database can be downloaded, from www.friendsofed.com/books/1590595173/code.html. Once you have the web service project created, let's move to the Server Explorer window in Visual Studio. The Server Explorer window is typically docked in the upper-left corner of the Visual Studio interface, or available from the View ➤ Server Explorer menu. As we'll see in this chapter, the Visual Studio Server Explorer provides easy access to database connections.

In order to use the Server Explorer to create database connections, it's first necessary to add the connection to the Server Explorer using the Add Connection option, available by right-clicking on the Data Connections item in the Server Explorer, as shown in Figure 9-1.

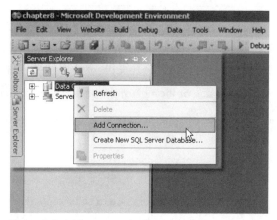

Figure 9-1. Adding a new database connection using Server Explorer

In the Add Connection window, we will choose the specifics of the database connection, in this case making an Access connection using the OLE DB data provider. Since the Server Explorer defaults to the SQL Server data provider, it will be necessary to click the Change button on the right side of the Add Connection window and select the Microsoft Access Database File option in the resulting window, as shown in Figure 9-2.

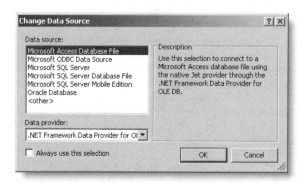

Figure 9-2. Choosing the Access database file

Once you have this data provider selected, you can select the location of your Access database, which should be located in the same directory as your web service project (see Figure 9-3). You can leave the User name and Password fields blank, since we won't be creating one for our Access database.

Figure 9-3. Configuring the database connection properties

And with that, the connection to the Access database has been created in the Solution Explorer. If you'd like to confirm that the connection works, try clicking the Test Connection button on the bottom of this screen—if there's a problem, the Solution Explorer will let you know!

One of the great features of the Solution Explorer in Visual Studio is that it creates a connection string for its connections, which, as we will see, can be used to connect to a database from C#. You can obtain this connection string by right-clicking on the database name in the Solution Explorer and then copying the ConnectionString property value from the Properties window, as shown in Figure 9-4. Select this string and copy it to the clipboard using the CTRL+C keys, and then close this screen by clicking OK.

Figure 9-4. Obtaining the ConnectionString from the Properties window

Now that we have the connection string to our Access database stored in our clipboard, let's jump to the code for the default web service file in our web service project, Service.cs. When you get to this file, it might be easiest to paste the connection string from your clipboard to a commented area on this page, just so you don't lose it!

In the Service.cs file, the first thing we'll do is modify the HelloWorld web service method that Visual Studio has created for us, creating a new method called TestAccessConnection. Within this method, we'll create a new instance of the OleDbConnection class and set the ConnectionString property of that instance to the connection string that we copied from the Solution Explorer. Once we have created the OleDbConnection instance, we'll try opening a connection to the Access database using the Open method.

```
[WebMethod]
public bool TestAccessConnection()
{
  OleDbConnection conn = new OleDbConnection();
  conn.ConnectionString = @"Provider=Microsoft.Jet.OLEDB.4.0;
➡ Data Source=C:\foundationaspnet\chapter9\Data\chapter9.mdb;
➡ Persist Security Info=False";
  try
  {
    conn.Open();
    conn.Close();
    return true;
  }
  catch
  {
    return false;
  }
}
```

In this codeblock, we are making use of a try-catch block to attempt to open and close a connection to the database, and to return a Boolean true value if this connection is successful. If the attempt is not successful, however, the try statement will fail and the catch statement will execute, returning a false value.

Let's try this method in a web browser by clicking the Start arrow in Visual Studio .NET. If the method executes successfully, the results should look similar to those in Figures 9-5 and 9-6.

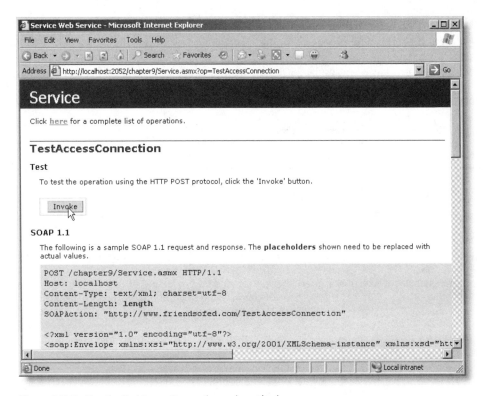

Figure 9-5. Testing the TestAccessConnection web method

Figure 9-6. Result of the TestAccessMethod test

Working with commands

While it's very important to understand how the Connection classes work, they alone don't allow us to execute any database operations. To accomplish these operations, we need to make use of the Command classes. The Command classes encapsulate SQL statements and use an existing connection object to perform the SQL operation. The Command object has a number of important members, which are used to execute SQL statements on an open connection—some of these are listed in Table 9-4.

Table 9-4. Useful members of the Command class

Member	Description
CommandText	The SQL statement to be executed.
CommandType	The type of the command that will be executed. This can be either command text, a stored procedure, or undefined.
Connection	Used to specify the connection object to be used for this command object.
ExecuteNonQuery	Executes a query that performs data processing (it doesn't return rows). Returns the number of rows affected by the query. This is typically used for UPDATE, DELETE, and INSERT statements.
ExecuteReader	Executes a query, returning a rowset. This is typically used for SELECT statements.
ExecuteScalar	Executes a query, returning a single record.
ExecuteXmlReader	Executes a query, returning an XML result.
Parameters	If the CommandType is a stored procedure, the Parameters property is used to specify the stored procedure parameters.

A command object can be created with or without specifying a SQL query and connection in the constructor, as shown here:

```
// creating a new Command
// and setting the Connection and CommandText properties
SqlCommand cmd = new SqlCommand();
cmd.Connection = myConnection;
cmd.CommandText =
  "INSERT INTO Products (ProductId, ProductName, ProductPrice)
➥ VALUES ('PRO121', 'Red Socks', 12)";

// creating a new Command by passing the connection
// and CommandText to the constructor
SqlCommand cmd =
  new SqlCommand(
➥ "INSERT INTO Products (ProductId, ProductName, ProductPrice)
➥ VALUES ('PRO121', 'Red Socks', 12) ", myConnection);
```

A command object that will be executing a query which does not return values (such as an UPDATE, INSERT, or DELETE statement) can be executed on the database using the ExecuteNonQuery method, as shown here:

```
// rowsAffected will contain the number of rows
// that were affected by the SQL statement
int rowsAffected = cmd.ExecuteNonQuery();
```

Working with DataReaders

If we want to execute not only a command on a database but also a SELECT statement that retrieves values from that database, we need to make use of the ADO.NET DataReader classes. DataReader provides a *forward-only* stream of data from the database that you can cycle through to retrieve the values returned from your query. Since a DataReader is *forward only*, the data retrieved by the DataReader can only be read sequentially (you can't just jump to the tenth row in a DataSet), and once a row has been read, it is freed from memory, making it impossible to access again. For this reason, the DataReader is very good for quick, memory-efficient data access that does not require a large amount of in-memory storage and manipulation.

Like the other classes in ADO.NET, the DataReader classes come in three flavors—SqlDataReader, OleDbDataReader, and OdbcDataReader. Table 9-5 lists the common methods of the ADO.NET DataReader class.

Table 9-5. Useful methods of the ADO.NET DataReader class

Method	Description
Close	Closes the DataReader object
GetBoolean	Retrieves a Boolean value from a column
GetByte	Retrieves a byte value from a column
GetChar	Retrieves a character from a column
GetDateTime	Retrieves the value of a column as a DateTime object
GetDecimal	Retrieves a decimal value from a column
GetDouble	Retrieves a double value from a column
GetInt32	Retrieves a 32-bit signed integer from a column
GetName	Retrieves the name of the specified column
GetString	Retrieves a string from a column
GetValue	Retrieves the value of a column in its original format
IsDBNull	Indicates whether the value of a column is null
NextResult	Moves the pointer to the beginning of the next result set
Read	Moves the pointer to the next record, if there is one

These methods are used to extract the data retrieved by a DataReader from a Command object's query result. A typical use of a DataReader object follows the same fundamental steps (although these are not required) as follows:

1. Open a Command object's connection, allowing the command to execute:

   ex: myConn.Open();

2. Create a new instance of a DataReader from a Command's ExecuteDataReader method:

   ex: DataReader dr = myCommand.ExecuteDataReader()

3. Loop through the entries within the DataReader, typically using a while loop and the DataReader's Read method:

   ex: while (dr.Read())

4. Use the DataReader's GetInt32, GetString, GetDouble, etc., methods to retrieve the values for each column in the DataReader:

   ex: { int myInt = dr.GetInt(0); // 0 is the column's index }

5. Close the DataReader:

   ex: dr.Close();

6. Close the Connection object:

   ex: myConn.Close();

Although this might seem a bit confusing at first, it's a pretty easy approach to get used to. Let's take a look at a simple example of a web service that uses this approach to retrieve data from a SQL database. In this example, we'll first create a struct object, Product, which will be used to return an object readable by the Flash Web Service Connector.

```
public struct Product {
  public string ProductName;
  public int ProductPrice;
}

[WebMethod]
public Product[] GetProducts () {
  SqlConnection conn = new SqlConnection(... a connection string ...);
  SqlCommand cmd =
    new SqlCommand(
➥ "SELECT ProductName, ProductPrice FROM Products", conn);

  // create an ArrayList to hold the Products temporarily
  ArrayList al  = new ArrayList();

  Conn.Open();
  SqlDataReader dr = cmd.ExecuteDataReader();
  while (dr.Read())
  {
    Product prod = new Product();
    prod.ProductName = dr.GetString(0);
```

```
    prod.ProductPrice = dr.GetInt(1);

    // add the product to the ArrayList
    al.Add(prod);
  }
  dr.Close();
  conn.Close();

  // create a product array, the size of the ArrayList
  Product[] products = new Product[al.Count];
  for (int x=0; x<al.Count; x++)
  {
    products[x] = (Product) al[x];
  }

  return products;
}
```

In this example, once a connection to a SQL database has been established, and a SqlCommand object has been created, a SqlDataReader is created in the following line of code:

```
SqlDataReader dr = cmd.ExecuteDataReader();
```

With this SqlDataReader now in existence, and containing the results of the query defined by the SqlCommand object, we can cycle through the rows of the query's results by using the line

```
while (dr.Read()) {
```

Since the DataReader's Read method returns a Boolean value denoting whether it was able to successfully read another row of data, a while loop is a perfect way to read through all of the records in the DataReader. When the DataReader contains no more rows of data, the DataReader's Read method will return false, causing our code execution to move on.

In the following lines:

```
Product prod = new Product();
prod.ProductName = dr.GetString(0);
prod.ProductPrice = dr.GetInt(1);
al.Add(prod);
```

a new Product structure is created and the data is retrieved from the current row (as retrieved by the DataReader's Read method), using the GetString and GetInt methods. These methods take the column number of the data to retrieve as a parameter and return the typed data from that column. Using this combination of a while loop and GetXXX commands, it is possible to obtain the values returned by a database query. Once the data has been extracted using the GetString and GetInt commands, the new Product is added to the ArrayList.

It is very important to note the following line in the DataReader example:

```
dr.Close();
```

Once a DataReader begins reading values using a Connection object, that object cannot be used for another operation until the DataReader object is closed. This is a very easy operation to overlook, but doing so will avoid headaches and keep your DataReader operations running effectively.

251

Finally, since our web method has been created to return an array of Products, we need to come up with a method for converting from the variable-dimension ArrayList we have created into a dimensioned array. This can be done using a for loop—first we create a new array of Products and then set each item in this array to each product we have added to the ArrayList:

```
Product[] products = new Product[al.Count];
for (int x=0; x<al.Count; x++)
{
    products[x] = (Product) al[x];
}
```

DataAdapters and DataSets

As we've seen in the previous section, the .NET Command classes, along with Connection and DataReader, provide a solid groundwork for performing SQL operations on a database. The ADO.NET framework also provides two other classes that help when working with larger database operations: DataAdapter and DataSet.

Using DataAdapters

The ADO.NET DataAdapter provides a bridge between a data source and a DataSet object. The DataAdapter object uses the Connection and Command objects covered in the previous sections, and provides some of the functionality of the DataReader object, but the DataAdapter provides a *set* of commands that are capable of filling a local DataSet object and updating changes made to that DataSet on the data source, as shown in Figure 9-7. This set of commands consists of *SelectCommand*, *InsertCommand*, *UpdateCommand*, and *DeleteCommand*, each of which is a Command object used to perform specific operations on the data source.

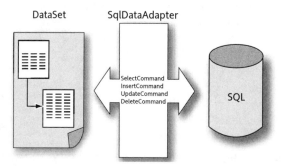

Figure 9-7. SqlDataAdapter functioning between a DataSet and SQL Server

Using the DataAdapter, a DataSet object can be filled with data, or a database's contents can be updated based on the data contained locally in a DataSet object. Before we look further into the DataAdapter, let's take a closer look at the DataSet object.

Using DataSets

A DataSet is an ADO.NET object that can be thought of as a local copy of data from a database. The DataSet object is actually a collection of ADO.NET DataTable objects, which hold data in a very similar manner to the way a database would hold it, allowing you to access that data *without being constantly connected* to the data source. Like database tables, the tables within a DataSet can contain relationships and constraints.

A typical interaction between a DataAdapter, DataSet, and data source consists of the following steps:

1. A DataAdapter instance fills a DataSet instance using the DataAdapter's Fill method, which uses the DataAdapter's SelectCommand to obtain the data from the data source. The SelectCommand connects to the data source using its Connection object (as described earlier in this chapter), and after it obtains the data, immediately disconnects. This connection and disconnection is a completely hidden process when using the DataAdapter.

2. Data is retrieved, updated, deleted, or inserted into the DataSet's DataTable objects using the DataTable's DataRows.

3. If the DataSet is being used to update, insert, or delete data from the database, the DataAdapter's Update method is called, which executes the necessary Update, Delete, and Insert commands to update the data in the data source.

Filling a DataSet and passing it to Flash using a web service

Let's take a look at an example of an ASP.NET application that retrieves data from a database using a DataAdapter/DataSet and allows Flash to access that data by posting it as a web method. As mentioned in the previous section, being able to send data stored in a DataSet to Flash will require that the records in the DataSet be converted to a format that can be read by Flash (a struct) and returned as an array of structs instead of a DataSet.

Creating a struct to use as a return type for a .NET web service is very easy, requiring only that you know the data types of each of the columns you would like to return from your database query. In this example, we're going to pull data from the Northwind Access database, specifically from the Customers table. For this example, we'll only return a few columns from the table: CustomerId, CompanyName, ContactName, ContactTitle, Address, City, and Country.

```
public struct Customer
{
    public string CustomerId;
    public string CompanyName;
    public string ContactName;
    public string ContactTitle;
    public string Address;
    public string City;
    public string Country;
}
```

With this struct created, we can create a new WebMethod that returns an array of these structs, as in the following lines:

```
[WebMethod]
public Customer[] GetCustomersDataSet()
{ ... }
```

Next, we'll need to do a couple of things in order to create a DataAdapter and fill a DataSet (which will be used to create the array of structs):

1. Create an OleDbConnection, which will define the database connection for the DataAdapter.

2. Create an OleDbCommand object, which will define the SelectCommand of the DataAdapter.

3. Set the Connection property of the new OleDbCommand to the OleDbConnection we just created.

These tasks are accomplished in the following code:

```
// remember first to add the necessary using statements
using System.Data;
using System.OleDb;
...

// create a new Connection
OleDbConnection conn = new OleDbConnection();
conn.ConnectionString =
  @"Provider=Microsoft.Jet.OLEDB.4.0;
➥ Data Source=C:\foundationaspnet\chapter9\Data\Northwind.mdb";

// create a new Command
OleDbCommand cmd = new OleDbCommand();
cmd.CommandText =
  "SELECT CustomerID, CompanyName, ContactName, ContactTitle,
➥ Address, City, Country FROM Customers";

// set the command's Connection property to "conn"
cmd.Connection = conn;
```

Now, with a new Command created, which will serve as the SelectCommand for a DataAdapter, let's create a new DataAdapter and set this SelectCommand property:

```
// create the DataAdapter
OleDbDataAdapter da = new OleDbDataAdapter();
// set the SelectCommand property
da.SelectCommand = cmd;
```

And with that, we've created a basic DataAdapter that is capable of performing one function—filling a DataSet based on the query contained in its SelectCommand. Next, let's create a DataSet and fill it:

```
DataSet ds = new DataSet();
da.Fill(ds);
```

At this point, we now have a DataSet instance that contains the rows resulting from the SELECT statement we defined. All we have left to do at this point is to create a new customer array and populate the elements of that array from the rows of the table we filled in the DataSet object. To accomplish this, we'll make use of the C# foreach loop to iterate through each row of the table. When using the foreach loop, we are able to obtain an instance of the ADO.NET DataRow object each time through the loop, and retrieve the data from each DataRow by specifying the DataRow's column name as an indexer, as in the following code:

```
Customer[] customers = new Customer[ds.Tables[0].Rows.Count];
int ct=0;
foreach (DataRow dr in ds.Tables[0].Rows)
```

```
{
  Customer cust = new Customer();
  cust.CustomerId = (string)dr["CustomerId"];
  cust.CompanyName = (string)dr["CompanyName"];
  cust.Address = (string)dr["Address"];
  cust.ContactName = (string)dr["ContactName"];
  cust.ContactTitle = (string)dr["ContactTitle"];
  cust.City = (string)dr["City"];
  cust.Country = (string)dr["Country"];
  customers[ct] = cust;
  ct++;
}
return customers;
}
```

You'll also notice that each time we retrieve a value from a DataRow instance, we must *cast* that instance as the data type we mean to retrieve.

When we publish this code, you'll see that we are able to retrieve the data from the Customers table of the Northwind Access database and publish it as an XML web service (see Figure 9-8).

```
<?xml version="1.0" encoding="utf-8" ?>
- <ArrayOfCustomer xmlns:xsi="http://www.w3.org/2001/XMLSchema-instance"
    xmlns:xsd="http://www.w3.org/2001/XMLSchema"
    xmlns="http://tempuri.org/">
  - <Customer>
      <CustomerId>ALFKI</CustomerId>
      <CompanyName>Alfreds Futterkiste</CompanyName>
      <ContactName>Maria Anders</ContactName>
      <ContactTitle>Sales Representative</ContactTitle>
      <Address>Obere Str. 57</Address>
      <City>Berlin</City>
      <Country>Germany</Country>
    </Customer>
  - <Customer>
      <CustomerId>ANATR</CustomerId>
      <CompanyName>Ana Trujillo Emparedados y helados</CompanyName>
      <ContactName>Ana Trujillo</ContactName>
      <ContactTitle>Owner</ContactTitle>
      <Address>Avda. de la Constitución 2222</Address>
      <City>México D.F.</City>
      <Country>Mexico</Country>
    </Customer>
  - <Customer>
      <CustomerId>ANTON</CustomerId>
      <CompanyName>Antonio Moreno Taquería</CompanyName>
      <ContactName>Antonio Moreno</ContactName>
```

Figure 9-8. Result of the GetCustomerDataSet web method

Summary

In this chapter, we've learned the basics of database access in .NET, ranging from SQL statements to ADO.NET DataSets. Through the examples in this chapter, you should be getting a taste of how easy it is to retrieve data using ADO.NET and pass that data along to Flash using a .NET web service. The skills that we've covered in this chapter will provide a basis for the advanced data-driven applications we'll be using in the rest of this book.

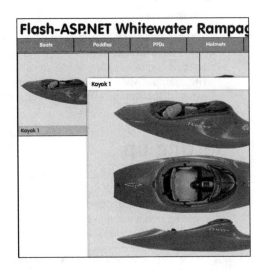

Chapter 10

PRODUCT VIEWER APPLICATION

What this chapter covers:

- Using an Access database to store information for an online storefront
- Retrieving the information from the Access database using ASP.NET web services
- Displaying the information and images for the storefront using Flash and the Flash Web Service Connector

In the past several chapters, we've learned how to create and consume web services using Flash and ASP.NET, as well as how to access databases using ADO.NET. In this chapter, we'll combine these two skills to create our own online storefront using Flash, ASP.NET web services, and an Access database. The methods we'll use in this example will provide a great framework for setting up many different types of applications—from e-commerce to interactive learning systems.

Setting up

By using the combination of Flash, ASP.NET web services, and Access for this application, we are provided with a well-defined model to create our presentation, logical, and data tiers. Since we do have this well-organized model, we'll be able to work through this application in a very structured manner, which will make the development process as simple as possible. Let's kick off this example by defining the functionality that each of the three application tiers will be designed to accomplish:

- **Presentation tier**: The presentation tier for this project will be accomplished with a Flash interface. The presentation tier will be responsible for displaying buttons representing the categories of products in our store, and when a category button is selected, displaying the products that exist within that category. The presentation tier will also be responsible for displaying a "detailed" view of each product when the product is selected by the user.

- **Logical tier**: The logical tier will be implemented by an ASP.NET web service. The logical tier will be responsible for retrieving category and product information from the data tier and sending it to the presentation tier. The methods that will be required of the logical tier will be

  - GetCategories—Takes no input parameters and returns a list of the product categories

  - GetCateogoryProducts—Takes a category ID as a parameter and returns a list of the products that fall into that category

- **Data tier**: The data tier for this project will be a Microsoft Access database. The data tier will be responsible for storing the information describing the products in our store.

With the division of functionality well defined, it's pretty easy to see what we'll have to accomplish in order to create this storefront. We'll attack this project from the bottom up, first creating the data tier, followed by the logical tier, and finally, the Flash presentation tier. As a first step, I'm going to create a new folder, C:\foundationaspnet\chapter10\, to house this new project, and then within this directory, create two new folders, Flash and Data. The Flash folder will hold the Flash files for this application, and the Data folder will hold the Microsoft Access database.

Creating the Microsoft Access data tier

Creating the data tier for this and other Flash/ASP.NET applications requires careful consideration, since making a change to the data tier once the other two tiers are created often requires cascading these changes in the logical and presentation tier. As mentioned earlier, the data tier will be created using Microsoft Access. Access databases are easy to create, deploy, and work with, but should not be used in high-traffic environments—in the case of a high-traffic environment, a more stable database option should be used, such as SQL Server, which will be covered in the next chapter.

In the Data folder of this project, I'm going to create a new Access database called store.mdb. In this database, I'm going to define two tables, Categories and Products. The Categories table will store the names of the categories of products in our store, and the Products table will store the information about the products themselves.

> *If you do not have Microsoft Access available, you can download this Access database from the friends of ED website at* `www.friendsofed.com/books/1590595173/code.html`.

Listed next are the columns that we will create for each table:

Categories

- CategoryId: An auto-incrementing number that will be the index for the Category table
- CategoryName: A text value that will be the name of the category (see Figure 10-1)

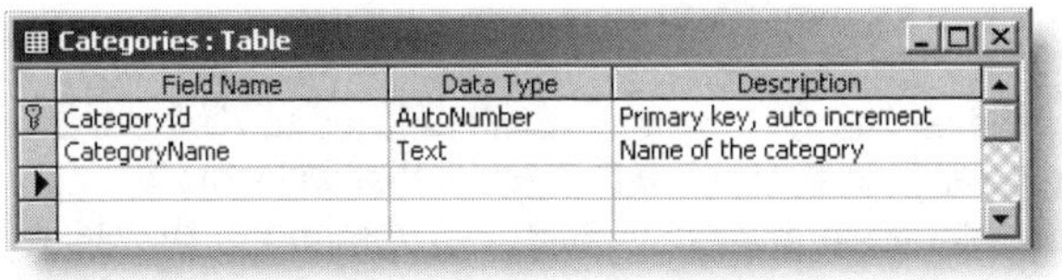

Categories : Table

Field Name	Data Type	Description
CategoryId	AutoNumber	Primary key, auto increment
CategoryName	Text	Name of the category

Figure 10-1. Categories table design

Products

- ProductId: An auto-incrementing number that will be the index for the Products table
- ProductName: A text value that will hold the name of the product
- ProductDescription: A text value that will contain a detailed description of the product
- ProductPrice: A number that will contain the price of the product
- ProductCategory: A number referencing the index of the Category table that the product belongs to
- ProductImage: A text value containing the name of the product's image (see Figure 10-2)

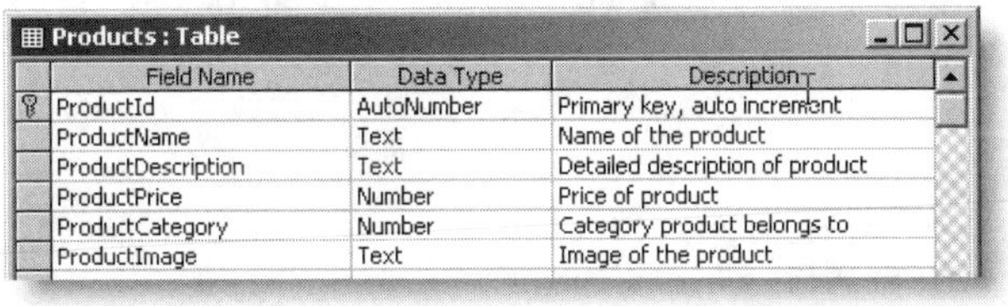

Products : Table

Field Name	Data Type	Description
ProductId	AutoNumber	Primary key, auto increment
ProductName	Text	Name of the product
ProductDescription	Text	Detailed description of product
ProductPrice	Number	Price of product
ProductCategory	Number	Category product belongs to
ProductImage	Text	Image of the product

Figure 10-2. Products table design

As you'll notice, the Products table contains a ProductCategory column, which defines the category that each product belongs to—known as a *foreign key* relationship between the Categories and Products tables. As we work through the logical tier, we'll see how we use this foreign key relationship in our SQL queries to return products from a specific category.

Creating the ASP.NET logical tier

With our data tier created, we can move into the logical tier with a pretty clear view of the functionality we need to implement. As defined earlier, we want to create two public methods for our web service, the GetCategories and GetCategoryProducts methods, which will retrieve data from the tables within the "store" database and publish this data as web service methods. We'll start off the logical tier by creating a new ASP.NET web service project, in the Chapter10 folder. If you're using Visual Studio .NET, there will be a web service file, Service.asmx, which we'll use to create our web service.

In the Service.asmx file, I'm going to add a Name attribute to the WebService declaration, as shown in the following codeblock:

```
[WebService(Namespace = "http://www.friendsofed.com",
            Name="Chapter_10_Storefront")]
```

Changing this attribute makes it easier to inspect your web services from the Flash Web Services panel, since Flash will show this more detailed description instead of just the name of the file, service.

Next, we should define the connection string that will be used to connect to our Access database. I'm going to create a string variable in this web service class that will store the connection string, and then set the value of the connection string in the constructor method of the class.

```
public class service : System.Web.Services.WebService {
    string _connString;

    public service () {
        _connString = @"Provider=Microsoft.Jet.OLEDB.4.0;
➥ Data Source=C:\foundationaspnet\chapter10\data\store.mdb";
    }
```

In this string, you'll see that I've set the Provider to use the Microsoft.Jet.OLEDB.4.0 provider, which is the provider typically used to connect to Microsoft Access databases. I've also set the Source to an absolute directory on my hard drive. You may need to change this value, depending on where you have set up your Access database.

The next step we should take is to make sure we have the proper .NET base class library namespaces included in our project. Listed here are the libraries we will need for this web service:

```
using System;
using System.Web;
using System.Collections;
using System.Web.Services;
using System.Web.Services.Protocols;
using System.Data;
using System.Data.OleDb;
```

Of these libraries, the most essential to this project is the System.Data.OleDb library, which contains the ADO.NET classes specific to OleDb connections—which we will be using to connect to our Access database.

Before making use of the connection string we have created and the OleDb classes, let's create C# structs that will define what a Category and Product consist of. As mentioned in Chapter 8, a structure is the easiest and most efficient way of returning data objects to Flash from ASP.NET web services. This structure will be a virtual mirror image of the columns created in the Products and Categories databases. Listed next is the code used to create the Product and Category structures. This struct should be placed in the same class file as our web service, Service.asmx.

```
public struct Product
{
  public int ProductId;
  public string ProductName;
  public string ProductDesc;
  public double ProductPrice;
  public int ProductCategory;
  public string ProductImage;
  }
public struct ProductCategory
{
  public int CatId;
  public string CatName;
}
```

With these structures created, we are now ready to create the web methods that will provide our presentation tier with access to the information in our Access database. First, let's create the GetCategories method:

```
[WebMethod]
public ProductCategory[] GetCategories()
{
    // GetCategories logic here!
}
```

As defined earlier in this chapter, the GetCategories method will take no input parameters and return a list of the product categories in our online storefront. We'll return this list of product categories in the form of an array of ProductCategory structs.

Within this method, we'll need to create a connection to the database using an OleDbConnection object and then, using an OleDbCommand object, we'll get an OleDbDataReader instance that will contain the information from the Categories table. This method will be very similar to the examples in the Chapter 9 "Working with DataReaders" section.

```
// create a connection object using the defined connection string
OleDbConnection conn = new OleDbConnection(_connString);

// create a new command object, setting the connection property
// to the conn object
OleDbCommand cmd = new OleDbCommand();
cmd.CommandText = "SELECT CategoryId, CategoryName FROM Categories";
cmd.Connection = conn;
```

```
// open the connection and create a new DataReader from the cmd object
conn.Open();
OleDbDataReader dr = cmd.ExecuteReader();
```

In this codeblock, after the OleDbCommand object was created, I set the CommandText property of that object to a SQL statement that will simply retrieve the CategoryId and CategoryName fields from the Categories table—note that it is usually easier to list all of the fields in a SQL query instead of using the * wildcard when executing a DataReader. This is because the DataReader requires you to know the index of the column that you would like to retrieve, and with the wildcard character, it's not easy to remember in what order the columns will be retrieved. Because this syntax is well defined, it can also save a good deal of trouble if you ever make changes to the schema of your database.

Next, I'm going to iterate through each of the rows in the DataReader object, creating a new ProductCategory object for each. I'll then add each of these new objects to a new ArrayList object, which will house the data until we create a ProductCategory array:

```
ArrayList al = new ArrayList();
while (dr.Read())
{
  ProductCategory pcat = new ProductCategory();
  pcat.CatId = dr.GetInt32(0);
  pcat.CatName = dr.GetString(1);

 al.Add(pcat);
}
```

And now, with an ArrayList filled with ProductCategory objects, we can create the ProductCategory array, which we return when the GetCategories method is called:

```
// create a new ProductCategory array, the same length as
// the al ArrayList object
ProductCategory[] pCatRet = new ProductCategory[al.Count];
for (int x = 0; x < al.Count; x++)
{
  pCatRet[x] = (ProductCategory)al[x];
}
return pCatRet;
```

And that's it for the GetCategories method. Next we'll define the GetCategoryProducts method, using very similar logic:

```
[WebMethod]
public Product[] GetCategoryProducts(int catId)
{
  OleDbConnection conn = new OleDbConnection(_connString);
  OleDbCommand cmd = new OleDbCommand();
  cmd.CommandText = "SELECT ProductId, ProductName, ProductDescription,
➥ ProductCategory, ProductImage, ProductPrice FROM Products
➥ WHERE ProductCategory=" + catId.ToString();
  cmd.Connection = conn;
```

```
   conn.Open();
   OleDbDataReader dr = cmd.ExecuteReader();
```

This codeblock looks almost exactly the same as the GetCategories method, with the exception that the CommandText's SQL statement uses the catId input parameter to specify a specific category to return products from, using the WHERE SQL keyword.

> *In the previous codeblock, I am creating my* CommandText *string by concatenating a* SELECT *statement with an integer input parameter. This practice, although relatively safe with integer parameters, can be very dangerous with string inputs—opening a vulnerability to SQL injection attacks. More information on SQL injection attacks can be found at* http://msdn.microsoft.com/msdnmag/issues/04/09/SQLInjection/. *In Chapter 13, we'll cover a more secure method of creating SQL queries, using stored procedures, which prevents many of the dangers of SQL injection attacks.*

The following code is used, just like in the GetCategories method, to create new Product structures, add them to a new ArrayList, and return a new array of Products:

```
ArrayList al = new ArrayList();
while (dr.Read())
{
   Product prod = new Product();
   prod.ProductId = dr.GetInt32(0);
   prod.ProductName = dr.GetString(1);
   prod.ProductDesc = dr.GetString(2);
   prod.ProductPrice = dr.GetDouble(3);
   prod.ProductCategory = dr.GetInt32(4);
   prod.ProductImage = dr.GetString(5);

   al.Add(prod);
}

Product[] retProd = new Product[al.Count];
for (int x = 0; x < al.Count; x++)
{
   retProd[x] = (Product)al[x];
}

return retProd;
```

Not too hard, right? As you can see by the simplicity of these methods, ADO.NET takes much of the complexity out of data access—and web services take the complexity out of structured data formatting!

The complete code for the Service.asmx.cs page is listed here:

```
using System;
using System.Web;
using System.Collections;
using System.Web.Services;
using System.Web.Services.Protocols;
using System.Data;
using System.Data.OleDb;

[WebService(Namespace = "http://www.friendsofed.com/",
             Name="Chapter_10_Storefront")]
[WebServiceBinding(ConformsTo = WsiProfiles.BasicProfile1_1)]
public class service : System.Web.Services.WebService {
  string _connString;

  public service () {
    _connString = @"Provider=Microsoft.Jet.OLEDB.4.0;
➥ Data Source=C:\foundationaspnet\chapter10\data\store.mdb";
  }
  public struct Product
  {
    public int ProductId;
    public string ProductName;
    public string ProductDesc;
    public double ProductPrice;
    public int ProductCategory;
    public string ProductImage;
  }
  public struct ProductCategory
  {
    public int CatId;
    public string CatName;
  }

  [WebMethod]
  public Product[] GetCategoryProducts(int catId)
  {
    OleDbConnection conn = new OleDbConnection(_connString);
    OleDbCommand cmd = new OleDbCommand();
    cmd.CommandText = "SELECT ProductId, ProductName, ProductDescription,
➥ ProductCategory, ProductImage, ProductPrice FROM Products
➥ WHERE ProductCategory=" + catId.ToString();
    cmd.Connection = conn;

    conn.Open();
    OleDbDataReader dr = cmd.ExecuteReader();

    ArrayList al = new ArrayList();
    while (dr.Read())
```

```csharp
      {
        Product prod = new Product();
        prod.ProductId = dr.GetInt32(0);
        prod.ProductName = dr.GetString(1);
        prod.ProductDesc = dr.GetString(2);
        prod.ProductPrice = dr.GetDouble(3);
        prod.ProductCategory = dr.GetInt32(4);
        prod.ProductImage = dr.GetString(5);

        al.Add(prod);
        }

      Product[] retProd = new Product[al.Count];
      for (int x = 0; x < al.Count; x++)
       {
        retProd[x] = (Product)al[x];
      }

      return retProd;
    }

  [WebMethod]
  public ProductCategory[] GetCategories()
  {
    OleDbConnection conn = new OleDbConnection(_connString);
    OleDbCommand cmd = new OleDbCommand();
    cmd.CommandText = "SELECT CategoryId, CategoryName FROM Categories";
    cmd.Connection = conn;

    conn.Open();
    OleDbDataReader dr = cmd.ExecuteReader();

    ArrayList al = new ArrayList();
    while (dr.Read())
    {
      ProductCategory pcat = new ProductCategory();
      pcat.CatId = dr.GetInt32(0);
      pcat.CatName = dr.GetString(1);

       al.Add(pcat);
     }

    ProductCategory[] pCatRet = new ProductCategory[al.Count];
    for (int x = 0; x < al.Count; x++)
    {
      pCatRet[x] = (ProductCategory)al[x];
    }
    return pCatRet;
  }
}
```

In order to test these web service methods, let's put some test data into the Access database, as shown in Figure 10-3.

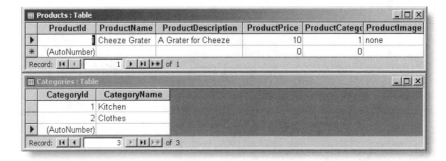

Figure 10-3. Test data

And, with this sample data inserted, we can test the result in Internet Explorer, as shown in Figure 10-4.

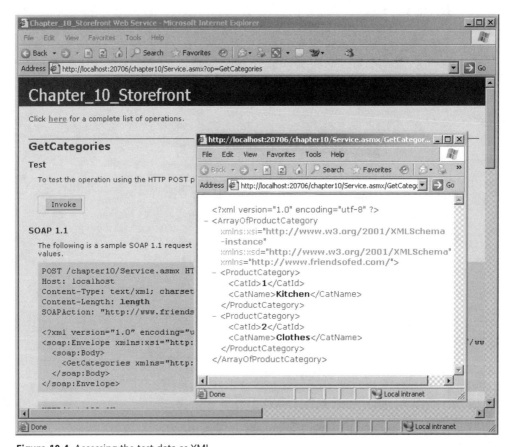

Figure 10-4. Accessing the test data as XML

Creating the Flash presentation tier

Now that we've completed the data and logical tiers, all we have left is to create our Flash presentation tier. In this Flash movie, we'll create an interface that will load the list product categories from the ASP.NET GetCategories web method and display them as navigational buttons for the storefront. When a category button is selected, the interface will load the products contained within that category from the GetCategoryProducts web method and display them as thumbnail images. If a product is clicked, the page will open a detailed view to display the full product information.

We'll get started by creating a new folder called Flash in the same folder as your ASP.NET web service project. Within this folder, create a new Flash Movie called storefront.fla. I have created this file with dimensions of 980×590, and a frame rate of 30 frames per second. In this file, I have created three layers, one titled actions, another background, and a third, zigo. In the zigo layer, I have dragged an instance of the Zigo engine (see Chapter 6), and in the background layer, I have created a simple wireframe for the storefront, with a solid header that is 30 pixels tall, as shown in Figure 10-5.

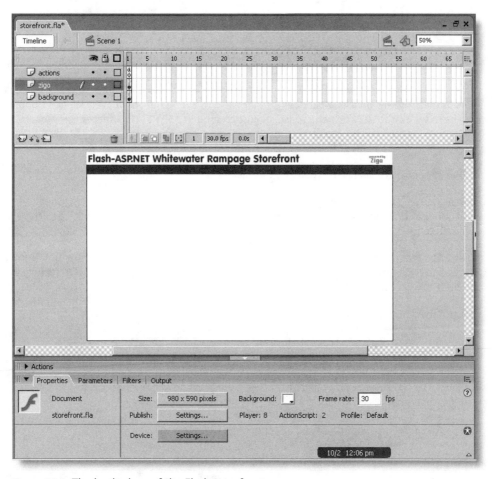

Figure 10-5. The beginnings of the Flash storefront

Using the same class application framework that I presented in Chapter 8, let's create a new ActionScript 2.0 class file, Application.as. I have saved this file in the same Flash folder that I saved the storefront.fla file in. In this file, I have created a static function, main; a constructor function; and a setup function:

```
dynamic class Application extends MovieClip {
  function Application(owner)
  {
    owner.__proto__ = this.__proto__;
    owner.__constructor__ = Application;
    this = owner;

    setup();
  }
  private function setup()
{   }
  public static function main(createdBy:MovieClip) {
    var app = new Application(createdBy);
  }
}
```

The first thing we're going to want this Flash storefront interface to do is load the category names for the items in the store. To do this, we'll need to make use of the ActionScript Web Service Connector component so we can access the web service we just created in ASP.NET. To use this component, we'll need to import the web service classes into the Application.as file we're working on, by adding the following code to the top line of the class:

```
import mx.data.components.WebServiceConnector;
```

In order for these classes to be available in our Flash movie, we'll also have to go back out onto the stage in Flash and drag an instance of the Flash Web Service Connector component onto the stage, and then delete it—so it will be available in the movie's library.

Let's create a function in the Application.as class that will load the list of categories from the ASP.NET web service. In this function, we'll need to call the GetCategories web method (which we know doesn't take any parameters) and wait for a response.

```
function LoadCategories()
{
  // create a handler to wait for the web service's result
  function res(ev) {   }

  var _catServ:WebServiceConnector = new WebServiceConnector();
  // note that this WSDLURL will be different on your system
  _catServ.WSDLURL =
    "http://localhost:20706/chapter10/Service.asmx?WSDL";
```

```
        _catServ.addEventListener("result",res);
        _catServ.operation = "GetCategories";
        _catServ.params = [];
        _catServ.suppressInvalidCalls = true;
        _catServ.trigger();
    }
```

This codeblock should look pretty similar to the examples in the previous chapter. An instance of WebServiceConnector is created, configured, and triggered, with an event listener added to wait for the service's response. Once we receive the response from the web service, we'll want to create the category buttons on our storefront interface. Before creating the web service event handler, let's create a new MovieClip and class for the Category buttons. I'm going to name this symbol CategoryButton and give it an AS 2.0 class named category_button, as shown in Figure 10-6.

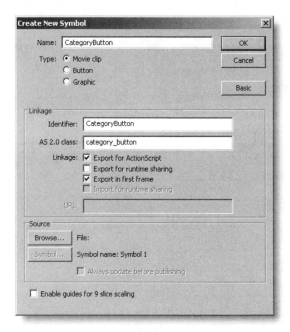

Figure 10-6. Configuring the category buttons

On the timeline for the CategoryButton, I'm going to create two layers, text and bg. In the text layer, let's create a dynamic text field called title_txt. I have made this text field white and centered, and have embedded the fonts within the file. In the layer beneath this text field, I have created a gray rectangle with a width and height of 120×28. I have placed the text field in the center of this rectangle, as shown in Figure 10-7.

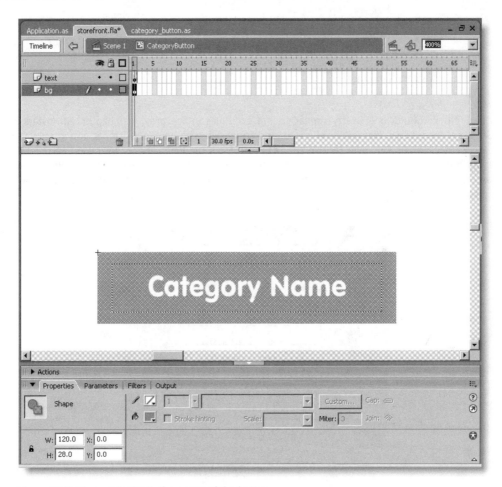

Figure 10-7. The text field is in the center of the button.

Next, let's create the class file for the CategoryButton instance. I have created a new file called cate-gory_button.as and saved it into the same folder as the storefront.fla file. In this file I have cre-ated a new class extending the MovieClip class, as shown in this codeblock:

```
dynamic class category_button extends MovieClip {
  var title_txt:TextField;

  function category_button() {
  }
}
```

Within this class, I'm going to create a new method called SetInfo, which will initialize the CategoryButton with a string value for its title_txt field and also assign it a CategoryID, which we'll need in a moment. I'm also going to create event handlers for the rollOver, rollOut, and onRelease events of this MovieClip:

```
dynamic class category_button extends MovieClip {
  private var _catId:Number;
  var title_txt:TextField;

  function category_button() {
    this.onRelease = gotClick;
  this.onRollOver = gotRoll;
  this.onRollOut = gotRollOut;
  }
  function SetInfo(catId:Number, catTitle:String)
  {
    title_txt.text = catTitle;
    this._catId = catId;
  }
  function gotClick()
  {
      // code to execute when a button is selected
  }
  function gotRoll()
  {
    this.brightnessTo(30, .4, "easeOut");
  }
  function gotRollOut()
  {
    this.brightnessTo(0, .4, "easeOut");
  }
}
```

In the gotRoll and gotRollOut methods of this codeblock, I have made use of the Zigo engine classes to produce a rollover brightening effect for the button.

Now that we have created the CategoryButton (except for the gotClick function, which we'll be completing shortly), let's jump back to the LoadCategories function in the Application.as file and complete the web service result event handler. In this event handler, we will be retrieving the listing of categories from the ASP.NET web service (as an array of ProductCategory objects) and using this array to create new instances of the CategoryButton MovieClip. Once the instances of the CategoryButton have been attached to the _root timeline, we'll make use of the CategoryButton's SetInfo function to initialize the category ID and category name for that instance.

```
function LoadCategories()
{
  function res(ev) {
    var x:Number;
    var res = ev.target.results;
    for (x=0; x<res.length; x++) {
      var nn:String = "cb"+x.toString();
      _root.attachMovie("CategoryButton",nn,50+x);
      _root[nn]._x = 122*x;
      _root[nn].SetInfo(res[x].CatId, res[x].CatName);
    }
  }
.. }
```

With this event handler created, let's modify the setup() function in the Application.as file to call the LoadCategories function:

```
public function setup()
{
    LoadCategories();
}
```

Now, let's jump to the Actions layer we created on the _root timeline of the Storefront.fla file and add a line of code to initialize our application:

```
Application.main(this);
```

Upon starting, our storefront.fla file will now create a new instance of the Application.as file, which will subsequently call the LoadCategories method and get the ball rolling! Let's try testing the application as it sits right now (see Figure 10-8). (If you don't have any test data in the Categories table of your Access database, you'll need to put some in now for the application to work!)

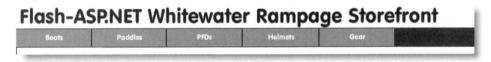

Figure 10-8. The menu of the storefront

Not too bad—just that easily, we have translated the contents of an Access database table into a menuing system in Flash! You might notice that there is a delay between when you start testing your application and when the CategoryButtons appear on the screen. This is when our application does its dirty work. Flash is calling the GetCategories method of the Service.asmx web service, the web service is retrieving values from the database, and the well-formatted XML result is returned to Flash. If you use a method similar to this one to create a live application, you will most likely want to create a "loading" function to run while this process is taking place—you don't want to leave the users of your app in the dark!

The next step we'll take is to create a MovieClip class that will represent the individual items in each category when a category button is selected. I am going to create a MovieClip called SmallItem that has an identifier of SmallItem and uses an AS 2.0 class file called small_item.as. In a very similar layout to the CategoryButton MovieClip, I will be creating two layers in this MovieClip, one called text and a second called bg. In the bg layer, I am creating a 196×173 rectangle, and in the text layer, a dynamic text field again named title_txt, as shown in Figure 10-9.

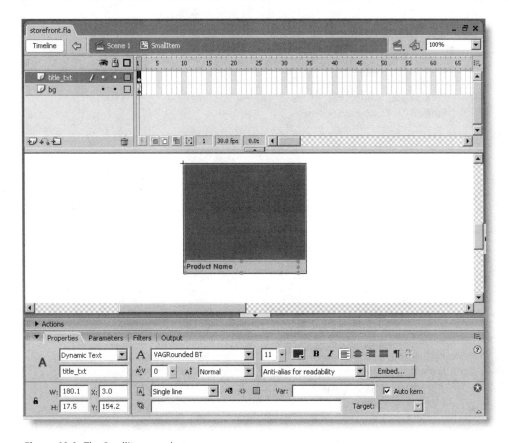

Figure 10-9. The SmallItem movie

Along with this MovieClip, I'm going to create the small_item.as file, which will look pretty similar to the class for the CategoryButton MovieClip:

```
dynamic class small_item extends MovieClip {
  private var _id:Number;
  private var _title:String;
  private var _price:Number;
  private var _desc:String;
  private var _image:String;
  var title_txt:TextField;

  function small_item() {
    this.onRelease = gotClick;
    this.onRollOver = gotRoll;
    this.onRollOut = gotRollOut;
  }
  function SetInfo(id:Number, title:String,
              price:Number, desc:String, image:String)
  {
```

```
        _id=id;
        _title=title;
        _price=price;
        _desc=desc;
         // this line will need to be changed
         // based on where the product images are stored
        _image= "../images/" + image;

        title_txt.text = title;

        // code to load the thumbnail image for the items
      }
    function gotClick() {
      // respond to a click
    }
    function gotRoll() {
      this.alphaTo(50, .5, "easeOut");
    }
    function gotRollOut() {
      this.alphaTo(100, .5, "easeOut");
    }
  }
}
```

Actually, this class is almost *exactly* the same as the CategoryButton class, with the exception of a few more private properties set through the SetInfo function. I've also created a slightly different rollover effect for this MovieClip using the alphaTo instead of the brightnessTo method. Since this MovieClip will be responsible for displaying a thumbnail image of a product, we'll need to create a new MovieClipLoader to load the image. In our Access database, I am going to store the name of the full-sized product image, which will be the string passed to this class. The image we'll want to load here is the thumbnail image, which we'll create with the same name as the full-sized image, but with a _tmb suffix before the .jpg extension. (For example, a product's full image might be myproduct.jpg, and the thumbnail would be myproduct_tmb.jpg.) Let's create the MovieClipLoader within the SetInfo function, as shown in the following codeblock:

```
function SetInfo(id:Number, title:String,
                 price:Number, desc:String, image:String)
{
    ...
    // load the image
    this.createEmptyMovieClip("loader", 10);
    this["loader"]._x=2;
    this["loader"]._y=2;
    var mcl:MovieClipLoader = new MovieClipLoader();
    mcl.loadClip(_image + "_tmb.jpg", this["loader"]);
}
```

In this codeblock, I have created a new MovieClip instance, loader, using the MovieClip's creatEmptyMovieClip method, and I am loading the .jpg thumbnail image into this instance using the MovieClipLoader's loadClip method. With this code created, let's go back to the Application class and create a function that will load a list of products from the ASP.NET web service when a category button is selected:

```
function LoadProducts(catId:Number)
{
  function res(ev) {
    // place the products on the interface
  }
  var _itemServ:WebServiceConnector = new WebServiceConnector();
  //Don't forget to change your URL here
  _itemServ.WSDLURL =
      "http://localhost:20706/chapter10/Service.asmx?WSDL";
  _itemServ.addEventListener("result",res);
  _itemServ.operation = "GetCategoryProducts";
  _itemServ.params = [catId];
  _itemServ.suppressInvalidCalls = true;
  _itemServ.trigger();
}
```

This method is again very similar to the LoadCategories method, with the exception that the GetCategoryProducts web service requires a parameter—the category ID. Again, we want to receive the results from the web service call using an event listener, and create new instances of the SmallItem MovieClip, which we just created. When we create new instances of SmallItem, we'll then set the information for the items using the SetInfo method.

```
function LoadProducts(catId:Number)
{
  function res(ev) {
    var x:Number;
    var res = ev.target.results;
    var curx:Number = 0;
    var cury:Number = 71;

    for (x=0; x<res.length; x++) {
      var nn:String = "si"+x.toString();
      _root.attachMovie("SmallItem",nn,100+x);
      _root[nn]._x = curx*196;
      _root[nn]._y = cury;
      _root[nn].SetInfo(res[x].ProductId, res[x].ProductName,
                        res[x].ProductPrice,
                        res[x].ProductDesc, res[x].ProductImage);

      if (curx>4)
      {
        curx=0;
        cury += 173;
      }
      curx++;
    }
    _root._itemCt=res.length;
  }
... }
```

As in the GetCategories method, this handler receives the Array of Product objects from the web service and, for each Product, attaches an instance of SmallItem to _root. You'll notice that there is some extra code in this method that handles the location of the attached products—if there are more than four objects in a row, we need to start a new row of products.

One more thing we'll need to do in the GetProducts method is to remove any MovieClips that we attached in previous calls to GetProducts (when another category button is clicked). To do this, let's create a simple for statement that makes use of the RemoveMovieClip method to eliminate all of the previously attached MovieClips. To record the number of previously attached MovieClips, you'll see that I've created a variable called _itemCt on the _root, which records the number of items in the last GetProducts call:

```
function LoadProducts(catId:Number)
{
  function res(ev) {
   ... }
  // first clear the old items
  if (this._itemCt!=undefined)
  {
    var x:Number;
    for (x=0; x<this._itemCt; x++)
    {
      var nn:String = "si"+x.toString();
      _root[nn].removeMovieClip();
    }
  }
  ...
}
```

With our GetProducts method complete, we need to "hook up" the CategoryButton class to call this function when clicked. Modify the gotClick method of the category_button.as file to look like the following:

```
function gotClick()
{
  _root.LoadProducts(this._catId);
}
```

And with that, let's publish the Flash movie and see what happens now when we select a CategoryButton (see Figure 10-10).

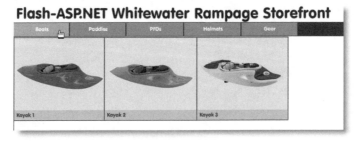

Figure 10-10. Selecting a category button

Voilà! When a CategoryButton is selected, our code successfully loads the products from the GetProducts web method, creates a new SmallItem for each product, and loads the image specified for each. Again, if you are planning on using a similar method for a live application, you will probably want to create a loading function that will execute both when a category button is selected and while each image is loading into the SmallItem MovieClipLoaders.

The last function we'll need to create in this application is one that will display the full-sized image and detailed product description of a product when it is selected. For this function, we won't even need to load any data from the web service, as it was all sent with the GetProducts method and is now contained within each SmallItem object. Let's start this step by creating another new MovieClip in the storefront.fla file, LargeItem, which will have an AS 2.0 class called large_item.as. As Figure 10-11 shows, in the LargeItem MovieClip, I have created four layers: text, close_btn, bg, and drop_shadow. In the text layer, I have created three dynamic text fields—title_txt, price_txt, and desc_txt—along with two static text fields—Price and Description. In the close_btn layer, I have created a new button called close_btn, which will be used to close the product detail. The bg and drop_shadow layers are used for creating the backdrop for the product detail. The size of the entire background is 680×382, with an area of 455×354 left open on the lower left for the large product images to display.

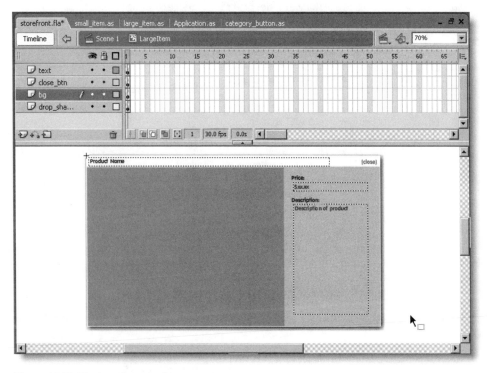

Figure 10-11. The LargeItem movie

In the file `large_item.as`, we'll create the class file that will contain the code for this MovieClip:

```
class large_item extends MovieClip {
  var title_txt:TextField;
  var price_txt:TextField;
  var desc_txt:TextField;
  var close_btn:Button;
  var _id:Number;

  function large_item()
  {
    // sets up the close_btn to close the item detail
    close_btn.onRelease = function ()
    {
      this._parent.removeMovieClip();
    }
  }
  function SetInfo(id:Number, title:String,
                   price:Number, desc:String, image:String)
  {
    _id = id;
    title_txt.text = title;
    price_txt.text = "$" + price.toString();
    desc_txt.text = desc;

    // load the image
    this.createEmptyMovieClip("loader", 10);
    this["loader"]._x=2;
    this["loader"]._y=27;
    var mcl:MovieClipLoader = new MovieClipLoader();

    mcl.loadClip(image + ".jpg", this["loader"]);
  }
}
```

This code is set up in the same way as the SmallItem class, loading the image passed into the object's SetInfo method into an empty loader MovieClip. The only additional code used in this class is the onRelease handler assigned to the close_btn instance in the constructor. This call to the RemoveMovieClip method will remove the LargeItem instance when selected.

Finally, we'll create a method in the Application class to "launch" an instance of the LargeItem when a SmallItem is selected:

```
function ItemDetail (id:Number, title:String,
                     price:Number, desc:String, image:String)
{
  if (this["li"]!=undefined){
    this["li"].removeMovieClip();
  }
  this.attachMovie("LargeItem", "li", 500);
  this["li"]._x=149;
```

```
        this["li"]._y=124;
        this["li"].SetInfo(id, title, price, desc, image);
    }
```

This method takes a title, price, description, and image as parameters and attaches a new instance of the LargeItem to the _root, passing its parameters. This method also checks to make sure there isn't already an instance of the LargeItem created, and if there is, removes it. In one last modification to the SmallItem class, we'll create a call to this method in the gotClick handler:

```
    function gotClick() {
        _root.ItemDetail(this._id, this._title,
                        this._price,this._desc,this._image);
    }
```

And with that, our Flash front-end is complete! Let's try publishing this file again to see our results (see Figure 10-12).

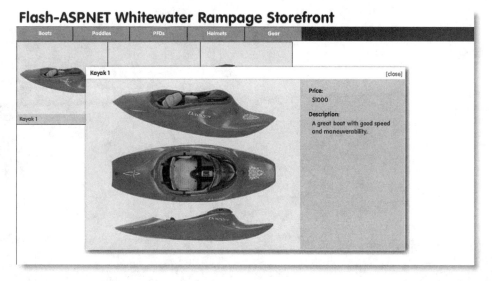

Figure 10-12. The finished storefront

Success! When a SmallItem instance is selected, the Application class's ItemDetail method attaches a new instance of LargeItem, passing the product's information. The LargeItem then loads the correct image for that item, and we're set!

Summary

In this chapter, we've created an example that loads a store's inventory from an Access database using ASP.NET web services and displays an interface for navigating through the inventory. By dividing the logical tiers of this application between Flash, ASP.NET, and Access, we were able to keep the presentation, logical, and data tiers very cleanly separated, making this application easy to maintain in the future. In the next chapter, we'll learn about session state in Flash and ASP.NET and then extend this application to contain a shopping cart.

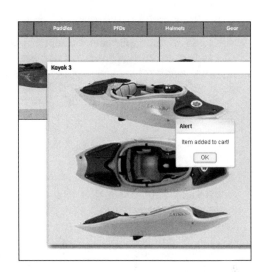

Chapter 11

SESSION STATE AND SECURITY

What this chapter covers:

- The ASP.NET Session class
- The ASP.NET Application class
- The global.asax file
- Using session state in ASP.NET web services
- Adding a session-based shopping cart to the Whitewater Rampage application
- Securing Flash and ASP.NET web service interactions using session state

In nearly any application distributed over the World Wide Web, *session state*, or the ability for a web server to recognize the status of a user's interaction with an application, is of utmost importance for providing a meaningful user experience. In this chapter, we'll take a look at the ASP.NET Session and Application classes and walk through examples of how they can be used to maintain state in an application that uses Flash as a presentation tier. In the final example in this chapter, we'll extend the storefront example from the previous chapter to include a session-based shopping cart.

Session state

Because web presentation tiers—whether it's a Flash application or an HTML interface—are not persistently connected to a web server (unless you're using a persistent connection, such as a Flash Socket connection), one of the biggest challenges for developers traditionally has been the ability to maintain *state* between the pages of a web application. In HTML, for example, the ability to maintain state allows you to fill in information on a web form and have the server "remember" the information you entered when you navigate to the next page, just like when you're using a desktop application. Because Flash applications, even when running in browsers, essentially *are* desktop applications, they are much better equipped to deal with the stateless nature of the Web. As I'm sure you know, when developing a Flash application, you don't have to invent mechanisms to pass information from one "state" of your application to the next—a Flash application can pass stateful variables within itself.

The idea that an application using Flash does not ever require an additional method for session management is a misconception, though. Session state does become an issue in a few circumstances, even when using Flash. Let's say you're developing an ASP.NET web forms application that has multiple pages (like a typical HTML-based website), with Flash elements on each page. In this scenario, as the user navigates from page to page, the Flash elements won't be able to maintain state—their information will be refreshed with each page refresh. An additional mechanism must be put in place to maintain state within the application. Also, when dealing with Flash and ASP.NET applications, you will often need to share information between Flash and other, HTML-based elements on an ASP.NET page, or even share information with *all the users* connected to a specific web application. For these scenarios, we need to pick from one of the session-storing mechanisms available from Flash and ASP.NET.

A number of mechanisms are available to maintain state in Flash and .NET, each of which has a distinct advantage depending on the scenario you're planning on implementing. Generally, these mechanisms can be divided into two categories: server-side and client-side. The client-side mechanisms include the Flash SharedObject and HTML-based cookie objects. In this chapter, though, we will focus on the server-side, ASP.NET mechanisms for maintaining the state of applications.

ASP.NET server-side state management

ASP.NET provides some of the most advanced techniques available for maintaining session state in a web application. In this chapter, we'll explore two of these techniques: using HttpApplicationState and HttpSessionState classes. These classes are available to ASP.NET developers within each .aspx page through the Page object, as well as to ASP.NET web services through the WebServices object. The following list explains the difference between the HttpApplicationState object (also referred to as the Application object) and the HttpSessionState object (also referred to as the Session object):

- **Application object**—Stores a list of objects that will be available to all users of an application. This object is useful for situations in which data must be shared between a large number of users, but a database is not accessible or applicable.

- **Session object**—Stores a list of objects that will be available for a specific user's *session* of interactions with the web server. A session generally begins when a user first requests a page from an ASP.NET web application and ends either when the user navigates away from the application, or when the session reaches its *timeout* limit, as set by the application developer. Unlike cookies or Flash SharedObjects, the next time a user visits the application, the information stored in a Session object will no longer be available.

By default, ASP.NET stores Application and Session objects in the web server's working memory. This type of storage is referred to as in-process storage in ASP.NET. When using in-process storage, it's very important to understand that when the ASP.NET process is restarted or reset, the Application and Session objects stored in memory will be lost. This loss can be detrimental to applications that rely on the storage of these objects—if you're going to make use of these objects, it's best to also create a "fail-safe" response to the scenario that your data has been lost.

There is another method that can be used to store ASP.NET Session and Application objects, which uses a Microsoft SQL Server (we'll cover SQL Server in Chapter 13) instead of the web server's physical memory to store the objects. This method is much more reliable than the in-process method, since your data, stored as database information, will not be lost when the ASP.NET application restarts. This method is also more applicable when deploying a very large application, which will be hosted on multiple web servers, known as a *web farm*. When using the in-process mode, the application and session data will only be stored on a single server, making it impossible to develop applications that use these features. Using the SQL Server method, however, each web server can access the same, shared database, making the use of these objects possible.

For more information on setting up and configuring SQL-based session management on your ASP.NET applications, please see http://msdn.microsoft.com/msdnmag/issues/05/09/SessionState/default.aspx.

ASP.NET application state

The ASP.NET HttpApplicationState class stores a collection (see "Collections" in Chapter 2) of C# objects and makes those objects available to *all sessions* connected to the ASP.NET application. Stated more clearly, when using the HttpApplicationState class, you can store certain information on the ASP.NET web server and make that information available to all users who are connected to a specific application—very similar to storing values in a database. The application state is created the first time a client accesses an application making use of application state, and is maintained until an event occurs that resets the ASP.NET state objects (such as a server reboot). Table 11-1 lists some of the most common methods of the HttpApplicationState object.

Table 11-1. Common methods of HttpApplicationState

Method	Description
Add	Adds a new value to the dictionary collection
Clear	Removes all values from the dictionary
Get	Takes as a parameter either a key or an index and returns the value of the item at that index
GetKey	Gets the string key of the item at a specific indexed position
Lock	Locks writing access to the dictionary collection until an UnLock command is called
Remove	Removes the item whose key matches the specified string
RemoveAt	Removes an item at a specified position
Set	Sets a value to an item with a specific key
UnLock	Unlocks writing access locked by a Lock command

Some typical application operations might look like the following:

```
// add an int value to the Application, with a key of "myKey"
int myInt = 2;
Application.Add("myKey", myInt);

// complex values can be added too
// add a "person" struct to the Application
person myPerson = new person();
Application.Add("myKey2", myPerson);

// retrieve a string that was set to the key "uName" in a previous page
string userName = (string) Application["uName"];

// remove a value that was set previously
Application.Remove("uName");
```

As shown in the previous examples, in order to access the value of an application variable that has been previously set, you use the string indexer syntax: ["keyValue"]. If, for example, you have previously placed an object in the application collection, with a key name of myKey, you could access that object using the like Application["myKey"].

You'll also notice that the Application object has two methods, Lock and Unlock, which are used to restrict access to the Application object from other browser sessions. These commands are necessary when you would like to manipulate an application variable without running the risk of having another session trying to manipulate that same object while you're working with it. An example of the Lock and UnLock methods looks like this:

```
Application.Lock();
// now, no one can access the Application objects while
// we're accessing them
Int anInt = (int) Application["myInt"];
If (anInt!=anotherInt)
{
  Application["myInt"] = anInt++;
}
Application.UnLock();
// now, everyone's free to access the Application objects again
```

If you are just performing a single command, however, the Lock and UnLock methods are not needed:

```
// this is a safe operation
Application["myInt"] = 5;
```

Specifically in Flash/ASP.NET development, the Application class can come in very handy for sharing information between all users currently using your application—especially when a database is not available or not practical. Some example tasks that application variables would be useful are

- Keeping track of the people currently logged on to your application
- Recording the current high score in a game
- Sharing information between users of an application

ASP.NET session state

The ASP.NET HttpSessionState class is very similar to the HttpApplicationState class, except that instead of storing objects across all current instances accessing an application, the Session object stores information specific to a single browser session. A single browser session might be most easily described as the time period that you are interacting with a specific web application. A session *can* extend between pages in an application; therefore, session values stored in one page of an application can be accessed on subsequent pages of that same application. When, however, you return to an application after leaving it (let's say by closing your browser), your session variables will be lost, as the session state mechanism is only specific to a single session.

Tables 11-2 and 11-3 list some properties and methods, respectively, of the HttpSessionState object (again, this object is also known as Session in ASP.NET). You'll notice that this object functions in a very similar manner to the Application object. You'll also notice, however, that there is an additional property, SessionId, which returns a unique identifier for the current browser session. This property can be useful when it's necessary to uniquely identify user interactions with an ASP.NET application.

Table 11-2. Properties of HttpSessionState

Property	Description
Count	Returns the number of items currently stored in the session state.
Item	Indexed property; provides access to a session value. Can be specified by either name or index.
Keys	Gets a collection of all values stored in the session.
SessionId	Gets a string with the current ID for the session.
Timeout	Gets or sets the number of minutes that the session module should wait between requests before eliminating the session.

Table 11-3. Methods of HttpSessionState

Method	Description
Abandon	Instructs the session module to abandon the current session
Add	Adds a new item to the session state
Clear	Clears all items from the session state
Remove	Deletes the key-indexed item from the session state
RemoveAt	Removes the specified item from the session state based on a numeric index

Like the Application object, values in the Session object can be accessed using the string indexer syntax. Some example Session statements are shown in the following codeblock:

```
// adding an int to a Session
Session.Add("myKey", myInt);

// retrieving a string from Session
string myVal = (string) Session["aString"];
```

There's another property of the Session object that's important to point out—the Timeout property. The Timeout property is an integer value that determines the amount of minutes allowed between requests to an ASP.NET page or web service before the ASP.NET server will clear the contents of the Session object. This value can be very important in Flash/ASP.NET session interaction, because when a user is interacting with a Flash application, depending on how you have designed your application, it might be quite a long period between requests to an ASP.NET server. Setting the timeout value to an effective value will be essential to the functionality of your application!

The ASP.NET global.asax file

Many times, when making use of Application or Session objects in a Flash/ASP.NET application, it's necessary to not only be able to get and set the values of these objects, but also to react to more "global" events, such as the first instantiation of an application or the end of a session. In order to monitor and react to these events, a file called global.asax must be added to your ASP.NET application. This file, also known as the ASP.NET application file, is an optional file that handles application-level events including, but not limited to, session and application events.

The global.asax file, when used, resides in the root of an ASP.NET web application. This file is configured in a way that an HTTP request for it will be denied by a web application—just like .cs files, your global.asax file cannot be viewed by a user navigating your site. Table 11-4 lists some of the events available in the global.asax file, specifically those that relate to the Application and Session classes.

Table 11-4. Events from global.asax that relate to the Application and Session classes

Event	Description
Application_Init	Fired the first time an application is initialized or created
Application_Disposed	Fired when an application is destroyed
Application_Error	Fired when an unhandled error has been encountered by the application
Application_Start	Fired when an application is requested for the first time
Application_End	Fired when the last instance of an application is destroyed
Session_Start	Fired each time a user starts a browser session with an ASP.NET application
Session_End	Fired when a user's session with an ASP.NET application is terminated

> *When using the event handlers in the* global.asax *file, it's important to note that these events apply to the entire application you are creating, rather than just a single page.*

Adding a global.asax file to an ASP.NET project

In Visual Studio .NET 2003/ASP.NET 1.1, the global.asax file is automatically added to a project upon creation. With Visual Studio .NET 2005, though, the file must be added manually, just as you would add a new web form. Remember, the global.asax file is optional—your application will run just fine without one! Figure 11-1 shows the Visual Studio .NET Add New Item dialog box, used to add a new global.asax file to a web application.

> *Note that this file will respond to the application-level events for either ASP.NET web forms (*.aspx *pages) or ASP.NET web services (*.asmx *files). It's only necessary to add one file to a project to handle events from all pages and services in an application.*

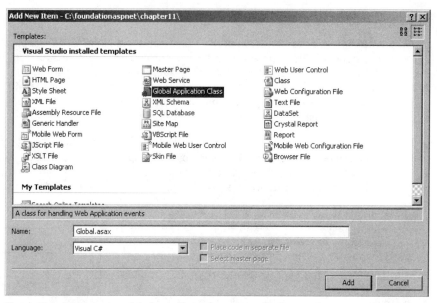

Figure 11-1. Adding a new global.asax file to the web application

By default, Visual Studio .NET places some of the application- and session-level event handlers into the `global.asax` file for us, as shown in Figure 11-2. These event handlers make it very easy to react to "global" events in an ASP.NET-based application.

```
<%@ Application Language="C#" %>

<script runat="server">

    void Application_Start(Object sender, EventArgs e) {
        // Code that runs on application startup

    }

    void Application_End(Object sender, EventArgs e) {
        //  Code that runs on application shutdown

    }

    void Application_Error(Object sender, EventArgs e) {
        // Code that runs when an unhandled error occurs

    }

    void Session_Start(Object sender, EventArgs e) {
        // Code that runs when a new session is started

    }

    void Session_End(Object sender, EventArgs e) {
        // Code that runs when a session ends.
        // Note: The Session_End event is raised only when the sessionstate mode
        // is set to InProc in the Web.config file. If session mode is set to StateServer
        // or SQLServer, the event is not raised.

    }
```

Figure 11-2. Event handlers in the global.asax file

Within these event handlers of the global.asax file, code can be written to accomplish various types of tasks, ranging from logging the errors in your application to clearing resources when your application is no longer in use. Although we won't be covering any further examples of the global.asax file in this chapter, the knowledge of its existence and potential is essential for further usage of Application- and Session-based development in ASP.NET.

Using session state in ASP.NET web services

Session and application state, although typically associated with individual sessions using web pages, can also be used in interactions with ASP.NET web services. By making use of session and application variables, it's possible to maintain state between calls to a web service. As mentioned earlier in the chapter, using ASP.NET Session and Application objects can be especially effective when your application requires data to be passed between pages in an application, and accessed interchangeably in either Flash or ASP.NET.

Session and application variables in ASP.NET web services are disabled by default, and you must specifically enable them in each method in which you would like to use them. This can be accomplished by adding the following attribute in the [WebMethod] declaration tag:

```
[WebMethod(EnableSession = true)]
```

After adding this attribute, any session or application variable can be accessed or assigned in your web service method. Let's test this by creating a simple example, in which we'll call an ASP.NET web method from a Flash movie, embedded in an ASP.NET page. In each call to the web method, we'll retrieve the value of an integer session variable we have stored, and increment that value.

Let's start by creating a web service project in a new folder, c:\foundationaspnet\chapter11\. Again, by default, Visual Studio .NET will create a file called session_service.asmx, which will be fine to use. In this file, we'll add a new web method, named Clicker, as shown here:

```
[WebMethod (EnableSession=true)]
public int Clicker()
{
  // if it's the first click, set "clicks" to 1
  int clicks = 1;

  // check to see if the clicks varaible is already in existence
  if (Session["clicks"] != null)
  {
    // increment it
    clicks = ((int)Session["clicks"]) + 1;
  }
  // set the session varaible
  Session["clicks"] = clicks;

  // return the current number of clicks
  return (clicks);
}
```

289

In this method, I simply check for the existence of the clicks session variable and, if it is available, I retrieve its value and increment it. Once the value has been incremented, I reset the value of the session variable, and finally return its value as an integer.

Now, let's create a simple Flash front-end to call this method. In the same directory (c:\foundationaspnet\chapter11\), I am going to create a new folder called flash. In this flash folder, I have created a new Flash movie called session.fla, which has a stage size of 250×125. On the stage of this file, I have placed a Flash Button component, which I have given an instance name of servBut, and a dynamic text field, called result_txt. I have also created a new layer called actions, in which I have placed the following code, used to call the web method we just created:

```
import mx.data.components.WebServiceConnector;
function gotClick()
{
  function res(ev)
  {
    // display the results of the web method in the dynamic textfield
    _root.result_txt.text = "Got Result: " + ev.target.results;
  }
  // when the button is clicked, create a new web serivce
  // connector and call the "Clicker" web method
  var _wsc:WebServiceConnector = new WebServiceConnector();
  _wsc.addEventListener("result", res);
  _wsc.WSDLURL =
    "http://localhost:2912/chapter11/session_service.asmx?WSDL";
  _wsc.operation = "Clicker";
  _wsc.trigger();
}
// listen for the click of the button
servBut.addEventListener("click", gotClick);
```

This codeblock will call the Clicker web service method each time the servBut button is clicked. Each time it is clicked, we should get a result telling us how many times we've clicked!

To test this example, let's embed this Flash movie in an .aspx page—testing ASP.NET session variables from the Flash IDE can be very misleading, since the ASP.NET server is not able to distinguish between multiple testing sessions. First, let's publish the Flash movie to create an .swf file, then back in Visual Studio .NET, we'll create a new ASP.NET web form called default.aspx. In this file, let's drag an instance of the epicFlashControl (see Chapter 3), and set it to display the session.swf file. Figure 11-3 shows the result of four instances of this file running in browsers—each is incrementing its own session variable!

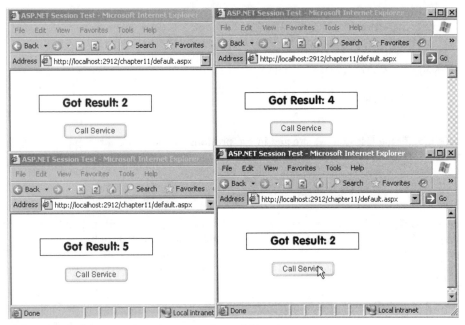

Figure 11-3. Each browser shows its own session variable value.

> When testing session variables on your local development machine using multiple Internet Explorer browsers, be sure to start each instance up separately—don't use the File ➤ New ➤ Window option. Using this command will cause the instances of Internet Explorer to share the same application variables, since they will both have the same session identification.

In this example, we see that each instance of a website can track ASP.NET session variables using web services—next, let's see how this application differs when we track application variables.

Using application state in ASP.NET web services

In this example, we'll be able to use nearly the exact same code as in the session state example with just a few modifications. Let's start by adding a new web method to the session_service.asmx file we created. This method, instead of accessing the clicks session variable, will access the clicks application variable, as shown in the following codeblock:

```
[WebMethod(EnableSession = true)]
public int ApplicationClicker()
{
    // if it's the first click, set "clicks" to 1
    int clicks = 1;

    if (Application["clicks"] != null)
```

```
    {
      // increment it
      clicks = ((int)Application["clicks"]) + 1;
    }
    Application["clicks"] = clicks;

    return (clicks);
  }
```

Next, let's modify the Flash file we created in the previous example to call the ApplicationClicker web method instead of the Clicker method. Before doing this, we'll save a copy of the session.fla file, in the same directory as application.fla. In this file, let's just modify one line of code:

```
    _wsc.operation = "ApplicationClicker";
```

This line will configure the Web Service Connector instance to call the ApplicationClicker method instead of the Clicker method from the previous example. Once this change has been made, publish the Flash movie, this time creating the file application.swf. We'll then create a new ASP.NET web form, application.aspx, in which we'll embed an epicFlashControl object to display the application.swf Flash movie.

Figure 11-4 shows the difference between this file and the default.aspx page. In this page, each time *any* of the Call Service buttons are clicked, the value of the returned value is incremented—this shows how easy it is to share variables between browsers using ASP.NET application variables!

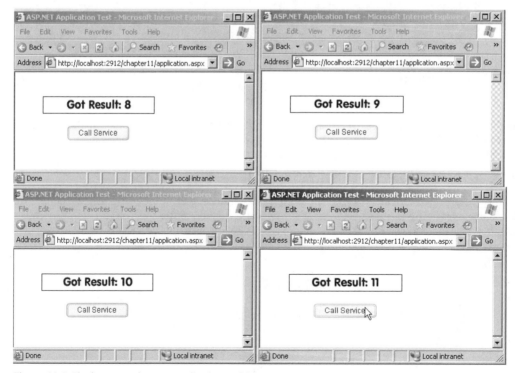

Figure 11-4. The browsers share an application variable.

Adding a shopping cart to the storefront example

In the previous chapter, we created a storefront application that allowed a user to view the contents of a store's inventory. This inventory data was supplied to the Flash presentation interface by an ASP.NET web service, which was obtaining data from an Access database. Now, we'll modify the example, adding an ASP.NET session-based "shopping cart." Because we're storing the shopping cart data in ASP.NET instead of Flash, the information will be ready to send to a .NET payment processing gateway, if we plan to integrate one into our application.

We'll start our renovation from the ASP.NET side, modifying the service.asmx file with some new methods to handle the functionality specific to the shopping cart. Let's start by creating a new method called AddItemToCart, which will require an item ID as a parameter. This web method will use an ArrayList, stored in a session variable, to keep track of the items and quantity that have been added to the user's shopping cart. In order to keep track of both the item type and quantity, we'll need to create a new struct, which will store not only a Product structure (which we defined in the previous chapter), but also an integer, Quantity.

```
public struct CartItem
{
  public Product Product;
  public int Quantity;
}
[WebMethod(EnableSession = true)]
public bool AddItemToCart(int itemId)
{
  ArrayList al = new ArrayList();

  // test the session variable, "cart"
  if (Session["cart"] != null)
  {
    // if the "cart" variable is not null, get its value
    al = (ArrayList)Session["cart"];
  }
```

In this codeblock, we have tested to see whether the cart session variable has been initialized, and if it has been, we obtain the information stored within it (if it's not, the al variable will just be an empty ArrayList). Next we'll create a loop that will go through each element in the ArrayList and determine if an item with the same ID as the one being added has already been added to the cart. If it has, we'll increment the quantity of that CartItem, as shown here:

```
// go through the current cart to see if this item
// has already been added
bool found = false;
for (int x = 0; x < al.Count; x++)
{
  CartItem ci = (CartItem)al[x];
  // found the item
  if (ci.Product.ProductId == itemId)
  {
    // increment the item's quantity
    ci.Quantity++;
```

```
        al[x] = ci;
        found = true;
        // get out of the loop, since the item won't be listed twice
        break;
    }
}
```

As you'll notice in this code, I have also created a new Boolean variable, found. This variable is initialized to false, but will be set to true if our search through the cart ArrayList finds an item matching the ItemId we are searching for. Next, we'll check the status of the found variable, and if it is still false, we'll retrieve the full information for that item, create a new CartItem structure, and add it to the ArrayList instance. In order to retrieve an item's information, we'll also create a new method, GetProductInfo, which will return a Product structure when passed a product ID. The Product structure is filled with details from the Access database.

```
    if (!found)
    {
        CartItem ci = new CartItem();
        // get the information for the new product
        ci.Product = this.GetProductInfo(itemId);
        ci.Quantity = 1;
        al.Add(ci);
    }

// this method is created outside of the AddItemToCartMethod
private Product GetProductInfo(int prodId)
{
    OleDbConnection conn = new OleDbConnection(_connString);
    OleDbCommand cmd = new OleDbCommand();
    cmd.CommandText =
        "SELECT * FROM Products WHERE ProductId=" + prodId.ToString();
    cmd.Connection = conn;

    conn.Open();
    OleDbDataReader dr = cmd.ExecuteReader();

    Product prod = new Product();
    while (dr.Read())
    {
        prod.ProductId = dr.GetInt32(0);
        prod.ProductName = dr.GetString(1);
        prod.ProductDesc = dr.GetString(2);
        prod.ProductPrice = dr.GetDouble(3);
        prod.ProductCategory = dr.GetInt32(4);
        prod.ProductImage = dr.GetString(5);
    }
    dr.Close();
    conn.Close();

    return prod;
}
```

And, now that we have an ArrayList containing the current CartItems, we'll set the cart session variable to this ArrayList:

```
Session["cart"] = al;
   return true;
}
```

The entire AddCartItem method is listed here:

```
[WebMethod(EnableSession = true)]
public bool AddItemToCart(int itemId)
{
  ArrayList al = new ArrayList();

  // test the session variable, "cart"
  if (Session["cart"] != null)
  {
    // if the "cart" variable is not null, get its value
    al = (ArrayList)Session["cart"];
  }

  // go through the current cart to see if this item
  // has already been added
  bool found = false;
  for (int x = 0; x < al.Count; x++)
  {
    CartItem ci = (CartItem)al[x];
    // found the item
    if (ci.Product.ProductId == itemId)
    {
      // increment the item's quantity
      ci.Quantity++;
      al[x] = ci;
      found = true;
      // get out of the loop, since the item won't be listed twice
      break;
    }
  }

  if (!found)
  {
    CartItem ci = new CartItem();
    // get the information for the new product
    ci.Product = this.GetProductInfo(itemId);
    ci.Quantity = 1;
    al.Add(ci);
  }

  Session["cart"] = al;
  return true;
}
```

Now that we have a method that can be used to add an item to the cart, we'll need to create a method to view the items currently in the cart. This method, GetCart, will return an array of the CartItem structs we just created, which will be specific to the current user's ASP.NET session.

```
[WebMethod(EnableSession = true)]
public CartItem[] GetCart()
{
  ArrayList al = new ArrayList();
  // check to see if any items have been added
  if (Session["cart"] != null)
  {
     al = (ArrayList)Session["cart"];


     // create an array, the size of the current cart
     CartItem[] ci = new CartItem[al.Count];
     for (int x = 0; x < al.Count; x++)
     {
       // add each item to the array
       ci[x] = (CartItem)al[x];
     }

  return ci;
}
```

And that's all the code we'll need on the ASP.NET web service side—let's move to the storefront.fla file and modify our presentation tier to provide a shopping cart that communicates with the ASP.NET web service.

Let's get started with the storefront.fla file by adding some new functions to the Application.as file. In this file, we'll add a new function, AddToCart, which will call the ASP.NET AddItemToCart method, as well as a GetCart function, which will be in charge of retrieving the cart information from the ASP.NET GetCart web method. In the AddToCart function, we'll take a product's ID as a parameter, and pass this parameter to the AddItemToCart web method, to add it to the ASP.NET cart session variable.

```
function AddToCart(itemId:Number)
{
  function res(ev) {
    Alert.show("Item added to cart!", "Alert", Alert.OK);
  }
  var _cartServ:WebServiceConnector = new WebServiceConnector();
  _cartServ.WSDLURL =_wsdl;
  _cartServ.addEventListener("result",res);
  _cartServ.operation = "AddItemToCart";
  _cartServ.params = [itemId];
  _cartServ.trigger();
}
```

You'll notice that this function is almost identical to the previous web service connector calls we have made—pretty easy to learn something that is so repeatable! You'll also notice that in the result handler of this call, we're making use of the Flash Alert component by calling the Alert.show method. In order to use the Alert class, it is necessary to pull an instance of the Alert component onto the stage in your Flash movie and then delete it—this will make the class available in your movie's library.

Next, we're going to add a function that will be used to call the ASP.NET GetCart web method. In this function, we'll follow the exact steps as in the AddToCart function, but we'll leave the result handler empty for now—we'll be using the GetCart function to retrieve the current user's shopping cart from ASP.NET. When we receive the result, we'll want to display this information, which we'll be tackling shortly.

```
function GetCart()
{
  function res(ev) {
    // we'll add code to display the cart
  }
  var _cartServ:WebServiceConnector = new WebServiceConnector();
  _cartServ.WSDLURL = _root._wsdl;
  _cartServ.addEventListener("result",res);
  _cartServ.operation = "GetCart";
  _cartServ.params = [];
  _cartServ.trigger();
}
```

Now that we have the functions necessary to interface with the ASP.NET shopping cart web service methods, let's modify our interface to support both adding items to a shopping cart, and viewing the items that exist in the shopping cart. We'll start by modifying the interface of the LargeItem MovieClip we created in the previous chapter. In this interface, we'll add a new button that simply displays the text Add to Cart, as shown in Figure 11-5.

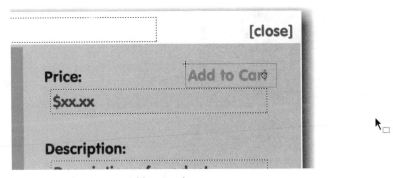

Figure 11-5. We have an Add to Cart button.

I have assigned this new button an instance name of cart_btn—next, let's add some code to the large_item.as file to handle the click of this button. In the constructor function for the large_item class, we'll create a new assignment for the onRelease event of the button. Then we'll create a function within this class to handle the button selection:

```
Function large_item() {
  ...
  cart_btn.onRelease = addToCart;
}
function addToCart()
{
  _root.AddToCart(_parent._id);
}
```

Now, when an item is viewed, and this Add to Cart button is clicked, the AddItemToCart web service method will be called, adding the item to the ASP.NET session variable. When the confirmation result is received from the ASP.NET web service, our Flash interface should display an alert message, notifying us that an item has been added to the cart. Figure 11-6 shows the storefront.fla interface after an item's Add to Cart button has been clicked.

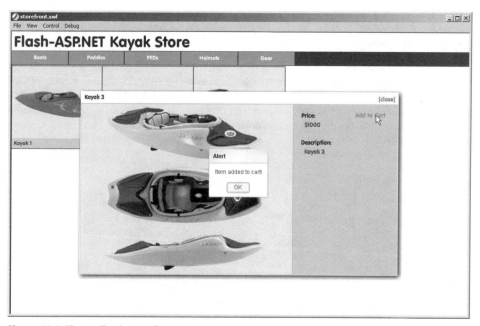

Figure 11-6. The application confirms when an item is added to the shopping cart.

Now that we are able to add items to the cart through the detailed product view, let's add a "View Cart" feature to our application. We'll start by adding a button, right on the _root timeline. Let's give this button an instance name of view_btn, as shown in Figure 11-7.

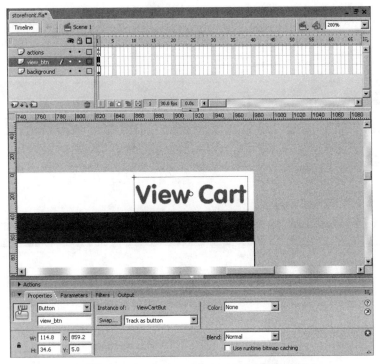

Figure 11-7. The View Cart button has an instance name of view_btn.

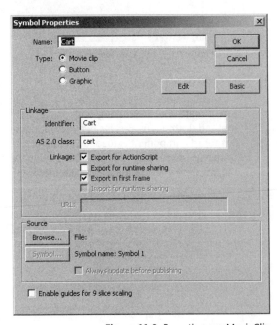

Figure 11-8. Exporting our MovieClip

And, in order to "hook up" this button to trigger the GetCart function, let's add the following line to the setup function of the Application.as file:

```
public function setup()
{
  view_btn.onRelease = GetCart;
  LoadCategories();
}
```

Finally, we're ready to create the shopping cart display. To accomplish this, we'll create a new MovieClip in the library named Cart. We will be exporting this MovieClip for ActionScript with the name Cart, and with an ActionScript 2.0 class file of cart, as shown in Figure 11-8.

In this new Cart MovieClip, we're going to create interface elements very similar to the LargeItem MovieClip, but instead of a large image, we'll place a Flash DataGrid component instance on the stage, with an instance name of cart_dg, and a dynamic text field with an instance name of total_txt, as shown in Figure 11-9.

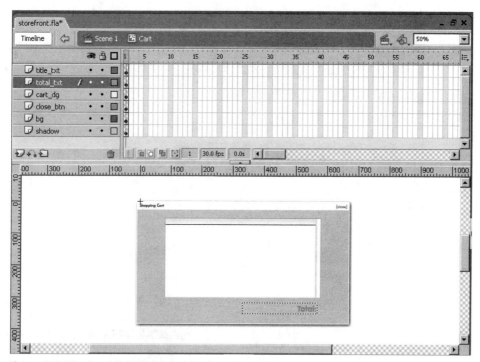

Figure 11-9. The Cart MovieClip's interface elements

In this MovieClip, we want to perform two fundamental tasks: display the contents of the shopping cart, and display the tallied total price of the contents of the cart. Accomplishing this will be easy; it's just a matter of formatting data, once we have received the result from the GetCart web service method. In the cart.as file, we'll create essentially just one function, onLoad, that will fire when the DataGrid component is loaded. Within this function, we'll iterate through each element in an internal property, _provider, which we'll set when we attach the Cart MovieClip. The contents of the cart.as file are shown in the following codeblock:

```
import mx.controls.DataGrid;
import mx.controls.gridclasses.DataGridColumn;
dynamic class cart extends MovieClip {
  var cart_dg:DataGrid;
  var _provider:Object;
  var close_btn:Button;
  var total_txt:TextField;

  function cart(_) {
    close_btn.onRelease = function ()
```

```
          {
            this._parent.removeMovieClip();
          }
     }
     function onLoad()
     {
          // first, create 4 data columns for the data grid
          var c1:DataGridColumn = new DataGridColumn("ItemName");
          c1.width = 140;
          c1.headerText = "Item";
          cart_dg.addColumn(c1);

          var c2:DataGridColumn = new DataGridColumn("ItemPrice");
          c2.width = 140;
          c2.headerText = "Price";
          cart_dg.addColumn(c2);

          var c3:DataGridColumn = new DataGridColumn("Quantity");
          c3.width = 100;
          c3.headerText = "Quantity";
          cart_dg.addColumn(c3);

          var c4:DataGridColumn = new DataGridColumn("Total");
          c4.width = 140;
          c4.headerText = "Total";
          cart_dg.addColumn(c4);

          var x:Number;
          var grandTotal:Number = 0;
          // go through each element of the _provider object
          for (x=0; x<_provider.length; x++)
          {
            var total:Number =
              _provider[x].Product.ProductPrice * _provider[x].Quantity;
            // add the item's total to the grand total for the order
            grandTotal+=total;
            var price_str:String = "$" + _provider[x].Product.ProductPrice;
            var total_str:String = "$" + total.toString();
            // add a new item to the data grid with the specified columns
            cart_dg.addItem({ItemName:_provider[x].Product.ProductName,
 ➥ ItemPrice:price_str,Quantity:_provider[x].Quantity,
 ➥ Total:total_str});
          }
          // set the total_text field
          total_txt.text = "TOTAL: $" + grandTotal.toString();
     }
}
```

And finally, we need to modify the GetCart function in the Application.as file to display the cart when the web service method call has completed. When attaching the Cart MovieClip, we'll set the _provider property of the MovieClip, through a parameter of the attachMovie function:

```
function GetCart()
{
  function res(ev) {
    _root.attachMovie("Cart", "cart",
                      150, {_provider:ev.target.results});
  }
  var _cartServ:WebServiceConnector = new WebServiceConnector();
  ...
}
```

And that should be all that is needed to complete the shopping cart addition to our storefront! The last thing we'll do is publish this movie and create a new ASP.NET web form page, default.aspx, to embed the Flash file within. Again, let's use the epicFlashControl to embed the Flash file—the final result is shown in Figure 11-10.

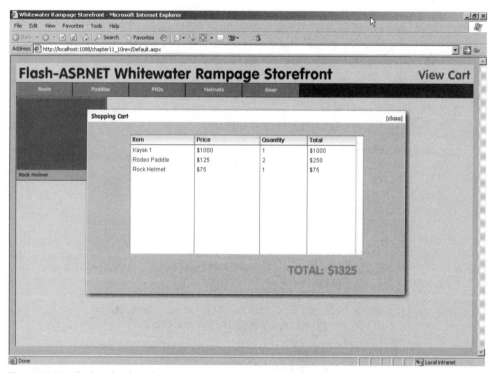

Figure 11-10. Viewing the shopping cart

In this example, you can see how easy it is to integrate ASP.NET state management into a Flash application. Although this example does not provide a complete "e-commerce solution" (you'd want to add Flash loading functions and a checkout, among other things), it does give you a great foundation to build upon for building an e-commerce application.

Securing an ASP.NET web service using session state

One of the great things about web services is their ability to provide access to services and data to applications around the world, regardless of the operating system or programming architecture they reside on. This tremendous ability also leaves a great task for developers—securing the web services that should not be accessible by the "public," and instead only allowing authorized parties to obtain data from the service. A perfect example of this would be a web service method that updates, inserts, or deletes items from a database. If access to such a service would fall into the wrong hands, you run the risk of compromising your entire database.

How, then, can we secure our web services to avoid unauthorized access? How about accepting a "key" as a parameter to each web service method? The key could function as an authorization code, to validate the application's security privileges . . . but web services are transferred between your Flash client and web server via SOAP, which travels as plain text over HTTP. This plain text is legible to any sinister third party sitting between your Flash client and your web server, making it possible for your key to be read, stolen, and reused by an unauthorized application.

One answer to the web service security problem is to encode all of the information exchanged between the Flash client and the web server using Secure Socket Layers (SSL). Using SSL, the information that is sent between the Flash client and .NET server can still be intercepted, but it cannot be read—it will look like a bunch of garbage instead of legible text. This allows you to pass a "key" parameter with each web method call, and validate that key on the server without worrying that the key has been compromised during its travels. This method is generally very secure—as long as your key is not compromised, there should be very little possibility for unauthorized access.

SSL, although very safe and secure, is not always a practical method. Because of the large amount of data encryption and decryption, both on the client and server side, data-exchange operations over SSL can take significantly longer than normal operations, decreasing the usability of your applications. SSL also might not be available in all of the applications we develop, increasing the need for an alternative method for securing our web services. Although there is no mechanism that provides 100 percent security without SSL, there are some methods we can use in Flash/ASP.NET applications that will make it extremely difficult for a user to obtain access to our web service methods. The method that follows is easy to implement with ASP.NET, and makes use of the ASP.NET session variables we have learned to use in this chapter.

The steps involved in performing this security method are as follows:

1. Embed a Flash movie into an ASP.NET page.
2. Set an ASP.NET session variable in that ASP.NET page, recording the IP address of the requesting browser.
3. When a web service method is called, validate that the IP address of the request is from the same IP address that was recorded in the initial page request.
4. If the above is true, return the web method result; otherwise, return an error message.

In concept, this method is very simple. When a user requests a page from a browser, the IP address of the browser is recorded as an ASP.NET session variable. Each web method that is contained in the web service file used by the application implements a validation method that checks for the existence of this session variable, and verifies that this variable is equal to the value of the original IP address. Using this simple authentication, we can do a very effective job of ensuring that the requests coming to our ASP.NET web service methods are being initiated by our Flash applications and not from a malicious third-party source.

To demonstrate this security method, let's create an ASP.NET web service method that employs this session-based validation mechanism. We'll then create a Flash movie that calls this protected web method and perform two tests—one in which the Flash movie calls the web method from within the Flash IDE (not within a browser), and another that calls the method while embedded within an ASP.NET web page, which sets the session variable necessary to allow the Flash movie to call the web method.

For the ASP.NET side of this example, we can use the same web service file we created earlier in this chapter, session_service.asmx. In this file, we'll create a new web method, ValidSessionEcho. This method will perform the same simple functionality as the EchoString web methods we've created in previous chapters, but for this example, we're going to "secure" the method, only passing results if a security validation has been passed. The code for this method is shown here:

```
[WebMethod(EnableSession = true)]
public string ValidSessionEcho(string echoString)
{
  if (ValidateUser())
  {
    return "Success: " + echoString;
  }
  else
  {
    return "Invalid access";
  }
}
```

You'll notice that in this method, before any logic is performed, we've made a reference to a second method, ValidateUser. It will be in this method that we will test for the existence of the IP address in the session variable and return a Boolean value indicating whether the authentication test was passed. This method, which we've added to the session_service.cs file, is shown here:

```
private bool ValidateUser()
{
  if (Context.Request.UserHostAddress == (string)Session["flashSec"])
  {
    return true;
  }
  else
  {
    return false;
  }
}
```

With this simple method created, let's now move into Flash, creating an interface that will call the web method. I have created a new Flash file in the flash folder within my c:\foundationaspnet\chapter11\ directory, called security_session.fla. On the stage of this Flash movie, I have added a dynamic text field, which I have given an instance name of result_txt. I have also added a Button component, which I have given an instance name of ServBut, as shown in Figure 11-11.

Figure 11-11. The results text field and the button to call the web service

Since we're using the web service connector class, don't forget to drag an instance of the Flash Web Service Connector component onto the stage and then delete it, so it is available in your library!

Next, I have added a new layer to this file called Actions, in which I have placed the following code:

```
import mx.data.components.WebServiceConnector;
function gotClick()
{
  function res(ev)
  {
    _root.result_txt.text = ev.target.results;
  }
  var _wsc:WebServiceConnector = new WebServiceConnector();
  _wsc.addEventListener("result", res);
  _wsc.WSDLURL =
    "http://localhost:2912/chapter11/session_service.asmx?WSDL";
  _wsc.operation = "ValidSessionEcho";
  _wsc.params = ["Foundation ASP.NET for Flash"];
  _wsc.trigger();
}
servBut.addEventListener("click", gotClick);
```

With this code, the application essentially does two things; it calls the session_service.asmx ValidSessionEcho method, and it displays the results of that method call in the result_txt text field. This simple interface is all we will need to test our security mechanism.

Now, let's perform the first of our tests, calling the web service method from within the Flash IDE. When the Flash WebServiceConnector calls the ASP.NET web method from within the Flash IDE, there has been no session variable set, and therefore we can expect that the method will not pass the ValidateUser method we created. Figure 11-12 shows the results of this test.

Figure 11-12. The results of using the Flash IDE to call the web service

As expected, our request to the ASP.NET web method was denied access! This is a perfect example of an unauthorized user's attempt to access our method—they will not be allowed to access the functionality of the method. Next, let's move back into Visual Studio and create an ASP.NET web form that will both embed the Flash movie into the page, and set a session variable, allowing the Flash movie to access our web method.

Back in Visual Studio .NET, let's add a new web form to our project, named security.aspx. In this web form, we'll drag an instance of the epicFlashControl (see Chapter 3), the properties of which are shown in Figure 11-13.

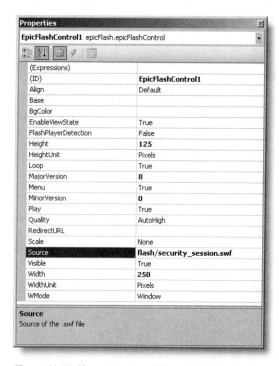

Figure 11-13. The properties of the epicFlashControl

In the code-behind file for this page, security.aspx.cs, we'll now add the essential code, setting the flashSec session variable equal to the UserHostAddress property of the page's Request class:

```
public partial class security : System.Web.UI.Page
{
  protected void Page_Load(object sender, EventArgs e)
  {
    Session["flashSec"] = Request.UserHostAddress;
  }
}
```

Now, when we test this page, we should expect that our web method will no longer return the "Invalid access" error, but instead return the proper result of the echostring method. Figure 11-14 shows this page tested within a web browser.

Figure 11-14. Successfully calling the web service

Success! Now that we have a Flash movie embedded within an ASP.NET web page, which has set a session variable, the call to our web method is successful. As you can see in this example, by using this simple method, we can provide a mechanism for protecting sensitive web services much more securely than with a password passed using clear text. Again, this method should never be used as a direct replacement for SSL, but should be used in situations where SSL is unavailable or not practical.

Summary

In this chapter, we've covered a very interesting topic in ASP.NET: session management. Using ASP.NET to provide session management in Flash/ASP.NET applications allows us to accomplish some very important tasks, especially when we're dealing with applications that require data to be passed through more than one page, or among users in an application. We've also learned how to extend our Whitewater Rampage application from the previous chapter, by adding a session-based ASP.NET-based shopping cart, and how to provide an extra level of security for the web services that we create in .NET. Using all of this information, it's possible to accomplish some very advanced tasks when creating Flash/ASP.NET web service-based applications.

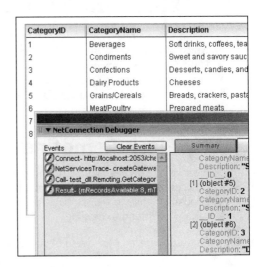

Chapter 12

FLASH REMOTING

What this chapter covers:

- The Flash Remoting technology
- ActionScript Messaging Format
- Flash Remoting using ASP.NET pages
- Accessing ASP.NET session variables with Remoting
- Flash Remoting using .NET DLLs
- Using Remoting to pass DataTables from .NET to Flash
- Using ASObjects in Flash Remoting
- Calling web services using Flash Remoting

In the last several chapters, we've been communicating between Flash and ASP.NET using web services, which transmit data using SOAP over HTTP. Although this is a very applicable and efficient method, Flash Remoting provides an even faster alternative to web services that does not require you to expose your code as a public web service. In this chapter, we'll learn about Flash Remoting and how to use it to access your server-side ASP.NET code.

Why Flash Remoting?

If we've already learned a great method for communication between ASP.NET and Flash with web services, why is it necessary to learn another? There are a number of reasons why Flash Remoting is a good alternative to web services (or the other) data access methods, depending on the type of application you intend to develop:

Previously written code doesn't have to be transformed into a web service.

Let's say you currently have a web application written in ASP.NET that uses HTML as a presentation tier and you would like to transfer that presentation tier to a more interactive Flash interface. If you have written the logical tier for your existing ASP.NET site using code-behind files, it would be necessary to re-code your files to expose your code's functionality (data access, etc.) as web service methods. In some circumstances, this can be very time consuming and difficult to accomplish, as well as a potential security hazard since your web services will be exposed publicly. Using Flash Remoting, under most circumstances, it's not necessary to re-code your logical tier! Given proper permissions, Flash Remoting can directly access .NET DLL files and access the classes within them—making a much more hassle-free and secure deployment.

Flash Remoting is faster than web services.

In most circumstances, Flash Remoting will transfer information significantly faster than web services. Instead of text-based SOAP messages, Flash Remoting uses a binary format to transmit data between the Flash movie and your ASP.NET code. This binary format requires less bandwidth than SOAP to transfer the same amount of data and is therefore more efficient than SOAP.

Since, as we discovered in Chapter 2, Flash and .NET do not share *exactly* common data types, when data is exchanged between Flash and ASP.NET, it first has to go through a process called *serialization* before it is transported, and another process called *deserialization* when the data is handled by the recipient. When data is serialized, it is translated from the native data types of the sender into "common" language—like XML. This common language is then sent to the recipient, where it is deserialized, or translated, from the common language into the recipient's native data types. When the Flash web service classes are used to transport information, this serialization is accomplished *by the web service classes*, which are compiled into your Flash movie, increasing its file size. With Flash Remoting, data serialization and deserialization is performed *by the Flash Player*, providing a much more efficient method of serialization without increasing the size of your Flash movie.

It's easier to debug Flash Remoting applications.

Communication between Flash and ASP.NET is so easy that it's not necessary to do much debugging, right? Well, maybe not that easy. In any application that requires communication between two completely different technologies, it's going to be necessary to monitor and debug that communication very efficiently. Using the NetConnection Debugger, Flash Remoting applications can be debugged in a much more sophisticated manner than any of the alternative communication methods.

The technology behind Remoting

One of the advantages of Flash Remoting over other communication mechanisms are the methods it employs to transfer data between the Flash client and remote ASP.NET application. Flash Remoting uses a binary message format for transferring messages between the Flash client and server-side ASP.NET code, called ActionScript Messaging Format (AMF). AMF, like any of the other methods we've discussed, travels between the client and server over HTTP, so you don't have to worry about security mechanisms (such as firewalls) interfering with your communication. Although modeled on the same protocol as web services, AMF is much more lightweight, and therefore travels much more quickly than calls using the Web Service Connector. AMF is also securable using SSL, so it is a great option for security-sensitive applications.

> *Flash Remoting requires that the end user have the Flash Player 6.0r40 or later installed on their system.*

Flash Remoting, like the other communication methods we've discussed, is also an *asynchronous* method, meaning that it doesn't wait around for a response from your .NET application when it makes a request. Instead, the Flash application can continue execution and react when the result is received back from the ASP.NET server. This type of model makes it possible to keep your applications "alive" while interacting with a web server—a feature previously impossible on the Web.

In Figure 12-1, the general architecture of a Flash Remoting application is shown. Flash, acting as a presentation interface, is able to request information from an ASP.NET web server by transmitting messages encoded with the AMF. When the ASP.NET server receives the AMF message, it passes the request directly to the *Flash Remoting Gateway*, a .NET DLL that handles the deserialization of the AMF messages and transfer to the requested ASP.NET application. Once your ASP.NET application receives the request from the Flash Remoting Gateway, it performs the method requested by your Flash interface and (optionally) returns a result to the Remoting Gateway, which then serializes the result back into AMF and sends it to the requesting Flash application.

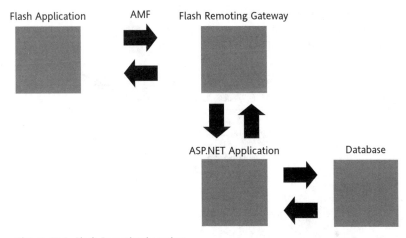

Figure 12-1. Flash Remoting in action

311

When the Flash Remoting Gateway receives a message from Flash, it must convert the parameters sent from ActionScript data types to C# data types. As we've talked about throughout this book, many of the ActionScript data types "play well" with C# data types while others don't. Table 12-1 lists the data type conversions between ActionScript and C#. You'll notice that one of the ActionScript data types, RecordSet, can't even be sent to .NET using Remoting—we'll discuss an alternative to RecordSets in the "Passing objects from .NET to Flash via Remoting" section of this chapter.

Table 12-1. Data type conversions between ActionScript data types and C# data types

ActionScript Data Type	C# Data Type
Null	Null
Undefined	null
Boolean	System.Boolean
String	System.String
Number	Any appropriate numeric type
Date	System.DateTime
Array	System.Collections.ArrayList
Associative array	System.Collections.HashTable
RecordSet	Cannot be sent to server
Object	FlashGateway.IO.ASObject
XML	System.Xml.XmlDocument

When messages are passed back from .NET code to a Flash client through the Remoting Gateway, they too must be transformed, this time into ActionScript variable types. Table 12-2 lists the valid C# return data types, along with their corresponding ActionScript data type.

Table 12-2. C# and ActionScript return data types

C# Data Type	ActionScript Data Type
Null	null
System.Boolean or bool	Boolean
Any numeric type (int, float, etc.)	Number
System.Char	string
System.String	string

C# Data Type	ActionScript Data Type
System.DateTime	Date
System.Collections.HashTable	Associative array
System.Data.DataSet	Associative array of RecordSets
FlashGateway.IO.ASObject	Object
FlashGateway.IO.ASObject with type property set	Typed object
System.Xml.XmlDocument	XML

Examining the methods for using Flash Remoting

Since ASP.NET is such a unique server-side language, Flash Remoting for .NET has features that are different from that of other Remoting-compatible languages, such as Java and ColdFusion. These features include a choice of three ways to transfer data from ASP.NET to Flash—each of which has its strengths and weaknesses. These methods include the following:

- *Directly connect to a DLL.* This method allows a Flash client to directly call methods from classes within a .NET DLL instead of having to work with any intermediate "interface." Using this method, Flash can access any method within a class (or a number of classes), making it a very powerful and flexible method.

- *Connect to an ASP.NET page.* Using this method, the Flash client makes a call directly to an ASP.NET page instead of a DLL file. The main difference between this and the DLL method is that an ASP.NET page can contain only a single ASP.NET method.

- *Connect to a web service.* Yes, you heard (or read) me right—Flash Remoting provides another method for accessing web services. Why would we use Flash Remoting to access a web service when we already have the Web Service Connector components? Because the Web Service Connector components are bulky and their XML parsing methods can consume precious CPU cycles. Using Flash Remoting, it's possible to retrieve the results of a web service method in a much more efficient manner than with the Web Service Connector components. With Flash Remoting, it's also not necessary to create a "proxy" to connect to a third-party service like we did in Chapter 7. Instead, Flash Remoting serves as the proxy, and you can make calls from a Flash client directly to a third-party service.

Ultimately, if you're working on an application that will be calling a large number of ASP.NET methods through Remoting, the DLL option is probably the best fit. If your application only requires a few methods, the ASP.NET page might be the best option, and if you will be consuming information from a third-party web service, you will want to connect directly using Flash Remoting. In this chapter, we're going to learn how to use each of these methods to create server-powered Flash Remoting applications!

Setting up Flash Remoting .NET

Whereas all of the other technologies we've talked about to this point come installed with Flash Professional, Flash Remoting requires a completely separate installation with two parts: the Flash Remoting components and the Flash Remoting service. In this section, we'll walk through the setup of Flash Remoting on your system from both the Flash and the .NET side.

Installing the Flash Remoting service

In order to use Flash Remoting in your applications, you'll have to have the Flash Remoting service installed on your development system, which needs to have Internet Information Services (IIS) running (instructions on installing IIS can be found in Chapter 1). It is the Flash Remoting service that allows your ASP.NET code to send and receive calls from a Flash movie running in a browser. The Flash Remoting service is available as a free trial download from the Macromedia website at www.macromedia.com/ software/flashremoting/. The trial version of Flash Remoting will be fully functional for 30 days, and after 30 days will work only from the localhost—which still works fine for testing and development. Installing the Flash Remoting service is easy—just download the package, follow the steps indicated, and you will be ready to go!

Once you have Flash Remoting installed, you'll find the installed files within the IIS root directory, typically at C:\Inetpub\wwwroot\flashremoting\, as shown in Figure 12-2.

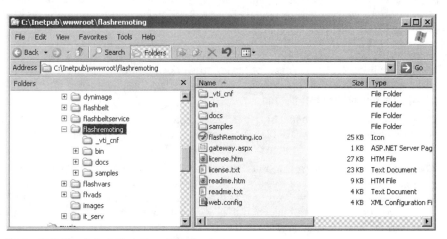

Figure 12-2. The default Flash Remoting directory

You can easily test the installation by opening the default.htm file found within the Samples folder in the flashremoting directory. We don't want to open this page directly, however. Instead you should type in the local URL for the page (http://localhost/flashremoting/samples/), which is now set up to run on your local instance of IIS. On the default.htm page, you'll see three examples to choose from—ASP.NET Page Example, ADO.NET Example, and ASP.NET Web Service Example. Selecting the first, ASP.NET Page Example, should bring up a screen similar to that in Figure 12-3.

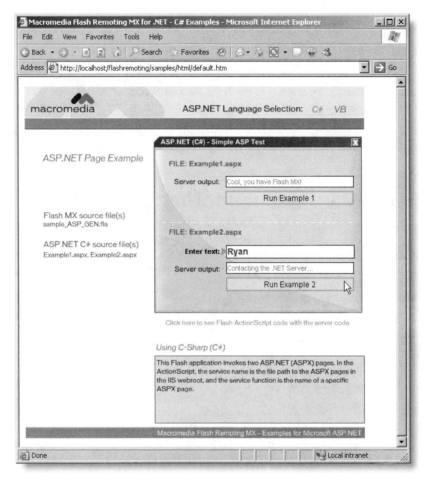

Figure 12-3. Testing the Flash Remoting installation

If you click the Run Example 1 button and see Cool, you have Flash MX! as shown in Figure 12-3, then you have successfully run your first Flash Remoting sample and are set to go!

Examining the files within the flashremoting directory

For the most part, after you run the sample files to confirm that Flash Remoting is working correctly, you won't need to use the Flash Remoting installation directly again. There are, however, two files that will be necessary to use in each application that you will build using Flash Remoting. These files are

- bin/flashgateway.dll
- gateway.aspx

In each of the examples in this chapter, you'll need to copy the flashgateway.dll file into your site's bin directory and gateway.aspx into the site's root folder in order for Flash Remoting to run success-fully. You'll also need to grab a couple of lines from the web.config file that is in this flashremoting folder—we'll see how to do this later in the chapter.

Installing the Flash Remoting components

As I mentioned, the Flash Remoting system consists not only of server-side components (which we just installed), but also client-side Flash components. These Flash Remoting components for ActionScript 2.0 are available at www.macromedia.com/software/flashremoting/downloads/components/. Download this component package and run the installer to install the Flash Remoting components. Be sure to shut down the Flash IDE if you have it open *before* you install the components, so the installation can do its magic.

To test that your installation succeeded, try firing up Flash again and hit the *F1* key to pull up the Help contents. If you see a section called Using Flash Remoting you are set to go!

ActionScript 2.0 Flash Remoting Connector

In the examples in this chapter, we're going to be using the Flash Remoting Connector component to perform our operations between Flash and ASP.NET. The Flash Remoting Connector works almost exactly the same way as the Web Services Connector, which we've covered extensively in the previous chapters, so the transition to Remoting should be pretty painless.

> *The Flash Remoting Connector requires that you have Flash Professional edition. If you don't have the Professional edition, the combination of the Flash Remoting Connection, Service, and Service Responder classes provide equivalent functionality and are configured in a very similar manner. More information about these classes can be found in the Flash Remoting documentation.*

Once the Flash Remoting components are installed, you can find the Remoting Connector in the Data Components section of the Components panel in the Flash IDE. Like the Web Services Connector, the Remoting Connector can be set up and triggered either using the visual Component Inspector panel or ActionScript. In this chapter, we will look only at the ActionScript method. When using the ActionScript method to create new instances of the Remoting Connector, it is always necessary to drag an instance of the Remoting Connector from the Data Components section of the Flash Components panel into the library of your Flash application so the classes are available at runtime.

Table 12-3 lists the properties of the Remoting Connector component. We'll be exploring these properties in depth throughout this and the next chapter.

Table 12-3. The properties of the Remoting Connector

Property	Data Type	Description
MultipleSimultaneousAllowed	Boolean	If this value is false, the Flash Remoting Connector will throw a CallAlreadyInProgress status event if you try calling a method through a Remoting Connector instance before a previous call has returned a result. If set to true, the Remoting Connector will allow multiple calls to be performed at the same time.

Property	Data Type	Description
ShareConnections	Boolean	If set to true, allows multiple Flash Remoting Connector instances to share a single connection to a common Flash Remoting Gateway.
SuppressInvalidCalls	Boolean	If true, the Flash Remoting Connector will attempt to validate the data types of parameters before performing a method call. If an invalid parameter is used, the instance will throw an InvalidParams status event.
GatewayUrl	String	The URL of the Flash Remoting Gateway that the Connector will be connecting to.
MethodName	String	The name of the ASP.NET method to call. If an ASP.NET page is being used, the methodName parameter should be set to the name of the ASP.NET page without the .aspx extension.
ServiceName	String	Specifies the name of the Flash Remoting service. You can find more details on this parameter in the following sections.

NetConnection Debugger

As mentioned earlier in the chapter, one of the features that makes Flash Remoting so cool is the advanced ability you have to debug applications at runtime. Using the Flash Remoting NetConnection Debugger, you can monitor calls from Flash to a .NET Remoting application, and you can view details about the events. This feature can remove hours of tedious trace operations, and make the application-creation process a more enjoyable one. To use the NetConnector Debugger, drag an instance of the RemoteDebugClass component into your library. This will ensure the debugger works properly. Listed next are the general steps necessary to enable the NetConnection Debugger in your applications.

Enabling the Flash Remoting NetConnection Debugger

1. Drag an instance of the RemotingDebugClass from the Other Panels ➤ Common Libraries ➤ Remoting menu in the Flash IDE.
2. Add the following import command to the Flash class: import mx.Remoting.debug.NetDebug;.
3. Call NetDebug.Initialize(); before any Remoting code to initialize the debugger.
4. Open the NetConnection Debugger window before publishing your Flash movie.

> *Although the RemoteDebugClasses are extremely helpful while you're building and debugging your Remoting application, it's a very good idea to remove them from your library before publishing your Flash movie on a production server. There are two reasons for this: 1) The classes will add unnecessary file size to your .swf, and 2) they could provide a potential security hole in your live application.*

Connecting to an ASP.NET page

Let's start off our Flash Remoting work with an example of how to connect to a method from an ASP.NET page. In this type of project, we'll be using a different method of ASP.NET programming than we've been using in this book so far—the C# code will be written within the ASP.NET page, instead of in the code-behind file. To accomplish this, we have to simply place a Flash Remoting server control in an ASP.NET page and specify a value to return to Flash when the page is called. As I mentioned earlier in this chapter, when using ASP.NET pages to transfer data between Flash and .NET, only one method can be executed per page—as we'll see momentarily!

Creating the ASP.NET

To get started, let's create a new ASP.NET website in the C:\foundationaspnet\chapter12\ folder. Within this chapter12 folder, let's create a folder named flash, which will house the Flash elements of this project.

Next, let's add a new web form to the project called test_asp.aspx. When adding this web form, be sure to specify that the code for this file *will not* be in a code-behind file, as shown in Figure 12-4.

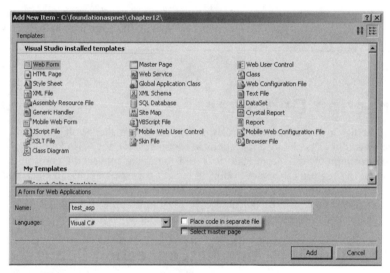

Figure 12-4. Creating a new web form with inline code

By not selecting the Place code in separate file option, we are telling Visual Studio to set up the page in a manner that allows us to put our code inline with the HTML on the .aspx page. With this page created, switch to the HTML Source view and modify the page contents to the following:

```
<%@ Page Language="C#" %>
<%@ Register TagPrefix="MM" Namespace="FlashGateway"
            Assembly="FlashGateway" %>
<MM:Flash ID="flash1" runat="server" />
<%
    string retVal = "Foundation ASP.NET for Flash!";
    flash1.Result = retVal;
%>
```

In this codeblock, we're registering the Flash Remoting server control in the page using the <%@Register %> tag, just like we used to register the epicFlashControl in Chapter 3. Then, using the value specified by the TagPrefix attribute, MM, we are creating a new instance of the Flash Remoting control, giving it an ID of flash1. The code that appears between the <% and %> symbols tells the ASP.NET server, "This is C# code that should be executed." In this section, we are simply creating a new string, "Foundation ASP.NET for Flash!", and binding that string to the Flash Remoting control's Result parameter—meaning that when this ASP.NET page is called by Flash, it will return the value assigned to its Result parameter.

The final thing we'll need to do on the ASP.NET side is to add the necessary Flash Remoting files to the ASP.NET site and configure the web.config file so that Flash Remoting requests from a Flash client get sent directly to the Flash Remoting DLL.

The first file we'll need to add will be the FlashGateway DLL—which you'll notice is referenced in the Register tag earlier, with the attribute Assembly="FlashGateway". To add this DLL to our site, go to the Solution Explorer in Visual Studio and right-click on the directory which the project resides in— C:\foundationaspnet\chapter12\. Then select Add Reference. When the Add Reference dialog box appears, select the Browse tab and navigate to the C:\inetpub\wwwroot\flashremoting\ directory, and then choose the flashgateway.dll file, as shown in Figure 12-5.

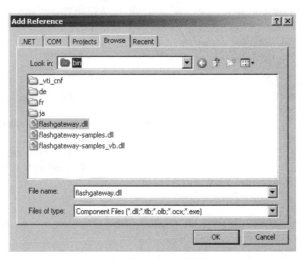

Figure 12-5. Selecting the flashgateway.dll file

After adding this reference, you'll notice that there is a new folder in your Solution Explorer, called bin. Within this bin folder will reside the flashgateway.dll file, along with its dependent files, including the de, fr, and ja folders.

Next, we'll need to add the gateway.aspx file to the project, which serves as the "Remoting gateway" for the Flash Remoting communication. The gateway.aspx file is simply a blank .aspx page—nothing tricky about it. You can either copy the gateway.aspx page from the C:\inetpub\wwwroot\flashremoting directory or just create a new, blank file called gateway.aspx and save it into your project's root directory (C:\foundationaspnet\chapter12\).

The last thing that we'll need to borrow from the Flash Remoting directory will be a couple of lines from the web.config file. As mentioned, these lines will be used to tell the ASP.NET web server that it should direct requests for Flash Remoting to the flashremoting.dll file that is in our bin directory. The lines we'll need from the C:\inetpub\wwwroot\flashremoting\web.config file are shown in bold here:

```
<configuration>
  <system.web>
  ...
  <httpModules>
    <add name="GatewayController"
➡ type="FlashGateway.Controller.GatewayController,flashgateway" />
  </httpModules>
 </system.web>
</configuration>
```

These lines can be placed, as shown in this codeblock, right before the end tag of the system.web element in the web.config file for our site.

Creating the Flash

Now, let's start a new Flash movie from which we'll call the ASP.NET page and retrieve the string value we just passed. In this Flash movie, we won't need any interface elements, just some ActionScript on the first frame of Layer 1. We'll get started by importing the classes that we'll need to do any Remoting functions in this chapter: the RemotingConnector and NetDebug classes.

```
import mx.data.components.RemotingConnector;
import mx.remoting.debug.NetDebug;
```

Figure 12-6. Flash Remoting Connector and Flash Remoting debug classes

And, in order to import these classes, we'll also need to add the RemotingConnector and NetDebug components to this Flash movie by dragging an instance of the Remoting Connector component onto the stage from the Data Components section of the Components window, and an instance of the RemotingDebugClasses from the Common Libraries ➤ Remoting panel. These components are shown in Figure 12-6.

Now we can move forward by creating an instance of the Remoting Connector and initializing the NetDebugger as shown in the following code:

```
// initialize the NetConnection Debugger
NetDebug.initialize();

// create a new Remoting Connector
var asp_rc:RemotingConnector = new RemotingConnector();
```

And with an instance of the Remoting Connector created, we are ready to set the parameters of the connector, in a very similar manner to the Web Service Connector that we've examined in the previous chapters.

```
// specify the gateway connection—
// You'll want to change this port number!!
asp_rc.gatewayUrl = "http://localhost:2053/chapter12/gateway.aspx";
```

```
// specify the name of the page we're going to be calling
asp_rc.methodName = "test_asp";
// specify the name of the sub-directory from the site's root
asp_rc.serviceName = "chapter12";
```

In this codeblock, we're setting three parameters of the Remoting Connector instance: gatewayUrl, methodName, and serviceName. The gatewayUrl parameter is simply the URL to the gateway.aspx file we copied (or created) in our site's directory. This parameter tells the Remoting Connector the location of the resource it will be communicating with. In the methodName parameter, we are specifying the name of the .aspx page that we'd like to call. You'll notice that this parameter doesn't use the .aspx suffix. Be careful, because by adding the .aspx suffix, your call will not work and you'll have some painful debugging on your hands! The final parameter, serviceName, is used to specify the subdirectory of the site's root that the Flash Remoting service resides in. Although this may seem confusing, as a general rule, serviceName will always be the directory that is specified in the URL of your site *after* the first quadrant of the URL. Table 12-4 gives examples of site URLs and the corresponding serviceName.

Table 12-4. Example URLs and their corresponding serviceName settings

URL	serviceName
http://localhost:2053/chapter12/	chapter12
http://localhost/flashremoting/samples/	flashremoting.samples
http://www.flashasp.net	""
http://www.friendsofed.com/foundationaspnet/remoting/	foundationaspnet.remoting

With the Remoting Connector component properly configured, just like with the Web Service Connector, the next step will be to add event listeners to wait for certain responses from the Remoting Connector. The two specific events we're going to be waiting for will be Result, which will be fired when we receive results from our .NET Flash Remoting service, and Status, which will fire when the status of the Remoting Connector changes—when an error is received, for example.

```
function gotResult(ev:Object) { .. }
function gotStatus(stat:Object) { .. }
asp_rc.addEventListener("result", gotResult);
asp_rc.addEventListener("status", gotStatus);
```

Within the gotResult and gotStatus functions, let's do a simple trace that will output the result or error of our call to the .NET Remoting service.

```
function gotResult(ev:Object)
{ trace("Got Result - "+ev.target.results); }
function gotStatus(stat:Object)
{ trace("Error - "+stat.code+" -  "+stat.data.faultstring); }
```

And finally, we'll set the ball in motion by calling the Remoting Connector's `trigger` method, which will cause the connection to the service to take place, and the remote method to be called.

```
trace("Triggering...");
asp_rc.trigger();
```

Before testing the movie, let's open the NetConnection Debugger window, located in the Other Panels ➤ NetConnection Debugger menu. By opening this window, we'll be able to monitor the progress of our calls as they occur. Now, testing the movie gives the results shown in Figure 12-7.

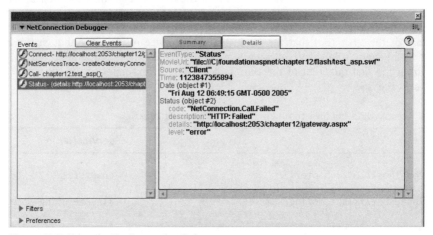

Figure 12-7. Using the NetConnection Debugger

Not exactly what we were expecting! As you can see by the Status event shown in Figure 12-7, my call to the remote server failed! Not to worry, though—I just wanted to show what it looked like when there *was* an error (since we won't be designing any more errors in our Remoting applications). I actually didn't have my local web server instance running—I'll fire it up now and try testing the movie again (see Figure 12-8).

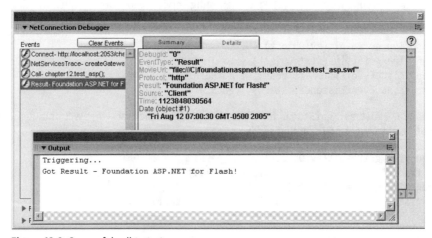

Figure 12-8. Successful call to test_asp

This time we're getting a different response in the NetConnection Debugger—a Result event, with a result of Foundation ASP.NET for Flash!, just like we placed in our ASP.NET code. You'll also see other events in the NetConnection Debugger: Connect, NetServicesTrace, and Call. Selecting these events in the debugger will display information useful for debugging purposes.

Accessing ASP.NET session state via Remoting

As we saw in the previous chapter, ASP.NET session state can be very useful in an application, especially when designing multipage applications that contain Flash elements on each page. When using Flash Remoting and ASP.NET, it is possible to retrieve the ASP.NET session state variables from the Flash client for maintaining state within your applications. In this example, we're going to set up another very simple Remoting application that will consist of a Flash interface containing a button and a text field. When the button is clicked, we'll call an ASP.NET page that will access a .NET session variable, clicks, increment its value, and return it to the Flash client. Upon receiving the result, the Flash client will display the new value of the clicks session variable.

Setting up the ASP.NET page

Setting up this ASP.NET page will be very similar to the ASP.NET code-behind example we covered earlier with the Flash Remoting server control. We'll create a new ASP.NET web form called test_session.aspx, with the code placed in a separate file. In the HTML source view of this page, we're going to modify the code to look like the following:

```
<%@ Page Language="C#" AutoEventWireup="true"
➥ CodeFile="test_session.aspx.cs" Inherits="test_session" %>
➥ <%@ Register TagPrefix="MM" Namespace="FlashGateway"
 Assembly="FlashGateway" %>

<MM:Flash ID="flash1" runat="server">
</MM:Flash>
```

Again, this page contains nothing more than the Flash Remoting server control—it will be in the code-behind page that we'll be doing the session magic. Next, let's go to the code-behind file test_session.aspx.cs and place some code within the Page_Load event handler, which will retrieve the value of an ASP.NET session variable, much like we did in Chapter 11.

```
protected void Page_Load(object sender, EventArgs e)
{
  // if it's the first click, set "clicks" to 1
  int tmpClicks = 1;

  if (Session["clicks"] != null)
  {
    // increment it
    tmpClicks = ((int)Session["clicks"]) + 1;
  }
  Session["clicks"] = tmpClicks;

  // set the flash control's Result parameter to the
  // current number of clicks in this Session
  flash1.Result = tmpClicks;
}
```

In this codeblock, I am simply creating a new variable, tmpClicks, and initializing that variable to 1—which will be the value of the clicks session variable the first time this page is selected. If the clicks session variable is tested and found not to be null (the user has already clicked and set the session variable), we're going to grab the value of that session variable and set the value of our tmpClicks variable to that value plus 1. After this comparison is made, I am setting the clicks session variable to its incremented value, and then setting the value of the Flash server control's Result parameter to the tmpClicks variable.

> Note that I am setting the value of the Flash server control's Result parameter to the value of the tmpClicks variable instead of the value of the Session["clicks"] variable, since this modified value is not available immediately after it is set.

That's it for the ASP.NET side of our example. Next we'll look at how to call this page from a Flash client using the Flash Remoting connector.

Creating the Flash interface

For the Flash side of this example, we'll create a new Flash movie in the flash folder of the C:\foundationaspnet\chapter12\ folder, called test_session.fla. In this movie, we'll create a simple interface consisting of a Button component, which we will give an instance name of inc_btn, and a Dynamic text field, which we will give an instance name of result_txt. Again, we're also going to drag instances of the Flash Remoting Connector component and the RemoteDebugClasses onto the stage, so we can use the Flash Remoting Connector and debugging classes in our example.

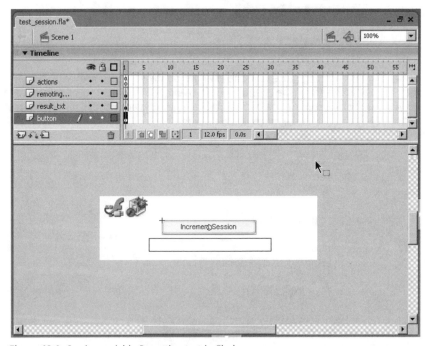

Figure 12-9. Session variable Remoting test in Flash

As shown in Figure 12-9, I have also created a layer called actions; in the first frame I will place the code used to retrieve our ASP.NET session variables via Remoting. The first thing we'll need to do in this code is to import the RemotingConnector and NetDebug classes, initialize the NetDebugger, and create a new instance of the Remoting Connector. We'll also set up the Remoting Connector instance with the same event listeners and properties as in the previous example, with the exception of the methodName property, which we will set to test_session so the test_session.aspx page is called instead of the test_asp.aspx page.

```
import mx.data.components.RemotingConnector;
import mx.remoting.debug.NetDebug;
NetDebug.initialize();
var myRemConn_rc:RemotingConnector = new RemotingConnector();

myRemConn_rc.addEventListener("result", gotResult);
myRemConn_rc.addEventListener("status", gotStatus);
myRemConn_rc.gatewayUrl =
➥ "http://localhost:2053/chapter12/gateway.aspx";
myRemConn_rc.methodName = "test_session";
myRemConn_rc.serviceName = "chapter12";
```

Next, let's create the gotResult and gotStatus event handlers. When the gotResult event handler is fired, we'll set the value of the result_txt text field to display the result we retrieved from the ASP.NET page.

```
function gotClick()
{
  _root.myRemConn_rc.trigger();
}
function gotResult(ev:Object) {
  result_txt.text = "'clicks' Session variable: " + ev.target.results;
}
function gotStatus(stat:Object) {
  result_txt.text = "crror: " +stat.code+" -  "+stat.data.faultstring;
}
```

And finally, we'll add an event handler to respond to the click of the Button component:

```
inc_btn.addEventListener("click", gotClick);
function gotClick()
{
  _root.myRemConn_rc.trigger();
}
```

In the gotClick event handler, we're simply going to call the Trigger method of the myRemConn Remoting Connector instance to start the Flash Remoting process. At this point, the example is ready—but because session variables require an active web browser session, we're going to need to add this movie to an .aspx page and do our testing there. First, publish the Flash movie (generating the test_session.swf file), and then we'll jump back into ASP.NET.

Testing the code

Back in Visual Studio, we'll create a new web form called session_page.aspx, into which we'll drag an instance of the epicFlashControl (see Chapter 3). We're going to set the source property of this instance of the epicFlashControl to flash/test_session.swf, and define the control's width and height accordingly. The final HTML source view of the session_page.aspx page is shown here:

```
<%@ Page Language="C#" AutoEventWireup="true"
➥ CodeFile="session_page.aspx.cs" Inherits="session_page" %>
<%@ Register Assembly="epicFlashControl"
➥ Namespace="epicFlash" TagPrefix="cc1" %>

<!DOCTYPE html PUBLIC "-//W3C//DTD XHTML 1.1//EN"
➥ "http://www.w3.org/TR/xhtml11/DTD/xhtml11.dtd">
<html xmlns="http://www.w3.org/1999/xhtml" >
<head runat="server">
    <title>Flash Remoting Session Test</title>
</head>
<body>
    <form id="form1" runat="server">
    <div>
        <cc1:epicflashcontrol id="EpicFlashControl1"
➥ runat="server" height="100" majorversion="8"
➥ minorversion="0" source="flash/test_session.swf" width="350">
        </cc1:epicflashcontrol>
    </div>
    </form>
</body>
</html>
```

Finally, let's test this page in a browser to see our code come together!

Figure 12-10 is shown after the Increment Session button has been clicked four times—the state of our session is successfully being tracked using Flash Remoting!

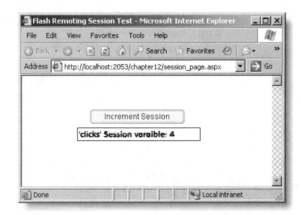

Figure 12-10. Session variables using Remoting

Connecting to a .NET DLL via Flash Remoting

One of the most useful methods of executing .NET server-side functionality in Flash using Flash Remoting is through the use of a precompiled .NET DLL file. Unlike in the previous example where we connected to a specific ASP.NET page, when connecting to a .NET DLL, we are able to access multiple methods through a single connection. This ability is very similar to the web services we set up in the previous chapters—we can create multiple methods in a .NET class and access each of them directly through our ActionScript code, just as if they existed in the Flash file.

Creating a .NET DLL

Creating a DLL file in .NET is going to be a slightly different process than any of the previous ASP.NET work we've done in this book. When creating a .NET DLL file in Visual Studio .NET for use with Flash Remoting, we're actually going to create two separate projects—one website project, just like we did in the previous examples in this chapter, with a gateway.aspx file and the flashremoting.dll file, and another class library project that will contain the classes we wish to connect to through our Flash code. In this example, we'll use the same website project we've been using for the previous examples, and we'll create a new class library project.

To create a new class library project, right-click on the name of the current solution in the Visual Studio .NET Solution Explorer and select Add ➤ New Project, as shown in Figure 12-11.

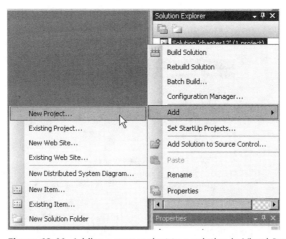

Figure 12-11. Adding a new project to a solution in Visual Studio .NET

In the following dialog box, you'll need to specify a location for the new project. Although this project does not need to exist within the same folder as your current website, I am going to create it in a new folder called remote_dll, within the C:\foundationaspnet\chapter12\ directory. I have also given this project a name of test_dll, as shown in Figure 12-12.

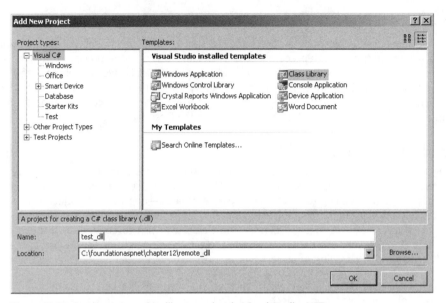

Figure 12-12. Creating a new class library project in Visual Studio .NET

When this project is created, you will see a new project appear in the Solution Explorer containing a new .cs file, Class1.cs, as shown in Figure 12-13.

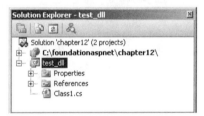

Figure 12-13. test_dll class library project
in Solution Explorer

Let's rename the Class1.cs file to Remoting.cs, so it better describes our project. This class file will contain the classes that will be available to our Flash client, exposed through Flash Remoting. Upon opening this file, you'll notice that there is some code automatically generated by Visual Studio .NET. Let's modify this code to look like the following:

```
namespace test_dll
{
  public class Remoting
  {
    public string EchoString(string orig)
    {
      return "Flash Remoting " + orig;
    }
  }
}
```

As shown in this codeblock, I have added a new method to the Remoting class, called EchoString. This method performs a very simple function—it takes in a string parameter, and returns that same parameter with the string "Remoting:" appended to it. For now, that's all we're going to do in this class file— next, we'll tell Visual Studio .NET to build this DLL file for us (similar to telling the Flash IDE to build an .swf) by selecting Build test_dll from the Build menu. If you navigate to the bin\debug\ folder of the directory that we've created this new DLL project in, you'll see that there has been a new file created, called test_dll.dll, as shown in Figure 12-14.

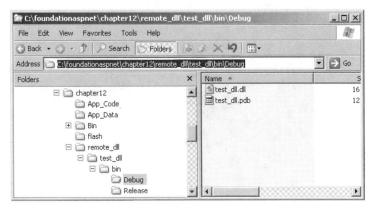

Figure 12-14. The test_dll file after compilation

This DLL file now contains all of the information we just coded into the Remoting class. The next (and last) step we'll need to take to make this class accessible for a Flash Remoting client is to add a reference to it in our website!

Adding this DLL file to our website project is a very easy task. In the Visual Studio .NET Solution Explorer, right-click on the Bin directory and select Add Reference, as shown in Figure 12-15.

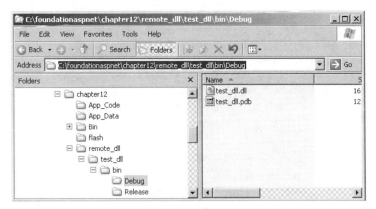

Figure 12-15. Adding a reference to a DLL file

When the Add Reference dialog box appears, select the Projects tab and choose the class project we just created, as shown in Figure 12-16.

After clicking OK, you should see a new file appear in the Bin directory of your Visual Studio .NET Solution Explorer—test_dll.dll. Because this DLL file is now residing in the same directory as the flashremoting.dll file, it is accessible through Flash Remoting.

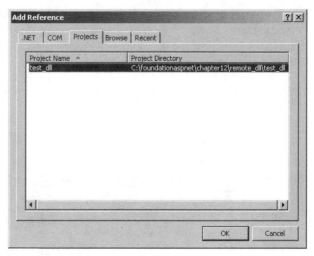

Figure 12-16. Adding a reference to the test_dll class library

Calling DLLs from Flash

Now that we have a DLL file created and ready in our website's Bin directory, we can create code in a Flash movie to access the methods of that class. For this example, we can make use of the same code we used in the test_asp.fla file in the "Connecting to an ASP.NET page" example earlier in this chapter, with the exception of the lines listed in bold in the following codeblock:

```
import mx.data.components.RemotingConnector;
import mx.remoting.debug.NetDebug;
NetDebug.initialize();
var myRemConn_rc:RemotingConnector = new RemotingConnector();

myRemConn_rc.addEventListener("result", gotResult);
myRemConn_rc.addEventListener("status", gotStatus);
// remember to change the port of the Gateway URL!
myRemConn_rc.gatewayUrl =
  "http://localhost:2053/chapter12/gateway.aspx";
myRemConn_rc.methodName = "EchoString";
myRemConn_rc.serviceName = "test_dll.Remoting";
myRemConn_rc.params = ["for .NET Rocks!"];

trace("Triggering...");
myRemConn_rc.trigger();
function gotResult(ev:Object) {
  trace("Got Result From .dll - "+ev.target.results);
}
function gotStatus(stat:Object) {
  trace("Error - "+stat.code+" - "+stat.data.faultstring);
}
```

In this codeblock, all I had to change was the methodName and serviceName parameters (and the params as desired), to connect to the DLL file *instead* of the .aspx page! Figure 12-17 shows the logic that should be used to determine the value of the serviceName parameter.

Finally, let's open up the NetConnection Debugger and test this Flash file (see Figure 12-18).

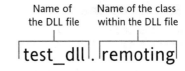

Name of   Name of the class
the DLL file   within the DLL file

test_dll . remoting

Figure 12-17. The process for determining the name of the serviceName parameter

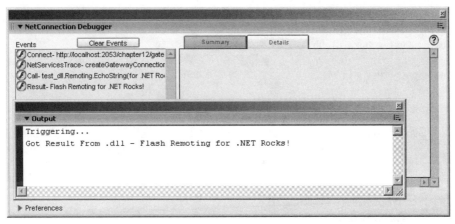

Figure 12-18. NetConnection Debugger

We have successfully connected from a Flash client to a .NET DLL using Flash Remoting! This is a pretty simple example—simply returning a string value. In the next section, we'll add some more complex code to our DLL file, returning a .NET DataSet.

Passing data from a .NET DLL to Flash

In each of the examples we've looked at so far in this chapter, we've been sending some pretty basic data types from .NET to Flash. In this example, we're going to see how we can pass a DataSet created in a .NET class file to a Flash client via Remoting.

As we discussed in Chapter 9, the combination of .NET DataAdapters and DataSets can be a very efficient method of retrieving data from a database. When using .NET web services, however, we had to convert those DataSets to arrays of structs, since the Flash web service classes cannot deserialize DataSet properly. Flash Remoting, however, can handle the DataTable object contained within .NET DataSet objects without a problem. When .NET DataTables enter Flash, they are serialized to become Flash RecordSets, which function in nearly the same way as ADO.NET DataTables—as a two-dimensional array of rows and columns.

> RecordSets *cannot be passed from Flash back to .NET. For this type of functionality, it is best to create an array of Flash objects, which are serialized as* ASObjects, *which we will cover in the next section.*

Setting up the DLL

In this example, we'll make use of the same class project test_dll that we created in the previous example, but we'll add another method, GetCategories, which will retrieve data from the Northwind Access database we used in Chapter 8. Shown in the following codeblock is the new code necessary to fill a DataSet with values from the Customers table of the Northwind database. I will not explain this process in detail, as it is the same as our DataAdapter example in Chapter 9.

```csharp
using System;
using System.Collections.Generic;
using System.Text;
using System.Data;
using System.Data.OleDb;

namespace test_dll
{
  class Remoting
  {
    public string EchoString(string orig)
    {
      return "Flash Remoting " + orig;
        }
    public DataTable GetCategories()
    {
      string _connString =
        @"Provider=Microsoft.Jet.OLEDB.4.0;Data Source=
➥ C:\foundationaspnet\chapter9\data\Northwind.mdb";
      OleDbConnection conn = new OleDbConnection(_connString);
      OleDbCommand cmd = new OleDbCommand();
      cmd.CommandText = "SELECT CategoryID,
➥ CategoryName, Description FROM Categories";
      cmd.Connection = conn;

      OleDbDataAdapter da = new OleDbDataAdapter();
      da.SelectCommand = cmd;

      DataSet ds = new DataSet();
      da.Fill(ds);

      return ds.Tables[0];
    }
  }
}
```

And, as easily as that, we have created a new DataSet in a .NET class that can be accessed via Flash Remoting. Before we move to the Flash interface for this example, we'll need to rebuild the *entire solution*, not just the test_dll project, so our website project will pull the newly compiled DLL file into its Bin folder. To build the entire solution, select Build Solution from the Build menu in Visual Studio .NET.

Retrieving the DataSet in Flash

Even though the DataTable is a more complex type than a string, retrieving this type in Flash is no more complicated than the previous examples in this chapter. For this front-end, we're going to create a new Flash file, test_datatable.fla, in the C:\foundationaspnet\chapter12\flash\ directory. In this Flash Movie, I'm going to create two layers, actions and DataGrid. In the DataGrid layer, we'll drag an instance of the Flash DataGrid component, to which we'll assign an instance name of dg1. Make this DataGrid 540×300 for visual purposes.

In the actions layer, we'll add code that is almost exactly the same as the previous examples in this chapter, with the exception of the lines notated in bold in this codeblock:

```
import mx.data.components.RemotingConnector;
import mx.remoting.debug.NetDebug;
NetDebug.initialize();
var myRemConn_rc:RemotingConnector = new RemotingConnector();

myRemConn_rc.addEventListener("result", gotResult);
myRemConn_rc.addEventListener("status", gotStatus);
// remember to update the port for the gateway!
myRemConn_rc.gatewayUrl =
➥ "http://localhost:2053/chapter12/gateway.aspx";
myRemConn_rc.methodName = "GetCategories";
myRemConn_rc.serviceName = "test_dll.Remoting";

trace("Triggering...");
myRemConn_rc.trigger();
function gotResult(ev:Object) {
   dg1.dataProvider = ev.target.results;
}
function gotStatus(stat:Object) {
   trace("Error - "+stat.code+" -  "+stat.data.faultstring);
}
```

In this codeblock, you'll notice that we've changed the methodName of the myRemConn instance to GetCategories, the name of the method we created in our .NET Remoting class. We've also modified the gotResult handler to set the dataProvider property of the DataGrid instance, dg1. The DataGrid component, like other Flash components, can accept a RecordSet as a dataProvider, making it a very quick way of binding data to a user interface element. Through this event handler, the DataGrid will display the results of the GetCategories method when the response is received.

Let's again try opening the NetConnection Debugger and testing the Flash movie (see Figure 12-19).

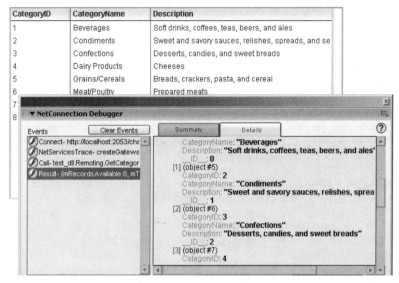

Figure 12-19. Viewing the results of the Remoting call in the NetConnectionDebugger

No problem! With a very minimal amount of code, we were able to send data retrieved directly from an Access database to a Flash client and bind that data to a DataGrid interface element.

Passing objects from .NET to Flash via Remoting

Another option for passing information from .NET to Flash using Remoting is through the use of ASObjects. ASObjects are objects, passed from .NET to Flash and serialized as Flash objects, which will have properties as assigned in .NET. ASObjects are very useful in situations where complex objects need to be exchanged or when the use of DataTables are not practical.

> The .NET ASObject *also requires that you add the* flashremoting.dll *file to your project, as we did earlier in the "Connecting to an ASP.NET page" section. When using the* ASObject *class, we'll actually be using a member of this* flashgateway.dll *file—the* ASObject *class residing within the* FlashGateway.IO *namespace.*

The use of ASObjects for Flash Remoting is very similar to the use of structs with web services. When a new ASObject is created, it is essentially a "blank" object, to which we can add any number of properties. Typically, properties are added to an ASObject instance using the Add method, which takes as inputs the name and value of the property to be assigned to the object. For example, a new ASObject representing a car could be created using the following:

```
FlashGateway.IO.ASObject aso = new FlashGateway.IO.ASObject();
Aso.Add("VehicleType", "Car");
Aso.Add("Doors", 4);
Aso.Add("Color", "Red");
Aso.Add("Year", 2005);
```

In this example, a new ASObject has been created by first creating a new instance of the ASObject class from the FlashGateway.IO namespace—remember that you could omit the FlashGateway.IO portion of this line by simply adding the following using statement at the beginning of a class file:

```
using FlashGateway.IO;
```

Next, let's take a look at an example where we modify the GetCateogries method we created in the previous section. In this example, instead of returning a DataTable object, we'll return an array of ASObjects, which will encapsulate the data from the Categories table in the Northwind database.

```
public FlashGateway.IO.ASObject[] GetCategoriesAS()
{
    string _connString = @"Provider=Microsoft.Jet.OLEDB.4.0;Data
➥ Source=C:\foundationaspnet\chapter9\data\Northwind.mdb";
    OleDbConnection conn = new OleDbConnection(_connString);
    OleDbCommand cmd = new OleDbCommand();
    cmd.CommandText = "SELECT CategoryID, CategoryName,
➥ Description FROM Categories";
    cmd.Connection = conn;

    OleDbDataAdapter da = new OleDbDataAdapter();
    da.SelectCommand = cmd;

    DataSet ds = new DataSet();
    da.Fill(ds);

    // create a new array of ASObjects
    FlashGateway.IO.ASObject[] ret = new
➥ FlashGateway.IO.ASObject[ds.Tables[0].Rows.Count];
    for (int x = 0; x < ds.Tables[0].Rows.Count; x++)
    {
        DataRow dr = ds.Tables[0].Rows[x];

        // for each row of data, create a new ASObject
        FlashGateway.IO.ASObject aso = new FlashGateway.IO.ASObject();
        aso.ASType = "Category";
        aso.Add("CategoryID", (int)dr["CategoryID"]);
        aso.Add("CategoryName", (string)dr["CategoryName"]);
        aso.Add("Description", (string)dr["Description"]);

        // add the new ASObject to the array
        ret[x] = aso;
    }
    return ret;
}
```

In this method, an array of ASObjects is created, with the same dimensions as the number of rows in the table we would like to pass to Flash. We then traverse through the rows in the DataTable, creating a new ASObject for each DataRow and creating a property for each column in the DataRow. Finally, the array of ASObjects is returned, containing all of the CategoryID, CategoryName, and Description fields from the Categories table.

Retrieving the objects in Flash

The ActionScript code used to retrieve data from .NET is again not any different than in the previous examples, except for the value assigned to the methodName property. For this example, I have created a Flash file called test_asobject.fla, saved in the same chapter12\flash directory. This time, we'll display the results of the Flash Remoting call in a new TextArea instance, which we'll give an instance name of resultTxt. For formatting purposes, set the HTML property of the resultTxt instance to true.

```
import mx.data.components.RemotingConnector;
import mx.remoting.debug.NetDebug;
NetDebug.initialize();
var myRemConn_rc:RemotingConnector = new RemotingConnector();

myRemConn_rc.addEventListener("result", gotResult);
myRemConn_rc.addEventListener("status", gotStatus);
myRemConn_rc.gatewayUrl =
    "http://localhost:2053/chapter12/gateway.aspx";
myRemConn_rc.methodName = "GetCategoriesAS";
myRemConn_rc.serviceName = "test_dll.Remoting";

myRemConn_rc.trigger();
function gotResult(ev:Object) {
  var x:Number;
  var txtVal:String = "";
  for (x=0; x<ev.target.results.length; x++) {
    txtVal += "<b>ASObject #"+x.toString()+"</b><br>";
    txtVal += "<b>CategoryID:</b> "+ev.target.results[x].CategoryID;
    txtVal +=
      "<br><b>CategoryName:</b> "+ev.target.results[x].CategoryName;
    txtVal +=
      "<br><b>Description:</b> "+ev.target.results[x].Description;
    txtVal += "<br><br>";
  }
  _root.resultTxt.text = txtVal;
}
function gotStatus(stat:Object) {
  trace("Error - "+stat.code+" -  "+stat.data.faultstring);
}
```

The result of this codeblock is shown in Figure 12-20. As you can see, the data contained in the ASObject array that was sent from ASP.NET is easily parsed and displayed!

CategoryID: 1
CategoryName: Beverages
Description: Soft drinks, coffees, teas, beers, and ales

ASObject #1
CategoryID: 2
CategoryName: Condiments
Description: Sweet and savory sauces, relishes, spreads, and
seasonings

ASObject #2
CategoryID: 3
CategoryName: Confections
Description: Desserts, candies, and sweet breads

ASObject #3
CategoryID: 4

Figure 12-20. The objects have been retrieved in Flash

Passing objects from Flash to .NET via Remoting

Passing complex objects created in ASP.NET is one thing, but is it possible to pass the same, complex objects the other way? It sure is! Flash objects can be passed as parameters to Flash Remoting methods, just like any other input parameter, and they are serialized in .NET as ASObjects, making them easy to work with in .NET code. This type of functionality can come in very handy when you're updating large sets of data, for example.

Let's try a simple example of this, starting by adding a new method to the Remoting class in our test_dll.dll file. In this method, which we'll name SendObject, we'll take an ASObject as a parameter, and return a string that will list the keys and values of the properties contained in the ASObject. In order to retrieve the keys and values from the ASObject, we're going to make use of the ASObject's Key and Values properties, which are implemented as C# HashTables (see Chapter 2). From the HashTables, we've used the CopyTo method, which copies all members of the HashTable to a string array, which we can then traverse through, retrieving the keys and values. For the purposes of this example, we'll use the keys and values to create an HTML-formatted string, which we'll send back to Flash as a return value.

```
public string SendObject(FlashGateway.IO.ASObject aso)
{
  string ret = "<b>" + aso.Keys.Count.ToString() +
➥  " Properties Found</b><br><br>";

  // create new string arrays
  string[] vals = new string[aso.Keys.Count];
  string[] keys = new string[aso.Keys.Count];

  // copy the keys and values to the string arrays
  aso.Keys.CopyTo(keys, 0);
  aso.Values.CopyTo(vals, 0);
```

337

```
    // go through each key/value pair and add it to the string
    for (int x = 0; x < keys.Length; x++)
    {
      ret += "<b>" + keys.GetValue(x).ToString() + ":</b> "
               + vals.GetValue(x).ToString();
      ret += "<br>";
    }

    return ret;
}
```

Next, rebuild the .NET project, and let's head to Flash to create an interface!

Sending an object from Flash

To send an object from Flash to this new .NET method, we can again make use of nearly the same code as in our previous examples. In this Flash file, test_send_asobject.fla, we have created a TextArea instance, resultTxt, which we're going to use to display the HTML-formatted string returned from the .NET Remoting SendObject method.

In the codeblock that follows, we've created a new object, to which we've added three properties: FirstName, LastName, and Team. Using the params property of the RemotingConnector instance, we've then passed this object to .NET, in the same way we have passed parameters in the previous examples.

```
import mx.data.components.RemotingConnector;
import mx.remoting.debug.NetDebug;
NetDebug.initialize();

// first, create the object we're going to send
var myObject:Object;
myObject = new Object();
myObject.FirstName = "Babe";
myObject.LastName = "Ruth";
myObject.Team = "Yankees";

var myRemConn_rc:RemotingConnector = new RemotingConnector();
myRemConn_rc.addEventListener("result", gotResult);
myRemConn_rc.addEventListener("status", gotStatus);
myRemConn_rc.gatewayUrl =
  "http://localhost:2053/chapter12/gateway.aspx";
myRemConn_rc.serviceName = "test_dll.Remoting";
myRemConn_rc.methodName = "SendObject";
myRemConn_rc.params = [myObject];

resultTxt.text = "Loading...";
myRemConn_rc.trigger();

function gotResult(ev:Object) {
  _root.resultTxt.text = ev.target.results;
}
```

```
function gotStatus(stat:Object) {
    trace("Error - "+stat.code+" -  "+stat.data.faultstring);
}
```

The results of this codeblock are shown in Figure 12-21. To recap what has actually happened in this example: An object was sent from Flash to a .NET class library, which, upon reception, went through each property of the object and added it to an HTML-formatted string. This string was then sent back to Flash, as a result, and we've used Flash to display these results in a TextArea instance.

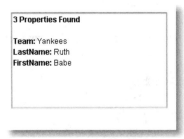

Figure 12-21. The string as displayed in a Flash TextArea

Connecting to a third-party web service using Remoting

As mentioned earlier in this chapter, Flash Remoting can even be used as a method for connecting to third-party web services—like the Google web service we connected to in Chapter 8. When connecting to a third-party web service using Flash Remoting, it's not necessary to create a web service proxy like we did in that chapter. When using Flash Remoting to invoke remote web service methods, it's not even necessary to create any code in ASP.NET—the Flash Remoting DLL takes care of all the work!

Another advantage of using Flash Remoting instead of the Flash web service classes to connect to web services is that, through Remoting, the data exchanged between Flash and the web service is serialized and deserialized natively by the Flash Player, rather than the web service classes. This feature causes web services that are invoked from Flash Remoting to respond faster than those called by the Web Service Connector classes, and also require less overhead, since the Web Service Connector classes do not have to be compiled into your .swf file.

Making a call to a third-party web service using the Flash Remoting Connector in ActionScript is very similar to the methods we've used earlier in this chapter. The gatewayUrl property of the Remoting Connector remains the same gateway.aspx as in the previous examples, the methodName property becomes the name of the method of the web service you wish to invoke, and the serviceName property is set to the WSDL URL of the service.

An example of a call to a third-party web service, provided by www.sheshkiran.com, is shown here. This web service provides a single method, GetQuote, which takes no parameters and returns a famous quotation as a string value. For this example, we've created a new Flash file, test_webserivce.fla, to which we've added both the Flash Remoting Connector classes and the RemotingDebugClasses, as we've done earlier in this chapter. We've also added a Button component with an instance name of quoteBtn, and a TextArea component with an instance name of resultTxt. In the first frame of a new layer we've called Actions, we've added the following ActionScript:

```
import mx.data.components.RemotingConnector;
import mx.remoting.debug.NetDebug;
NetDebug.initialize();
var myRemConn_rc:RemotingConnector = new RemotingConnector();
myRemConn_rc.addEventListener("result", categoryResult);
myRemConn_rc.addEventListener("status", categoryStatus);
// don't forget to change the port number!
myRemConn_rc.gatewayUrl =
   "http://localhost:2053/chapter12/gateway.aspx";
myRemConn_rc.methodName = "GetQuote";
myRemConn_rc.serviceName =
➥ "http://www.seshakiran.com/QuoteService/QuotesService.asmx?wsdl";
myRemConn_rc.suppressInvalidCalls = true;

function categoryResult(ev:Object) {
  trace("Got Result - "+ev.target.results);
  resultTxt.text = ev.target.results;
}
function categoryStatus(stat:Object) {
  trace("Error - "+stat.code+" -  "+stat.data.faultstring);
}
quoteBtn.addEventListener("click", gotClick);
function gotClick() {
  trace("Triggering...");
  _root.myRemConn_rc.trigger();
}
```

In this codeblock, we've set the gatewayUrl property of the myRemConn_rc Remoting Connector instance to the same gateway as we've used in the previous chapters, http://localhost:2053/ chapter12/gateway.aspx. For the serviceName property, we've used the WSDL URL of the quotation service we plan to call, http://www.seshakiran.com/QuoteService/QuotesService.asmx?wsdl. By inspecting this service using the Flash Web Services panel (which we covered in Chapter 7), you can find that the only method exposed by this service is GetQuote, which we have set as the value of the methodName parameter. The results of this example are shown in Figure 12-22. (If you have problems getting this code to work correctly, please skip ahead to "Potential problems with web services and Flash Remoting.")

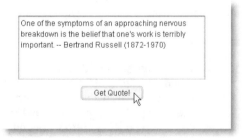

Figure 12-22. The results of calling the web service

And, just that easily, you can use Flash Remoting to incorporate return values from a remote web service into your Flash projects! After a successful execution, you will see by looking in the bin directory of this example's root folder that two new files have been generated alongside the FlashGateway.dll, as shown in Figure 12-23. These files, Quotes.cs and Quotes.dll, are files that have been generated by FlashGateway.dll, using one of the tools that comes with the .NET SDK—WSDL.exe. This executable, known as the Web Services Description Language Tool, generates code for XML web services and XML web service clients from a WSDL URL—very similar to creating a web service proxy, just like we did in Chapter 8.

Figure 12-23. FlashGateway.dll has created the Quotes.cs and Quotes.dll files.

Potential problems with web services and Flash Remoting

If you're running into issues connecting to third-party web services using Flash Remoting, don't worry, you're not alone! In many circumstances the default setup of Visual Studio .NET, the .NET Framework, and Flash Remoting isn't quite right to make web service calls work on the first try. Listed here are a couple of common problems and possible solutions to get web service calls to work through Flash Remoting.

Unable to create web service proxy. Please ensure the Microsoft.NET Framework SDK is installed.

If you get an error from Flash that notifies you to install the .NET SDK, you will most likely need to add a new PATH variable to your system, which will allow Flash Remoting to find the .NET Framework's WSDL.exe tool, used to generate the class library necessary to perform the call to the remote web service. This PATH variable can be added by going to Control Panel ➤ System, then selecting the Advanced tab. In the Advanced tab, select Environment Variables, then in the pane titled System Variables, scroll down to Path and select Edit, as shown in Figure 12-24. In the following Edit System Variable dialog box, you'll need to add a reference to the path of the SDK\bin directory within your Visual Studio .NET installation (or .NET Framework SDK installation). On my system, this path is C:\Program Files\ Microsoft Visual Studio 8\SDK\v2.0\Bin. Be sure to put a semicolon (;) between the previous entry and the Visual Studio SDK directory.

After you add this reference in your system's PATH variable, it will most likely be necessary to reboot your system for the changes to take effect.

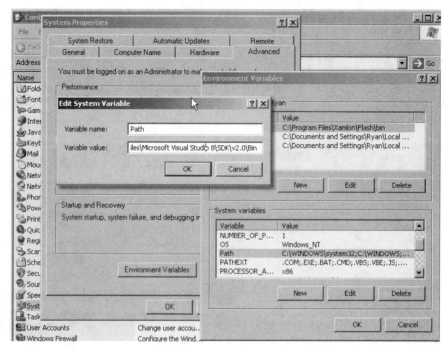

Figure 12-24. Editing the Path environment variable

Could not load file or assembly x.dll

If you have already tried the previous fix, try either republishing the Flash file or rebooting your system. It is most likely that the WSDL.exe program didn't generate the new DLL file soon enough for Flash's taste.

Any error relating to "access denied"

If you are receiving an error that appears to be related to access issues, you will need to make sure that the aspnet_wp user account on your system has full write privileges to your application's bin directory. This problem does not normally occur when using the ASP.NET development server in Visual Studio .NET 2005, but is more common when tested using IIS. For more information on setting the user access level of the aspnet_wp user account, please see http://msdn.microsoft.com/library/default.asp?url=/library/en-us/vsdebug/html/vxgrfaspnetdebuggingsystemrequirements.asp.

Summary

In this chapter, we've covered a load of information relating to Flash Remoting! From simple data access to complex objects and web services, we've learned how to use ASP.NET along with the Flash Remoting Connector to pass information between Flash and ASP.NET using the most efficient method available to Flash/ASP.NET developers. As you've seen in many of these examples, developing Flash Remoting–based applications isn't really any more difficult than the previous methods we've examined. In the next chapter, we'll look at a more in-depth Flash Remoting example, a video weblog, which will use Flash Remoting to execute methods that will access and manipulate data in a SQL database!

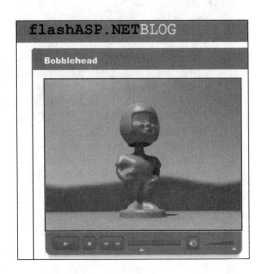

flashASP.NETBLOG

Bobblehead

Chapter 13

CREATING A VIDEO WEBLOG USING SQL SERVER AND FLASH REMOTING

What this chapter covers:

- File uploading in Flash/ASP.NET
- SQL Server
- SQL stored procedures
- Creating a video weblog using Flash Remoting and SQL Server

We've certainly covered a lot of information in the past few chapters! In Chapter 9, we learned how to connect to and retrieve information from an Access database, and in Chapter 10, we integrated information from an Access database into an e-commerce application using web services. In Chapter 12, we covered a new method for communicating between Flash and ASP.NET with Flash Remoting. Now, we're going to tie much of this knowledge together, by creating a video weblog application that makes use of Flash Remoting and Microsoft SQL Server as a database engine. In this application, we'll also learn how to create and execute SQL stored procedures, which are a very safe and efficient method for executing queries on a SQL Server. Before we get started with the weblog application, however, we're going to cover an exciting topic in Flash and ASP.NET—file uploading using Flash as a presentation tier. Then, we'll make use of this skill to create an administrative panel to upload videos to our video weblog!

File uploading with Flash and ASP.NET

In recent years, the term "file upload" has been almost nonexistent in the world of Flash development. Instead of providing file upload capabilities through the Flash presentation tier, developers have typically been forced to rely on a combination of server-side code and HTML to provide the ability to upload files from a user's file system to a directory on the server. The ability to accomplish this type of file upload using Flash has been one of the top requests of developers, and with the release of Flash 8, Macromedia added this feature to the list of Flash's capabilities.

As we've seen with many of the other powerful features of Flash in this book, file uploading also can't be accomplished by Flash alone—it requires the help of a server-side partner like ASP.NET. When Flash is used to complete a file upload, the Flash Player takes care of the majority of the process—the steps in this process are listed here:

1. Browse for the file on the user's filesystem. When the user selects a file, information about that file (size, etc.) can be obtained through ActionScript.

2. Upload the file from the user's filesystem to a web server using HTTP. Again, this process is initiated by the Flash Player, and the progress of this upload can be monitored through ActionScript.

3. When the file upload has completed, the process is handed off to the server-side process—in this case, the ASP.NET page. ASP.NET handles the uploaded file, performs any necessary logic necessary for the file, and moves the file to the correct location on the server.

With Flash 8, file uploading is built into the ActionScript 2.0 Flash library through the use of the flash.net.FileReference class. This class allows us to browse for a file using a standard browsing dialog box, select a file, and upload it to a web server, while monitoring its progress and potential errors.

The Flash.net.FileReference class

Before we examine the ASP.NET side of the Flash file upload process, it's important that we understand the capabilities of the flash.net.FileReference class. This class allows not only file uploads through the Flash Player, but also downloads—a feature we won't cover in this chapter, but one that might be very useful in many Flash applications! Listed in Tables 13-1 and 13-2 are the methods and events of the ActionScript FileReference class.

Table 13-1. Methods of the FileReference class

Method	Description
AddListener	Registers an object to receive notification when a FileReference event handler is invoked.
Browse	Brings up a dialog box that allows a user to select a file from their local filesystem. This method takes an optional array parameter that specifies the types of valid files that can be uploaded.
Cancel	Cancels any current file upload or download by this FileReference object.
Download	Brings up a dialog box that allows a user to download a file from the web server. This method takes two parameters: url and defaultFileName. url specifies the location to download the file from, and defaultFileName provides the suggested name for the file on the user's filesystem.
RemoveListener	Removes an object that has been added using the AddListener method.
Upload	Starts the upload of a file to the web server. Takes a string parameter, url, which specifies the page to POST the file to.

Table 13-2. Events of the FileReference class

Event Name	Description
OnCancel	Fired when the user closes the file selection dialog box without selecting a file
OnComplete	Fired when an upload or download operation has completed
OnHTTPError	Fired when an upload fails because of an HTTP type error
OnIOError	Fired when an IO error occurs
OnOpen	Fired when an upload or a download operation begins
OnProgress	Fired intermittently during the file upload or a download operation to monitor the progress of the operation
OnSecurityError	Fired when an upload or a download error occurs because of a security error
OnSelect	Fired when a user selects a file from the selection dialog box

Handling file uploads in ASP.NET

As mentioned earlier in this chapter, when files are sent from a presentation tier (like Flash or HTML) to a server-side ASP.NET web application, it's necessary to create code for an ASP.NET page that will be receiving the file upload to copy the uploaded file to its intended location. To accomplish this in ASP.NET, we again make use of the ASP.NET Page.Request object, this time taking advantage of the Files property. The Files property contains an HttpFileCollection object, which is, in essence, an array of HttpPostedFile objects. HttpPostedFile objects provide direct access to the files that have been uploaded to a page, as well as methods for moving the files to their final destination on the web server. Table 13-3 lists several of the members of the HttpPostedFile class.

Table 13-3. Members of the HttpPostedFile class

Member	Description
ContentLength	Gets the size of an uploaded file in bytes.
ContentType	Gets the MIME type of an uploaded file.
FileName	Gets the name of an uploaded file on the client's computer—for example, turtle.jpg. In ASP.NET 1.1, the FileName property returned the fully qualified file name—for example, c:\temp\turtle.jpg.
SaveAs	Saves the uploaded file to a location on the web server.

When using the Files property of the Page.Request object, the uploaded file (or files) can be accessed using a numerical indexer, as shown here:

```
// if there are files posted to the page
if (Page.Request.Files.Count > 0)
{
  // get the name of the first file using the 0 indexer
  string fileName = Page.Request.Files[0].FileName;
  // save the file to a location on the server
  Page.Request.Files[0].SaveAs(
    ➥ Server.MapPath("~/uploads/" + fileName));
}
```

You'll notice that in the preceding codeblock, the Server.MapPath method is used in conjunction with the SaveAs method to save the file to a location on the web server. This method is used since the SaveAs method requires a full filesystem path to the file it will be saving, instead of just a relative path from the current location. The MapPath method does just that—it returns the full path of a file located on the web server.

Uploading a file from Flash to ASP.NET

Now that we understand how the Flash FileReference object can be used to browse for and upload a file to an ASP.NET page, and how to handle an uploaded file in ASP.NET, let's take a look at an example of a basic file upload instantiated and monitored by a Flash interface, and handed off to an

ASP.NET page for server-side processing. In this example, we'll create an interface that will allow a user to select a .jpg image from their filesystem, then upload that image to a predetermined uploads directory on an ASP.NET website.

Let's get started with this example from the .NET side. There really won't be too much for the ASP.NET code to accomplish—it will simply check to see if there is a file uploaded, and place it in a directory if there is. For this project (and for the remainder of the projects in this chapter), we'll be creating our website using the local Internet Information Services (IIS) web server instead of the standalone Visual Studio .NET integrated server. This is due mainly to security restrictions of the Visual Studio server when accepting file uploads from an unknown source, like a Flash interface. To start a website project in Visual Studio using IIS instead of the integrated web server, select HTTP as the location type in the New Website dialog box of Visual Studio .NET. This will prompt Visual Studio to contact the local web server and create a *virtual directory* on that web server for your project.

> *A virtual directory created on your local IIS instance will appear as a subdirectory of the localhost domain, e.g.,* http://localhost/fileupload/. *For the use of local ASP.NET testing, a virtual directory is almost the same as creating a completely new website domain—URL paths relative to the "root" directory of an ASP.NET website project will resolve to file paths relative to the virtual directory's root directory. Also, you can have a separate* bin *directory and* web.config *file in each virtual directory.*

Figure 13-1 shows the selection of HTTP in Visual Studio to create a website project on the local Internet Information Services website root.

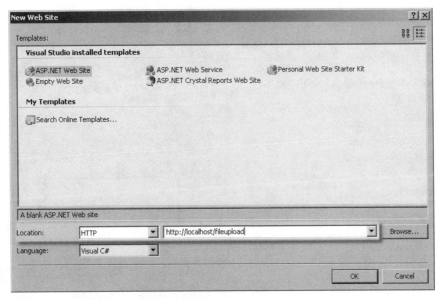

Figure 13-1. Using IIS to host a Visual Studio website project

With the project created, let's create a new folder inside this directory's root, called uploads. This folder will be used in this example to house the files uploaded from Flash to the ASP.NET page. On my system, the virtual directory I've just created is located at C:\Inetpub\wwwroot\fileupload (yours may be different depending on the directory you've installed IIS to), so the new folder will be C:\Inetpub\wwwroot\fileupload\uploads\. Once you have created this folder, it is necessary to make sure that the ASP.NET worker process has the permissions necessary to write files to that folder. The steps needed to ensure that the ASP.NET process has these permissions are listed next. It is necessary to check for these permissions any time you are creating an ASP.NET application that needs to have write access to a folder on a filesystem.

1. Right-click on the uploads directory. Select Properties, then select the Security tab.

2. In the Group or User Names box, look for a name title ASP.NET Machine Account. If you see this account, go to step 4; if not, proceed to step 3.

3. Click the Add button, and in the following dialog box, enter the name of your system followed by \ASPNET, as shown in Figure 13-2.

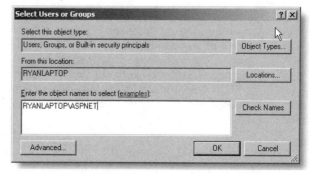

Figure 13-2. Adding the ASP.NET machine account

4. Select ASPNET Machine Account, and change the permissions to allow Read & Execute, List Folder Contents, Read, and Write permissions for the folder, as shown in Figure 13-3.

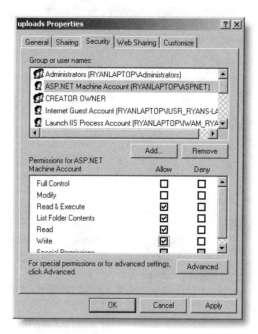

Figure 13-3. Changing permissions for the ASP.NET machine account

Now that we have the directory structure ready for our project, let's jump to the Page_Load event handler of the default.aspx page, which Visual Studio has created for us, and add some code to handle a file upload. The following codeblock shows all the code necessary to handle a single uploaded file and save it to a directory on the server's filesystem:

```
protected void Page_Load(object sender, EventArgs e)
{
  if (Page.Request.Files.Count > 0)
  {
    string fn = Page.Request.Files[0].FileName;
    try
    {
      // save the file to the "uploads" directory
      Page.Request.Files[0].SaveAs(
        ➥ Server.MapPath("~\\uploads\\" + fn));
    }
    catch (Exception e2)
    {
      // add code to handle an error
    }
  }
}
```

In the third line of this codeblock, if (Page.Request.Files.Count > 0), we're simply checking to see if there have been files POSTed to the page. If the Count property of the Page.Request.Files object is greater than 0, then we know that there is a file upload to handle. In the following line, string fn = Page.Request.Files[0].FileName;, the FileName property of the first Files object is used to obtain the name of the file that has been uploaded. This property retrieves the name without the original full file path, and with the file extension. Finally, the file is saved to the uploads directory of our site's root using the SaveAs method in combination with the Server.MapPath method, which is used to obtain the full path to our uploads directory. Generally, this is all the code that is needed to handle a file that is uploaded from Flash ASP.NET. Other functions that you might want to perform when receiving an uploaded file in ASP.NET include recording the name of the file in a database entry and renaming the file, to prevent unintentional file overwrites. Next, let's move to Flash (remember that you'll need Flash 8 in order to do file uploads!), to create an interface that will allow a user to select a file from their filesystem and upload that file to the ASP.NET page we just created. Let's get started by creating a new flash folder within the root directory of the ASP.NET website we just created—c:\inetpub\wwwroot\fileupload\. Within this folder, we'll create a new Flash movie, 480×350 pixels, called fileupload.fla. On the stage of this file, we'll create a new layer called components, in which we'll place a few components—a TextInput, two Buttons, and a ProgressBar, along with a dynamic text field, arranged as shown in Figure 13-4.

Figure 13-4. The fileupload.fla interface

Let's give these components instance names of fileTxt, browseBtn, uploadBtn, progressBar, and statusTxt, respectively. For the progressBar instance, set the mode parameter to manual, so we can update the status of this progress bar with ActionScript. Let's also create a layer called actions and on the first frame place the following ActionScript, used to initialize our application:

```
Application.main(this);
```

Next, we'll create the Application class, which will provide the ActionScript functionality for this application. Create a new file, Application.as, and save it in the same directory as the fileupload.fla file. In this file, place the following code:

```
dynamic class Application extends MovieClip {
  var fileRef:flash.net.FileReference;
  var fileUpload:Object;
  var uploadBtn:mx.controls.Button;
  var browseBtn:mx.controls.Button;
  var fileTxt:mx.controls.TextInput;
  var statusTxtTxt:TextField;
  var progressBar:mx.controls.ProgressBar;

  function Application(owner)
  {
    owner.__proto__ = this.__proto__;
    owner.__constructor__ = Application;
    this = owner;

    setup();
  }

  public static function main(createdBy:MovieClip) {
    var app = new Application(createdBy);
  }
```

```
private function setup()
{
  // fileRef is the FileReference object used to select
  // and upload a file
  fileRef = new flash.net.FileReference();

  // fileUpload will be the fileRef listener
  fileUpload = new Object ();
  fileUpload.onSelect = fileSelected;
  fileUpload.onProgress = fileProgress;
  fileUpload.onComplete = fileComplete;
  fileUpload.onError = fileError;
  fileRef.addListener (fileUpload);

  browseBtn.addEventListener("click", onBrowse);
  uploadBtn.addEventListener("click", onUpload);
}
private function fileError(file:flash.net.FileReference,
                           errorCode:Number)
{
  // error has occurred
  status_txt.text += "\ronHTTPError: " + file.name
    + " HTTP Error Code: " + errorCode;
}
private function fileProgress(file:flash.net.FileReference,
                              bytesLoaded:Number,
                              bytesTotal:Number) {
  // update the file upload progress bar
  var percent = Math.round (bytesLoaded / bytesTotal * 100);
  _root.progressBar.setProgress(percent, 100);
}
private function fileComplete(file:flash.net.FileReference)
{
  // file has uploaded successfully
  _root.statusTxt.text += "\r" + file.name
    + " uploaded successfully!";
  _root.fileTxt.text = "";
}
private function onUpload()
{
  if (_root.fileTxt.text.length>0)
  {
    // upload the file to the waiting .NET page
    _root.fileRef.upload (
      ➥ "http://localhost/fileupload/Default.aspx");
  }
}
private function onBrowse()
```

```
    {
      _root.fileRef.browse([
        ➡ {description: ".jpg file", extension: "*.jpg"}]);
    }
    private function fileSelected(file:flash.net.FileReference)
    {
      _root.status_txt.text += "File selected: " + file.name;
      _root.fileTxt.text = file.name;
    }
  }
}
```

For the most part, this class should look very similar to many of the other examples we've covered throughout this book. Essentially, when the browseBtn is selected, the browse method of a FileReference object, fileRef, is fired, prompting the user to select a file. You'll also notice that we've specified the file browser to only display files of the .jpg type, as highlighted in this code:

```
    _root.fileRef.browse([{description: ".jpg file", extension: "*.jpg"}]);
```

In the setup method of this class, we've created an object, fileUpload, which will be an event listener for the fileRef object. This object is assigned several event handlers to monitor events such as onSelected, onComplete, and onHttpError. When these events occur, the user interface is updated to reflect the change in status of the file upload progress.

Finally, let's go back to the .NET code and embed the Flash movie we've just created into the default.aspx page, using the epicFlashControl (as covered in Chapter 3). You'll notice that we are able to embed the Flash movie into the same ASP.NET page that contains the file upload logic we defined earlier. Because of the line if (Page.Request.Files.Count > 0), when this page is requested and there is no file being uploaded through HTTP, the page does not attempt to process the upload, but instead just displays the contents of the Flash interface.

The default.aspx page is shown in Figure 13-5, after being tested in Internet Explorer. In this example, I have selected a .jpg file, called msnet.jpg, and clicked Upload. After the upload completed successfully, you can see that the file has been copied by ASP.NET into the uploads directory, just as planned!

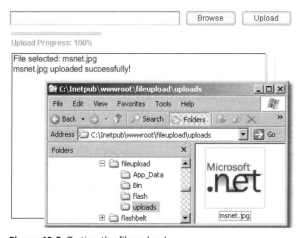

Figure 13-5. Testing the file upload

Creating a video weblog using .NET Flash Remoting and SQL Server

Since one of the hottest topics on the Web today is blogging, why not take advantage of the great presentation-tier video abilities of Flash, along with the necessary back-end power of ASP.NET and Microsoft SQL Server to create a video blogging system? In this example, we'll make a video weblog front-end and administration panel using a combination of Flash, Flash Remoting, ASP.NET, and SQL Server. The weblog will make use of the Flash/ASP.NET file uploading skills we've learned in this chapter—and we'll also learn how to use SQL Server to store the entries and provide the database tier for the blog.

To get started, let's define the functionality of the two sections of the video blogging system, and what functions each will accomplish:

- **Blog interface**: The front-end interface of the blog will provide the interface between the end user of the blog, navigating to the application using a browser. The interface will be capable of displaying blog entry posts (text values), blog entry titles, blog entry post dates, and videos attached to blog entries. The front-end interface will display the entries in chronological order, with the most recent being first, and be capable of scrolling through the older blog entries in a page-based style.

- **Administrative interface**: This interface will be available only to the administrator of the blog and will provide the administrator with an interface for adding and maintaining blog entries. Using the administrative interface, the blog administrator can upload new videos to the weblog (which are stored in a designated folder on the web server). The administrative interface will be password protected so unauthorized users cannot gain access.

Let's start the attack on this example from the ground up again, beginning with the data tier, then creating the ASP.NET logical tier, and finally moving up to the weblog front-end and administrative presentation tiers. Since we'll be using SQL Server for the data tier of this application, let's learn a bit about it first.

SQL Server

Microsoft SQL Server, which we learned how to install in Chapter 1, is a very powerful database engine that can be used in conjunction with Flash and ASP.NET to provide data-driven applications. SQL Server, as compared to Microsoft Access, is a much more robust and reliable database engine, especially for high-traffic or e-commerce applications. Visual Studio .NET 2005 also has very tight integration with SQL Server, making it a favorable choice when building Flash/ASP.NET applications.

In the next sections, you'll learn how to create databases on the SQL Server you have installed on your development system, and how to add tables and stored procedures to that database. As we're building this database, we'll also be building the foundation for our video weblog example.

SQL Server, like Flash and C#, has its own set of data types that it can use to store information. For the most part, SQL data types correspond to the .NET data types. You will notice that some .NET data types, like int and text, are broken into smaller subsets of data in SQL, making it possible to store certain fields most efficiently. Listed in Table 13-4 are the 27 SQL supported data types.

Table 13-4. SQL Server data types

Type	Description
tinyint	Integer data from 0 through 255
smallint	Integer data from -2^{15} through $(2^{15}) -1$
int	Integer data from -2^{31} through $(2^{31}) -1$
bigint	Integer data from -2^{63} through $(2^{63}) -1$
bit	Integer data with either a 1 or 0 value
decimal	Fixed precision and scale numeric data from $(-10^{38})+1$ through $(10^{38}) -1$
numeric	Fixed precision and scale numeric data from $(-10^{38})+1$ through $(10^{38}) -1$
smallmoney	Monetary data values from −214,748.3648 through +214,748.3647
money	Monetary data values from -2^{63} through $(2^{63}) -1$
float	Floating precision number data from $-1.79E + 308$ through $1.79E + 308$
real	Floating precision number data from $-3.40E + 38$ through $3.40E + 38$
smalldatetime	Date and time data from January 1, 1900, through June 6, 2079, with an accuracy of 1 minute
datetime	Date and time data from January 1, 1753, through December 31, 9999, with an accuracy of 3.33 milliseconds
char	Fixed-length character data with a maximum length of 8,000 characters
nchar	Fixed-length Unicode data with a maximum length of 4,000 characters
varchar	Variable-length data with a maximum length of 8,000 characters
nvarchar	Variable-length Unicode data with a maximum length of 4,000 characters
text	Variable-length data with a maximum length of $2^{31} - 1$ characters
ntext	Variable-length Unicode data with a maximum length of $2^{30} - 1$ characters
binary	Fixed-length binary data with a maximum length of 8,000 bytes
varbinary	Variable-length binary data with a maximum length of 8,000 bytes
image	Variable-length binary data with a maximum length of $2^{31} - 1$ bytes
cursor	A reference to a cursor
sql_variant	A data type that stores values of various data types, except text, ntext, timestamp, and sql_variant

Type	Description
table	A special data type used to store a result set for later processing
timestamp	A database-wide unique number that gets updated every time a row gets updated
uniqueidentifier	A globally unique identifier

Creating a new database on SQL Server with Visual Studio .NET 2005

Let's kick off our work with SQL Server by learning how to create a new SQL Server database right from Visual Studio .NET. (This assumes that you already have the SQL Server Express Edition running on your local system, as we covered in Chapter 1.) A SQL database, conceptually, is very similar to an Access database—except that a single SQL Server instance can contain many databases, which can be used to power any number of applications. The two simple steps for creating a database, which we will use for our video weblog application, are shown here:

1. Go to Server Explorer in Visual Studio .NET (this is called "Database Explorer" in the Web Developer Edition). Right-click Data Connections and select Create New SQL Server Database, as shown in Figure 13-6.

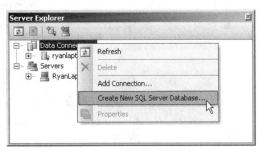

Figure 13-6. Creating a new SQL Server database in Server Explorer

2. In the following dialog box, as shown in Figure 13-7, enter either localhost or the name of your system for the server name, and video_blog for the database name. Depending on the type of authentication you configured your SQL Server to use when you set it up, you can either select Use Windows Authentication or Use SQL Server Authentication. If you choose SQL Server authentication, you will be required to provide a valid username and password for the SQL Server.

Figure 13-7. Creating the new video_blog SQL Server database

357

And just like that, we have created a database on our SQL Server. A database alone doesn't do us much good, though—the next logical step is to add tables to it. Luckily, adding tables to the database using Server Explorer is just as easy as creating it. The steps for adding a new table to our video_blog database are as follows:

1. Expand the video_blog database in the Visual Studio .NET Server Explorer.

2. Right-click Tables and select Add new table.

3. The SQL Server table view will appear in the main Visual Studio .NET pane. Fill in the column names, data types, and properties as desired. (We'll go through this step for a table that we'll use in our video blog in the next section.)

4. Click the Close button in the upper-right corner of the table designer. When Visual Studio .NET prompts you to save the table, select Yes and fill in the desired table name.

Again, pretty painless! For use with our video weblog, we'll create a new table called blog_posts with the following columns:

- item_id: Integer value that will function as the unique identifier for posts on our blog. This column will be the primary key for the table, and also used as an identity.

- item_title: Nvarchar data type column that will house the title of a blog post.

- item_post: Text type column that will house the full text for a post in our blog.

- item_video: Nvarchar data type column that will store the file name of a video that has been posted to the weblog.

- post_date: DateTime data type column that will store the date that the blog entry was posted.

Next, let's create this table using the SQL Design view. Using the SQL Design view is very similar to designing a database table in Access. At the simplest level, a column name and data type are required to create a new data column. Additionally, many other properties of a column can be specified, such as Allow Nulls, which determines whether the column will allow null values to be inserted, and Is Identity, which is highlighted in Figure 13-8. By choosing the item_id column to be an identity, we have put the task of "auto-assigning" a unique primary key for our table into the hands of the SQL Server. As shown, we have specified that the Vbid column should have an Identity Seed of 1—meaning that the first key assigned should be 1—and an Identity Increment of 1—meaning that as more rows are added to the table, the key will be incremented by 1 for each row.

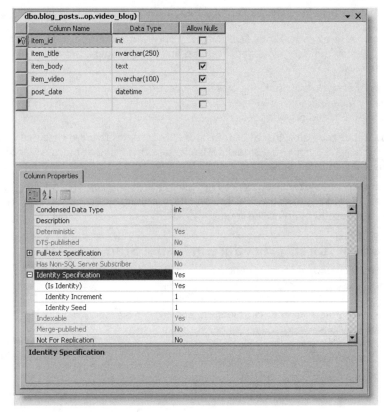

Figure 13-8. The Blog_posts table

Stored procedures

Back in Chapter 9, we learned how to interact with database information using SQL statements that were created in our ASP.NET/C# code. This practice, known as inline-SQL, is generally not the most secure or efficient method for performing database queries. Stored procedures are SQL statements that are stored on a SQL Server (as compared to in a .NET compilation), and can be passed values and executed through your .NET code. On the SQL Server, stored procedures are compiled only once, the first time the procedure is called, making them very processor efficient.

Stored procedures are created using a language called Transact-SQL, or T-SQL, which is a superset of the standard SQL language. Transact-SQL is a language proprietary to Microsoft's SQL Server, but creating queries using T-SQL (at least for the purposes of this book) is essentially the same as using industry-standard SQL statements. Using Transact-SQL, however, multiple statements and conditional logic can be combined into a Transact-SQL stored procedure, reducing the computational load on your logical tier.

Here are some of the benefits gained by using stored procedures instead of "inline" SQL statements:

- **Efficient reuse of code**: When SQL statements are written using stored procedures, they can be accessed by different pages, applications, and programmers, providing an efficient model for code reuse.

- **Reduced network traffic**: Using stored procedures reduces the size of the packages sent between your application and the SQL Server, lowering the amount of network traffic and increasing the speed of your application.

- **Can be debugged using Visual Studio**: Stored procedures that are executed on a SQL Server can be debugged using Visual Studio .NET, a feature that makes it much easier to troubleshoot your data-driven .NET applications.

- **Precompiled code execution**: Stored procedures are compiled only once by the SQL Server, then reused upon each execution. This results in a dramatic speed increase, especially when the stored procedures are called frequently.

Creating a new stored procedure in Visual Studio

Just like SQL databases and tables, stored procedures can be created easily using the Visual Studio .NET Server Explorer. In order to create a new stored procedure, you can right-click the Stored Procedure folder in Server Explorer and select Add New Stored Procedure, as shown in Figure 13-9.

Figure 13-9. Creating a new stored procedure using Visual Studio .NET

In the following screen, Visual Studio provides us with the basic template for a new stored procedure. In Figure 13-10, the general sections of a stored procedure are notated.

```
CREATE PROCEDURE dbo.StoredProcedure1
    /*
    (
    @parameter1 int = 5,
    @parameter2 datatype OUTPUT
    )
    */
AS
    /* SET NOCOUNT ON */
    RETURN
```

Figure 13-10. Sections of a new stored procedure

In the first line of this figure, you'll notice the T-SQL keyword CREATE PROCEDURE, used to begin the creation of a new stored procedure. The text that follows this keyword will be the name of the new stored procedure. The name of a stored procedure must be unique within the database and its owner. You'll notice that the default name of this stored procedure, StoredProcedure1, is preceded by dbo.—this prefix is the optional name of the stored procedure's owner. If, for example, we wanted to create a new stored procedure named MyStoredProcedure, we would modify the default procedure stored here with the following line:

```
CREATE PROCEDURE dbo.MyStoredProcedure
```

The next section in this stored procedure codeblock, which is referred to as "input and output parameters" in Figure 13-10, is used to declare the variables that will be either passed into the stored procedure by your .NET code or returned from the procedure to .NET. These parameters must begin with the @ identifier, and must be assigned a data type, as defined in Table 13-4. All parameters that are declared in a stored procedure must be passed to the procedure by your .NET code, unless the parameter is assigned a default value. Three parameters are defined here, one without a default value defined, one with a default value, and a third that is defined as an output parameter, used to pass a specific value back from a stored procedure:

```
/* parameter, declared as nvarchar of length 50,
    without a default value */
@parameter1 nvarchar(50),
/* parameter, declared as int with a default value */
@parameter2 int = 5,
/* parameter, declared as an output value */
@parameter3 OUTPUT
```

In this chapter, we won't be declaring any parameters for OUTPUT. This parameter type is typically used for more complex T-SQL statements, which we won't need in our video weblog example.

The final section of the stored procedure statement, which appears between the AS and RETURN T-SQL keywords, is where the actual SQL statement that you would like the stored procedure to execute will reside. You'll notice that, by default, Visual Studio inserts a statement in this section that is commented out, SET NOCOUNT ON. This statement determines whether or not the T-SQL statement will return the number of rows affected by the query to your .NET code. Generally, this statement can be deleted, as the NOCOUNT will default to OFF, allowing your .NET code to retrieve the number of affected rows in your query.

The following T-SQL statement shows a new procedure with a SELECT SQL query inserted, which could be to retrieve some rows from a table that match a certain condition, as passed in by an input parameter:

```
CREATE PROCEDURE dbo.MyStoredProcedure
(
@parameter1 int
)
AS
SELECT * FROM myTable WHERE myColumn=@parameter1
RETURN
```

You'll notice that the next time you edit a stored procedure (which now appears in the Stored Procedures folder in Server Explorer), the keyword CREATE will change to ALTER. The ALTER keyword is used, as you might expect, to alter a preexisting stored procedure. The last statement in this stored procedure codeblock, RETURN, is used to exit the T-SQL statement, returning any query values to the calling procedure.

Creating stored procedures for the video weblog

Since we've already created the database table that we'll be using to store the blog entries for this example, and now understand how to create stored procedures, we can move right along to the creation of the T-SQL statements that we'll use to perform our database queries. The queries we'll use should be fairly easy to define, consisting of the following:

- GetPosts: This procedure will take no parameters, and simply return all of the blog posts in the table.

- InsertBlogPost: This procedure will take as parameters a post title, body, post date, and (optional) video, and will run an INSERT statement, creating a new entry in the database table.

- DeleteBlogPost: This procedure will take a single parameter, the ID of a blog post, and run a DELETE procedure, deleting the specified entry.

- UpdateBlogPost: This procedure will take as parameters the ID, title, body, and video for a blog post and execute the necessary UPDATE query to update the stored values for the table entry with the corresponding ID.

To create these stored procedures in the video_blog database, let's use the Add Stored Procedure method as shown earlier, in the Visual Studio Server Explorer. The code for the GetPosts, DeleteBlogPost, UpdateBlogPost, and InsertBlogPost procedures are shown in the codeblock here:

```
- GetPosts procedure
CREATE PROCEDURE dbo.GetPosts
AS
  SELECT item_id, item_title, item_body, item_video, post_date
➥ FROM blog_posts ORDER BY post_date
RETURN


- DeleteBlogPost procedure
CREATE PROCEDURE dbo.DeleteBlogPost
(
  @id int
)
AS
  DELETE FROM blog_posts WHERE item_id=@id
RETURN


- EditBlogPost procedure
CREATE PROCEDURE dbo.EditBlogPost
(
  @id int,
  @title nvarchar(250),
  @body text,
```

```
    @video nvarchar(100),
    @post_date datetime
)
AS
    UPDATE blog_posts SET item_title=@title, item_body=@body,
➥ item_video=@video, post_date=@post_date WHERE item_id=@id
RETURN

- InsertBlogPost procedure
CREATE PROCEDURE dbo.InsertBlogPost
(
    @title nvarchar(250),
    @body text,
    @video nvarchar(100),
    @post_date datetime
)
AS
    INSERT INTO blog_posts (item_title, item_body, item_video,
➥ post_date) VALUES (@title, @body, @video, @post_date)
RETURN
```

Creating the ASP.NET logical tier

Now that we've created a new SQL database, table, and several stored procedures for storing information relating to our video weblog, let's move on to the ASP.NET logical tier, which will be used to
access the stored procedures we've just created. To get started, we'll create a new website project in
Visual Studio, which should again be created on the local IIS server, as shown in Figure 13-11.

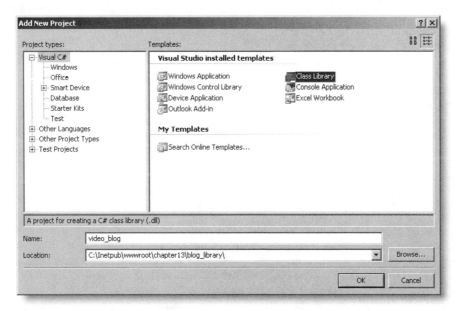

Figure 13-11. Starting a new website project using IIS

363

As defined earlier in the chapter, we're going to expose these stored procedures to the Flash interfaces we will be creating using Flash Remoting. As you saw in the previous chapter, when exposing multiple methods for Flash Remoting, the most convenient method is to create a separate DLL class library. For this project, as shown in Figure 13-12, let's create a new class library project in a folder called `blog_library` within the root of our website (you can create the project anywhere on your system; I'm just adding it to my website's root directory for convenience). After you create this library, create a new C# class file within the project, called `BlogEntries.cs`, and delete the default file created by Visual Studio.

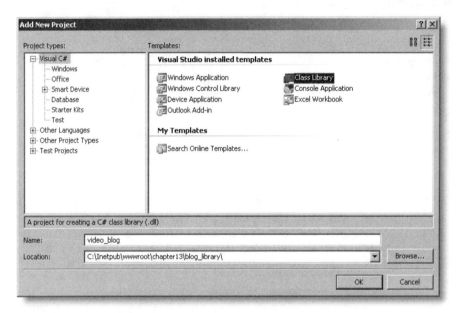

Figure 13-12. Creating the video_blog class library

Executing a stored procedure using a SqlCommand

Executing a SQL stored procedure is done in a very similar manner to the methods that we used to execute SQL commands using the `OleDbCommand` object in the previous chapters. In order to specify that a `SqlCommand` object should use a stored procedure rather than a text command, the command object's `CommandType` parameter must be set to the `StoredProcedure` `CommandType`, which is shown in this codeblock:

```
SqlCommand cmd = new SqlCommand();
cmd.CommandType = CommandType.StoredProcedure;
```

As you saw in Chapter 2, `CommandType` is an enumeration, which provides choices for the valid `CommandType` properties for a `Command` object. You might notice that we have never set the `CommandType` parameter when we were dealing with the `OleDbCommand`—this is because the `CommandType` parameter defaults to Text, which is used for text-based queries created within our C# project. Once we have set the `CommandType` property to specify a `StoredProcedure`, it's then necessary to provide the name of the stored procedure that we would like to execute, using the `CommandText` property, as shown here:

```
cmd.CommandText = "StoredProcedureName";
```

Now that we have picked the stored procedure that we will be executing, the only remaining step is to configure the parameters that will be passed to the stored procedure (assuming that the stored procedure has parameters!). In order to pass the parameters, it's necessary to use the Command object's Parameters object, which allows us to easily set the values of a stored procedure's parameters before execution. Specifically, in this chapter, we'll be using the Parameters object's AddWithValue method, which takes the name of a parameter and the value that the parameter should be set to as parameters:

```
cmd.Parameters.AddWithValue("@ParameterName" , paramValue);
```

It's important here to notice two things about the parameter name—it must be a string value, and must be proceeded with an @ symbol, just like it is in the stored procedure definition. Forgetting about this @ can make for some frustrating debugging sessions.

Creating the BlogEntries.cs file

Once we have added the necessary parameters to the SqlCommand, the command can be executed in the same way as a text-based command—possibly using the ExecuteReader, ExecuteScalar, or ExecuteNonQuery methods. Let's try this out by creating the methods that will access our weblog's entries within the BlogEntries.cs file we created. We're going to start with the InsertBlogPost method, which will access the InsertBlogPost stored procedure:

```
using System;
using System.Collections.Generic;
using System.Text;
using System.Data;
using System.Data.SqlClient;
using FlashGateway.IO;
using System.Collections;

namespace video_blog
{
    class BlogEntries
    {
        // your connecting string may be different
        // depending on your SQL installation
        private string _connString =
           "Data Source=localhost;Initial Catalog=video_blog;
➥ Persist Security Info=True;User ID=[insert SQL user name];
➥ password=[insert SQL password];Pooling=False";

        public bool InsertBlogPost(string title, string body,
                                   DateTime postDate, string video)
        {
            SqlConnection conn = new SqlConnection(_connString);
            SqlCommand cmd = new SqlCommand();
            cmd.CommandType = CommandType.StoredProcedure;
            cmd.CommandText = "InsertBlogPost";
            cmd.Connection = conn;
            cmd.Parameters.AddWithValue("@title", title);
            cmd.Parameters.AddWithValue("@body", body);
```

365

```
        cmd.Parameters.AddWithValue("@video", video);
        cmd.Parameters.AddWithValue("@post_date", postDate);

        try
        {
            conn.Open();
            cmd.ExecuteNonQuery();
            conn.Close();
            return true;
        }
        catch (Exception e)
        {
            return false;
        }
    }
```

No problem, right? As shown in this method, once its methods have been set, a stored procedure can be executed using the same ExecuteNonQuery method we used previously. Next, we'll add methods to access the DeleteBlogPost, UpdateBlogPost, and GetPosts procedures. You'll notice that for the GetPosts procedure, we make use of the ASObject as covered in the previous chapter to pass complex values from ASP.NET to Flash using Flash Remoting. As you learned in the previous chapter, in order to use the ASObject, we need to also add a reference to the FlashGateway.IO namespace in our class.

```
using System;
using System.Collections.Generic;
using System.Text;
using System.Data;
using System.Data.SqlClient;
using FlashGateway.IO;
using System.Collections;

namespace video_blog
{
    class BlogEntries
    {
        private string _connString =
            "Data Source=localhost;Initial Catalog=video_blog;
➥ Persist Security Info=True;User ID=[insert SQL user name];
➥ password=[insert SQL password];Pooling=False";

        public bool InsertBlogPost(string title, string body,
                                    DateTime postDate, string video)
        {
            // InsertBlogPost
        }
        public bool DeleteBlogPost(int bpid)
        {
            SqlConnection conn = new SqlConnection(_connString);
            SqlCommand cmd = new SqlCommand();
```

```
        cmd.Connection = conn;
        cmd.CommandType = CommandType.StoredProcedure;
        cmd.CommandText = "DeleteBlogPost";
        cmd.Parameters.AddWithValue("@id", bpid);

        try
        {
            conn.Open();
            cmd.ExecuteNonQuery();
            conn.Close();
            return true;
        }
        catch
        {
            return false;
        }
    }
    public bool UpdateBlogPost(int bpid, string title, string body,
                               string video, DateTime postDate)
    {
        SqlConnection conn = new SqlConnection(_connString);
        SqlCommand cmd = new SqlCommand();
        cmd.Connection = conn;
        cmd.CommandType = CommandType.StoredProcedure;
        cmd.CommandText = "EditBlogPost";
        cmd.Parameters.AddWithValue("@id", bpid);
        cmd.Parameters.AddWithValue("@title", title);
        cmd.Parameters.AddWithValue("@body", body);
        cmd.Parameters.AddWithValue("@video", video);
        cmd.Parameters.AddWithValue("@post_date", postDate);

        try
        {
            conn.Open();
            cmd.ExecuteNonQuery();
            conn.Close();
            return true;
        }
        catch
        {
            return false;
        }
    }

    public ASObject[] GetPosts()
    {
        SqlConnection conn = new SqlConnection(_connString);
        SqlCommand cmd = new SqlCommand();
        cmd.CommandType = CommandType.StoredProcedure;
```

```
                    cmd.CommandText = "GetPosts";
                    cmd.Connection = conn;

                    conn.Open();
                    SqlDataReader dr = cmd.ExecuteReader();

                    ArrayList al = new ArrayList();
                    while (dr.Read())
                    {
                        ASObject aso = new ASObject();
                        aso.Add("item_id", dr.GetInt32(0));
                        aso.Add("item_title", dr.GetString(1));
                        aso.Add("item_body", dr.GetString(2));
                        aso.Add("item_video", dr.GetString(3));
                        aso.Add("post_date", dr.GetDateTime(4));

                        al.Add(aso);
                    }
                    dr.Close();
                    conn.Close();

                    ASObject[] rets = new ASObject[al.Count];
                    for (int x = 0; x < al.Count; x++)
                    {
                        rets[x] = (ASObject)al[x];
                    }

                    return rets;
                }
            }
        }
```

Let's add another method to this class, which will be used in the administrative interface of our weblog, to validate the credentials of a user attempting to modify the weblog entries using the admin interface. This method, called ValidateUser, will simply take two string input parameters, username and password, and return a Boolean value indicating whether the combination was valid.

```
        public bool ValidateUser(string userName, string pw)
            {
                if ((userName == "admin") && (pw == "flash"))
                {
                    return true;
                }
                else
                {
                    return false;
                }
            }
```

With this class file completed, the next step will be to build this project and then add the resulting DLL file to our website project, allowing it to be accessed using Remoting. As shown in Figure 13-13, this DLL is added as a reference to the project (we saw this in Chapter 12) by selecting the Projects tab in the Add Reference dialog box, which you access by right-clicking the name of the project in the Visual Studio .NET Solution Explorer.

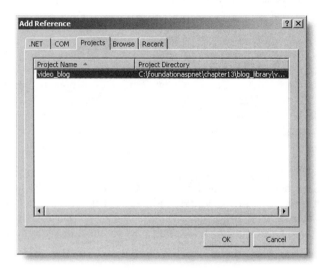

Figure 13-13. Adding a reference to the video_blog

Next, let's complete some of the setup of the ASP.NET website, adding the necessary references for Flash Remoting. Again, using the Add Reference dialog box, navigate to the flashgateway.dll file, which will most likely be located in your C:\Inetpub\wwwroot\flashremoting\bin directory. Once this reference is added, add the existing gateway.aspx file from the Flash Remoting directory to your project. The last step necessary for our Flash Remoting setup will be to add the Remoting section to our web.config file, placed just inside the <system.web> tag:

```
<httpModules>
    <add name="GatewayController"
        type="FlashGateway.Controller.GatewayController,
        ➥ flashgateway"/>
</httpModules>
```

And with that, we can leave Visual Studio (for now) and head to Flash to create the administration section for the video blog! Before we do, create a new folder in the project called admin, which will be used to house the administration page of the site.

Creating the Flash admin presentation tier

The administration screen for our video weblog will be the place that a user will come to in order to add, delete, and edit weblog entries they've created. This Flash movie will interface with the Blog_Entries class we've just developed to create and modify values in our SQL database, and use the Flash/ASP.NET file uploading ability we've covered earlier in this chapter to upload .flv video files to a directory on our web server.

> For our video blog, we're going to use Flash 8 Video (.flv) files so we can take advantage of the dynamic playback features of Flash Video. Using the Flash 8 Video Encoder that ships with Flash 8 Professional edition, it's easy to convert from many video formats to create .flv files. For more information about .flv video files, see the following article on the Macromedia Flash Developer Center: www.macromedia.com/devnet/flash/articles/video_guide.html.

This administrative screen will consist of a single Flash file, which we'll name application.fla and save in a new directory called flash in our site's admin directory. Set the size of this application.fla file to 660×450, and set a frame rate of 12 fps. On the _root timeline of the application.fla file, let's create a new MovieClip with an instance name of login_mc, which will contain two TextInput components, userTxt and passTxt, along with a Button component instance, submitBtn, as shown in Figure 13-14.

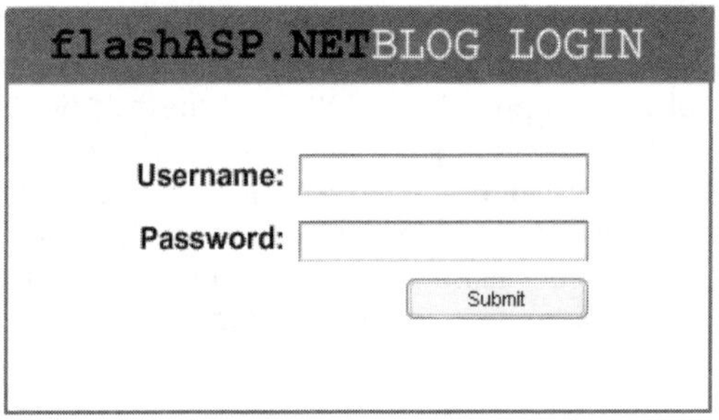

Figure 13-14. login_mc

Also in login_mc, in a layer below the TextInput and Button components, let's create a button, bg_btn, which will be white and will cover the entire 660×450 stage. This button, which we will be disabling in our ActionScript class, will be used to "protect" the interface elements we will create next, therefore keeping an unauthorized user from accessing our administrative control panel.

Also on the _root of the application.fla timeline, on a layer *below* the login_mc MovieClip, we'll create a new layer called components, containing an instance of the Flash List component, postsLst, and three Button components, newBtn, editBtn, and deleteBtn, along with some background interface elements and an instance of the Zigo engine (see Chapter 6), as shown in Figure 13-15. Also, since we are using the Flash Remoting Connector and will be using the Alert component, now is a great time to drag an instance of each of these onto the stage and delete them, so the classes are available for our application.

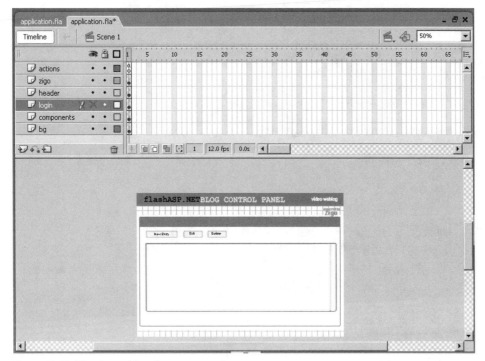

Figure 13-15. Blog Control Panel

Now that we have the elements created for the main interface to our application, let's create the class file that will power it—named `Application.as`. In this file, we'll create five `RemotingConnector` instances: `new_rc`, `edit_rc`, `delete_rc`, `post_rc`, and `login_rc`, one for each remote method that we will be potentially invoking. We'll also configure the `shareConnections`, `methodName`, `serviceName`, and `gatewayUrl` properties of these connector instances to work properly with the ASP.NET service we have created for use with the Flash Remoting Connectors:

```
import mx.data.components.RemotingConnector;
import mx.remoting.debug.NetDebug;
import mx.controls.*;

dynamic class Application extends MovieClip {
  var _gateway = "http://localhost/chapter13/gateway.aspx";
  var _posts:Array = [];

  var newBtn:Button;
  var editBtn:Button;
  var deleteBtn:Button;
  var postsLst:List;
  var login_mc:MovieClip;
```

```
var new_rc:RemotingConnector;
var edit_rc:RemotingConnector;
var delete_rc:RemotingConnector;
var post_rc:RemotingConnector;
var login_rc:RemotingConnector;

function Application(owner)
{
  owner.__proto__ = this.__proto__;
  owner.__constructor__ = Application;
  this = owner;

  setup();
}

public static function main(createdBy:MovieClip) {
  var app = new Application(createdBy);
}

private function setup()
{
  NetDebug.initialize();
  // new entry connector
  new_rc = new RemotingConnector();
  new_rc.addEventListener("result", newRes);
  new_rc.gatewayUrl = _gateway;
  new_rc.shareConnections = true;
  new_rc.methodName = "InsertBlogPost";
  new_rc.serviceName = "video_blog.BlogEntries";

  // edit entry connector
  edit_rc = new RemotingConnector();
  edit_rc.addEventListener("result", editRes);
  edit_rc.gatewayUrl = _gateway;
  edit_rc.shareConnections = true;
  edit_rc.methodName = "UpdateBlogPost";
  edit_rc.serviceName = "video_blog.BlogEntries";

  // delete entry connector
  delete_rc = new RemotingConnector();
  delete_rc.addEventListener("result", deleteRes);
  delete_rc.gatewayUrl = _gateway;
  delete_rc.shareConnections = true;
  delete_rc.methodName = "DeleteBlogPost";
  delete_rc.serviceName = "video_blog.BlogEntries";

   // all posts
  post_rc = new RemotingConnector();
  post_rc.addEventListener("result", gotPosts);
```

```
            post_rc.gatewayUrl = _gateway;
            post_rc.shareConnections = true;
            post_rc.methodName = "GetPosts";
            post_rc.serviceName = "video_blog.BlogEntries";

            // login screen
            login_rc = new RemotingConnector();
            login_rc.addEventListener("result", gotLogin);
            login_rc.gatewayUrl = _gateway;
            login_rc.shareConnections = true;
            login_rc.methodName = "ValidateUser";
            login_rc.serviceName = "video_blog.BlogEntries";

            // disable the bg_btn - this will prvoide a "shield" from
            // the components on the _root
            login_mc.bg_btn.enabled=false;
        }
    }
```

Since we're using an Application class with this application, we can't forget to add the following line of ActionScript onto a layer on the _root timeline:

```
    Application.main(this);
```

Next, let's add an onLoad function to the Application class, which will fire when the components on the stage have completely loaded. In the onLoad function, add event listeners to the Button and List instances, so we can react to their selections. Let's also add a call to a new method, which we'll add to the class DoLoad. DoLoad will be responsible for triggering the GetPosts method—which will populate our interface with the current blog entries in the SQL database.

```
    function onLoad()
    {
      newBtn.addEventListener("click", newEntryClick);
      editBtn.addEventListener("click", editEntryClick);
      deleteBtn.addEventListener("click", deleteEntryClick);

      login_mc.submitBtn.addEventListener("click", loginClick);

      postsLst.addEventListener("change", listClick);

      DoLoad();
    }

    function DoLoad()
    {
      // disable the delete and edit while we're loading data
      deleteBtn.enabled=false;
      editBtn.enabled=false;
```

```
        // remove all of the items from the List
        postsLst.removeAll();
        postsLst.addItem("Loading...");
        // trigger the ASP.NET GetPosts method
        post_rc.trigger();
    }
```

At this point we have completed the setup of our application and, upon loading, have initiated the process of loading the current entries from the SQL database through the use of the GetPosts method we created in the C# BlogEntries class. Next, before we create the event handlers that will fire for each of the elements we have already created, let's create the functions that will power our initial "login" interface—sending a username and password value to the ASP.NET ValidateUser method we have created.

```
    // user login functions
    private function loginClick()
    {
      // set the parameters of login_rc and trigger it!
      _root.login_rc.params =
        [_root.login_mc.userTxt.text, _root.login_mc.passTxt.text];
      _root.login_rc.trigger();
    }

    private function gotLogin(res:Object)
    {
     // if the result==true, it's a valid
     // username/password combination
      if (res.target.results)
      {
        _root.login_mc._visible=false;
      }
      else
      {
        Alert.show("Invalid username / password", "ALERT");
      }
    }
```

In the loginClick function, which fires when the login_mc's submitBtn instance is selected, we are simply setting the parameters of the login_rc connector and triggering that service—when the result is returned to the gotLogin function, the results property is tested, and if it is true, we can remove the login_mc instance, allowing access to the main interface. If results is not true, a new Alert window is shown, indicating that an invalid username/password combination has been entered.

Next, let's add a couple of functions—listClick and gotPosts. The listClick function will handle the selection of an item in the List box (which will be displaying all of the current blog entries), and the gotPosts function will handle the results of the GetPosts Remoting method call. In the gotPosts function, we'll set the value of the Application class's _posts variable to the results object we receive from the Remoting call. The _posts array will allow us to store the information sent from the SQL database for editing—as we'll soon see.

```
// get posts functions
private function gotPosts(res:Object)
{
  _root._posts = [];
  _root._posts = res.target.results;

  var posts = _root._posts;

  var x:Number;
  _root.postsLst.removeAll();
  for (x=0; x<posts.length; x++)
  {
    var lbl:String = posts[x].item_title + " - " +
    ➥ posts[x].post_date.getMonth()+ "/"
    ➥ + posts[x].post_date.getDate()
    ➥ + "/" + posts[x].post_date.getFullYear();
    _root.postsLst.addItem({data:posts[x].item_id, label:lbl});
  }
}

function listClick()
{
  // if the item selected has a data value greater than 0
  // it must be legit - enable the edit and delete buttons
  if (_root.postsLst.selectedItem.data>0)
  {
    _root.deleteBtn.enabled=true;
    _root.editBtn.enabled=true;
  }
  else
  {
    _root.deleteBtn.enabled=false;
    _root.editBtn.enabled=flase;
  }
}
```

Now that we have created the functions that will populate the List component with our blog entries, we'll add a new MovieClip to the Flash file that will be used to insert and edit our blog entries. This MovieClip, which will be called BlogEntry, will also have a linkage identifier and AS 2.0 class of BlogEntry. In this MovieClip, add the following interface elements; the result is shown in Figure 13-16:

- EntryBg: The white rounded-rectangle with the drop shadow, used as the container for the interface

- bg_btn: A semitransparent button, which will cover the entire stage, 550×400

- close_btn: An "X" button in the upper-right corner of the interface

- titleTxt: A TextInput component

- videoTxt: A TextInput component

- selectBtn: A Button component

- postDate: A DateField component

- postTxt: A TextArea component

- postBtn: A Button component

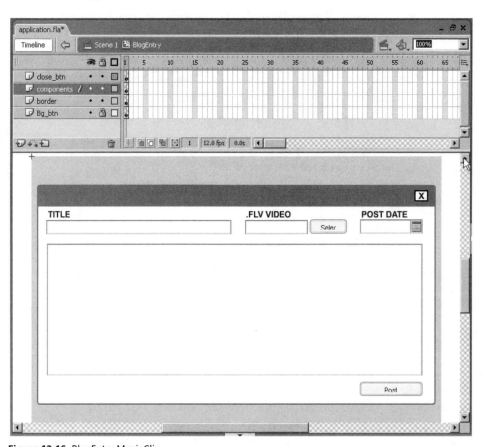

Figure 13-16. BlogEntry MovieClip

Next, let's create the class file for this MovieClip, BlogEntry.as. The code for this class is listed a bit later—I'm not going to walk through this class file, but I would like to point out a few things. In this code, you'll see a reference to the UploadProgress MovieClip—we will be creating this MovieClip in the next step. You'll also notice that I am referring to this clip as _root.entry—when we complete the Application.as class, you'll see that this will be the name given to this MovieClip as it is attached to the _root timeline.

In this class, we're also making use of the Flash/ASP.NET file upload skills we learned earlier in this chapter. You'll notice that we've added a variable to the class, _uplDir, which specified the file that will handle the file upload from Flash. We will be creating this file later in this example, and will add the logic necessary to handle the file upload.

```
import mx.controls.*;
dynamic class BlogEntry extends MovieClip {
  var titleTxt:TextInput;
  var postDate:DateField;
  var videoTxt:TextInput;
  var selectBtn:Button;
  var postTxt:TextArea;
  var postBtn:Button;
  var bgBut:Button;
  var close_btn:Button;

  var _uplDir = "http://localhost/chapter13/admin/Default.aspx";
  var _id:Number;
  var _fileRef:flash.net.FileReference;
  var _fileUpload:Object;

  var _update:Boolean = false;

  function Blog_entry()
  {

  }

  function onLoad():Void {
    postDate.selectedDate = new Date();
    bgBut.enabled=false;
    close_btn.onRelease = function() {
      _root.entry.removeMovieClip();
    }

    _fileRef = new flash.net.FileReference();
    _fileUpload = new Object ();
    _fileUpload.onSelect = fileSelected;
    _fileUpload.onProgress = fileProgress;
    _fileUpload.onComplete = fileComplete;
    _fileUpload.onError = fileError;
    _fileRef.addListener(_fileUpload);
```

```
    if (_update)
    {
      var selObj:Object = _root._posts[_root.postsLst.selectedIndex];

      _id = selObj.item_id;
      titleTxt.text = selObj.item_title;
      videoTxt.text = selObj.item_video;
      postDate.selectedDate = selObj.post_date;
      postTxt.text = selObj.item_body;

      postBtn.label = "Update";
    }
    else
    {
      _id=undefined;
      postBtn.label = "Post";
    }
    selectBtn.addEventListener("click", fileBrowse);
    postBtn.addEventListener("click", postClick);
}

private function fileBrowse()
{
  _parent._fileRef.browse([{description:
  ➥ ".flv video", extension: "*.flv"}]);
}

private function fileError(file:flash.net.FileReference,
  ➥ errorCode:Number)
{
  mx.controls.Alert.show("HTTP Error: " + file.name
                            + " HTTP Error Code: " + errorCode);
}

private function fileSelected(file:flash.net.FileReference)
{
  _root.entry.videoTxt.text = file.name;
}

private function fileProgress(file:flash.net.FileReference,
                              bytesLoaded:Number,
                              bytesTotal:Number) {
  var percent = Math.round (bytesLoaded / bytesTotal * 100);
  _root.prog.progBar.setProgress(percent, 100);
};

private function fileComplete()
{
  _root.prog.progBar.label = "Sending Data...";
  if (_root.entry._update)
```

```
    {
      _root.entry.editEntry();
    }
    else
    {
      _root.entry.addEntry();
    }
  }

  function postClick()
  {
    _parent.postBtn.enabled=false;
    _parent.postBtn.label = "Loading...";

    if (_parent._fileRef.name.length>0)
    {
      _root.entry.brightnessTo(-25);
      _root.entry.postBtn.enabled=false;
      _root.attachMovie("UploadProgress", "prog", 11);
      _root.prog.progBar.setProgress(0, 100);
      _root.entry._fileRef.upload(_parent._uplDir);
    }
    else
    {
      if (_parent._update)
      {
        _parent.editEntry();
      }
      else {
        _parent.addEntry();
      }
    }
  }

  function addEntry()
  {
    _root.NewEntry(_root.entry.titleTxt.text,
                   _root.entry.postTxt.text,
                   _root.entry.postDate.selectedDate,
                   _root.entry.videoTxt.text);
  }
  function editEntry()
  {
    _root.EditEntry(_root.entry._id,
                    _root.entry.titleTxt.text,
                    _root.entry.postTxt.text,
                    _root.entry.videoTxt.text,
                    _root.entry.postDate.selectedDate);
  }
}
```

As I mentioned, this `BlogEntry` class references the `UploadProgress` MovieClip—in the Flash file, let's add a new MovieClip by that name to the library, with a linkage identifier of `UploadProgress`, and to this MovieClip, add a Progress Bar component, with an instance name of `progBar`, as shown in Figure 13-17. When you add the Progress Bar instance, be sure to change the mode property of the component from event to manual. This will allow us to manually set the status of our upload through ActionScript.

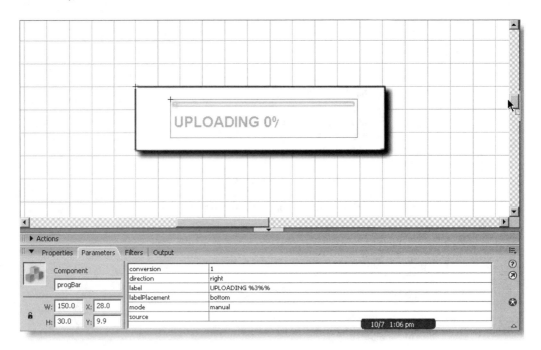

Figure 13-17. ProgressBar MovieClip

Next, let's jump back to the `Application.as` file and complete the creation of this class file by adding the event handlers needed for the Button and Remoting Connector instances. With this code, our Flash movie will call the `DeleteBlogEntry` or `EditBlogEntry` Flash Remoting method when either the Delete or Edit button is clicked. After a delete or edit operation has completed, the interface is refreshed by making another call to the `DoLoad` method.

```
// edit post functions
private function editEntryClick()
{
  _parent.attachMovie("BlogEntry", "entry", 10, {_update:true});
}

private function EditEntry(id:Number, ttl:String, body:String,
                          video:String, postDate:Date)
{
  _root.edit_rc.params = [id, ttl, body, video, postDate];
  _root.edit_rc.trigger();
}
```

```
private function editRes() {
  if (_root.prog!=undefined)
  {
    _root.prog.removeMovieClip();
  }
  _root.entry.removeMovieClip();
  _root.DoLoad();
}

// delete post functions
function confirmDelete(evt:Object)
{
  switch (evt.detail) {
  case Alert.YES :
    _root.deleteEntry();
    break;
  case Alert.NO :
    break;
  }
}

private function deleteEntry()
{
  _root.delete_rc.params = [_root.postsLst.selectedItem.data];
  _root.delete_rc.trigger();
}

private function deleteEntryClick()
{
    Alert.show("Are you sure you'd like to delete this post?",
               "Confirm Delete",
               Alert.NO | Alert.YES, _root, _root.confirmDelete);
}

private function deleteRes()
{
  _root.DoLoad();
}

// new post functions
public function NewEntry(ttl:String, post:String,
                         postDate:Date, video:String)
{
  new_rc.params = [ttl, post, postDate, video];
  new_rc.trigger();
}
private function newRes()
{
```

```
        _root.prog.removeMovieClip();
        _root.entry.removeMovieClip();
        _root.DoLoad();
    }
    private function newEntryClick()
    {
        _parent.attachMovie("BlogEntry", "entry", 10, {_update:false});
    }
```

And, with this, the Flash side of our blog administration is complete! With this code completed, you can now publish the application.fla file, creating application.swf. The last thing that we'll need to do is jump back into Visual Studio .NET and create an .aspx page to house the Flash movie, as well as the code-behind necessary to process the file upload, as required by our BlogEntry MovieClip.

In Visual Studio .NET, let's add a new web form, called default.aspx, to the admin folder. In the design interface of this file, we'll drag an instance of the epicFlashControl (see Chapter 3), and configure the properties to display the application.swf file. In the PageLoad event of the code-behind file for this page, we'll need to add code similar to the example presented earlier in this chapter, which will copy a file uploaded from Flash into a folder called uploads in our website's root directory.

```
public partial class _Default : System.Web.UI.Page
{
    protected void Page_Load(object sender, EventArgs e)
    {
      if (Page.Request.Files.Count > 0)
      {
        string fn = Page.Request.Files[0].FileName;
        Page.Request.Files[0].SaveAs(
          ➥ Server.MapPath("~\\uploads\\" + fn));          }
      }
}
```

> Don't forget to create the uploads folder in the root of the website and set the security permissions as we did earlier in the chapter, or the upload will fail!

And, with this file created, we are ready to test our weblog administration application! Figures 13-18 through 13-21 show this application in progress, effectively administering our weblog entries, and uploading new videos to the web server, as needed.

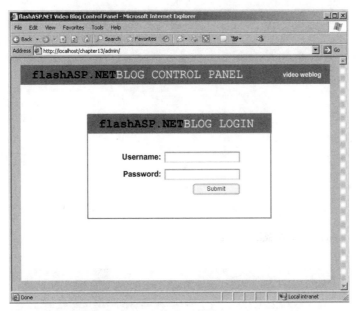

Figure 13-18. Admin login screen

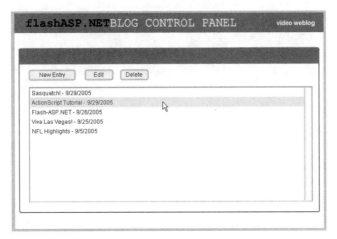

Figure 13-19. Main Administration screen

Figure 13-20. Edit/Insert Blog Entry screen

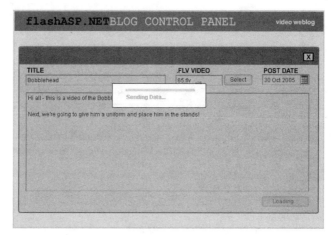

Figure 13-21. Progress bar when adding a blog entry

Creating the video weblog front-end

Now that we've created the back-end administration application for our video weblog, we can move to the front-end user interface. This interface, oddly enough, will be less complicated to create than the administration application, since we only need to make use of a single method from our C# BlogEntry class, GetPosts. For this interface, we'll create a new Flash file, application.fla in a new folder, flash, in the root of the Chapter 13 website—on my system, this folder is C:\inetpub\wwwroot\chapter13\ flash\. Set the dimensions of this Flash file to 720×1100, with a frame rate of 30 fps.

> *You may want to create this MovieClip with a height less than 1100 when testing, since a clip this big is hard to test in the Flash IDE.*

On the _root timeline of this file, let's create the interface elements shown in Figure 13-22. We'll also add a new MovieClip with an instance name of loading, which contains the text Loading blog entries.

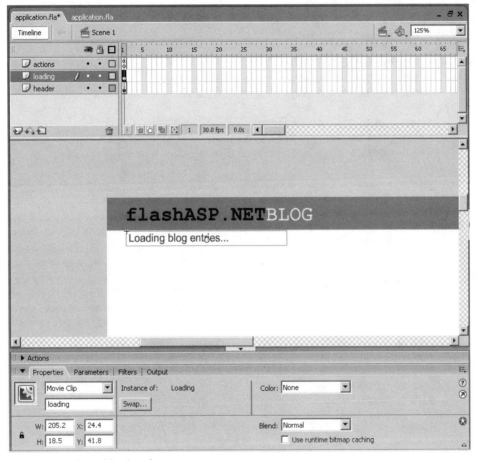

Figure 13-22. The weblog interface

Next, let's add an Application class for this file—Application.as. In this file, we'll use very similar methods to those we used for the administrative interface. Create a Remoting Connector instance, post_rc, and using this connector, call the GetPosts method from our ASP.NET class library. When this class file is initiated, it immediately makes a call to the ASP.NET GetPosts method, and after receiving the result, attaches an instance of the PageNav MovieClip, which we will create next.

```
import mx.data.components.RemotingConnector;
import mx.remoting.debug.NetDebug;

dynamic class Application extends MovieClip {
  var post_rc:RemotingConnector;
  var _posts:Array;
  var loading:MovieClip;

  function Application(owner)
  {
    owner.__proto__ = this.__proto__;
    owner.__constructor__ = Application;
    this = owner;

    setup();
  }

  public static function main(createdBy:MovieClip) {
    var app = new Application(createdBy);
  }

  private function setup()
  {
    NetDebug.initialize();

    post_rc = new RemotingConnector();
    post_rc.addEventListener("result", gotPosts);
    post_rc.gatewayUrl = "http://localhost/chapter13/gateway.aspx";
    post_rc.methodName = "GetPosts";
    post_rc.serviceName = "video_blog.BlogEntries";

    GetPosts();
  }

  private function gotPosts(res:Object)
  {
    // clear the loading MovieClip
    _root.loading._visible = false;
    _root._posts = [];
    _root._posts = res.target.results;

    // attach the Page navigation
    _root.attachMovie("PageNav", "PageNav", 40, {_x:597, _y:42});
```

```
      }
    }

    private function GetPosts()
    {
      post_rc.trigger();
    }
  }
```

One of the essential things we'll need to be able to do in our weblog is to scroll through the pages of entries that are displayed. In order to accomplish this, we'll create a MovieClip called PageNav, as shown in Figure 13-23. We'll create this MovieClip with a linkage identifier of PageNav, and an ActionScript class of PageNav.

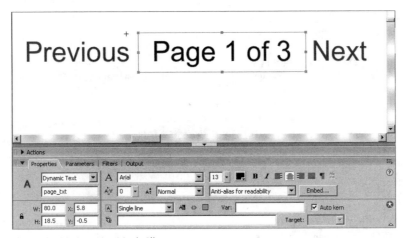

Figure 13-23. PageNav MovieClip

In this MovieClip, we'll create two Button instances, next_btn and prev_btn, along with a dynamic text instance, page_txt. Along with this MovieClip, let's create a new .as file in the same flash directory, as shown in the codeblock that follows. I'm not going to explain this class in detail, but I have highlighted the updatePage function, which calls a new function, PlacePage, in the application.as file. We'll add this function to the application class next.

```
dynamic class PageNav extends MovieClip {
  var page_txt:TextField;
  var next_btn:Button;
  var prev_btn:Button;

  var _curPage:Number;
  var _totalPages:Number;

  function PageNav()
  {
    next_btn.onRelease = nextPage;
```

```
      prev_btn.onRelease = prevPage;
      prev_btn._visible = false;
      next_btn._visible = false;
    }

    function SetPageCount(ct:Number)
    {
      _curPage = 0;
      _totalPages = ct - 1;
      if (ct>1)
      {
        next_btn._visible = true;
      }
      updatePage();
    }

    function nextPage()
    {
      this._parent._curPage++;
      if (this._parent._curPage == this._parent._totalPages)
      {
        this._parent.next_btn._visible = false;
      }
      this._parent.prev_btn._visible = true;
      this._parent.updatePage();
    }

    function prevPage()
    {
      this._parent._curPage--;
      if (this._parent._curPage == 0)
      {
        this._parent.prev_btn._visible = false;
      }
      this._parent.next_btn._visible = true;

      this._parent.updatePage();
    }

    function updatePage()
    {
      page_txt.text = "Page " + (_curPage+1).toString() +
    ➥ " of " + (_totalPages+1).toString();
      _root.PlacePage(_curPage);
    }
}
```

When the blog entries have loaded, and we know which page of entries should be displayed, we'll need to create a function that will display the requested entries on our interface. In order to do this, we can simply iterate through the _posts array we stored from the GetPosts method results. For each new blog entry, we'll add a new MovieClip, BlogEntry, which again, we will be creating next.

```
private function PlacePage(pg:Number)
{
  var x:Number;
  var ct:Number = 0;
  for (x=pg*5; x<((pg+1)*5); x++)
  {
    var nn:String = "be" + ct.toString();
    if (_root[nn] != undefined)
    {
      _root[nn].removeMovieClip();
    }
    if (x<_root._posts.length)
    {
      _root.attachMovie("BlogEntry", nn, 50+ct);
      _root[nn]._y = 100+(ct*185);
      _root[nn]._x = 30;
      _root[nn].SetInfo(_root._posts[x].item_title,
                        _root._posts[x].item_body,
                        _root._posts[x].post_date,
                        _root._posts[x].item_video);
      ct++;
    }
    else
    {
      break;
    }
  }
}
```

Now that we've created the code to call the GetPosts method, let's add a new MovieClip to the Flash file, called BlogEntry. This MovieClip should also have a linkage identifier of BlogEntry, as well as use BlogEntry for its AS 2.0 class file. The interface for the BlogEntry MovieClip is shown in Figure 13-24. This MovieClip contains the following elements in its interface:

- title_txt: A dynamic text field with embedded fonts
- date_txt: A dynamic text field with embedded fonts
- postTxt: A TextArea component
- video_btn: A Button instance

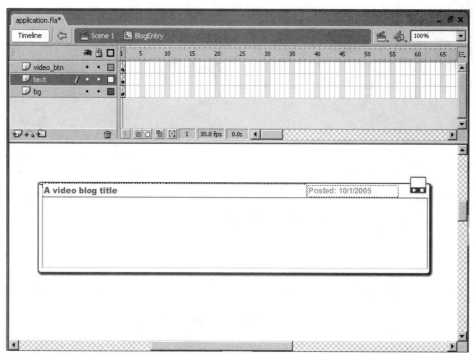

Figure 13-24. BlogEntry MovieClip

And, with this MovieClip, we'll create a new class file, BlogEntry.as. The SetInfo function of this class will be used to set the properties of the interface elements in the BlogEntry MovieClip, as well as attach a video player (which we'll create next!) when the video_btn instance is selected.

```
import mx.controls.TextArea;
dynamic class BlogEntry extends MovieClip {
  var title_txt:TextField;
  var postTxt:TextArea;
  var date_txt:TextField;
  var video_btn:Button;
  var close_btn:Button;

  private var _video:String;
  private var _post:String;
  private var _date:Date;
  private var _title:String;
```

```
function BlogEntry()
{
  video_btn.onRelease = gotClick;
  close_btn.onRelease = function()
  {
    this.removeMovieClip();
  }
}

function gotClick()
{
  _root.attachMovie("BlogVideoPlayer", "player", 100);
  _root["player"]._x=150;
  _root["player"]._y = this._parent._y-50;
  _root["player"].SetInfo(_parent._title,
    ➥ _parent._video, _parent._post);
}

function onLoad()
{
  postTxt.text = _post;
  title_txt.text = _title;
  date_txt.text = date_txt.text = "POSTED: " +
    ➥ _date.getMonth().toString() + "/"
    ➥ + _date.getDate().toString()
    ➥ + "/" + _date.getFullYear().toString();
}

function SetInfo(ttl:String, post:String, date:Date, video:String)
{
  _title = ttl;
  _post = post;
  _date = date;
  if (video!=undefined)
  {
    _video = video;
  }
  else
  {
    video_btn._visible=false;
  }
}
```

Next, let's create the BlogVideoPlayer MovieClip, as referenced in the BlogEntry class earlier. This MovieClip will also have a linkage identifier and AS 2.0 class of BlogVideoPlayer. This MovieClip will consist of five elements, as shown in Figure 13-25.

- EntryBg: A MovieClip that will be the background container for the video player.
- title_txt: A dynamic text field with embedded fonts.
- player: A Flash 8 FLVPlayback component. We've set the size of this video player to 320×240, which will be the required video size for this application.
- close_btn: A button instance.
- postTxt: A TextArea instance that will display the post text.

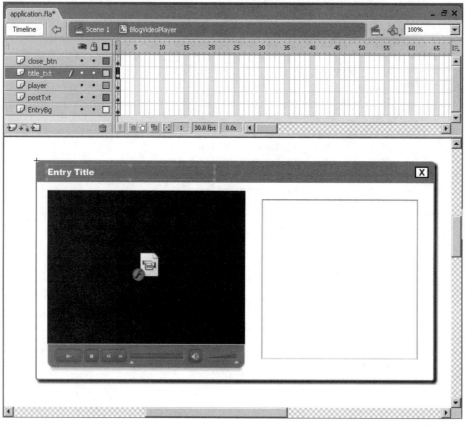

Figure 13-25. BlogVideoPlayer MovieClip

Next, we'll create the `BlogVideoPlayer.as` class file, as shown here:

```
import mx.video.*;
import mx.controls.TextArea;

dynamic class BlogVideoPlayer extends MovieClip {
  var title_txt:TextField;
  var player:FLVPlayback;
  var close_btn:Button;
  var postTxt:TextArea;

  private var _video;
  private var _title;
  private var _post;

  function BlogVideoPlayer()
  {
    close_btn.onRelease = function () {
      this._parent.removeMovieClip();
    }
  }

  function onLoad()
  {
    postTxt.text = _post;
    title_txt.text = _title;
    player.contentPath = "../uploads/" + _video;
    player.play();
  }
  function SetInfo(ttl:String, video:String, post:String)
  {
    _post = post;
    _title = ttl;
    _video = video;
  }
}
```

This class file consists of two methods—the `SetInfo` method, which sets the internal properties of the object, and the `onLoad` method, which, upon loading the FLVPlayback component sets the title field of the video, and sets the `contentPath` property of the FLVPlayback component, allowing it to play the video attached to the blog entry.

And that's it for the video weblog Flash front-end! The last thing we'll need to do to complete the application will be to publish this file as `application.swf`, and create another new `.aspx` page using Visual Studio .NET that will house this file. We've called this page `default.aspx`, and placed it in the root of the website project—`C:\inetpub\wwwroot\chapter13\`. In this file, we've used the epicFlashControl to embed the `application.swf` file, and have configured its properties accordingly. In order for the FLVPlayback component to work correctly in a page outside of the `flash` folder, we must copy the skin file (I chose the SteelExternalAll skin) that was used for the playback component into our site's root folder, as shown in Figure 13-26.

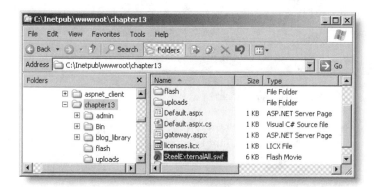

Figure 13-26. Copy the skin FLVPlayback skin to the site's root.

Finally, the `default.aspx` page, opened in Internet Explorer, is shown in Figure 13-27.

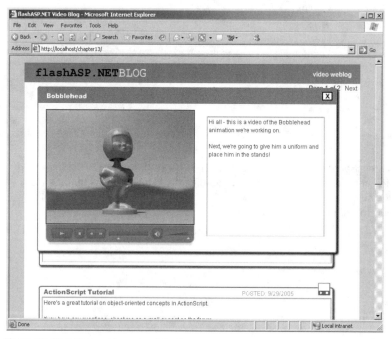

Figure 13-27. Video weblog completed!

Summary

Well, we've really covered a lot of exciting material in this chapter, ranging from file uploading in Flash to SQL Server access using Flash Remoting. In our video weblog application, we've tied these concepts together and also integrated many of the concepts we learned throughout this book. In this example, we created some of the basic functionality for a video weblog—we hope, with the skills you've learned in this book, you can extend it even further, to include features like comments, links, RSS feeds, and direct linking to posts. As we've seen throughout this book, there's almost no limit to the extent of the capabilities we can give our applications using Flash and ASP.NET!

INDEX

A

Abandon method, HttpSessionState, 286

AcceptTypes property, Request object, ASP.NET, 103

Access databases, 243, 246, 258–260, 263

access denied errors, 342

ActionScript
Application class, 226–227
Data Type, 312–313
file uploading, 352–354
front-end, video weblog application, 384–394
version 2.0, vs. C#, 15–16, 89, 91
with web services, 212–217

ActionScript Messaging Format (AMF), 311, 313

Add method
HttpApplicationState, 284
HttpSessionState, 286

AddListener method, FileReference class, 347

admin tier, video weblog application, 370, 372–374

ADO.NET
Access databases, 243–247
commands, 242, 248
connections, 242
ConnectionString property, 242–243
data providers, 241–242
DataAdapter, 239, 241–242, 252
DataAdapter/DataSet
steps for using, 253
using with Flash, 253–255
DataReader class, 239–242
DataReaders class, 249–252
DataSet, 239–241
OdbcConnection, 242–243, 246
OdbcDataReader, 249
OleDbCommand, 261, 263
OleDbConnection, 260–261, 263
OleDbDataReader, 261, 263
overview, 239

AMF (ActionScript Messaging Format), 311, 313

App_WebReferences, Google web service API, 223

Application object and session state, 282–283, 285

application state, in web services, 291–292

Application_Disposed event, global.asax file, 287

Application_End event, global.asax file, 287

Application_Error event, global.asax file, 287

Application_Init event, global.asax file, 287

Application_Start event, global.asax file, 287

ArrayList collection in C#, 58–59

arrays in C#, 55, 57

AsObject .NET class with Flash, 334, 336–339

ASP, classic, 5–6

ASP.NET
code-behind files, 72–87
complete example program, 87–97
creating a new website, 62–63
creating a web service proxy, 220–221
designing a website in Visual Studio, 63, 65
developer features, 7–8
file processing, 382
file uploading, 348–354
Flash interface, 177–189
Flash server control, 79–80
generated HTML, 70
GET and POST variables, 101–102
global.asax file, 287–289
HTTP request, 100–101
HTTP response, 102
IIS mail configuration, 115–117
language support, 7
loadVars object, 117–121
open standard, 7
overview, 2, 7
page tag, 163, 167, 169
Page_Load event, 76, 107
performance, 7
Request object, 102–104
request-response model, 100
scalability, 8
server controls, 66
server-side code, 168–176
System.Exception class, 110
System.Web.Mail, 113
testing web pages in Visual Studio, 68, 72
try-catch-finally, 109–113
two-way Flash communication overview, 100
Web.config file, 70
XML socket server, 117

Attachments property, MailMessage object, ASP.NET, 114

friendsofed.com/forums

Join the friends of ED forums to find out more about our books, discover useful technology tips and tricks, or get a helping hand on a challenging project. *Designer to Designer*™ is what it's all about—our community sharing ideas and inspiring each other. In the friends of ED forums, you'll find a wide range of topics to discuss, so look around, find a forum, and dive right in!

■ **Books and Information**

Chat about friends of ED books, gossip about the community, or even tell us some bad jokes!

■ **Flash**

Discuss design issues, ActionScript, dynamic content, and video and sound.

■ **Web Design**

From front-end frustrations to back-end blight, share your problems and your knowledge here.

■ **Site Check**

Show off your work or get new ideas.

■ **Digital Imagery**

Create eye candy with Photoshop, Fireworks, Illustrator, and FreeHand.

■ **ArchivED**

Browse through an archive of old questions and answers.

HOW TO PARTICIPATE

Go to the friends of ED forums at **www.friendsofed.com/forums**.